The Wesleys in
Cornwall, 1743–1789

ALSO BY SAMUEL J. ROGAL

The Wesleys in Cornwall, 1743–1789

A Record of Their Activities Town by Town

SAMUEL J. ROGAL

McFarland & Company, Inc., Publishers

Jefferson, North Carolina

LIBRARY OF CONGRESS CATALOGUING-IN-PUBLICATION DATA

Rogal, Samuel J.
   The Wesleys in Cornwall, 1743–1789 : a record of their activities
town by town / Samuel J. Rogal.
      p.   cm.
   Includes bibliographical references and indexes.

   ISBN 978-0-7864-9971-7 (softcover : alkaline paper) ∞
   ISBN 978-1-4766-2367-2 (ebook)

   1. Wesley, John, 1703–1791—Travel—England—Cornwall (County)
2. Wesley, Charles, 1707–1788—Travel—England—Cornwall (County)
3. Methodist Church—Missions—England—Cornwall (County)—History—18th century.   4. Missionaries—England—Cornwall (County)—
History—18th century.   5. Cornwall (England : County)—Church
history—18th century.   6. Methodist Church (Great Britain)—History—18th century.   7. Great Britain—Church history—18th century.
I. Title.

BX8495.W5R596 2015
287.09423'709033—dc23   2015034056

BRITISH LIBRARY CATALOGUING DATA ARE AVAILABLE

On the cover: (top, left to right) John and Charles Wesley;
(bottom) Land's End in Cornwall, England (Thinkstock)

Printed in the United States of America

McFarland & Company, Inc., Publishers
   Box 611, Jefferson, North Carolina 28640
   www.mcfarlandpub.com

Table of Contents

Prefatory Note   1

1. Cornwall: An Introduction   3
2. Methodism in Eighteenth-Century Cornwall   17
3. The Wesleys in Cornwall: The Places   26
4. Summary, Conclusion and Assessment   199

Appendices

   Table 1: Preachers, Cornwall Circuit (1746–1791)   205

   Table 2: Membership, Cornwall Methodist Societies (1765–1791)   210

   Table 3: Funds Allocated to Cornwall (1766–1791)   211

   Table 4: Places in Cornwall Visited by Charles Wesley/ John Wesley   212

Chapter Notes   214

Bibliography   225

Index to Citations from Scriptures   229

Index of Persons, Places and General Topics   231

William the Conqueror gave to his brother Robert almost the whole shire of Cornwall, out of which arose that great Earldom, and afterwards Duchy, of Cornwall, which was deemed too powerful to be trusted in the hands of any but men closely akin to the royal house and the remains of which for ages formed the appanage of the heir apparent to the Crown.

—Edward Augustus Freeman (1823–1892),
William the Conqueror (1888)

You do not know the Cornish yet. Many of them have little sense and a great inclination to criticize.

—John Wesley to John Valton,
6 November 1790

Prefatory Note

The Wesleys in Cornwall, 1743–1789 comprises the fifth title that I have produced that features the specific activities of the eighteenth-century English Methodist leadership in a particular section of the British Isles. The previous publications concern the work in London (1988), Scotland (1988), Ireland (1993), and Wales (1995), and they focus almost exclusively upon John Wesley. The obvious reason for excluding brother Charles from those publications arose from the simple fact that during those years, there existed little in the way of essential and reliable published primary sources related and essential to observing Charles Wesley's thoughts, words, and work during his travels on the missionary rounds. Although there arises little doubt that, in terms of the length of time spent on the Methodist itinerancy, Charles Wesley performed a subordinate role (but yet a fairly effective one) to that of his older brother John, relatively recent scholarship has permitted one the opportunity to bring the two together upon the same fields, enjoying similar successes and failures, enduring similar hardships, and confronting similar threats and dangers to their own limbs and lives. Specifically, the scholarly community can embrace the advantages gained from two volumes of John Wesley's *Letters* (1980–1982); seven volumes of his *Journal and Diaries* (1988–2003); four volumes of analyses and discussions of his *Teachings* (2012–2014) and of works related thereto; and four volumes of his *Sermons* (1984–1987). There have reached the press two volumes of Charles Wesley's *Manuscript Journal* (2007–2008); one volume of his *Letters* (2013); a critical edition of his *Sermons* (2001); and a miscellaneous collection of his prose and verse (1989). One must not ignore a volume of primary sources concerning *The Methodist Societies* (1989) and another, a one-thousand-page-plus tome and

1

companion to the latter, *The Methodist Societies: The Minutes of Conference* (2011). Thus, scholars can survey a more dimensional and more accurate scene of the labors of John and Charles Wesley than they could through the earlier literary and editorial efforts of the likes of Robert Southey, Luke Tyerman, Nehemiah Curnock, and John Telford.

Eighteenth-century Cornwall certainly must have appealed to both Wesleys within their overall scheme to evangelize as many of their countrymen as possible through teaching, preaching, and organizing. That elongated peninsular shire of England housed fishermen, miners, farm workers, and general laborers—men, women, and children for whom religious commitment and practice did not rank high among their priorities. However, the varying degrees of successes and failures experienced by the Wesleys in dispensing their brand of practical religion, as anchored firmly to the sound and sense of Holy Scriptures, derived from their collective determination to assess the spiritual needs of people, from young to old, particularly those who dwelt among the middle and lower social and financial classes, as well as those possessed of limited educations. In the end, judging if the Wesleys' periodic missions to Cornwall actually achieved their evangelical ambitions cannot be determined solely upon partisan or enthusiastic generalizations. Their individual journeys to that shire must be viewed from town to town, through detailed observations of the activities of Cornish Methodist societies, through the reactions of Church of England priests who strove to maintain a spiritual hold upon their parishioners, and even from the perspective of those anti–Methodist Cornish inhabitants—mobs, on occasion—who stood as defiant and active deterrents to their efforts.

Thus, this book gathers from various sources to re-create, on paper, a spiritual journey and an arduous trek—a record of a determined religious mission to a particular region of their nation, undertaken by two brothers who did not always agree with the purposes and the plans of each other. It offers the reader the opportunity to engage in and to complete the journey, and thus allows for the assessment of the contributions of that mission to the religious and social backgrounds of the broad narrative of eighteenth-century England.

Cornwall: An Introduction

Physically, the county (shire) of Cornwall—the name derives from the pre-tenth-century Old English *Cornweallas* ("Corn-welsh")[1]—1,376 square miles, appears as a peninsula, bounded seaward by the English Channel and the Atlantic Ocean, and landward by Devonshire. Its length, from east to west, extends to seventy-four miles, and its largest breadth measures approximately forty-three miles. The shire terminates in the southwest with two promontories: the Lizard Point and the rugged Land's End. The region reveals a low-lying plateau, rising to its highest point at Brown Willy, 1,375 feet, in the barren Bodmin Moor. Cornwall claims as its principal rivers the Tamar, which forms the major portion of the border with Devonshire; the Fowry; the Fal; and the Camel, which flows northwest for approximately thirty miles into the Atlantic Ocean. The fact that the sea surrounds Cornwall on three sides creates fairly even temperatures; thus, travellers to Cornwall seldom found themselves exposed to severe frosts or radically extreme heat, and spring came earlier there than to the remainder of England. Nevertheless, the county has tended to endure exposure to severe storms, as well as an abundance of rainy and foggy weather.

Traditionally, the Cornish river valleys have given rise to productive vegetable and dairy farms, while the uplands yielded to sheep and cattle pasturage, although, historically, the growth of corn and the numbers of cattle have not been considered significant. The centuries-old Cornish tin and copper deposits, known by the ancient Greeks and Romans even before the Roman invasion of Britain, and the mines arising from them, continued to prove quite active during the eighteenth and early nineteenth centuries. Indeed, the principal economic importance of Cornwall developed from its mineral wealth. The valuable copper mines within the county even increased their worth on those rare occasions in which miners occasionally uncovered small deposits of gold and silver, as well as lead, iron, zinc, and arsenic. However, the tin mines, from antiquity, became the most extensive and celebrated.

From a purely artistic perspective, one might wish to examine a painting, *A Gentleman and a Miner*, executed by the portrait and historical painter and illustrator John Opie (1761–1807), born in the copper-mining village of St. Agnes, Cornwall, and known as "the Cornish Wonder,"[2] that hangs in the Royal Institution of Cornwall at Truro. The piece depicts a gentleman on the right, perhaps age sixty-five or so, attired in a white lace shirt beneath a black jacket, extending his left hand slightly to receive, from a young miner, on the left and facing him, a specimen of copper ore held in his left hand. The miner has his right arm bent and extended slightly, pointing at his opposite with his index finger. The older man expresses a slight frown, and the younger person appears expressionless. The "gentleman" has been identified as Thomas Daniell, a merchant and leading mine speculator from Truro; the miner, known as Thomas Morecom, worked in the Polperro mine at St. Agnes. Neither name appears in the journals, diaries, or correspondence of either John or Charles Wesley.

The earth of Cornwall also yielded numerous varieties of rock quarried there, mainly for building construction—granite and freestone, slates for roofing, and grit (sand, gravel) to produce millstones (circular stones for grinding corn in a mill). Further, a species of extremely clear crystal also became associated with the county, known to jewelers of the time as "the Cornish diamond."

Before proceeding further with this discussion, the reader might wish to pause, and to consult the pages of a late eighteenth- or early nineteenth-century volume of English county maps, thus devoting the time to becoming familiar with what geographers would label "the lay of the land" and implanting in the mind a clear topographical image of the county of Cornwall. As a recommendation, one such collection and its topographer-compiler appear particularly worthy of bibliographical and biographical mention. An excellent map of Cornwall will be found in *England's Topographer; or, Moule's English Counties in the Nineteenth Century* (London: George Virtue, Ivy Lane/Simpkin and Marshall, Stationers Court, 1836). The author and compiler, Thomas Moule (1784–1851), born in the Marylebone section of London on 14 January 1784, eventually became a clerk in the General Post Office, where he served as an inspector of "blind letters" (letters with illegible or indecipherable names and/or addresses), retiring after forty-four years of service. He also operated a bookselling business

(1816–1823) in Duke Street, Grosvenor Square, London, and from 1822 until his death, he occupied the office of chamber-keeper in the Lord Chamberlain's department. A member of the Numismatic Society, Moule authored *A Table of Dates for the Use of Genealogists and Antiquaries* (1820), published anonymously; *Bibliotheca Heraldica Magnae Britanniae, an Analytical Catalogue of Books in Genealogy, Heraldry, Nobility, Knighthood, and Ceremonies, with a List of Provincial Visitations, Pedigrees, Collections of Arms, and Other Manuscripts, and a Supplement Enumerating the Principal Foreign Genealogical Works* (1822); *Antiquities in Westminster Abbey* (1825); *The English Counties Delineated, or, a Topographical Description of England*, 2 vols. (1837); and *The Heraldry of Fish* (1842). He also contributed the letter-press to *Views of Noble Mansions in Hampshire* (1825), by Henry (?) Hewetson; wrote the texts for such illustrated plate books as William Westall's *Great Britain Illustrated* (1830), *The Illustrations of the Work of Walter Scott* (1834), and R.B. Winkle's *Architectural and Picturesque Illustrations of the Cathedrals of Salisbury, Canterbury, St. Paul's, York, Wells, Rochester, Winchester, Lincoln, Chichester, Ely Petersborough, Exeter, Norwich, Bristol* (1835–1838); and authored an essay on "Roman Villas of the Augustan Age." Moule died in his official residence in the Stable Yard, St. James's Palace, London, in January 1851.[3]

Given the position of the shire of Cornwall on the map of England, one can certainly understand it having been, traditionally, considered the most remote and the least significant of the counties of England; yet, equally traditional romantics have associated the area with tin mining, natural stone monuments, smugglers, and wreckers. The remnants of the Cornish language will be found in place names and in the surnames of families beginning with *pen* (head)—Pendennis, Penhale, Penzance; *pol* (pool, hole)—Polkerris, Polmassick, Polperro; *porth* (port)—Porthallow, Porthcothan, Porthcorno); *tre* (farm)—Tremain, Tresillian, Trevelyan. One cannot discount, in addition, the number of place names beginning with *Saint*—St. Agnes, St. Austell, St. Buryan, St. Cleer, St. Columb Major.[4] The county once stood among the retreats of the ancient Britons when the West Saxons seized the eastern part of the isle of Britain, carried their arms to the Land's End, and extinguished for good the kingdom of Cornwall. Within the first two centuries following the withdrawal of Roman legions from Britain, the West Saxons had fairly well conquered about two thirds of England, counting from east to west. They had penetrated from the tidal Severn near Gloucester, and the tidal Dee near Chester, and in so doing had severed the British kingdom into three distinct parts: West Somerset, Dorsetshire, Devonshire and Cornwall; Wales; and Cumbria, or Strathclyde (identified as Lancashire north of the Ribble, Westmorland, and all of Galloway).[5]

Nonetheless, by the end of the eighteenth century and into the opening decade of the century following, the last remnant of the old Celts dialect had almost reached extinction. One significant tradition remained, however, that of ceding to the eldest son of an English sovereign the ducal title, and as revenue, he would receive the proceeds of a duty charged on all of the tin raised within the shire. Thus, for example, by 1858, when Albert Edward (1841–1910; later Edward VII), Prince of Wales, became of age, the revenue from the estates of the Duchy of Cornwall that he would receive amounted to £60,000 per year.[6]

The history of Cornwall remains essentially distinct from that of the remaining English counties, beginning with its organization, in the fourteenth century, as a duchy. When Henry VII (1457–1509; reigned 1485–1509), in 1497, considered an invasion of Scotland, and Parliament voted him a heavy tax to support it, an insurrection erupted in Cornwall, and its leaders marched to London to demand its repeal. Slow to accept the Reformation, in 1549 thousands of Cornishmen marched to defend the Roman Catholic Church; at the outset of the Civil War (1642–1649), Cornwall stood as a principal recruiting area for Charles I; and, as we shall notice throughout the discussions that follow, Wesleyan Methodism, in the eighteenth century, exercised a significant influence there, particularly upon the middle and lower classes.

Finally, one might wish to consider examples from what might be termed the literature (including books of prints) of Cornwall, as well as certain practices (various editions, costs, et al.) within the early English book trade, particularly those books published before, during, and shortly following the Wesleys' missions to that southwestern county of England. The principal source for the following short list derives from works (but not all of them first editions) on English topography set down, **numbered**, and **priced** throughout various sections of A Catalogue of Books by Henry G. Bohn (London: Henry G. Bohn, York Street, MDCCCXLI [1841]). Henry George Bohn (1796–1884), born of German parentage in London, began his career, in 1831, as a second-hand bookseller. In 1841, he issued his noted "Guinea [£1.1s] Catalogue," containing 23,208 published items in various languages. Five years later, he initiated the library of inexpensively priced reprints of standard works of fiction and nonfiction (including poetry and drama), the titles of which bear his name. An accomplished scholar, Bohn, himself, translated a number of the foreign classics in history, science, philosophy, and theology, and he compiled a dictionary of quotations. Although Bohn placed those titles under the broad category of "English Topography," not all of them tend to be limited to that area of study. As one will note, the following survey also ranges into such areas as Cornish language and history. For Bohn, in 1841, the term "topography" applied to physical descriptions of locales and, as well, to their historical and cultural features. For the titles discussed below, listed in chronological order by year of publication, the figures preceding refer to Bohn *Catalogue* number.

No. 15353. Carew's (R.) *Survey of Cornwall*, original edition, 1602— Spelman's *Villare Anglicanum; or, A View of the Cities, Towns, and Villages in England* published anonymously 1656 (another edition in 1678), 2 vols. in 1, small 4to., nt. 8s. "Although more histories of Cornwall have been written than of any other county, they are all wretched productions; and the Survey of Carew remains beyond all comparison the most accurate and satisfactory."—*Lowndes.* (1) The poet and antiquary Richard Carew (1555–1626), the son of Thomas Carew, Esq., studied at Oxford and served in Parliament in 1584, as well as High Sheriff of Cornwall (1856). He published a number of translations from the Italian, including five cantos from Tasso's *Jerusalem Delivered* (1594), and wrote *A True and Ready Way to Learn the Latin Tongue.* However, Carew's best work came forth in his *Survey of Cornwall* (London, 1602), with further editions in 1723, 1769, and 1811—the last undertaken by Francis, Lord De Dunstanville. (2) Sir Henry Spelman (1562–1641), a native of Norfolk and educated at Trinity College, Cambridge, entered Lincoln's Inn, London, in 1580, at age eighteen for the study of the law. Two years later he returned to Norfolk, where he became (1604) High Sheriff. Spelman engaged in business in Ireland and held appointments from James I in England. He settled in London in 1612 and devoted the remainder of his life to antiquarian research and publication. (3) The London bookseller and bibliographer William Thomas Lowndes (1798?-1843), born in London, achieved his reputation as the author and compiler of the four-volume *The Bibliographer's Manual of English Literature, Containing an Account of Rare, Curious, and Useful Books, Published in and Relating to Great Britain and Ireland* (1834)— the first systematic work of its kind in England, as well as a labor of fourteen years of research prior to completion—and *The British Librarian* (1839–1842), a literary product left unfinished at his death, but revised and enlarged by Henry George Bohn in 1857–1858.[7]

No. 5554. William Lloyd, *Archaeologica Britannica (or Glossographica)*,[8] *Giving an Account of the Languages of the Original Inhabitants of Britain* (1707). Folio,[9] calf,[10] scarce. Oxford. *Contents*—Britain and Ireland—Armoric[11] Grammar—Armoric-Eng[lish]. Vocabulary—Welsh Vocabulary—**Cornish Grammar**—Etymologicon Britann[icae].—Ancient Scottish Grammar—Irish-English Dictionary. William Lloyd (1627–1717), a native of Berkshire, began his formal undergraduate education at Oriel College, Oxford before removing to Jesus College in 1640, where he became a fellow in 1646. He entered into Holy Orders of the Church of England and eventually received appointments as prebendary (canon of a cathedral or collegiate church who receives from either one a portion [a "prebend"] of the revenues from its lands or the tithes) of Sarum (Salisbury, Wiltshire) Cathedral (1667); dean (the head of a chapter [a body of canons] of a cathedral or a collegiate church) of Bangor, Wales (1672); Vicar of St. Martin-in-the-Fields, London (1676); Bishop of St. Asaph, Wales (1680); Bishop of Lichfield and Coventry (1692); and Bishop of Worcester (1699–1700). A person of considerable learning, Lloyd stood among the seven bishops of the Church committed to the Tower of London in June 1688 for refusing to commit to and advance the Declarations of Indulgence of King James II, but the Court acquitted them of the charge of seditious libel. Declarations of Indulgence, by the way, comprised royal decrees that suspended penal legislation against religious Nonconformity (including Roman Catholicism). Following an abortive attempt in 1662, the 1672 declarations permitted Protestant Dissenters to worship in licensed meeting-houses and Roman Catholics to worship in private. Parliament brought about their cancellation, but James II (1633–1701, reigned 1685–1688) revived the declarations in 1667, which brought about the case of the seven bishops (including William Lloyd) in 1688.

No. 19728. Norden's (John) *Speculi Britanniae Pars; a Topographical and Historical Description of Cornwall* (1728); royal (pertaining to a sheet of paper measuring 24" × 19" for writing, and for printing 24" × 25"); 4to. Large paper, frontispiece, maps and plates, neat. 18s. (No. 19728). A native of Somerset, the cartographer John Norden (1548–1625?) eventually entered into the legal profession, but at some point in c. 1580, he turned his attention and labor to the production of surveys of the English counties. He then published descriptions of several of those counties—Middlesex, Hertfordshire, Northamptonshire, Norfolk, et al.—and maps, the latter proving to have been the first printed English maps to indicate roads and to furnish a scale.

No. 14681. [Borlase, William]. (See the entry immediately following) *Observations on the Ancient and Present State of the Islands of Scilly and Their importance to the Trade of Great Britain* (1756) 4to, plates, bds [boards]. 9s. Oxford. The Isles of Scilly/Scilly Isles/Scilly Islands comprise a group of 140 small islands, six miles square, off of Land's End, Cornwall, its principal settlement being High Town. In the eighteenth century, the area appeared as a haven for prates and smugglers. Samuel Johnson reviewed this volume in *The Literary Magazine, or Universal Review*, 1:2 (1756), 91–97,[12] noting, "This is the most pleasing and elegant pieces of local enquiry that our country has produced."

No. 14677. Borlase's *Natural History of Cornwall* (1758); folio, plates, with the autograph and a few MS. notes by Peter Collinson, the friend of Linnaeus; hf. bd. [half board], old morocco; £1. 16s. In the bookbinding process, *boards* represent pieces of strong pasteboard covered with paper and applied as the covers of books; *morocco* refers to leather produced from goatskins tanned with sumac—as well as imitations of that process and material, produced from sheepskins and lambskins. Morocco had been, in the early seventeenth century, applied principally to shoemaking, but beginning later in that century, bookbinders adapted it.

(1) The clergyman and antiquary William Borlase (1695–1772), a native of Cornwall, received his formal higher education at Exeter College, Oxford, and following his entrance to Holy Orders of the Church of England, occupied, in 1722, the rectory of Ludgvan, Cornwall, and then, in 1732, added to his responsibilities the vicarage of St. Just, in that same county. After the poet and satirist Alexander Pope (1688–1744) had leased a villa at Twickenham, Middlesex, in 1719, he then turned his attention to the construction of a grotto, lined with rock crystals, in the grounds of St. Catherine's Convent of Mercy and beneath the Teddington Road, thus linking his gardens on either side. To that underground retreat Borlase contributed the following items—a list that adds significantly to the knowledge of the natural resources of eighteenth-century Cornwall: "Many pieces of sparry Marble of diverse Colours [the adjective *sparry* descriptive of "spar," a general term for a number of crystalline materials, fairly lustrous in appearance and easily split into fragments or particles] and between each Course of Marble, many kinds of Ores, such as Tin Ore, Copper Ore, Lead Ore, Soapy Rock [having the soft or greasy feeling of soap; chalk-like; also known as soap rock, consisting of streatite or magnesium clay], Kallan [the word does not appear in the *Oxford English Dictionary (OED)*; the nearest to it, "kalinite," refers to a native form of potash occurring in the form of an aggregate of minute crystals], and Wild Lead intermixed, with large Clumps of *Cornish* Diamonds, and several small ones of different Degrees of Transparency. The several sorts of figur'd Stones are rich white Spars, interlaced with black Cockle [a miner's reference to "Black Tourmaline"—a brittle mineral occurring in crystals, with

a blackish luster], or Spars shot into Prisms of different Degrees of Waters. Some very particular sorts of Fossils, of different Sizes and Colours; Copper Ore of a fine Purple Colour; several fine Pieces of granated white Mundic [the Cornish miners' name for "pyrites"—native disulphide of iron, crystallizing in isometric forms], intermixed with a plain Spar in a Copper Bed. A very uncommon sort of Mundic mix'd, or rather inclos'd in Wild Lead; several thin Crusts or Films of bright Spar, form'd on a Surface before shot into Protuberances; a Lump of Yellow Copper, that has a very bright Crust of Spar; some grains of Mundic interspers'd, of different Colours, some Yellow, some Purple, and others of a deep Blue, inclining to Black; all from the Reverend Dr. *William Borlase*."[13]

(2) Born at Hugal Hall, near Windermere, Westmorland, Peter Collinson (1694–1768), botanist and naturalist, initially entered the business of manufacturing hosiery. Eventually, however, he introduced American plant species into England and English species to British North America, thereby assisting agricultural progress in both lands.

(3) Carolus Linnaeus (originally Carl von Linne [1707–1778]), Swedish botanist and the founder of modern systematic botany, born in Rashult, Smaland, Sweden, the son of a Lutheran pastor, received his education at Lund (1727) and Uppsala (both in Sweden), where he became an assistant to Dr. Olaf Celsius (1670–1756) in compiling *Hierobotanicon*, a treatise on the plants of the Bible. Linnaeus also wrote an essay on sex in plants and in 1730 accepted the appointment as the assistant to the professor of botany at Uppsala. Two years later, he explored Lapland under the sponsorship of the Swedish Academy of Sciences, publishing the scientific results of that expedition in *Flora Lapponica* (1737). Further travel carried Linnaeus through Dalecarlia, Sweden, and upon his return he studied for and earned a doctor of medicine degree from the university at Harderwijk, Holland, in 1735. His publications included *Systema Naturae* (1737); *Hortus Cliffortianus*, as a result of studying the plants in a garden near Haarlem, the Netherlands, belonging to his patron, the Dutch merchant George Clifford; *Fundamenta Botanica* (1736), written in Holland; *Bibliotheca Botanica* (1736); *Critica Botanica* (1737); *Genera Plantarum* (1737); *Classes Plantarum* (1738). Linnaeus traveled to England and France, after which he returned to Sweden and established himself, in 1738, as physician at Stockholm; professor of medicine (1741) and professor of botany (from 1742) at Uppsala University, where he proved responsible for increasing the academic reputation of that institution. Another tour took him to Oland and Gotland, in Sweden, the results being published in *Olandska och Gothlandska Resa* (1745), in which specific

botanical names first appeared. Other important publications of Linnaeus include *Flora Swecica* (1745); *Fauna Swecica* (1745); *Hortus Upsaliensis* (1748); *Philosophia Botanica* (1750; and *Species Plantarum* (1753)—in which Linnaeus provided a complete account of specific botanical names and created a work that has long been considered the foundation for the modern system of botanical nomenclature. Essentially, he insisted upon the identification of plants by a limited, specific name, in addition to a generic reference.

No. 14578.—the same [Borlase's *Natural History of Cornwall* [1758], *wanting the plates, very neat*. 15s. [Oxford].

No. 14679.—[Borlase's] *Natural History and Antiquities of Cornwall* [1758–1769], 2 vols. in 1, folio, *plates, Russia* [an extremely desirable leather produced from skins impregnated with oil distilled from the birch bark and applied extensively to bookbinding] *extra, borders, gilt edges, by Clarke,* £5. 15s. 6d.

No. 14675. Borlase's (W.) *Antiquities, Historical and Monumental, of the Inhabitants, Druid-Superstition, Customs, and Remains of the Most Remote Antiquity in Britain and the British Isles, with a Vocabulary of the Cornish Language* (1769), folio, plates, hf. bd. [half-boards], russia, uncut, £1. 16s. Druids existed as the priests and judges of the ancient Celts in pre–Christian Gaul, Britain, and Ireland, responsible for the education of young Gauls. They proved proficient in natural philosophy and developed as practitioners of a religion that, supposedly, included human sacrifice. The Druids taught the immortality of the soul and a doctrine of reincarnation, studied ancient verse, and demonstrated considerable knowledge of astronomy. Suppressed in Gaul by the Emperor Tiberius (42 BC–37 AD, reigned 14–37 AD), they later suffered the same treatment in Britain. In Ireland, the Druids lost their priestly function following the establishing of Christianity in that land, and they survived for a time as poets and historians.

No. 14676.—the same [Borlase's *Antiquities* (1769)]. Folio, some of the plates wanting, several leaves; Manuscript, very neat in old russia, 15s.

No. 20497. Price's/Pryce's[14] (W.) *Mineralogia Cornubiensis, a Treatise on Minerals, Mines, and Mining, Containing the Theory and Natural History of Strata, Fissures, and Lodes, with the Methods of Discovering, Working, &c., with a Glossary of the Terms Used by the **Cornish** Miners* (1778), folio, plates, bds. [boards] £1. 7s. William Price/Pryce held the M.D. degree and practiced medicine at Redruth, Cornwall.

No. 20498.—the same (1778). [Price/Pryce, *Mineralogia Cornubiensis*], folio, very neat in calf, £1. 11s. 6d.

No. 4831. Price/Pryce, William. *Archaeologia Cornu-Britannica; or, An Essay to Preserve the Ancient Cornish Language; Containing the Rudiments of That Dialect, in a Cornish Grammar and Cornish-English Vocabulary* (1790). 4to., bds. [boards], 15s.

No. 18903. Lysons' (D. and S.) *Britannia Depicta, a Series of Views, with Brief Descriptions, of the Most Interesting and Picturesque Objects in Great Britain, from Original Drawings, Engraved by W. Byrne, to Illustrate Lysons' "Magna Britannia,"*[15] with Indexes Referring to That Work, 5 Parts Containing Bedfordshire, Berkshire, Buckinghamshire, Cambridgeshire, Cheshire, **Cornwall,** and Cumberland (1803–1815; all published), in 1 vol. oblong folio,[16] 98 plates, fine impressions, (pub. at £13. 9s.) hf. bd. [half board], calf, £4. 4s. (1) Daniel Lysons (1760?-1834), rector of Rodmarton, Gloucestershire (1804–1833)—and a nephew of Daniel Lysons the elder (?-1800), M.D., who practiced medicine at Bath, Somersetshire—achieved a modest reputation, during his time, and those close to his work described him as a learned, astute, judicious, and accurate antiquary. He held a fellowship in the Royal Society and membership in the Antiquarian Society. A biographical note will be found in the *Gentleman's Magazine*, May 1834, 558.[17] (2) His brother, Samuel Lysons (1763–1819), called to the Bar in 1798, became Keeper of the Records in the Tower of London (1803) while, at the same time, earning recognition for his ingenuity, tireless research, and publications in antiquarian studies.

No. 22871. *Whitaker's* (John) *Historical Survey of the Ancient Cathedral of Cornwall [The Ancient Cathedral of Cornwall Historically Surveyed]* (1804), 2 vols., 4to, plates, hf. bd. [half-boards], russia extra, uncut, by Kalthoeber, Fonthill copy, £1. 7s. Fonthill Abbey, the extravagant residence built in 1790 on Lansdowne Hill, near Bath, Somersetshire, had been occupied by the English novelist and art collector William Beckford (1760–1844), the author of the French language Gothic novel *Vathek* (1782), and designed by the English architect James Wyatt (1746–1813), who revived interest in Gothic architecture. Whitaker's *Historical Survey* has been described as "full of curious antiquarian research, respecting early British History" (1). John Whitaker (1735–1808), born at Manchester, Lancashire, became a fellow of Corpus Christi College, Oxford, in 1753, entered into Holy Orders of the Church of England, and served for a lengthy period as curate of Newton Abbot, Devonshire. During a brief period (November-December 1773), he held the pulpit as morning preacher of Berkeley Chapel, London, then removed to the rectory of Ruan Lanyhome, Cornwall. Whitaker died on 30 October 1808.[18]

No. 22982. Williams's (T.H.) *Picturesque Excursions in Devonshire and Cornwall* (1804); 2 parts in 1 vol., 8vo. [octavo], with 26 clever etchings by the author, hf. bd. [half-boards], morocco, full gilt, London. 14s. The majority of the limited number of publications by Thomas H. Williams, a resident of Plymouth, then of Exeter (both in Devonshire), appear to have been printed privately.

No. 18898. Lysons' (D. and S.) *Magna Britannia, Vols. 1–6, Containing Bedfordshire, Berkshire, Buckinghamshire, Cambridgeshire, and Cornwall, with the Volume of Additional Plates, and Corrections for Volume 1*, in 5 vols. (1806–1814); imperial (printing papers measuring 22" × 32" or of writing paper 22" × 30") 4to. LARGE PAPER, plates, bds. [boards] £3. 13s. 6d.

No. 18897. Lysons' (D. and S.) *Magna Britannia*. LARGE PAPER, WITH NUMBERED ADDITIONAL PLATES, including the whole of Byrne's *Britannica Depicta* (1808–1822). The first four counties interleaved and divided into 6 vols., forming together 12 vols., imperial 4to., numerous plates (pub. at upwards of 70 guineas [£73. 10s.]); bds. [boards] uncut, £12. 12s. The first edition of *Magnus Britannica* combined with *Britannica Depicta*, large paper, fetched £71. 10s.

No. 66. *Ordnance Maps of Devon and Cornwall, Divided into Sections and Mounted on Canvas* (1809–1813). Enclosed in 2 stout blue morocco cases, in fine condition, £7. 7s. "This is less than half the original cost." Ordnance referred to the branch of the public service concerned with the supply of military stores and materials and the management of the artillery. The Board of Ordnance, comprised partly of military and partly of civilians, managed all of the affairs related to the artillery and engineers, in addition to the materials available and supplied to the Royal Army. When dissolved in 1855, the major portion of its functions concerning materials went over to the Royal Army Ordnance Department. Finally, the *Ordnance Surveys of Great Britain and Ireland* originated with the government and underwent publication under the direction of the Master-General of the Ordnance.

No. 18896. Lyons' (D. and S.) *Magna Britannia, Being a Concise Topographical Account of the Several Counties of Great Britain, viz.*[19] *Bedfordshire, Berkshire, Buckinghamshire, Cambridgeshire, Cheshire, Cornwall, Cumberland, Derbyshire, and Devonshire* (1813–1822), 10 vols. in 8, 4to. Numerous plates, (pub. at £27. 4s.) bds. [boards], £6. 15s.

No. 20358. Polwhele's (Rev. Richard) *History of Cornwall, Civil, Military, Religious, Architectural, Agricultural, Commercial, Biographical, and Miscellaneous* (1816); new edition, corrected and enlarged, 7 vols. in 2, 4to. plates (pub. at £8. 8s.), bds. [boards], £2. 5s. Richard Polwhele

(1760–1838), born at Truro, Cornwall, received his formal higher education at Christ Church, Oxford, after which he underwent Holy Orders in the Church of England—ordained deacon in 1782 and, presumably, priest in 1783. He received ecclesiastical appointments as curate to Archdeacon John Sleech (?-1788) at Kenton, Suffolk (1783–1793); vicar of Manaccan, Cornwall (1793); curate of Kenwyn, Cornwall (1806); vicar of St. Newlyn, Cornwall (1821–1828). He then removed to his paternal seat, Polwhele, near Truro, where he resided for the remainder of his life, serving as magistrate and devoting time to literary labor.

No. 613. *Excursions in Essex, Norfolk, Surrey, Kent, Sussex,* **Cornwall,** *and Ireland* (1818–1824). 13 vols., royal (paper size measuring 24" × 19" for writing and 24" × c. 25" for printing) 4to., LARGE PAPER, 621 fine Views, INDIA PROOFS—India paper (or India proofs) refers to a soft absorbent paper of creamy yellow or pale buff color, imported from China, and applied to the *proofs* of engravings—*half-bound, morocco, uncut, top edge gilt,* £10. 10s. (*pub. at* £40. 19s.), *bds.*[boards], £19. 9s. *Excursions in ...* **Cornwall** *and Ireland* (1818–1824) [same title as above]. LARGE PAPER, INDIA PROOFS.

No. 3154. *Transactions of the Geological Society of Cornwall.* (1818–1828); 3 vols. 8vo., plates, bds., scarce, £2.

No. 17164. Gorham's (G.C.) *History and Antiquities of Eynesbury and St. Neot's, in Huntingdonshire, and of St. Neot's in Cornwall, with Some Critical Remarks on the Two Saxon Saints from Whom These Places Derived Their Names* (1820). 2 vols. 8vo., with 50 plates (pub. at 18s.), bds. [boards], 9s. (1) George Cornelius Gorham (1787–1857), born in St. Neot's, Huntingdonshire, the son of George James Gorham, a merchant, studied at St. Neot's School and Queens' College, Cambridge (B.A. 1808, M.A. 1812, B.D. 1820), and became a fellow of Queen's College (1809–1827). Following his entrance into Holy Orders of the Church of England, he held ecclesiastic appointments as curate of Beckenham, Kent (1814–1818); curate of Clapham, Surrey (1818–1827); curate of St. Mary's Chapel, Maidenhead, Berkshire (1840–1842); curate of Fawley, Oxfordshire (1843–1846); and vicar of St. Just, in Penwith, Cornwall (1846–1850). In November 1847, Lord Chancellor Charles Christopher Pepys, first Earl of Cottenham (1781–1851), presented Gorham with the vicarage of Brampford Speke, Devonshire, but the Bishop of Exeter refused to install him on account of his views denying unconditional baptismal regeneration. The Bishop's action resulted in two and one-half years of litigation, at the end of which the Rev. Gorham received his appointment from Sir H.J. Fust, judge of the Court of Arches—the ecclesiastical court of appeal for the province of Canterbury, formerly held at the Church of St. Mary-Le-Bow ("of the Arches"), London—so named for the arches that supported the steeple. Gorham died at Brampton Speke on 19 June 1857.[21]

No. 17091. Gilbert's (Davies) *Parochial History of Cornwall, Founded on the Manuscript Histories of Hals and Tonkin, with Additions, Including a Minute Geological Account of Each Parish, by Dr. Bose, and Various Appendices* (1838). 4 vols., 8vo. [octavo—the size of a book, or page, after the sheets have been folded so that each leaf measures *one-eighth* of a whole sheet; thus, a book or a volume "in octavo"] bds. [boards] £2. 12s. 6d. (No. 17091). Davies Gilbert (1767–1839)—original surname of "Giddy"—an English antiquary and a former president of the Royal Society, contributed a number of essays on Cornish topography to the *Proceedings of the Antiquarian Society*.

Viewed collectively, the preceding volumes would appear to proclaim to the reading public of the day those features of Cornwall that proved particularly attractive to the eyes and minds of the imaginative and the inquisitive: the ruins of the thirteenth-century Tintagel Castle at Bude, the legendary birthplace of King Arthur; Pendennis Castle at Falmouth, built by Henry VIII to guard the western coast of Carrick Roads, with an outer curtain wall and angle bastion added by Elizabeth I; the coastal fortification of St. Mawes Castle, also at Falmouth, begun by Henry VIII in 1540; the small Iron Age fortification of Castle Dore, at Fowey, reputedly the headquarters of the Cornish chieftain King Mark (Cunomorus) of the Arthurian legend, whose betrothed Iseult became the lover of Tristan; Innisidgen chambered tomb, Isles of Scilly, a partially covered Neolithic chambered tomb; Star Castle, St. Mary's Island, in the Isles of Scilly, an Elizabethan fortification designed by the Court engineer Robert Adams and built in 1593 to defend England against the possible return of a second Spanish Armada; Oliver Cromwell's castle on Tresco, the Isles of Scilly, a fortification built by Robert Blake in 1651–1652 to guard the west coast of England against Royalist privateers and landing parties; the late twelfth- or early thirteenth-century Launceston Castle, built by Richard, Earl of Cornwall, brother of Henry III; "The Hurlers" at Liskeard, a Bronze Age monument of three stone circles in a line—originally twenty-five to thirty-five stones in each circle; Carn Brae near Redruth, a hillside Iron Age fort extending to thirty-seven acres; the foundations of the Iron Age village of Chysauster, near St. Ives.

The words on the printed page and the images on the numerous plates would readily serve to satisfy the appetites of those who traveled with their eyes and their minds, rather than on foot, upon horseback, or in carriages. They would loom large for, say, readers in London or Birmingham or Manchester, for whom Cornwall might have seemed as far distant from their own lives as a portion of Africa or a province in Asia or a colony in North America. The authors of those volumes, however, demonstrated little attention and revealed even less interest in the spiritual states of the inhabitants of Cornwall, although a significant number of them had embraced Holy Orders in, and a lifelong commitment to, the Church of England. Such pursuits and endeavors, as we shall see, they willingly ceded to the missionaries of their day.

Methodism in
Eighteenth-Century Cornwall

In looking into the state of religion and life in eighteenth-century Cornwall, one must not react hastily and assume that the efforts toward a revival of religious discipline and practice in that county derived solely from the work of Methodists' hands. Certainly, there arises a tendency to think in that direction, principally because of the reputation (and one justly deserved) of John Wesley—and to a lesser extent of his brother Charles Wesley—and his significant and innovative contributions to religious and social reform throughout Britain during the last six decades of the eighteenth century. In other words, John Wesley included Cornwall on his regular Methodist missionary itinerancy, and therefore John Wesley planted Methodism in eighteenth-century Cornwall. However, remember that from John Wesley's theological perspective, Wesleyan Methodism meant evangelicalism within the extant boundaries of the Church of England—an emphasis upon religious conversion and salvation by faith in the atoning death of Jesus Christ. Wesley sought to build a religious organization that would inject reality into religion at a time when immorality had achieved too high a position upon the priorities of human conduct and activity, and when the clergy appeared openly negligent and excessively worldly. Actually, though, that "evangelicalism," or "Evangelical Revival," practiced and advanced by the Wesleys had come into the world long before the name "Wesley" had been imprinted upon the pages of Western world history.

Richard Heitzenrater has reminded us that the Evangelical Revival in England comprised but a portion of "a larger worldwide movement of the

Spirit." He identified German Pietism of the late seventeenth century and the Great Awakening in British North America in the early eighteenth century as among "the precursors" of the revival in England. Insofar as concerns Pietism, that late seventeenth- and early eighteenth-century movement, principally within German Protestantism, sought to supplement the emphasis upon institutions and dogma in orthodox Protestant religious organizations by concentrating upon the practice of piety. The founders and followers of the movement anchored their thinking to inner experience and to committing themselves to a life of religious practice. At the same time, however, the Protestant orthodox establishment began to initiate movements to a new reformation, or a revival of religious life. A principal leader in the Pietist movement emerged in the person of the German theologian, genealogist, and heraldic scholar Philipp Jakob Spener (1635–1705), whose tract *Pia Desideria* (1675) spread the movement far beyond the range of his personal influence.[1] Those two movements, especially, featured effective preaching, significant numbers of evangelical conversions, and "assorted manifestations of spiritual vitality" in forms and modes ranging from individual piety, individual and group piety, to outright and radical displays of human frenzy. Heitzenrater identified several "antecedents" to the characteristics that would, beginning in the early 1740s, become associated with the Wesleyan revival in England, Ireland, Scotland, and Wales: the small groups comprising the Church of England religious societies beginning in the 1670s; evidence of itinerant field preaching in Wales prior to the 1720s; the religious revival in Wales in the 1730s; and the spiritual revival that preceded the entrance of Charles Wesley and John Wesley into Cornwall and Scotland.[2]

To be fair to the reputations of the Wesleys, they never claimed to be the sole originators of their ideals, ideas, and methods. They simply labored longer than the majority of their predecessors and, as the result of John Wesley's organizational acumen, did so more efficiently—at least as efficiently as eighteenth-century conditions permitted them to do so. Further, by the time the Wesley's turned their individual attentions toward Cornwall, the obstacles to their achieving a successful mission to that far southwestern county had grown considerably. Enter into the discussion John Wesley's prominent but not always objective nineteenth-century biographer, the Yorkshire-born Methodist minister Luke Tyerman (1820–1889). Tyerman held Wesleyan Methodist pulpits at Iver, Buckinghamshire (1845–1848); the London district of Lambeth (1848–1851); Bristol, Gloucestershire (1851–1852); Newcastle-upon-Tyne, Northumberland (1852–1855); Sheffield, Yorkshire (1855–1858); Manchester, Lancashire

(1858–1861); Liverpool, Lancashire (1861–1864); supernumerary (non-traveling, semi-retired) at Brixton Hill, London (1864–1867); and Clapham, Surrey (1887–1889). He authored biographies of Samuel Wesley the elder (1866); John Wesley (1870–1871); the Oxford Methodists (1873), George Whitefield (1877); and John William Fletcher, vicar of Madeley, Shropshire (1882). Tyerman died at Stanhope House, Atkins Road, Clapham Park, on 20 March 1889.[3] Tyerman probably drew an accurate (though, perhaps, at the time, stereotypical) sketch of Cornwall in the first half of the eighteenth century, when he exclaimed, "Cornwall, at this period [c. 1743], was as imbruted as Staffordshire." His choice of the word "imbruted" reminds those familiar with John Milton's *Paradise Lost* (1667) of Satan's lament,

> O foul descent! That I who erst contended
> With Gods to sit the highest, am now constrain'd
> Into a Beast, and mixt with bestial slime,
> This essence to incarnate and **imbrute**,
> That to the highth of Deity aspir'd [9:163–167],

while the reference to Staffordshire points directly to the severity of the anti–Methodist mobs and riots at Wednesbury and Darlaston, in Stafford-shire, during June-October 1742.[4] "Smuggling," continued Tyerman, "was considered an honourable traffic, and the plunder of shipwrecked mariners was accounted a lawful prize. Drunkenness was general; and cockfighting, bullbaiting, wrestling, and hurling were the favourite amusements of the people."[5] For those particularly interested in the sporting life of provincial eighteenth century, hurling consisted of a game closely related to handball, extremely popular in Cornwall throughout the seventeenth and into the eighteenth centuries. Played by two parties, the object of the exercise focused upon being to "hurl" or carry a ball to a distant goal or to a goal in their own part of the country. A different form of it had been played in Ireland. John Wesley observed, as well as uttered the desire, in 1781, that "*hurling*, their [Cornish men's] favourite diversion, at which limbs were usually broke, and very frequently lives lost, is now hardly heard of: it seems in a few years it will be utterly forgotten."[6]

Another of the Wesleys' late nineteenth-century biographers, the Rev. John Telford (1851–1936), proved equally enthusiastic and subjective in his treatment of his subjects. Born at Wigton, Cumberland, the son of John Telford the elder and Frances Ross Telford, he received his education at private schools, Didsbury College, Manchester, and London University (B.A.). After entering the Wesleyan Methodist ministry, he served churches at Leytonstone, greater London; Hinde Street, Lewisham, greater London; Richmond, Surrey; Finchley, greater London; Guildford, Surrey;

Tunbridge Wells; and Redhill, Dorking. From 1878 to 1880, Telford functioned as an assistant to his father-in-law, Dr. James Harrison Rigg (1821–1899), president of the Wesleyan Methodist Conference; as one of the secretaries of the committee that prepared the 1904 *Methodist Hymn Book*; as the Wesleyan Methodist Connexional Editor and editor of *The Wesleyan Methodist Magazine*, the *Preacher's Magazine*, *The London Quarterly Review*, *The Church Record*, and a number of periodicals associated with the Wesleyan Methodist Church. In all, Telford published no less than eighteen book titles and twenty periodical essays devoted to the lives and works of John and Charles Wesley.[7] Nonetheless, Telford noted, with a fair degree of accuracy, the prevailing attitude of the Church of England establishment toward the Wesleys' missionary efforts in Cornwall: "The [Church of England] clergy were still opposed to the work. Some of them were enraged because the Methodists were so familiar with the Scriptures. One even expressed a wish that the Bible were in Latin only, so that none of the vulgar might be able to read it. A member [of the Methodist society] went to the Rev. Dr. [William] Borlase,[8] a magistrate, to seek redress, because a rioter had broken into his house and stolen his goods. 'They may burn thy house if they will,' was the doctor's reply; 'thou shalt have no justice.'"[9] Given the extent of the violent reactions in Cornwall to the initial visits into that county by the Wesleys and their subordinates, one might believe that the evangelical blades of early Methodism had come to plow uncultivated ground. To the contrary, as far back as the early 1730s, and extending into the very year of the Wesleys' first arrival, at least a dozen individuals had involved themselves, and had organized others, in efforts to cleanse the moral and spiritual climates of Cornwall. Those persons could not, technically, be labeled "Methodists," but their actions, their ideals, their methods, and their objectives ranged not too far beyond those of the brothers from Lincolnshire and Oxford.

For example, and reportedly,[10] an evangelically-minded sea captain, one Joseph Turner, a native of Bristol, arrived in St. Ives, Cornwall, early in 1743 and discovered a religious society there. He informed the members of the Wesleys' work, and they requested that a preacher be sent to them—which, in turn, led to the visitations into Cornwall by the Wesleys themselves. Two Church of England clerics, the Rev. John Bennet (1670?-1750), perpetual curate of North Tamerton, Cornwall, and curate of Tresmeer (from 1720) and of Laneast (from 1731)—a contemporary and acquaintance at Oxford University of the Wesleys' father, the Rev. Samuel Wesley the elder—and Rev. George Thomson (1698–1782), rector of St. Gennys (from 1732), who underwent evangelical conversion in. c. 1733 or 1734 and later engaged in itinerant preaching, had both undergone evangelical conversion well in advance of the Wesleys' influence and had preached religious and social reform independent of them. James Hervey (1714–1758), the former pupil of the Wesleys at Oxford, had preached at St. Gennys in 1738. Catherine Quick, a resident of or near St. Ives, led a group of eleven other evangelically-minded persons who met at St. Ives for prayer and the reading of the then popular *Expository Notes, with Practical Observations, on the New Testament of Our Lord and Saviour Jesus Christ* (1700?), by William Burkitt (1650–1703), vicar of Dedham, Essex. Captain Joseph Turner visited this group, and Catherine Quick afterward issued the invitation to the Wesleys to visit Cornwall. John Nance, another St. Ives evangelical resident, emerged to welcome Charles Wesley to that town on 16 July 1743, to serve as his host, and to introduce him to the religious society there.[11] Unfortunately, a considerable portion of the so-called details concerning the general state of Methodism in Cornwall during the eighteenth century tends toward the anecdotal from secondary and tertiary sources. That proves to be true, to an extent, even in the commentaries recorded in such primary sources as the Wesleys' own journal narratives and correspondence. Nonetheless, one can readily attempt to balance such speculation, opinion, and generalization against the details and statistics available from one of the more important documents in the history of eighteenth-century Methodism—the *Minutes*, both in manuscript and in print, of the Methodist Conferences from 1744 to 1791. Of course, even the numbers and details from that source might well stand eligible for questioning, since, as one should know, materials emerging from those annual meetings—whether in autograph copies or in print—did not come forth until examination by the steady and critical eye, and revision from the heavy hand, of John Wesley. At any rate, consider, within the substance of the text and tables that will follow, that (1) the manuscript minutes concern the Methodist Conferences from 1744 to 1764; (2) the printed volumes containing the Conference *Minutes* began in 1765; (3) the listing of preachers assigned to supply the various Methodist circuits began in 1746; (4) the listing of society membership statistics began in 1765; and (5) the publication of figures relating to the distributions of funds to the various societies began in 1769.[12]

Specific reference to Cornwall initially appeared upon the Agenda, dated 1 June 1744, for the first Methodist Conference, held at London on 25–29 June 1744. One will find it almost buried, listed under Section III, "Practice," item 47: "**Cornwall**? Wednesbury? To swear?"[13] In other words, the question to be considered concerned whether to develop a Methodist society in such religiously contentious corners of England as Cornwall and Wednesbury. That issue, or at least an item that came close to it, emerged on Thursday, 28 June, under the question, "What is the best way of spreading the gospel?"—which brought forth the answer from John Wesley, "To go a little farther from London, Bristol, **St. Ives**, Newcastle, or any other Society."[14] One might interpret the response to indicate that a Methodist society would be organized formally at St. Ives. The hard answer came in 1746, when one sees, in the *Minutes*, that Cornwall had become one of the seven original Methodist circuits, with specific preachers assigned—as well as indications of the lengths of their assignments (see Table 1 in "Appendices"). By 1748, Cornwall had become one of the nine "divisions" (recast as *circuits* in 1749) within John Wesley's Methodist organizations, to include the societies at Tavistock, Devonshire; Plymouth Dock, Devonshire; Trewint; St. Ewe; Gwennap; Illogan; St. Ives; and "The Western Societies."

From 1744 to 1791, the Methodist Conference (primarily John Wesley) dispatched a total of 146 preachers (excluding John Wesley, himself, but including Charles Wesley) to supply the spiritual needs of Cornwall Methodists. Of that number, 90 (62 percent) served in Cornwall for one year or less; 33 of them (22.6 percent) for two years; and 23 itinerant preachers (15.8 percent) labored in Cornwall for more than two years. Almost every one of those preachers carried with him anecdotal evidence of ministerial success and/or failures while on the Methodist hustings, but there exists little or no quantitative data by which to measure individual or collective work. Further, John Wesley tended to shift his itinerant preachers from one locale to another, lest they became overly complacent by settling in a particular circuit for too long a period. Nonetheless, realize that no matter from whatever the perspective one wishes to analyze the listing in Table 1, that roster of preachers and circuit assistants comprised the cast of characters who, more than anyone else—even more than the Wesleys themselves— bore the burdens of the success and the failures of the forty-six-year Methodist mission to Cornwall.

Certainly, the more revealing form of data to support the development and the degree of success of Methodism in eighteenth-century Cornwall would, naturally, assume the form of the numbers of members within the circuits and/or individual Methodist societies of that county. The absolute accuracy of those numbers, of course, will always remain under the shrouds of question and speculation until one can examine the membership lists and see (and *count*) the actual names of society members. However, such close scrutiny might not always be necessary, as revealed by just this single point of comparison: For the year 1770, as but one example, the Conference *Minutes* recorded a total Methodist membership throughout the British Isles as **29,181**. According to a later set of figures for that same year, gathered from a number of sources and published in 1977 by three British academics, the total number of Wesleyan Methodists in England, Wales, Scotland, and Ireland stood at **29,406**—a "mere" difference of **225** members. Thus, in the absence of more detailed analysis, one can, with varying degrees of confidence, rely upon the information housed in the Conference *Minutes*.[15] At any rate, figures for the membership within the various Methodist circuits and individual societies appeared in the published *Minutes* of the Methodist Conferences, beginning in 1765 (for Cornwall, see Table 2, "Appendices").

The membership statistics for Cornwall Methodism can readily be divided into two distinct parts: (1) According to the Conference count, from 1765 through 1783, the number of Methodists in Cornwall averaged 2,107 per year. (2) Then for 1784, the *Minutes* reported that the county had experienced an increase of five hundred persons over the previous year who claimed membership in John Wesley's religious organization, and thus, from 1784 through 1791 (the year of John Wesley's death) the average membership in Cornwall per year increased to 3,221. More than any other factor, that increase had to have come as the result of a combination of a significant change in attitude in the religious thoughts and practices of a percentage of the population of Cornwall in combination with the efforts of those preachers who engaged in the evangelical mission upon which the Methodist Conference had sent them. The specific details to support that claim will unfold in the discussions of Methodist activities that occurred in the towns and villages of Cornwall to which the principal sections of this volume have been devoted.

Finally, in the "Large" *Minutes* of the Methodist Conference of 1763, the question arose as to "How may we raise a General Fund?" John Wesley responded, "By a yearly subscription, to be proposed by every Assistant when he visits the classes at Christmas, and received at the visitation following." Various changes in that policy occurred in later years—e.g., in 1767, the collection would be gathered at Easter; in 1770, a policy of strict controls for spending on building; in 1772, collections gathered at every preaching house; in 1779, the fiat that each circuit must begin to "bear its own burden."[16] Figures concerning the funds distributed to the Methodist circuits throughout England, Wales, Ireland, and Scotland became available initially in the annual Conference *Minutes* of 1766, indicating the subscription for that year had yielded £695 2s. 11d.—against the general

Methodist building debt having risen to £11,383. The question then followed, "What places petitioned for help?" Although the Cornish Methodist societies at St. Hilary, Crowan, Stithians, and St. Just had submitted petitions, and the names of those towns appeared on the list, no amounts had been posted beside them—which means that Cornish Methodists received nothing in that year from the Conference coffers. Even so, subsequent listings (see Table 3, "Appendices") do provide indications of the levels of commitment of John Wesley and the Methodist Conference to the development and maintenance of Methodism in Cornwall.

Clearly, in 1769, the Conference allocation to Cornwall of £137 0s. 0d. comprised what one would label "seed money," a sign that the Conference (and John Wesley) seriously intended to support the Methodist missionary efforts in that county. However, the allotments that followed for Cornwall between 1770 and 1780 can only be termed, collectively, a mere pittance in contrast to what the Methodist patriarch and the annual Conference bestowed on more "profitable" fields of evangelical endeavor. For instance, in 1773, Methodists in Chatham, Kent, received from the Conference £120; Norwich, Norfolk, £180; Bradford, in the West Riding of Yorkshire, £149. 5s.; Whitby, in the North Riding of Yorkshire, £100; Edinburgh, Scotland, £143; and **Cornwall** (both East and West circuits), **£0. 0s. 0d.** Essentially, there arose no bias on the part of John Wesley and the Methodist Conference against Cornwall. Simply, as Methodism became a more complex organization, proceeds from the yearly contributions had to be applied to the support of such entities as assistance to preachers' wives and families, the elimination or reduction of general indebtedness, the building and maintenance of chapels, the Methodist publishing concern, the education of preachers' children, and partial stipends for the maintenance of preachers. As the organization developed, Wesley expected that individual societies, while continuing to contribute to the general fund, would become financially self-sufficient.

In mid–November 1781, John Wesley recalled the recent occasions wherein he had spoken with members of various Methodist societies in Cornwall, noting that "it pleased God, the seed that was then sown [prior to 1743[17]] has since produced an abundant harvest, Indeed, I hardly know any part of the three kingdoms [England, Ireland, Scotland] where there has been a more general change.... And that scandal of humanity, so constantly practised on all the coasts of Cornwall, the plundering [of] vessels that struck upon the rocks, and often murdering those that escaped out of the wreck, is now wellnigh at an end; and if it is not quite, the gentlemen, not the poor tinners, are to be blamed. But it is not harmlessness, or outward decency alone, which has within few years so increased, but the religion of the heart, faith working by love, producing all inward as well as outward holiness."[18] Therefore, before entering upon the discussions of the specific towns and village of Cornwall visited by the Wesleys between 1743 and 1789, one needs to raise the questions of whether the statistics from the Methodist Conference *Minutes* actually support John Wesley's positive view of the state of Methodism in Cornwall. How does one begin to measure such qualities as "inward holiness," "religion of the heart," and "faith working by love"? Can inquisitive minds be satisfied by declaring that in 1765 Cornwall housed a total of 2,321 Methodist society members, and a quarter of a century later, in 1791, that number had increased by 1,871 souls to a total of 4,192? Can such numbers prove sufficient to inject substance into the seemingly hazy idealism of "inward holiness," "religion of the heart," and "faith working by love"? The answers require more than theological phrases better fitted to sermon texts. On his initial visit to Cornwall in late August 1743, John Wesley had spent three weeks preaching to inhabitants of St. Just, Zennor, Morvah, St. Ives, Sennen, Gwennap, St. Mary's on the Isle of Scilly, and on several of the downs throughout the west of Cornwall. There, and in the ninety-two other towns, villages, and sites throughout that county will one find substantive results of the Wesleys' forty-six-year mission to Cornwall.

• 3 •

The Wesleys in
Cornwall: The Places

Bodmin

Bodmin, the county town of Cornwall, lay on the sheltered western edge of a considerable expanse of moorland—Bodmin Moor. Situated approximately in the center of the county, it measured twenty-six miles north-northwest of Plymouth, Devonshire, and stood between St. Columb Major, fifteen miles to the southwest, and Liskeard, twelve miles to the east. In the first quarter of the eighteenth century, Daniel Defoe (1660?-1731) identified Bodmin ("Bodmyn") as formerly one of the coining towns for tin—meaning a place for the transforming of metal (including tin) into currency by stamping the pieces by definite weight and value with authorized marks or characters, thus converting them into coins. A coining town also stood as a place where public officials stamped tin blocks of standard weight before exposing those objects for sale. Unfortunately, Bodmin lost that designation to Lestwithyel, four miles south of Bodmin. Defoe, nonetheless, claimed that "this town enjoys several privileges [which the writer-traveler never thought worthy of mention or description], some of which are also tokens of antiquity."[1] A century later, Bodmin would bear the description of, as well as be anointed with the reputation of, a town "seated in a bottom [a low-lying land; a valley; the lowest point or locality] between two high hills, which renders the air very unwholesome. It chiefly consists of one street, and the many decayed houses show that it has been a place of greater note; it formerly had the privilege [a grant of special rights, or the sole right, extended to a community] of the coinage of tin."[2] Nonetheless, as the county town, eighteenth-century Bodmin hosted the quarterly session of the district judges, as well as contained the principal house of correction—a facility not unknown to a number of John Wesley's itinerant preachers,[3] and, until 1909, a site of public executions. By 1830, the population of Bodmin stood at 4643; that number would increase to 12,148 by 1981[4]—or at a rate of 49.7 persons per year over a period of 151 years. One might add that the first *official* population count of England, Wales, and Scotland did not occur until 1801; following that year, the national census would be conducted every ten years.

Bodmin Church had been dedicated to the sixth-century St. Petrock, "the captain of the Cornish saints," supposedly the son of a Welsh chieftain, who after studying in Ireland, made his way to Cornwall, undertook missionary work, and founded monasteries at Padstow ("Petrockstow") and Bodmin. Reportedly, in 1177, a Breton canon removed Petrock's remains from Bodmin and turned them over to the abbey of St. Meen, but Henry II secured their restoration, and they continue to lie in Bodmin Church, housed in a twelfth-century ivory casket.[5] One should also be aware that, in the 1740s Bodmin housed a Presbyterian meeting-house, though it eventually fell into disuse when the number of adherents to that faith seriously declined.[6]

A much-traveled Charles Wesley set his weary body within the limits of Bodmin upon a single occasion—that and no more. On Friday, 15 July 1743, he had spent the previous day somewhere twenty miles outside of Exeter, Devonshire—perhaps Postbridge, Devonshire, which then lay approximately twenty miles southwest of Exeter and, more or less, on a line from Exeter to Bodmin. He then "set out alone, and by wandering made it threescore miles to Bodmin"—that Cornish town then lying approximately fifty-five miles southwest of Exeter. "Both horse and rider were worked down so that I slept till five the next morning without waking."[7] No further comment came forth from Charles Wesley, who left Bodmin behind him—and, trusting to the fragmented state of his extant manuscript journal, he never returned.

John Wesley, on the other hand, appeared a bit more attentive to Bodmin, although his initial visit to the town came under circumstances similar with those of his younger brother. Thus, on Monday, 29 August 1743, Wesley, in company with three of his itinerant preachers—William Shepherd (fl. 1740–1750), the Yorkshire stonemason John Nelson (1707–1774), and John Downes (1723?–1774)—found themselves at sunset "in the middle of the first, great, pathless moor [Bodmin Moor, north of the town] beyond Launceston. About eight [p.m.] we were quite out of our way. But we had not gone far before we heard Bodmin bell." Bodmin then lay nearly twenty miles southwest of Launceston, and thus the four of them must have ridden at least that far, for "directed by this [the church bell], we turned to the left and came to the town before nine." The stay there must not have been a long one, for Wesley recorded in his journal that on the next day, Tuesday, 30 August, his party reached St. Ives "in the evening." That meant that they had spent practically the entire day traversing the thirty-seven or thirty-eight miles southwest from Bodmin to St. Ives.[8]

More than a quarter of a century would pass before John Wesley would pause at Bodmin to perform his ordained and self-appointed primary task. On Wednesday, 30 August 1769, the Methodist leader rode, beginning from Launceston at 4:00 a.m., for four hours through "incessant rain, driven ... by a furious wind," arriving at Bodmin at approximately 8:00 a.m. There, "at the request of one of our friends, I preached to a small, serious company in the town hall." Almost immediately thereafter, without observation or comment, he left Bodmin for Truro (22:202). More rain and violent winds again provided the background scenery for John Wesley's next trek from Launceston to Bodmin, on Wednesday, 31 August 1774. At the least, on this occasion, he provided a glimpse of both the state of Methodism in the town and the condition of its principal building, reporting, "A little company are at length united here. At their request I preached [again] in the town hall (the most dreary one I ever saw) to a mixed congregation of rich and poor." The building in question, according to a note in *The Proceedings of the Wesley Historical Society* (1904:193), stood on Fore Street and featured a carved wooden doorway dating from the sixteenth century. Eventually, town officials improved the room in which Wesley preached by adding a circular stained-glass window.[9] At any rate, despite the gloom of the room, "All behaved very well—and who knows that some good may be done even at Bodmin!" (22:427). Such reaction by the leader of the Methodists reveals clearly the low state of religious reform in that part of the county at that time—three decades after Charles Wesley had first appeared there.

The elder Wesley tried again on Friday, 1 September 1775, but all he would recall in his journal extract for that day assumed the form of a cryptic "I preached at.... Bodmin" (22:464). He offered little more in the way of reaction or comment when he preached in the town at 10:00 a.m. on Friday, 22 August 1777 (23:66); again near the town hall to "a large and serious congregation" (23:104); and, for the final time, on Tuesday, 4 September 1781, he announced, in his journal extract, only that he had preached there (23:222).

One might justifiably conclude that neither Wesley demonstrated, personally, and at least in their manuscript and published journal entries, more than token interest in the spiritual states of the citizens of Bodmin. An exhausted Charles Wesley stopped there for a single good night's sleep, while John Wesley's several visits proved little more than stopovers on his way from Launceston to those towns and villages in Cornwall that promised the potential for, or actual evidence of, the revival of evangelical religion within the county. Nonetheless, they placed responsibility for the real work in Bodmin directly upon the initiatives and abilities of their itinerant preachers, who, in turn, responded (supposedly) to the direct advice, orders, and authority extended to them from John Wesley.

Brea

Brea has been identified in one instance as a mining village on the slopes of Carn Brae, in the parish of Illogan, near Redruth, which means that it lay approximately fifteen miles northeast of St. Ives. Another estimate (20:356) places it one mile east of Camborne, which translates into twenty-one miles northeast of St. Ives. In that village lived Richard Probis (or Provis), most likely a member of the Methodist society there or nearby (possible Redruth or Illogan). Thus, on Saturday afternoon, 13 September 1746, John Wesley left St. Ives and between one and two in the afternoon arrived for the first of his four recorded visits to Brea. There he preached in front of Richard Probis's house on "'the promise' which is 'given to them that believe.' Many were there who had been vehement opposers. But from this time they opposed no more" (20:141). The text of Galatians 3:22 reads, "But the scripture hath concluded all under sin, that the promise by faith by Jesus Christ might be given to them that believe" (KJV). One might wish for more specificity concerning how "*Many* were there," but in terms of numbers assembled, no matter where the locale, Wesley rarely offered specific counts, noting, instead, generalizations or inaccurate estimates. In his defense (should a defense be required), be aware that the composition of these published journal "Extracts" (edited versions of the actual events) reached the press years after the dates indicated. For example, *An Extract of the Reverend Mr. John Wesley's Journal, from October 27, 1743, to November 17, 1746*, bears the publication date of 1753.

John Wesley returned to Brea on or about noon on Monday, 6 July 1747, where he found that "neither the house nor the yard would contain the congregation. And all were serious"—meaning the lack of boisterous opposition. "The scoffers are vanished away. I scarce saw one in the county" (20:181–182). The word "scoffer" and its variant appear but twice in the

King James Version of Holy Scriptures—(1) Habakkuk 1:10. "And they [the Chaldeans] shall **scoff** at the kings, and the princes shall be a scorn unto them: they shall deride every strong hold; for they shall heap dust, and take it." (2) 2 Peter 3:3. "Knowing this first, that there shall come in the last days **scoffers**, walking after their own lusts."

The third visit to Brea by the Methodist leader occurred on Tuesday, 14 August 1750, but John Wesley saw fit only to indicate that he had preached there at "about six in the evening" (20:356). Finally, on Sunday, 14 September 1755, at 8:00 a.m., John Wesley preached at Brea "to a very numerous congregation. And I believe God spoke to the hearts of many— of backsliders in particular" (21:29). His stay in the village extended some two hours. There arises, at least on paper, no apparent reason as to why he never returned to Brea, and, again, his vague references to the numbers of persons who gathered to hear him provide little or no indication as to the state of Methodism in that village. One might always speculate as to whether Wesley omitted details from his published journal extract or if he entrusted further efforts in Brea to his itinerant preachers, determining that his own labors would be better expended in other locales.

Breage

Breage—identified on Thomas Moule's map[1] as "St. Breage"—existed as a parish situated three miles west from Helston, on the road to Marazion and two miles from the coast of Mounts Bay. Perhaps the single claim to industrial recognition for this town came in c. 1623 when William Lemon (1696–1760), of Germoe, Cornwall, then studying the effect of steam power in the mining industry, inspected a steam engine for pumping mine water erected at Wheal Vor, in Breage. That first successful commercial steam engine had been originally designed and constructed, in 1698, by Thomas Savery (1650?-1715), an English military engineer.[2]

John Wesley preached in Breage, but without comment, at "about noon" (20:357) on Wednesday, 15 August 1750, and departed shortly thereafter. He returned, five years later, at noon on Friday, 5 September 1755, and called upon William (?) Rowe, a resident of the village and, per-haps, a member of a Methodist society there—or of one in the vicinity. "'Twelve [eleven?] years ago,'[3] he said, 'I was going over Gulval Downs [sit-uated approximately between one and two miles northeast of Penzance and eight miles northwest of Breage], and I saw many people together. And I asked what was the matter. And they told me, "A man going to preach." And I said, "To be sure it is some *mazed* [crazed, stupefied, dazed, out of one's wits] man." But when I saw you, I said, "Nay, this is no mazed man." And you preached on God's raising the dry bones. And from that time I could never rest till God was pleased to breathe on *me* and raise my dead soul!'" (21:27). The applicable biblical passage here, Ezekiel 37:4, reads, "Again he said unto me, Prophesy upon these bones, and say unto them, O ye **dry bones**, hear the word of the Lord" (KJV). See, also, John 22:22, Luke 7:22, Acts 3:15. Wesley had not intended to preach at Breage on that day, but "seeing the poor people flock from every side, I could not send them empty away. So I preached at a small distance from the [preaching] house and besought them to consider our 'great high priest, who is passed through into the heavens.' [Hebrews 4:14. "Seeing then that we have a **great high priest** that **is passed into the heavens,** Jesus the Son of God, let us hold fast our profession" (KJV).] And none opened his mouth, for the lions of Breage, too, are changed into lambs. That they were so fierce ten years ago is no wonder. Since their wretched minister told them from the pulpit (seven years before I resigned my fellowship) that John Wesley was expelled at the college for a base child and had been quite mazed ever since; that all the Methodists at their private societies put out the lights, etc., with abundance more of the same kind. But a year or two since it was observed, he grew thoughtful and more melancholy. And about nine months ago, he went into his own necessary house and hanged himself!" (21:27). Obviously, Wesley had heard of past conditions at Breage from one of his itinerant preachers to, or a society member residing within, that area of Cornwall, since the time line described does not coincide with the dates of his visits to the village as recorded in his published journals. Further, John Wesley had to resign his fellowship at Lincoln College, Oxford, to which he had been elected in 1726, on 1 June 1751, because of his marriage, on 18 February of that year, to the widowed Mrs. Mary (Molly) Goldhawk Vazeille (1710–1781)—University fellows could not be married. The minister of Breage during the period to which Wesley referred, the Rev. Henry Lanyon (1711–1754), the son of a "gentleman," Tobias Lanyon of Gwinear, Cornwall (ten miles northwest of Breage), had received his higher education at Pembroke College, Cambridge (1727–1733). The rite of his burial occurred at Germoe, Cornwall (two miles northwest of Breage), on 23 August 1754 (21:27).

Finally, John Wesley's last visit to Breage occurred at noon on Tuesday, 10 September 1765, and at some moment during that portion of the day his attentive eye caught a glimpse of at least one specific object that Nature had bestowed upon the village. Nonetheless, he chose only to report that he preached "under a lovely shade of tree" (22:20). The sermon text, the number of those assembled, and the spiritual condition of the assembly had either escaped his thoughts or had proven unworthy of inclusion into the journal entry for that day—as well as the relationship between the "lovely shade tree" and his message.

Callestick/Callestock/Calstock

John Wesley's single visit to Callestick, identified as a hamlet four and one-half miles northwest of Truro, occurred on Monday, 12 September 1768. There he "preached about noon" and left shortly thereafter, without noting anything relative to the place or to its inhabitants. The Methodist leader might have noticed, even if he did not note in his journal extract, that Callestick had been, since the end of the seventeenth century, on the list of "coinage towns"[1] in Cornwall.

Camborne

The mining town of Camborne, during the forty-six-year period of the Wesleys' visits there, lay nine miles east-northeast of St. Ives and three miles south-southwest of Redruth. One might be interested to learn that the Church of England had clearly maintained its establishment in Camborne during the eighteenth century, as underscored by the fact that in 1779, the parish church presented 199 of its young citizens and adults for the triennial Confirmation service conducted by John Ross (?-1792), vicar of Frome, Somersetshire, and Bishop of Exeter (1778–1792).[1] At that time, all of Cornwall belonged to the see of Exeter. Ross had received his higher education at St. John's College, Cambridge, as well as the doctor of divinity degree from that university. He published six single sermons (1756–1785) and a valuable (in its day) edition of Cicero's *Epistles* (1749).

On Tuesday, 2 August 1743, Charles Wesley reported, "An elderly man pressed us to turn into his house, near Camborne. It was a large old country seat, and looked like the picture of English hospitality. When he could not prevail on us to stay longer, he would ride two or three miles on our way with us, and listened all the while to the word of reconciliation" (2:367). The term "reconciliation" implies that an estrangement between God and humankind has been overcome, leading to the possibility of reestablishing harmonious relations between God and humanity. The word also has meaning within the context of human beings' relationships with one another, as set forth in the directive of Jesus Christ, in Matthew 5:23–25—"be reconciled to thy brother" (KJV). That notion aside, Charles Wesley's words, unfortunately, do not create a sharp image for the reader, who learns little or nothing about the elderly man, his house, the town of Camborne, or the religious attitudes of the residents of the town. Further, the fragmentary condition of the younger Wesley's journal raises the question as to whether he ever returned to Camborne.

The initial visit of John Wesley offers even less. His extract journal entry for Saturday, 14 April 1744, notes only that he preached in the town at 2:00 p.m. However, following his practice of inserting into his published journal extracts accounts and correspondence related to the issues of the day, Wesley, then in London, provided in his journal entry for Sunday, 16 September 1744, a letter to him from Henry Millard, a native of St. Ives, Cornwall, and one of Wesley's itinerant preachers, dated 11 September 1744. Therein Millard described the ordeal of another itinerant preacher, Thomas Westell, who, in the midst of his sermon, suffered an attack by an anti–Methodist mob at Camborne. The mob pulled him from the house and carried him off to the magistrates at Penzance, who sentenced him for vagrancy to the jail at Bodmin. Westell eventually gained his release, while Millard died sometime afterward from the smallpox (20:40–41). From that incident comes the knowledge that early on, Camborne proved to have been a hostile and dangerous place for Wesleyan Methodist preachers.

On Thursday, 11 September 1746, John Wesley left Gwennap for Camborne, but he never recorded what he did or what he experienced upon or following his arrival. Less than a year later, on Monday evening, 7 July 1747, the Methodist leader preached at Camborne and, finally, provided a modicum of detail. Or, had he merely responded to an invitation to do so? "I looked about for John Rogers, the champion [of the local anti–Methodists], who had so often sworn I should never more preach in that parish. But it seems he had given up the cause, saying, 'One may as well blow against the wind'" (20:182). Conditions continued to improve for Methodism at Camborne, as Wesley noted on Friday, 24 August 1750, when he preached, at noon, "to the largest congregation I had ever seen there" (20:358)—but, as we know, "largest" means absolutely nothing unless it can be compared with or contrasted to specific numbers that preceded it. In addition, both the Wesleys and their itinerants attracted the curious and the mischievous to their preaching, as well as Methodist society members and Methodist sympathizers. Thus, to separate the choir from potential converts, and then those two groups from the stones, would have been a difficult task.

Arriving at Camborne on Wednesday afternoon, 4 September 1751,

John Wesley called upon a Mr. Harris at his home, Rosewarne, in Camborne parish. The journal extract does not contain entries for 5–6 September, and thus raises a number of questions: Why did Wesley seek out Harris at Rosewarne? What transpired there? Did Wesley remain in Camborne through 5–6 September? If so, how did he spend that time? Why did he not, in the published extract, provide readers with specific (or even general) details of his activities during 4–6 September? The now eighty-three-year-old "standard" edition of Wesley's *Letters* (8 vols., 1931), edited by John Telford, offers no possible answers. One observes therein (3:74–75) a letter "To a Friend" from Salisbury, Wiltshire, dated 21 August 1751; immediately following that a letter to John Downes from London on 7 November 1751; and between those two pieces—nothing! The reader can only speculate as to what occurred in Camborne, and, as we all know, speculation does not always proceed as a rational and worthwhile exercise. In any event, Wesley unexpectedly returned to Camborne on Monday, 23 September 1751, but, again, provided no information—not even a vague generalization or two—of what he did there or for how long he remained.

The tale takes on even a more frustrating aspect for readers when, on Saturday evening, Wesley *rode* from St. Just to Camborne, but the entry ends there (at least the Camborne part of it), for Wesley never even bothered to note if and when he ever arrived in the town, opting, instead, to report "a remarkable incident" (21:29) related to him on the way by his traveling companion, John Pearce of Redruth. However, events came to rhetorical life a bit during Wesley's next visit to Camborne, on Tuesday, 6 September 1757. There, he "rejoiced to hear that the gentleman who pressed Mr. Maxfield no longer persecutes the Methodists, nor will suffer [allow, permit, endure, sanction] anyone else to do it. And in the late dearth [famine; a period where a shortage of food exists], he relieved great numbers of the poor and saved many families from perishing" (21:122). Thomas Maxfield (?-1784), a native of Bristol, had become a full-time Methodist itinerant preacher in 1741. Impressed into the Royal Navy at Crowan, Cornwall, in June 1745, Maxfield found himself conveyed by the press gang first to Henry Tompkins' house, then off to Marazion, where he would have been thrust immediately aboard a man-of-war. However, the captain of the ship refused to accept him, and authorities then cast him into the dungeon at Penzance, from which he eventually gained his release on 3 July 1745.[2] The spiritually transformed "gentleman" who aided in the impressment of Maxfield most likely had been the aforementioned Henry Tompkins (21:122), a resident of a house situated some two miles from Crowan, Cornwall, in the vicinity of Redruth. After receiving the news of

Tompkins' reformation, Wesley apparently departed Camborne for a preaching session at Crowan.

John Wesley's interest in events natural and scientific cast a beam of light onto the portrait of Camborne during the middle of the eighteenth century when, on Friday, 19 September 1760, he rode from Helston to Illogan. "We had heavy rain before I began," he noted, "but scarce any while I was preaching. I learned several other particulars here relating to the water-spout." In the most general of terms, "water-spout" appears as a gyrating column of mist, spray, and water, produced by the action of a whirlwind on a portion of the sea and the clouds immediately above it. The word also has been applied to a sudden and violent fall of rain; a cloud-burst. One will encounter the word but once in the 1611 KJV, in Psalms 42:7—"Deep calleth unto deep at the noise of thy **waterspouts**: all thy waves and thy billows are gone over me." For those interested in editorial language changes, the editors of the 1989 New Revised Standard Version (NRSV) offered

> Deep calls to deep
>   At the thunder of your **cataracts;**
> all your waves and your billows
>   have gone over me.

The translator and editor of the *Complete Jewish Bible* (1998) rendered the verse as

> Deep is calling to deep
>   at the thunder of your **waterfalls**;
> all your surging rapids and waves
>   are sweeping over me.

At any rate, John Wesley continued to observe that the waterspout had been "seen near Mousehole about an hour before sunset. About sunset, it began traveling over the land, tearing up all the furze [a spiny evergreen shrub with yellow flowers, growing abundantly on wastelands throughout Europe] and shrubs it met. Near an hour after sunset, it passed (at the rate of four or five miles an hour) across Mr. Harris's[3] fields in **Camborne**, sweeping the ground as it went, about twenty yards in diameter at bottom and broader up to the clouds. It made a noise like thunder, took up eighteen stacks of corn with a large haystack and the stones whereupon it stood, and scattered them all abroad (but it was quite dry), and then passed over the cliff into the sea" (21:280–281). The reader certainly cannot mistake Wesley's reasoning for having inserted this passage into his journal—the message from God by way of the agency of Nature, as a reminder to mortals of their subservience to God, of their inadequacies in the face of God-created natural phenomena, and of the punishment that awaits them for the commission of their sins. The seventy-eight-year-old Wesley's final recorded visit to Camborne, on Sunday, 2 September 1781, appeared to punctuate that sentiment, as he preached at 11:00 a.m. and expressed the belief that "all the people were bowed down before the Lord" (23:222).

Camelford

Situated on the north-central section of Cornwall, on the Camel River, fifteen miles west-southwest of Launceston, Camelford functioned, in the eighteenth century, principally as a market town and a Parliamentary borough (the latter a town that, until the Reform Act of 1832, sent members to Parliament). Close by the town one would have found the successful and profitable Delabole Quarry, a producer, since ancient times, of a high quality of slate from a mine that would, by the end of the nineteenth century, measure four hundred feet deep and one mile in circumference. In 1662, Delabole Quarry achieved the reputation for yielding the best slate quarry in the nation, and its owners retained that national recognition for as long as slate remained in demand. By the middle of the eighteenth century its output had begun to expand rapidly. Unfortunately, in early December 1754, a collapse occurred that brought about the deaths of six miners and injury to two others. John Wesley would receive information about that incident in February 1755 and record, in his journal for 16 February 1755, a narrative of events sent to him in a letter from an unidentified friend.[1]

John Wesley had, initially, been in Camelford on Monday, 15 September 1746, but all he would note in his journal entry for that day concerned a guide meeting his fellow travelers and him there to conduct them to Week St. Mary. A year later, on Saturday, 25 July 1747, Wesley approached Camelford and paused at "a friend's house near the town." From there he proceeded on foot to the house of one Walter Mallet (1675–November 1747), who had formerly expressed the desire that if Wesley came to Camelford, he could preach either in his house or on the town bowling green. To the contrary, the mayor, a "gentleman" by the name of John Rowe, declared that if John Wesley did preach in Camelford, he would prosecute Mallet. Thus, finding no place within the town where he could preach, Wesley determined to leave and to proceed to Laneast.

Fortunately, the political climate of the town had shifted considerably by the time of Wesley's next visit there, on Monday, 19 September 1748. "I rode to Camelford, and preached about noon, none now offering to interrupt" (20:249). Evidence that Methodism had gained even a stronger foothold in Camelford presented itself two years later, when John Wesley "hastened" there from St. Gennys and preached in the main street in the midst of a steady rainfall. "But that neither drove the congregation away nor hindered the blessing of God. Many were in tears, and some could not help crying aloud, during the preaching and the meeting of the society" (20:359). The establishment of a Methodist society in any Cornish town or village demonstrated, at that relatively early period, a significant sign of potential success for the Wesleyan evangelical mission to Cornwall.

Nonetheless, John Wesley's thoughts could, on occasion, be carried away from that mission, even while physically engaged in it and riding toward it. For example, he reported in his journal for Monday, 2 September 1751, that on his way from Launceston to Camelford, he read *Saducismus Triumphatus; or, Full and Plain Evidence Concerning Witches and Apparitions, Proving Partly by Holy Scripture, Partly by a Choice Collection of Modern Relations, the Real Existence of Apparitions, Spirits, and Witches* (1666; first English ed., London, 1681), by Joseph Glanvill. A philosopher and a senior member of the Royal Society, Glanvill (1636–1680), born at Plymouth, Devonshire, studied at Exeter College (1652) and Lincoln College, Oxford, after which he entered into Holy Orders and became vicar of Frome, Somersetshire (1662); rector of the Abbey Church in Bath, Somersetshire (1666); and prebendary (a canon of a cathedral or collegiate church who receives from either one a portion [a "prebend"] of the revenues from its lands or the tithes) of Worcester Cathedral (1678). Joseph Glanvill died at Bath in November 1680. At least three other major English editions of *Saducismus Triumphatus* came forth in 1682, 1700, and 1726. "I wish the facts had had a more judicious relater—" remarked Wesley as he reacted to Glanvill's work, "one who would not have given a fair pretence for denying the whole by his awkward manner of accounting for some of the circumstances" {20:401).

That vague reaction aside, Wesley proceeded one step further by recording absolutely nothing relative to his activities once he had arrived at Camelford. Not only did Wesley's reading appear to cloud the specifics of missionary activity in Camelford, the health of the Methodist leader, as well as the weather, had similar effects. For instance, while once again on the road from Launceston to Camelford, on Tuesday, 24 July 1753, "I was taken with such a bleeding of the nose as I have not had since my return from Georgia [1 February 1738]. For a mile or two it increased more and more, and then once stopped of itself. So I rode on comfortably (though the day was extremely hot)" (20:468–469). Unfortunately, Wesley found himself unable to practice any one of his own dozen remedies cited to prevent bleeding of the nose, as published in his *Primitive Physick; or, an Easy and Natural Method of Curing Most Diseases* (London: Thomas Tyre, 1747)—an extremely popular work, one compiled to challenge the physicians of the times, that would reach its twenty-third London edition by the time of his death on 2 March 1791. Those remedies ranged from "put the legs and arms in cold water," through "steep a linen rag in sharp vinegar, burn and blow it up the nose with a quill," to "dissolve an ounce of alum powdered in a pint of vinegar; apply a cloth dipped in this to the temples, steeping the feet in warm water" (see Wesley, *Primitive Physick*, 33). Whether Wesley actually paused at Camelford on this day, one will never know.

We do know, however, that on Saturday, 11 August 1753, following a consistently heavy rainstorm that did not cease until noon, John Wesley found "an opportunity of preaching in the market-place at Camelford. I saw only one person in the congregation who was not deeply serious. That one (which I am sorry to hear) was the curate of the parish" (20:471). Although Wesley's last sentence might be viewed as an insignificant detail, W. Reginald Ward has noted that a licensed curate did not exist at Camelford during the 1750s, nor would there be an appointee for that office in the near future. The rector there, the Rev. William Phillips (1723-?), had studied at Balliol College, Oxford (20:471, note 1). W. Reginald Ward's source, as cited in his note, derives from William Pearce's *The Wesley's in Cornwall: Extracts from the Journals of John and Charles Wesley and John Nelson* (Truro, Cornwall: D. B. Barton, 1964). To continue upon the wheels of the bibliographical cart, Pearce, in turn, would have relied upon such then available sources as Nehemiah Curnock's edition of John Wesley's *Journal* (1909–1916); Thomas Jackson's edition of Charles Wesley's *Journal* (1849); and, possibly, William Reed's edition of the *Journal of John Nelson* (1870).

No matter: a positive spiritual environment continued through to Wesley's next visit to the town, on Tuesday, 16 September 1755, at which time (6:00 p.m.) he preached in the market-place on the text, "Ye must be born again"—or, in full, John 3:7: "Marvel not that I [Jesus Christ] said unto thee [Nicodemus], Ye must be born again" (KJV). "Some were much afraid there would be disturbance," he noted. "But the whole congregation was quiet and attentive" (21:30). Another bout of physical discomfort merely temporarily diverted his attention when he next came to Camelford on Tuesday, 30 August 1757, for on this occasion, "my toothache was cured by rubbing treacle upon my cheek." Treacle had been derived, during the seventeenth century, from the uncrystallized syrup, or molasses, from the process of refining sugar. From there it became a medicinal compound, originally in the form of a salve, as a treatment for venomous bites, general types of poisons, and malignant diseases. Interestingly enough, "treacle" does not exist among the nine treatments for the toothache listed in Wesley's *Primitive Physick* (1747)—those ranging from being "electrified through the teeth" to "put a leaf of betony [a plant of the mint family formerly credited with medicinal and magical virtues] up the nose," to "keep the feet in warm water, and rub them well with bran just before bed time" (119–120). With that discomfort seemingly eased, "At six I preached in the market-place. How are the lions in this town also become lambs!" Nonetheless, even lambs can prove difficult to control, particularly when but a single shepherd assumes the self-appointed responsibility for direction over all of them.

From Launceston on 4 September 1760, Wesley had written to his evangelically-minded friend, the Rev. Samuel Furly (?-1795), "I am entering into Cornwall, which I have not visited these three years, and consequently all things in it are out of order. Several persons *talk* about sharing my burthen, but none does it."[2] Thus, upon his next visit to Camelford, Friday, 5 September 1760, he came upon "the small remains of a dead, scattered [Methodist] society," lacking in Methodist discipline and suffering from irregular visits from Methodist preachers. In addition, "their deadness here was owing to bitterness against each other. In the morning [Saturday the 6th], I heard the contending parties face to face, and they resolved and promised on all sides to let past things be forgotten. O how few have learned to forgive 'one another, as God for Christ's sake hath forgiven' us!" (21:273–274)—the full text of Ephesians 4:32 reading, "And be ye kind one to another, tender-hearted, forgiving one another, even as God for Christ's sake hath forgiven you" (KJV). One can only speculate as to the specifics of the contention within the Camelford Methodist society and the reasons for Wesley having excluded those details from the publication of his extract journal. By the way, John Wesley might have been aware, to the advantage of his own travel plans, that in 1759, the English Parliament had passed an Act "for making a road, or repairing a road, from Launceston to **Camelford**, Wadebridge, St. Columb, and Truro." That route had become one of the significant through-roads in England, and the ministry expected it to carry heavy traffic, and thus connecting with the other main roads of southern England.[3]

Two years later, the negative state of Methodism in Camelford had completely reversed itself. On Friday, 24 September 1762, John Wesley found abundant evidence of God in that town after having preached there in the evening and at 5:00 on Saturday morning. "In the afternoon, the rain intermitting, I preached in the market-place. And it was a solemn season." He remained for the entire day, and following his sermon address at 8:00 a.m. on Sunday, 26 September, "I left Camelford, now one of the liveliest places in Cornwall" (21:390). On his next visit, Friday, 16 September 1765, Wesley had to change his venue from the marketplace to "a field near Camelford, it being the fair-day," and he addressed the gathering on the text "Come and buy wine and milk, without money and without price" (22:18)—Isaiah 55:1: "Ho, every one that thirsteth, come ye to the waters, and he that hath no money; come ye, buy, and eat; yea, come, buy wine and milk, without money and without price" (KJV).

Unfortunately, during John Wesley's absence, the efforts of Methodism in Camelford once more evidenced a serious decline. Following his 1765 visit to the town, he returned there on Friday, 26 August 1768, where he found "the society is shrunk once more from seventy to fourteen." Without further comment upon the loss of 80 percent of the society's membership, he "preached in the market-place on 'O that thou hadst known, at least in this thy day, the things that make for thy peace!'— Luke 19:42: "If thou [the Pharisees] hadst known, even thou, at least in this thy day, the things which belong unto thy peace! but now they are hid from thine eyes" (KJV). Continued Wesley, "Many were moved for the present, as they were the next day while I was applying those awful [awesome, wondrous] words, 'The harvest is past, the summer is ended, and we are not saved!'" [Jeremiah 8:20] (22:154). The two biblical citations might well have provided the substance for effective sermon addresses that "moved" a number of persons assembled to hear them, but, more importantly in this instance, the reader of this journal entry has no clue of measures (if any) taken by John Wesley to restore numerical strength to the Camelford Methodist society. Certainly he continued regular visits to Camelford: on Tuesday, 21 August 1770, but without a word of comment; again at some point during the week of 23 August 1773, also without comment; yet again on Wednesday, 7 September 1774, with the same rhetorical result and without mention of the membership of the Methodist society. He broke his rhetorical silence on Friday, 16 August 1776, noting, "I was going to preach in the Market-place at Camelford, where a few are still alive to God, when a violent storm drove us into the house—that is, as many as could squeeze in. The fire quickly kindled among them and seemed to touch every heart. My text was, 'What dost thou here, Elijah?'"—or, more fully, 1 Kings 19:9: "And he [Elijah] came thither [to Horeb] unto a cave, and lodged there; and, behold, the word of the Lord came to him, and he said unto him, What doest thou here, Elijah?" (KJV) and 1 Kings 19:13. "And it was so, when Elijah heard it ["a still small voice" (v. 12)], that he wrapped his face in his mantle, and went out, and stood in the entering in of the cave. And behold, there came a voice unto him, and said, What doest thou here, Elijah?" (KJV). Neither the biblical question nor the state of the Camelford Methodists proved worthy of response from Wesley during his visits to the town on Monday, 28 August 1780, or on Tuesday, 3 September 1782—on the latter preaching in the street but being quickly summoned to St. Gennys to attend his dying friend, the Rev. George Thomson.

The published extract of John Wesley's journal does not contain an entry for Tuesday, 30 August 1785, but his published diary reveals the details of his twenty-one-hour stay in Camelford: On Tuesday, 30 August, he left Port Isaac by chaise at 2:45 p.m.—that particular vehicle having been an important mode of transportation for the aging John Wesley. In its simplest form, the chaise represented a light open carriage for one or two persons, with a top ("calash"), drawn by a single horse. Whether Wesley actually owned one of those vehicles or relied upon benevolent followers for the loans of such cannot always be readily determined. If, indeed the former held to be true, his chaise would have been one of the earliest examples, in history, of the "company car." In any event, the Methodist leader arrived at Camelford by 4:00 that same afternoon, which means that the seven-mile ride from Port Isaac consumed one hour and fifteen minutes, at the approximate rate of speed (non-stop) of 10.4 miles per hour. Wesley then spent the remainder of the hour writing "notes," then, at 5:00, engaged in prayer for an hour before preaching, at 6:00 p.m. on 1 Corinthians 13:1–3—"Though I [Paul] speak with the tongues of men and of angels, and have not charity, I am become as sounding brass, or a tinkling symbol./And though I have the gift of prophecy, and understand all mysteries, and all knowledge; and though I have all faith, so that I could remove mountains, and have not charity, I am nothing./And though I bestow all my goods to feed the poor, and though I give my body to be burned, and have not charity, I am nothing" (KJV). He then met with the Methodist society—but no indication of numbers here—ate supper, engaged in religious conversation with unidentified persons, prayed privately, and, at 9:30 p.m. retired for the night. Up at 4:00 the next morning (Wednesday, 31 August), Wesley prayed and, shortly thereafter, wrote a letter; took tea at 8:00 a.m., then engaged in religious conversation with unidentified parties and worked on "accounts"—most likely those of the Camelford society. Concerning the letter—its intended recipient and its substance—John Telford's edition of Wesley's *Letters* (7:286) offers no epistolary text between a letter from Redruth, Cornwall, to Wesley's itinerant preacher, Christopher Hopper (1722–1802), at Bolton, Lancashire, dated 27 August 1785, followed immediately by an epistle, from Bristol, on 4 September 1785, to another of his itinerant preachers, Robert Costerdine (1736–1812), at an unidentified locale within the Birmingham circuit. At 11:00 a.m., John Wesley delivered a sermon on Matthew 12:43—"Then goeth he [an unclean spirit] and taketh with himself seven other spirits more wicked than himself, and they enter in and dwell there [an empty house]: and the last state of that man is worse than the first. Even so shall it be also unto this wicked generation" (KJV)—followed by dinner, prayer, and departure in his chaise for Launceston at 1:15 p.m. (23:534). When John Wesley returned to Camelford on Friday, 28 August 1789, the condition of Methodism in that town had changed again—this time for the better. He "preached at nine [a.m.] in our new house at Camelford, thoroughly filled, though at a short warning" (24:153). Wesley's diary for that day provides more depth to his one hour and forty-five-minute visit to the town. He had arrived, by chaise, in Camelford, at 8:15 a.m., and he found time for tea before preaching in the **new house** on Ecclesiastes 9:10—"Whatsoever thy hand findeth to do, do it with thy might; for there is no work, nor device, nor knowledge, nor wisdom, in the grave, wither thou goest" (KJV). Following that exercise, he met with the Methodist society before departing for Launceston at 10:00 a.m. (24:292). Thus ended John Wesley's almost two dozen recorded journeys to Camelford, with the Methodist leader having been convinced that he had succeeded in the struggle of his preachers and him to establish Methodism as a fixture there.

Cape Cornwall

Cape Cornwall, off of St. Just, in the eighteenth century, would have been (as it continues to be) situated on the west coast of Cornwall, approximately three and one-half miles north of Land's End. On Tuesday, 31 July 1744, Charles Wesley rode from Penzance to St. Just, and following arrival there, the evangelical Church of England clergyman John Meriton (1698?-1753) and he "climbed up and down Cape Cornwall ... to the needless hazards of our necks" (*Manuscript Journal*, 2:413). That occasion proved to have been the first and last mention of Cape Cornwall in the extant fragments of Charles Wesley's manuscript journal. Apparently, John Wesley saw no reason to attempt such an exercise.

Carn Brae

Located just one and one-half miles outside Redruth, to the southwest, Carn Brae existed as an Iron Age defensive hill fort built over a Neolithic settlement. The Iron Age, one will recall, represents the third stage in the classification of pre-historic periods (preceded by the Stone Age and Bronze Age), when persons fashioned weapons and tools from iron. The Hittites in Anatolia (Asia Minor) had been working with iron on a relatively small scale as early as c. 1400 BC, but they never really or fully understood the techniques or the potentials. By the twelfth century BC, iron, as a functional tool and weapon, had spread more widely: the Hebrews and Greeks knew of the metal by 1000 BC, but, again, iron did not become employed on a large scale until two centuries later. The application of the term "Iron Age" ceases, in Europe, at the outset of the Roman period. The term Neolithic refers to the latter part of the Stone Age, when ground or polished stone weapons and implements prevailed. The Neolithic Period, which witnessed the introduction of agriculture and the domestication of animals, has occasionally been referred to as "the Neolithic Revolution"— the transference of human beings from being dependent upon nature to the ability to control it, at least partially and indirectly. The change led to the establishment of settled communities, accumulation of food and wealth, the expansion of agriculture, and a noticeable growth in the world population.

In the eighteenth century, the site known as Carn Brae consisted of approximately thirty-six acres enclosed by a single rampart on the north and a double rampart around the south side of the hill. The term *rampart* identifies a defensive wall with a broad top and usually a stone parapet (a defense of stone or earth to conceal and protect troops); a walkway on that structure; or, in the broadest sense, a defense or protection—as seen in this declaration from Moliere's *Tartuffe* (1664): "There is no **rampart** that will hold out against malice" (1:1). The majority of citizens of the United States might occasionally recognize the word in a poem, "Defence of Fort M'Henry" (1814), by the American lawyer Francis Scott Key (1779–1843), which begins with the question,

> O! say can you see, by the dawn's early light,
>   What so proudly we hail'd at the twilight's last gleaming,
> Whose broad stripes and bright stars through the perilous fight,
>   O'er the **ramparts** we watch'd , were so gallantly streaming? [1:1–4].

Literary connections aside, both of those structures had been (and continue to be) well preserved. The western entrance to the inner rampart proved of particular interest because of it having been lined with large stone slabs and flanked by guard chambers.[1]

On Saturday, 1 September 1770, John Wesley "took a walk to the top of that celebrated hill, Carn Brae. Here are many monuments of remote antiquity, scarce to be found in any other part of Europe: Druid altars of enormous size, being only huge rocks, strangely suspended one upon the other; and rock-basins, hollowed on the surface of the rock, it is supposed, to contain the holy water." The Druids have been long remembered as the priests of the ancient Celts in Gaul, Britain, and Ireland who held political and judicial functions as well. Proficient in natural philosophy, the druids held responsibility for the education of young Gaulish nobles, a duty which they conducted in oral poetry. "It is possible," continued Wesley, "that these are at least coeval [of contemporaneous origin; equally old; existing at the same time] with Pompey's theatre [the large open air theater in the ancient town of Pompeii, by Mount Vesuvius] if not with the pyramids of Egypt. And what are they the better for this? Of what consequences is it either to the dead or the living, whether they have withstood the wastes of time for three thousand or three hundred years?" (22:247).

W. Reginald Ward identified Wesley's observations of Carn Brae as "a romantic interpretation of a rocky wilderness" (24:247) derived from having read, on Friday, 16 September 1757, *Observations on the Antiquities, Historical and Monumental, of the County of Cornwall* (Oxford, 1754), by William Borlase (1695–1772), who held, jointly, the appointments as rector of Ludgvan (1722–1772) and of St. Just (1732–1772)—also the brother of the violent anti–Methodist, Walter Borlase. John Wesley had labeled William Borlase "a fine writer and quite a master of his subject, who has distinguished with amazing accuracy the ancient Saxon monuments from the more ancient Roman and from those of the Druids, the most ancient of all" (21:124).

Crowan

Located between four and four and one-half miles south of Camborne and five and three-quarter miles north of Helston, in the southeastern section of Cornwall, eighteenth-century Crowan, which housed the parish church, offered little in the way of historical notice. However, one might recall that at some point in mid–June 1745, Thomas Maxfield, then one of John Wesley's itinerant preachers, had been impressed into the Royal Navy at Crowan (see p. 34 above).

Charles Wesley preached at Crowan on Thursday, 19 July 1744, before a gathering that he claimed numbered "between one and two thousand sinners." The size of the congregation reported by Charles Wesley (as well as by John Wesley) derived from his own estimate, a number most likely exaggerated or, at best, terribly overestimated. In other words, the number of "between one and two thousand" appears more a manifestation of wishful thinking than even that of a reasonable estimate (or so-called "educated guess"). Charles Wesley further described members of that congregation as persons "who seemed started [leaped, jumped, moved with a bound or sudden violent impulse from an inactive state or position, awakened from lethargy or apathy] out of the earth. Several hid their faces, and mourned inwardly, being too deeply affected to cry out. I concluded with a strong exhortation to continue in the ship—the shattered sinking Church of England—and my brother [John] Meriton [see Cape Cornwell], whose heart I spake, seconded and confirmed my saying, The poor people were ready to eat us up, and sent us away with many an hearty blessing" (2:409). The image of the Church of England as a "shattered sinking" "ship" proves an interesting figure here, revealing that Charles Wesley, a most loyal priest of the Church of England, nonetheless realized the fragile condition of that institution in terms of failing to fulfill its social and spiritual responsibilities. That occasion proved to have been the only recorded visit of Charles Wesley to Crowan.

John Wesley first preached at Crowan at 11:00 a.m. on Thursday, 12 April 1744, but recorded nothing in the way of a Methodist society there. However, on his return to the town a year later, on Sunday, 23 June 1745, he provided the readers of his journal extract with a sense of the religious climate of the place. At 5:00 a.m. he began to preach in (or outside of) what he considered to be "the headquarters of the people that delight in war"—Wesley here reaching into his large repository of the language and substance of Scriptures: Psalms 68:30—"When the company of the spearmen and multitude of the mighty are scattered abroad among the beasts of the people, so that they humbly bring pieces of silver: and when he hath scattered the people that delight in war" (BCP). He continued his worship service by "expounding part of the Second Morning Lesson," which, according to the calendar of "Proper Lessons to be Read at Morning and Evening Prayer on the Sundays, and other Holidays throughout the year," in the Book of Common Prayer (1662), the second morning lesson for Sunday, 23 June, would have been based upon Luke 7. In the midst of the sermon, one identified only as "Capt[ain] R——ds"—the term "Captain," in this context not associated with military rank, but applied, with a degree of sarcasm, to one who stands at the head of others; a chief or a leader—

in any event, that person, according to Wesley, "came with a party of men, ready for battle. But their master riding away in two or three minutes, their countenances [behavior, demeanor] quickly fell. One or another stole [past tense and past participle of "steal"—to remove gradually, so as to avoid observation] off his hat, till they were all uncovered, nor did they either move or speak till I had finished my discourse" (20:72). Fifteen months from that experience, Wesley preached at Crowan on Tuesday, 9 September 1746, and chose only to report, "The night came upon us while I was speaking, but none offered to go away" (20:139). He had even less to convey to readers concerning his visit there on Monday, 26 September 1748, only that he preached in the town at 6:00 p.m.

During his next scheduled round to Cornwall, Wesley remained in Crowan for a lengthier period—almost thirty-six hours, perhaps—arriving on Wednesday, 15 August 1750, preaching in the evening and continuing his stay until Thursday morning, 17 August. During a portion of that time he continued to "read over, with all the impartiality I could," the volume of a controversial collection of extracts, *Free and Candid Disquisitions Relating to the Church of England* (London, 1749; another edition in 1750), published anonymously by John Jones (1700–1770), rector of Boulne-Hurst, Bedfordshire, and vicar of Shephall, Hertfordshire, that focused upon the need for a revision of the Book of Common Prayer (1662) and the Thirty-Nine Articles. Specifically, the Thirty-Nine Articles (1536–1563) comprised a set of doctrinal formulae accepted by the Church of England in its attempt to define its dogmatic position in relation to the various theological controversies of the sixteenth century. The Articles appeared as short summaries of dogmatic tenets, each article concerning itself with an issue raised within the context of current controversies, setting forth in general terms the Church of England perspective on such issues as medieval corruptions of Catholic teaching; orthodox Roman Catholic doctrine; Calvinism; Anabaptist teachings; and predestination. Subscription to the Thirty-Nine Articles had never been required of any congregate member of the Church, with the exception of the clergy and, until the nineteenth century, members of the universities at Oxford and Cambridge.[1] According to Wesley's review of Jones' volume, "It is doubtless an exceedingly well wrote book, yet something in it I cannot commend. The author (for the representing himself as *many* and so speaking all along in the *plural* number, I take to be only a pious fraud, used to make himself appear more considerable) is far too great a flatterer for me, dealing in panegyric beyond all measure." The term "panegyric" identifies a public speech or writing in praise of another person, an object, or an achievement; also a formal, elaborate, or extremely inflated statement of praise; a eulogy or an extremely laudatory piece of writing. In the introductory comments of his *The Life of Samuel Johnson, LL.D.* (1791), James Boswell declared, with all honesty, that "he [Johnson] will be seen as he really was; for I profess to write, not his **panegyrick**, which must be all praise, but his Life; which, great and good as he was, must not be supposed to be entirely perfect."[2] "But in truth," continued the Methodist leader, Jones "is not much guilty of this with regard to the Book of Common Prayer. About one objection in ten appears to have weight, and one in five has plausibility. But surely the bulk of his satire, though keen, is by no means just, and even allowing all the blemishes to be real, which he has so carefully and skillfully collected and recited, what ground have we to hope that if we gave up this we should profit by the exchange? Who would supply us with a liturgy less exceptional than that which we had before?" (20:357).

One year later, on Tuesday, 10 September 1751, Wesley preached at Crowan, offering no comment, but the next visit, on Tuesday, 31 July 1753, found him there in a state of serious physical discomfort. He had been affected, for at least "several days" with "a looseness" of the bowels (diarrhea) which, by Sunday, 29 July, had "increased every hour." By Monday, 30 July, his malady had developed into "the flux"—an abnormally copious discharge or flowing of blood and excrement from the bowels or other organs; an early term for dysentery—complicated by "a continual headache, violent vomitings, and, several times in an hour, the cramp in my feet or legs—sometimes in both legs and both thighs together." On Tuesday, the 31st, "after living a day and a half on claret [originally identified with a yellowish or light red wine, as distinguished from pure red or white wines; from the outset of the seventeenth century, applied, generally and informally, to all red wines] and water I found myself so easy that I thought I could ride to Crowan [from Newlyn]. I found no inconvenience the first hour. But in the second my disorder returned. However, I rode on, being unwilling to disappoint the congregation, and preached on 'Be careful for nothing'" (20:469–470). The announced sermon text derived from Philippians 4:6. "**Be careful for nothing**; but in every thing by prayer and supplication with thanksgiving let your requests be made known unto God" (KJV). Wesley departed the town immediately following the sermon.

If one trusts solely to John Wesley's journal, more than four years passed before the Methodist leader returned to Crowan, preaching there on Tuesday evening (6:00), 6 September 1757, on "I will heal their backsliding"—Hosea 14:4. "**I will heal their backsliding,** I will love them freely: for mine anger is turned away from him" (KJV)—"and God applied his word. Several who had left the society for some years came after sermon and desired to be readmitted. O how should our bowels [hearts senti- ments, inward feelings] yearn over all who did once run [hasten, seek, commit to] well!" Recognize here the sound and the sentiment of Galatians 5:7—"Ye did run well: who did hinder you that ye should not obey the truth?" Continued Wesley, "This is the very thing we want—or how many souls might we yet pluck out of the jaws of the lion!" (22:122–123). One might wish to compare/contrast the second part of that sentence with/to Job 29:17—"And I broke the jaws of the wicked, and plucked the spoil out of his teeth" (KJV).

Following the passing of another five years, Wesley preached at Crowan on Thursday, 9 September 1762, and departed without comment, but a letter to Thomas Rankin (1738–1810), one of his itinerant preachers, written from London on 6 November 1764, reveals progress in that town. He instructed Rankin that if the Methodist Society at Crowan can "bear the expense of building [a preaching house] themselves, we have no objec- tion; but we must not increase our debt this year." A detailed account of the annual Methodist Conference for 1764, held at Bristol on 6–10 August, does not, currently, exist, either in a manuscript draft or in published form. Therefore, one cannot determine the Methodists' debt for that year. However, at the 1765 Conference, at Manchester, in late August, the ques- tion arose, "We are still overrun with debt. What can be done?" John Wes- ley's response: "Let no preaching-house anywhere be begun but by the advice of the Assistant. And let no Assistant consent thereto without an absolute necessity."[3] Returning to the matter of the Methodist debt at Crowan, John Wesley continued, "This is what we determined. If you do build, build large enough. In general we do not pay rent out of the publick stock, but get help from friends in the circuit. For once we may allow forty shillings [£2]" (*Letters*, 4:275).

Nonetheless, when John Wesley next came to Crowan on Monday, 9 September 1765, to preach at 6:00 p.m. his mind's eye focused upon mat- ters far removed from preaching houses. "I admire the depth of grace in the generality of this people: so simple, so humble, so teachable, so serious, so utterly dead to the world!" At 5:00 on the following morning, "they filled the house" (22:20). Speculative discussion might come forth as to what Wesley meant by these "simple" and "humble" people of Crowan being "dead to the world": Were they alive to matters of the spirit during their various tenures on earth, as well as aware of there being "life" beyond the grave? Were they totally unaffected by, or "dead to" the temptations of the world? Would their ignorance of the complexities of the world have been caused by their provincialism and their lack of sophistication? More importantly, did Wesley truly appreciate the fact that these "simple" and "humble" residents of this small Cornish town needed to view the world from the perspective of the maintenance and survival of themselves and their families—in other words, to feed and to clothe themselves? As such, even though Wesley and his itinerant preachers sought to inject life into their spirits, they, in turn, could not afford to live in a state "so utterly dead to the world." Finally, the fact that the residents of Crowan "filled" the Methodist preaching house on that Tuesday morning, 10 September 1765, proved that at least x number of them knew something, at the least, about one aspect of the world.

The new preaching house at Crowan, which John Wesley had conditionally approved, had been completed by the time the Methodist leader arrived in the town on Saturday, 13 September 1766. He preached in that building at noon—only because consistent storms prevented him from doing so outside. Apparently, though, even a cursory description of the new facility did not merit inclusion into the journal extract. A return to the town to preach at noon on Friday, 31 August 1770, yielded no comment from Wesley—and that appeared to have been his final visit to Crowan. One will never know why he never returned there (or failed to note the occasion if he did).

Cubert

Cubert, a Church of England parish presided over, in the mid-eighteenth century, by evangelical-minded clergy, lay approximately a mile and a half east of the west coast of Cornwall, three and one-quarter miles northeast of Newlyn. The original name of the town, St. Kubert, changed to Cubert, then to Cuthbert in the fourteenth century, and in the eighteenth century, "Cuthbert" became the common reference to the parish (but not the town!), derived from a local saint, Cubertus. In John Wesley's journal extract for 7 September 1765, the Methodist leader claimed "Cuthbert" to have been the true spelling for the name of the town (22:18). Thomas Moule, on his map of Cornwall (1830), spelled the name as *Cubert* (32).

John Wesley's initial visit to Cubert occurred on Wednesday morning, 18 September 1751. After his usual "preaching," he went on his way without noting what he had seen or heard—particularly concerning a Methodist society there. On the next visit, however (Sunday, 14 September 1755), Wesley reported that he arrived in Cubert "much tired. But I was now as fresh as in the morning"—the exercise of preaching no doubt claiming responsibility for his revival. The next day (Monday, the 15th), the elements of Nature caught his attention, and thus would, later, prompt the extension of the manipulation of his pen. He and his companions engaged in an hour-long walk "near the sea-shore, among those amazing caverns, which are full as surprising as Poole's Hole or any other in the Peak of Derbyshire. Poole's Hole might stand as a reference to the town of Poole, Dorsetshire, on Poole Harbour, the large, nearly land-locked bay of the English Channel, situated forty miles west of Portsmouth, Hampshire. In addition, the Peak District of Derbyshire, in the East Midlands and northwest of Derby, offered two distinct types of landscape: in the south, the gently rolling hills of the White Peak; to the north, west, and east, the wild, heather-clad moorlands of the Dark Peak peat bogs, superimposed on millstone grit. "Some part of the rock in these natural vaults glitters as bright and ruddy as gold," continued Wesley. "Part is a fine sky-blue, part green, part enameled, exactly like mother-of pearl; and a great part, especially near the Holywell (which bubbled up on the top of a rock and is famous for curing either scorbutic [of or pertaining to scurvy, a disease characterized by a general debility of the body, extreme tenderness of the gums, foul breath, subcutaneous (lying beneath the skin) eruptions, and pains in the limbs—all the result of mal-nutrition arising from the lack of suitable food] or scrofulous [scrofula, a disease characterized principally by chronic enlargement and degeneration of the lymphatic glands which, at one point in the seventeenth century, bore the term "the King's Evil"] disorders), is crusted wherever the water runs with a hard white coast like alabaster" (21:30). *Alabaster*, a term for sulphate of lime, or gypsum, appears white, yellow, red, or clouded. American singers of songs and hymns, particularly of the patriotic and romantic kind, quickly associate the word with the urban image found in the final verse of "America the Beautiful" (1895), by Wellesley College (Massachusetts) graduate and English professor, Katharine Lee Bates (1859–1929):

> O beautiful for patriot dream
> That sees beyond the years
> Thine **alabaster** cities gleam
> Undimmed by human tears!
> America! America!

Nehemiah Curnock mentioned (*Journal*, 4:136), and Reginald Ward cited from (21:30), a fragment from William Hals, et al., *A Complete Parochial[1] History of the County of Cornwall*. 4. vols. (Truro, Cornwall,

1867–1873), 1:273, concerning the Holywell, situated one and one-half miles from Cubert parish church. "In this parish is that famous and well-known spring of water called Holy-well (so named, the inhabitants say, for the virtues of this water was [*sic*] first discovered on All-hallows day)." All Saints Day—or **Allhallows Day**, Hollantide, or Hallowmas—occurs on 1 November. Occasional references to a Sunday of All Martyrs, later of All Saints, will be found in documents prior to the seventh century. The Orthodox Church celebrated the event on the Sunday after Pentecost until 609 or 610, at which time Pope Boniface IV dedicated the Pantheon as the Church of Sancta Maria ad Martyrs on 13 May, and for a period that date became the time of celebration for the Western world. The date of 1 November derived from the dedication of a chapel in St. Peter's Rome, to "all of the saints" by Pope Gregory III (731–741), and Pope Gregory IV (827–844) declared that date to be universal.[2] Curnock went on to explain, "The same stands in a dark cavern of the sea-cliff rocks ... from the top of which ... distils continually drops of water, from the white, blue, red, and green veins of those rocks ... in the place where those drops of water fall it swells to a lump of considerable bigness, and there petrifies ... [in] the several colours ... and is of a hard brittle nature, apt to break like glass. The virtues of this water are very great. It is incredible what numbers in summer season frequent this place and waters from counties far distant."

Seven years would pass before John Wesley found another opportunity to visit Cubert. He and his companions had been riding in the dark, through incessant rain, before "God brought us safe" to the town, "a little after eight" (21:390), on the evening of 19 September 1762. He preached there at 8:00 on Monday and departed on Tuesday, 21 September, without further word or comment upon his activities or observations during a stay that lasted for approximately thirty-six hours.

At this point in the discussion of Methodism in Cubert, one needs to dwell a bit upon the relationship between John Wesley and a person of that town whom the Methodist leader had readily embraced. Joseph Hosken (1698–1780), a wealthy farmer at Cairnes, in Cubert, and a prominent Methodist of the parish, had gone so far as to add a parlor and a bedroom to his own house to accommodate the Methodist itinerant preachers assigned to that part of Cornwall circuit. He also built a small chapel in Cubert church-town—the term "church town" designating the town of Cubert itself, thus separating it from the wider, or outlying "Cubert parish." John Haime (1708–1784), a native of Shaftesbury, Dorsetshire, and a professional soldier who had, in 1743–1744, formed a Methodist society among his fellow soldiers, and following his discharge from the military in

1746 or 1747, joined the Wesleyan Methodist itinerancy in late August 1750. However, he suffered from depression and spiritual doubt, and in August 1766, physically and mentally worn out, he left the itinerancy. Beginning in late September 1766, through arrangements executed by John Wesley, John Haime came to Cubert to become Joseph Hosken's domestic chaplain. On 16 September 1766, Wesley, then at St. Ives, Cornwall, had written to Haime at his home in Shaftesbury, strongly advising (ordering, perhaps), "I think you have no need to go to London; God has, it seems, provided a place for you here [in Cornwall]. Mr. Hoskins [*sic*] wants a worn-out preacher to live with him, to take care of his family, and to pray with them morning and evening" (5:27). Haime performed those functions until 1769 or 1770.

John Wesley's surviving and published correspondence indicates that the Methodist leader knew directly, or knew of, Joseph Hosken since mid–July 1765. Writing to his itinerant preacher Thomas Rankin, then stationed in Redruth, Cornwall, from Kilkenny, Ireland, on the 15th of that month, the leader of the Methodists indicated "no objection to what you proposed to Mr. Hoskins [*sic*], only my age. If he had left *that* gentleman trustee, I would not have given a groat for all his legacies." For the benefit of those interested in the history of currency, the "groat" stood as a denomination of a coin recognized from the thirteenth century onward in various European countries—its standard being, theoretically, one-eighth of an ounce of silver. The English groat, coined in 1351–1352, became equal to 4d., but it ceased to be issued for circulation in 1662—the year of the restoration of Charles II to the throne of England and the end of the Puritan Commonwealth. At any rate, John Wesley concluded, "I wish he would not delay. A day ought not to be lost" (4:309). Unfortunately, the letter conveys little meaning—and Telford's headnote mentions everything but the substance of Wesley's instructions. For that, one must assume and speculate—two dangerous exercises.

In any event, the name of Joseph Hosken worked its way upon the pages of John Wesley's journal extract and remained there throughout fifteen years of narrative. During that period, the man literally and alternately reposed in and rose out of his death bed. Thus, on Saturday, 7 September 1765, John Wesley came to Cubert to find Hosken "weak in body but happy in God. He was just able to ride to the Churchtown in the evening, where a serious congregation soon assembled" (22:18–19). There exists no mention of Hosken (or anyone or anything else) when Wesley preached at Cubert on Monday, 15 September 1766; or at some point between 21 and 25 August 1770; on Monday, 24 August 1773; or on Monday, 5 September

1774—but one must assume that if Wesley preached in the town, he must have had some contact with Joseph Hosken. However, a year later, on Wednesday, 6 September 1775, Wesley actually recorded his observation of "my good old friend, Mr. Hosken, quivering over the grave. He ventured, however, to the churchtown and, I believe, found a blessing under the preaching" (22:465). Hosken continued the fight, and when Wesley came again to Cubert on Saturday, 17 August 1776, he found him "alive, but just tottering over the grave." The Methodist leader then preached on that evening, his sermon text from 2 Corinthians 5:1–4: "For we know that if our earthly house of this tabernacle were dissolved, we have a building of God, an house not made with hands, eternal in the heavens./For in this we groan, earnestly desiring to be clothed upon with our house which is from heaven:/If so that being clothed we shall not be found naked./For we that are in this tabernacle do groan, being burdened: not for that we would be unclothed, but clothed upon, that mortality might be swallowed up of life" (KJV). According to Wesley, that would have been "probably the last sermon he will hear from me. I was afterward inquiring if 'that scandal of Cornwall, the plundering of wrecked vessels,' still subsisted. He [Hosken] said, 'As much as ever, only the Methodists will have nothing to do with it. But three months since, a vessel was wrecked on the south coast, and the tinners presently seized on all the goods—and even broke in pieces a new coach which was on board and carried every scrap of it away.' But is there no way to prevent this shameful breach of all the laws, both of religion and humanity? Indeed there is. The gentry of Cornwall may prevent it whenever they please. Let them only see that the laws be strictly executed upon the next plunderers, and, after an example is made of ten of these, the next wreck will be unmolested. Nay, there is a milder way. Let them only agree together to discharge any tinner or labourer that is concerned in the plundering of a wreck, and advertise his name, then no Cornish gentleman may employ him any more, and neither tinner nor labourer will any more be concerned in that bad work" (23:28–29).

When John Wesley came once more to Cubert a year later, on Friday, 22 August 1777, Joseph Hosken continued to remain among the living— "that venerable old man ... calmly awaiting his discharge from the body" (23:66). On the Methodist leader's next, and final, recorded visit to the town, Saturday, 29 August 1778, Hosken had not yet been "discharged." Wesley "found the venerable old man at Cubert pale, thin, and scarce half alive; however, he made shift to go in a chaise to the preaching and, deaf as he was, to hear almost every word. He had such a night's rest as he had not had for many months, and in the morning seemed hardly the same person. It may be God will give him a little longer life for the good of many" (23:104). Indeed, God did just that, for Joseph Hosken lived on until 6 March 1780, and, following Wesley's departure, Wesleyan Methodism at Cubert, also, endured "a little longer life for the good of many."

Falmouth

A principal port of Cornwall on the English Channel and at the mouth of the Fal River, Falmouth lay nine miles southwest of Truro and forty-four miles west-southwest of Plymouth, Devonshire. Situated on Falmouth Bay, the town enjoyed the physical benefits of that long, winding, branched estuary, commanded by Pendennis and St. Mawes castles on opposite sides of the harbor. Henry VIII built Pendennis Castle to guard the western coast of Carrick Roads ("roads" being a sheltered area of water near the shore where vessels, in cases of extreme weather, might lie at anchor in safety); it featured a thick three-hundred-foot circular tower with a surrounding gun platform. At some point within the reign of Henry's daughter, Elizabeth I (1558–1603), builders added the outer curtain wall and angle bastions, and in 1611, during the reign of James I (1603–1625), an extraordinarily large Italianate gatehouse underwent construction. As for St. Mawes Castle, Henry VIII ordered its construction in 1540, paying particular attention to its large circular tower surrounded by three semi-circular bastions.[1] The town gained considerable importance in the middle and late seventeenth century from mail packets from the West Indies, from North America, and from Portugal. During the English Civil War, Thomas Fairfax (1612–1671), 3rd Baron Fairfax of Cameron and commander-in-chief of the Parliamentary Army, besieged Falmouth for five months in 1646 before finally taking the town from the Royalists— the length of the siege owing, in part, to resistance strengthened by the effectiveness of the Elizabethan ramparts of Pendennis Castle. Granite quarries nearby yielded a fine quality of building stone, but eventually foreign competition forced a considerable number of laborers to leave the area and to look for work elsewhere—even to British North America.

Visiting Falmouth in the early 1720s Daniel Defoe observed the Cornish port town as "the richest and best trading town in this county ... owing to the situation, for that Falmouth [not only] lying upon the sea, but within the entrance, ships of the greatest burthen [weight and capacity] come up to the very quays, and the whole royal navy might ride safely in the road." Defoe noted further that "Falmouth is well built, has abundance of shipping belonging to it, is full of rich merchants, and has a flourishing and increasing trade. I say increasing, because by the late setting up the English packets [vessels traveling at regular intervals between two specific ports for the conveyance of mails, goods, and passengers] between this port and Lisbon [Portugal], there is a new commerce between Portugal and this town, carried on to very great value." Defoe's reference to "setting up" pointed to what has been termed the "Methuen Treaty" of 27 December 1703, one result of which led to the providing of four weekly packets between Falmouth and Lisbon. The Methuen Treaty consisted of a three-clause commercial treaty between England and Portugal, named for its negotiators, John Methuen (1650–1706), ambassador extraordinary to Portugal, and his son, Paul Methuen (1672–1757), envoy to Portugal since 1697. Under the terms, Portugal would remove its existing prohibition on English cloth, and admit it at a relatively inexpensive rate. In return, England undertook to import Portuguese wines at rates that would always be less by one-third than those charged on French wine. English merchants and manufacturers expressed their collective delight at a bargain that found a new outlet for their cloth, and sheep-breeding gentleman-farmers owning hundreds of acres and owners of small agricultural estates proved equally pleased. The cloth manufacturing industry of Portugal suffered near destruction, but that country found salvation in recognizing itself as an enormous vineyard to provide English dining tables with port.[2]

"It is true," added Defoe, himself a failed student and unsuccessful practitioner of commerce, "part of this trade was founded in a clandestine commerce, carried on by the said packets at Lisbon, where being king's [Peter II (1683–1706), John V (1706–1750)] ships, and claiming the privilege of not being watched or visited by the custom-house officers, they found means to carry off great quantities of British manufactures, which they sold on board to the Portuguese merchants, and they conveyed them on shore, as 'tis supposed without paying custom. But the government there, getting intelligence of it, and complaint being made in England also, where it was found to be very prejudicial to the fair merchant, that trade has been effectively stopped, but the Falmouth merchants having by this means gotten a taste of the Portuguese trade, have maintained it ever since in ships of their own. This is a specimen of the Portugal trade, and how considerable it is in it self, as well as how advantageous to England, but as that is not to present the case, I shall proceed [to Truro]."[3] On that note, "I shall proceed" to the discussion at hand—the Wesleys in Falmouth.

Unfortunately, so far as concerns Charles Wesley, only a single mention of Falmouth has been preserved upon the pages of his fragmented manuscript journal. On Thursday, 2 August 1744, he traveled five miles

west of Falmouth to "a large gentleman's seat near Penryn." A serious student of grammar and syntax might raise the question of whether the adjective "large" modifies the gentleman or his seat! And, to silence the wits
among the readership, the term "seat" refers solely to the unidentified gentleman's landed *estate*. In more precise terms, Wesley added to his narrative, "We saw the people come pouring in from Falmouth and all parts"
(2:414). Wesley went on to estimate the number of those assembled to
hear his sermon at 2,000; exactly how he managed to identify those who
came "pouring in" from Falmouth remains a question.

As for John Wesley, his initial visit to Falmouth provided the Methodist
leader with ample drama, as well as presented before his readers perhaps
one of the most detailed and graphic accounts to appear in a single entry
throughout all of his twenty-one published journal extracts. He rode to
the town on Thursday, 4 July 1745, and at approximately 3:00 p.m. went
to visit with "a gentlewoman who had been long indisposed. Almost as
soon as I was set down, the house was beset on all sides by an innumerable
number of people. A louder or more confused noise could hardly be at
the taking of a city by storm." Nehemiah Curnock, having consulted an
article from the *Proceedings of the Wesley Historical Society* (4:188),
claimed that the scene of the disturbance occurred "near Greenbank Terrace"—which means little to anyone unfamiliar with the physical particulars of eighteenth-century Falmouth. What proves more bothersome to
the inquiring mind, however, focuses upon the reasons, or motivation, for
a mob to form and to attempt an assault upon a single person, and John
Wesley in particular. From Robert Southey in 1820, through Luke Tyerman
in the late 1870s, and to Richard Heitzenrater in 2013, John Wesley's biographers and historical commentators have tended to agree in pointing the
accusing finger in the direction of a number of related causes: (1) a decade-
long anti-evangelical sentiment in Cornwall, supported by established and
conservative Church of England clerics and local magistrates; (2) the tensions throughout the nation, particularly in such seaport towns as Falmouth, created by inhabitants' fear of invasion from Roman Catholic
France during the Jacobite uprising of 1745; and (3) a combination of fear
and resentment fueled by a belief in Methodism as a means of separation
from the Church of England caused local populations to react radically
and unreasonably against outsiders. Simply, mobs could easily be gathered,
manipulated, and urged into action by authorities without pausing for due
thought or consideration.

With such questions of intra-town sites and intra-town politics put
aside, we can return to Wesley's narrative. "At first, Mrs. B. [the indisposed

woman?] and her daughter endeavoured to quiet them. But it was labour lost. They might as well have attempted to still the raging of the sea." The final phrase of the sentence derives from Psalms 89:10—"Thou rulest the raging of the sea: thou stillest the waves thereof when they arise" (BCP). Continued John Wesley, "They were soon glad to shift for themselves and leave K[itty]. E. and me to do as well as we could. The rabble roared with all of their throats, 'Bring out the *Canorum!* Where is the *Canorum?*' (an unmeaning word which the Cornish generally use instead of Methodist)." Professor W. Reginald Ward chose to accept John Wesley's explanation for the meaning of that word, but Nehemiah Curnock had turned to a source, *Lexicon Cornu-Britannicum* (p. 44) by a Rev. R. Williamson, and thus concluded, "'Canorum.' This 'unmeaning word' is perhaps derived from the Cornish *Canor* (Welsh *canwr*), a singer: an allusion to the love of singing among the Methodists" (*Journal*, 4:189, note 2)—as accurate and as logical a stab in the dark as any wanderer on or off the street might attempt. The most recent editors of the *Oxford English Dictionary (OED)* offer little beyond the Latin derivative *canor* (n), having to do with melody or sweet singing, and its adjectival relative, *canorous*, meaning singing, melodious, musical, resonant, or ringing. Professor Ward appears to have been well served by ignoring the matter and allowing Wesley to have the final word.

Again, returning to Wesley's narrative in Falmouth, the Methodist leader proceeded, "No answer being given, they quickly forced open the outer door and filled the passage. Only a wainscot partition was between us, which was not likely to stand long." "Wainscot" has generally been defined as a superior quality of foreign oak imported into England from Russia, Germany, and Holland, principally applied to the construction of fine panel work. Such material also includes logs, planks, or boarding of that type of oak; panel-work of oak; or other types of wood for lining the walls of rooms. Wesley undoubtedly had reference to one of the lower qualities of wainscot. In any event, he "immediately took down a large looking glass which hung against it, supposing the whole side of it would fall down at once. When they began their work with abundance of bitter imprecations [expletives, curses, blasphemies, profanity, insults] poor Kitty was utterly astonished and cried out, 'O Sir, what must we do?' I said, 'We must pray.' Indeed at this time, to all appearance, our lives were not worth an hour's purchase. She asked, 'But Sir, is it not better for you to hide yourself? To get into the closet?' [At 5'3" in height and c. 135 pounds in weight, Wesley would have fit easily into the majority of household closets.] I answered 'No. It is best for me to stand where I am.' Among those without were the crews of some privateers, which were lately come into the harbor. Some of these, being angry at the slowness of the rest, thrust them away, and coming up all together, set their shoulders to the inner door and cried out, 'Avast [hold, stop, stay, cease], lads, avast!' Away went all the hinges at once, and the door fell back into the room. I stepped forward at once into the midst of them and said, 'Here I am.'" Relying upon a combination of Scripture and the words of historical figures, Wesley's words certainly derive from (1) Isaiah 6:8. "Also I heard the voice of the Lord, saying, Whom shall I send, and who will go for us? Then said I, **Here am I**; send me" (KJV); and (2) echo the most popular translation of the concluding sentence of Martin Luther's declaration before the Diet of Worms on 18 April 1521: "**Here I stand**; I can do no other. God help me. Amen." ("*Hie stehe ich. Ich kan nicht anders. Gott helff mir. Amen.*") Wesley then confronted his assailants with a litany of questions: "'Which of you has anything to say to *me*? To which of you have I done any wrong? To you? Or you? Or you?' I continued speaking till I came, bareheaded as I was (for I purposefully left my hat, that they might all see my face), into the middle of the street, and then raising my voice, said, 'Neighbours, countrymen! Do you desire to hear me speak?' They cried vehemently, 'Yes, yes. He *shall* speak. He shall. Nobody shall hinder him.'" The scene, as well as the sound and the sense of it all, appears to have been cast from the noblest of all of England's playwrights. Compare with/contrast to, if you will, the brief exchange in William Shakespeare's *The Tragedy of Julius Caesar* (1623), immediately prior to Mark Antony's oft remembered and oft quoted "Friends, Romans, countrymen, lend me your ears" speech (3:2):

> *Fourth Plebeian*: Peace, let us hear what Antony can say.
> *Antony*: You gentle Romans.
> *All the Plebeians*: Peace, ho! Let us hear him [3:2:67–69].

"But having nothing to stand on and no advantage of ground," continued Wesley, "I could be heard by few only. However, I spoke without intermission, and as far as the sound reached." The final words of that sentence beg the introduction of a closely related incident that occurred an ocean away from the rural environment of Falmouth, Cornwall. One might recall that during the initial visit of George Whitefield to Philadelphia (beginning 2 November 1739), Benjamin Franklin, ever the scientist, arrived at a most interesting conclusion by way of a simple experiment: "He [George Whitefield] had a loud and clear voice, and articulated his Words and Sentences so perfectly that he might be heard and understood at a great Distance, especially as his Auditories, however numerous, observ'd the most exact Silence. He preach'd one Evening from the top of the Court House Steps, which are in the Middle of Market Street, and on the West Side of Second Street which crosses it at right angles. Both Streets were fill'd with his Hearers to a considerable Distance. Being among the hindmost in Market Street, I had the Curiosity to learn how far he could be heard, by retiring backwards down the Street towards the [Delaware] River, and I found his voice distinct till I came near Front-Street [c. 500 feet from the Court House steps], when some Noise from that Street, obscur'd it. Imagining then a Semi-Circle, of which my Distance should be the Radius, and that it were fill'd with Auditors, to each of whom I allow'd two square feet, I computed that he might well be heard by more than Thirty-thousand."[4] Leonard W. Labaree and his fellow editors of the 1964 edition of Franklin's *Autobiography* added a note (2, 179) to the effect that "on the basis of this distance Franklin's calculation is faulty; but in *Poor Richard* ['*s Almanack*], 1749, in discussing the same matter, he pointed out more accurately that 45,000 persons might stand in a space 100 yards square or 21,780 on an acre of ground."

Within the bounds of that same narrative, Wesley went on to claim that "the people were still, till one or two of their captains [leaders] turned about and swore not a man should touch him [Wesley?]. Mr. Thomas, a clergyman [otherwise unidentified], then came up and asked, 'Are you not ashamed to use a stranger thus?' He was soon seconded by two or three gentlemen of the town and one of the aldermen, with whom I walked down the town, speaking all the time, till I came to Mrs. Maddern's house." Jennifer Borlase Maddern (1700–1782), a native of Newlyn East, Cornwall, the daughter of Dr. John Borlase—the family of John Borlase (fl. 1730–1745), residents of Newlyn East, having lost property because of its refusal to attend Church of England services— physician, and a Roman Catholic, had married John Maddern, a Protestant, a native of Madron, Cornwall, and a reported spendthrift. "The gentlemen proposed sending for my horse to the door," continued Wesley, "and desired me to step in and rest the meantime. But on second thoughts they judged it not advisable to let me go out among the people again. So they chose to send my horse before me to Penryn and to send me thither by water, the sea running close by the backdoor in which we were."

"I never saw before, no, not at Walsall itself, the hand of God so plainly shown as here." Wesley filtered his comparison/contrast through the serious anti–Methodist riots at Walsall, Staffordshire, commencing 20 October 1743. "There," he explained, "I had many companions who were willing to die with me; here not a friend, but one simple girl [Kitty E.], who likewise was hurled away from me in an instant, as soon as ever she came out of Mrs. B.'s door. There [Walsall, Staffordshire] I received some blows, lost part of my clothes, and was covered with dirt. Here, although the hands of perhaps some hundreds of people were lifted up to strike or throw, yet they were one and all stopped in the midway, so that not a man touched me with one of his fingers. Neither was anything thrown from first to last, so that I had not even a speck of dirt on my clothes. Who can deny that God heareth the prayer? Or that he hath all power in heaven and earth?" The two questions derive from an equal number of passages from Scriptures: (1) Nehemiah 1:6. "Let thine ear now be attentive, and thine eyes open, that thou mayest **hear the prayer** of thy servant, which I pray before thee now, day and night, for the children of Israel thy servants, and confess the sins of the children if Israel, which we have sinned against thee: both I and my father's house have sinned" (KJV); (2) Matthew 28:18. "And Jesus came and spake unto them [his disciples], saying, All **power** is given unto me **in heaven and in earth**" (KJV). "I took boat about half an hour past five [p.m.]," concluded Wesley. "Many of the mob waited at the end of the town, who, seeing me escaped out of their hands, could only revenge themselves with their tongues. But a few of the fiercest ran along the shore, to receive me at my landing. I walked up the steep, narrow passage from the sea, at the top of which the foremost man stood. I looked him in the face and said, 'I wish you a good night.' He spake not, nor moved hand or foot till I was on horseback. Then he said, 'I wish you was in hell,' and turned back to his companions" (20:75–77). Wesley offered to his readers nothing in the form of his own moral commentary to that lengthy journal entry, instead allowing the final four sentences to perform that function.

A full decade and more passed before John Wesley returned to Falmouth, and he immediately remarked, in his journal entry for Tuesday, 2 September 1755, "The town is not now what it was ten years hence. All is quiet from one end to the other. I had thoughts of preaching on the hill near the church. but the violent wind made it impracticable, so I was obliged to stay in our own room. The people could hear in the yard likewise and the adjoining houses, and all were deeply attentive"—or so he imagined, since he had no way of determining without actually seeing. At 4:00 a.m. the next day, Wednesday, 3 September, Jennifer (Mrs. John) Maddern entered his room (most probably in her house) "all in tears and told me she had seen, as it were, our Lord standing by her, calling her by her name, and had 'ever since been filled with joy unspeakable.'" Note the clear echo from 1 Peter 1:8—"[Jesus Christ] Whom having not seen, ye love; in whom, though now ye see him not, yet believing, ye rejoice with

joy unspeakable and full of glory": (KJV). "Soon after came her sister,"
continued Wesley, "in almost the same condition, and afterward her niece,
who likewise quickly melted into tears and refused to be comforted. Which
of these will endure to the end?" The questions derive from (1) Matthew
24:13: "But he that shall **endure unto the end**, the same shall be saved"
(KJV); and from (2) Mark 13:13: "And ye shall be hated of all men for my
[Jesus Christ's] name's sake: but he that shall **endure unto the end**, the
same shall be saved" (KJV). However, Wesley had not quite finished with
Scriptures, even as he completed his journal commentary. "Now at least
God is among them" (21:26)— Exodus 29:45: "And I will dwell **among** the
children of Israel, and will be their **God**" (KJV). Later on that same day,
Wesley preached "again to a congregation who now appeared to devour
every word" (21:26). Afterward, he donned the garb of tourist and found
time to observe one of the features of Falmouth, Pendennis Castle, which
he described as "finely situated on a high point of and which runs out
between the bay and the harbor, might easily be made exceeding strong.
But our wooden castles are sufficient" (21:390). Professor Ward (21:390,
note 3) envisioned the possibility of Wesley having paraphrased a speech,
delivered on 17 June 1635, by Thomas Coventry, first Baron Coventry
(1578–1640), Lord Chancellor of England, who opined, "The wooden walls
are the best walls of this kingdom." An edition of the speech had reached
the press in *Historical Collections of Private Matters of State, Weighty
Matters in Law, Remarkable Proceedings in Five Parliaments, from 1618
to 1648*, 8 vols. (London, 1659–1701), compiled by the English historian
and Parliamentarian John Rushworth (1612–1690), ultimately confined
for debt in King's Bench Prison, London, where he died.

    Two years after that 1755 visit to Falmouth, John Wesley had to con-
tend with an issue raised by the Rev. Samuel Walker (1714–1761)—a native
of Exeter, Devonshire, educated at the Exeter grammar school and Exeter
College, Oxford (B.A. 1736), and ordained priest in the Church of England
(1737). He occupied the ecclesiastical living as curate of Doddliscombsleigh, Devonshire (six miles southwest of Exeter), but resigned that
appointment in 1738 so that he could accompany the youngest brother of
Lord Rolle, as his tutor and companion, on a two-year tour of the Conti-
nent. On his return to England in 1740, Walker obtained the curacy of
Lanlivery, Cornwall, succeeding there as vicar in that same year, where he
served actively until 1746—thereafter holding the living in trust. He
assumed the living of Truro in 1746, in combination with that of Tolland
in 1747. However, in 1752, Walker invoked his principles against pluralism
(the holding of more than a single ecclesiastical appointment) and resigned

the living at Tolland. At Truro, he eventually and totally embraced evangelical views that led to an evangelical revival in that town, and in 1754, he organized groups of his like-minded parishioners for weekly meetings for prayer, mutual self-examination, assistance, and encouragement. More importantly, he exercised care in the maintenance of the identities of the members of those societies as communicants of the Church of England.[6]

As both an evangelical and a strict loyalist of the Church of England, Walker observed carefully the formation of Wesleyan Methodist societies in his area of Cornwall, and, though generally favorable toward the efforts of George Whitefield and the Wesleys, he became suspicious lest John Wesley's societies would separate from the Church. Within that context, he wrote to John Wesley on several occasions, expressing his desire that the Methodist leader cede to his care the Methodist societies in his parish. A portion of one of Wesley's replies to Walker's request, with particular connection to Falmouth, appeared in the former's letter of 19 September 1757, written from Penryn, Cornwall: "Two years since [c. 1755], eleven or twelve persons of Falmouth were members of our Society. Last year [1756] I was informed that a young man there had begun to teach them new opinions, and that soon after offence and prejudice crept in and increased till they were all torn asunder. What they have done since I know not; for they have no connexion with us. I do 'exert myself' so far as to separate from us those that separate from the Church. But in a thousand other instances I feel the want of more resolution and firmness of spirit. Yet sometimes that may appear irresolution which is not so. I exercise as little authority as possible, because I am afraid of people's depending upon me *too much* and paying me more reverence than they might" (*Letters*, ed. Telford, 3:222). Despite Wesley's attempt at humility here, his extant correspondence, diary, journal extracts, prose tracts, "conversations" within the Conference *Minutes*, assignment of preachers to and within circuits, direction and distribution of finances, and even his editorial changes to his brother's verse—all of those and more—demonstrate clearly his attempts to "exercise ... authority" and to control Methodist affairs. Without that control, without that authority, Wesleyan Methodism would not have survived the eighteenth century and would not have remained a visible evangelical branch of the Church of England—although that Church would not admit or recognize that fact.

John Wesley did not attempt another visit to Falmouth until Thursday, 30 August 1770, at which time he preached, at 2:00 p.m. near the church and "to a greater number of people than I ever saw there before, except the mob five and twenty years ago" (22:245). He had nothing more to note about that visit. For a record of the eighty-six-year-old Wesley's final visit to the Cornish port town, one must turn to the diary entries (24:291) for Tuesday and Wednesday, 18–19 August 1789, to view the cryptic details of a stay that extended from 4:15 p.m. to 10:15 a.m. Beyond the usual tea, religious conversation, prayer, and meals, he delivered but a single sermon at Falmouth, that exercise occurring at some time after 6:00 p.m. on the 18th, the text of which he derived from John 4:24—"God is a Spirit: and they that worship him must worship him in spirit and in truth" (KJV). Thus, beyond the dramatic episode with the mob during his initial visit, the emotional outpourings of three local women, a brief look at historic Pendennis Castle, and correspondence concerning internal problems within the local Methodist society, the reader of Wesley's journal and diary entries does not enjoy an especially perceptive account from the Methodist leader of religious activities in eighteenth-century Falmouth. He simply did not plant his feet there often enough to do so.

Fowey

Situated on the east coast of central Cornwall, on the west side of the southeastern end of the River Fowey, the town of Fowey currently exists as a rest stop for those visitors to the Iron Age hill fort of Castle Dore, three miles to the northeast, and Tristan Stone, two miles to the south of the fort. Castle Dore, with its circular banks as high as seven feet, served, during the fifth century, as the headquarters of a Cornish chieftain, possibly Cunomorus—the King Mark of the Arthurian legend, whose betrothed Iseult became the lover of his nephew, Tristan. Tristan Stone, of course, takes his name from that Arthurian Tristan.[1] The inner portions of the town house revealed, in the eighteenth century, a tangle of small steep streets and featured the Church of St. Finbarrus, which marked the end of the ancient Saint's Way footpath from Padstow, twenty miles to the northwest—the route of the Celtic missionaries who arrived on the west coast of Cornwall to convert people to Christianity. Inside St. Finnbarrus one will still find memorials to the seventeenth-century Rashleigh family, whose landed estate bore the name Menabilly. A late eighteenth-/early nineteenth-century member of that family and resident of Menabilly, the Parliamentarian Philip Rashleigh (fl. 1790–1810) published *Specimens of British Minerals, Selected from His Cabinet, with Descriptions*, 2 "thin" vols. (London, 1797, 1802), with fifty-four colored plates, which sold for £5. 5s. the set. He also wrote three papers on the subject of "Antiquities in Archaeology" (1789, 1803).[2] In addition, one might be interested to learn that the London-born novelist Daphne du Maurier (1907–1989) lived for a time in Menabilly, and in her popular romantic novel *Rebecca* (1938), the Cornish estate assumes the name of "Manderley."

Daniel Defoe described Fowey (in the sixteenth, seventeenth, and early eighteenth centuries also known as "Foy") as "an ancient town, and formerly very large; nay, not large only, but powerful and potent for the Foyens, as they were then called, were able to fit out large fleets not only for merchant's ships, but even of men of war; and with these, not only fought with, but several times vanquished, and routed the squadron of the Cinque Port men, who in those days were thought very powerful." The Cinque Ports comprised a number of ports and towns on the coast of Kent and Sussex, England, important during the medieval period (the Middle Ages, c. 600–1500 or 1000–1400).

The original five had been Dover, Sandwich, Romney, Hastings, and Hythe—Winchelsea and Rye added afterward. Edward the Confessor (reigned 1042–1066) bestowed a charter upon the Cinque Ports, and throughout the period the English Crown endowed them with considerable benefits, especially in trade, in return for sea services in defense of the southeastern coast. "Edward IV [1442–1483, reigned 1461–1483]," continued Defoe, "favoured them much, and because the French threatened them, to come up river with a powerful navy, to burn their town, he caused two forts to be built at the public charge for security of the town and river, which forts at least some show of them remain there still, but the same King Edward was some time after so disgusted at the townsmen for officiously falling upon the French after a truce was made, and proclaimed, that he effectually disarmed them, took away their whole fleet, shops, tackle apparel and furniture; and since that time we do not read of any of their naval exploits, nor have they ever recovered, or attempted to recover their strength at sea.[3] However, Foy, at this time, is a very fair [pleasing to the eye in its appearance] town; it lies extended on the east side of the river for above a mile, the buildings fair; and there are a great many flourishing merchants in it, who have a great share in the fishing trade, especially for pilchards." Small sea fish, closely related to herrings, pilchards have been taken in large numbers on the coasts of Cornwall and Devonshire.

William Shakespeare reinforced the definition in his comedy, *Twelfth Night, or What You Will* (1623), at the point where Viola, the lady disguised as Cesario, asks Feste, Countess Olivia's court jester, "Art thou not the Lady Olivia's fool?" Feste replies, "No indeed, sir, the Lady Olivia has no folly, she will keep no fool, sir, till she be married, and fools are like husbands as **pilchards** are to herrings—the husband's the bigger" (3:1:27–30).[4] Defoe might have added that in such Cornish fishing towns as Fowey, the pilchard season extended from July to October, and for the lower classes, fresh or salted pilchards, combined with potatoes, barley bread and "pillez" (a variety of corn, akin to oatmeal), formed the staple diet for a number of families.[5]

During the decade of the 1740s and prior to the Wesley's evangelical missionary efforts in Cornwall, the citizens of Fowey appeared firmly anchored to the Church of England. For example, during 1744–1745, the church there held a monthly Communion celebration, with 180 *eligible* communicants, and the monthly average stood at between sixty and seventy, with 126 at Easter. At the other extreme, during the same general period, reports from Fowey indicated that only two Roman Catholic families resided within the town.[6]

The fragmented manuscript journal entries of Charles Wesley contain no evidence of a visit to Fowey, while John Wesley appears to have paused at the seaport town but once—on Monday, 25 August 1755. The Methodist leader recorded that "a little company met us [at Fowey] and conducted us to Luxulyan" (21:24). Whether the Methodist leader actually preached there cannot be determined. From that note, Fowey appears to have lost its place in the narrative records of eighteenth-century Wesleyan Methodism.

Goldstithney

The village of Goldstithney, in southern Cornwall, lay approximately five to six miles east of Penzance. John Wesley preached there on Wednesday, 29 August 1770, offered no comment or note of observation, and never returned.

Grampound

Grampound stood as a market town and a Parliamentary borough[1] divided between the two parishes of Probus and Creed, seven and one-half miles northeast of Truro and forty miles southwest of Launceston. The majority of the town came within the parish of Creed, the rector there during 1751–1774 being Walter Harte (1700–1774). Educated at Marlborough Grammar School, Wiltshire, and then at St. Mary's Hall, Oxford, where he eventually became vice-principal, he entered into Holy Orders of the Church of England and received Cornish appointments as vicar of

St. Austell and St. Blazy prior to occupying the rectory of Creed—in the same year as he began to serve as canon of Windsor. Harte's publications include *Poems on Several Occasions* (London, 1727, 1739); *An Essay on Satire* (1736)—with focus upon Alexander Pope's *The Dunciad* (1728, 1729, 1742, 1743)[2]; *An Essay on Reason* (1735); *The Union of Reason, Morality, and Revealed Religion: A Sermon* (1737); *A Fast Sermon* (1740); *The History of Gustavus Adolphus, King of Sweden, Surnamed the Great* (1759; 2 vols., 1767); *Essays on Husbandry* (1764, 1770); a volume of poems titled *The Amaranth* (1767)—an imaginary flower that never fades—and *An Essay on Painting* (1769).[3] The portion of Grampound in the parish of Probus came under the ecclesiastical jurisdiction of John Reynolds (?-1758?), vicar from 1730 to 1758. He also served at least one term as the mayor of Grampound, and in both capacities John Wesley would encounter him on one of his visits to the town.

Of prime importance to the Wesleys and their itinerants was the fact that in 1754, a new turnpike had undergone construction, southeast, from Truro to Falmouth, to be extended northeast from Truro to Grampound. However, as late as 1761, the southern portion of the road had reached only as far as Marazion, which had the effect of continuing the isolation of the St. Ives and Land's End districts.[4]

John Wesley initially reached Grampound on Thursday afternoon, 4 September 1746, leaving without any notation in his journal extract as to what he had done there. More than a decade later, though, when the next opportunity to visit the town occurred on Wednesday, 21 September 1757, he observed "a mean, inconsiderable, dirty village. However, it is a borough town!" Recovering from his surprise at learning that fact, Wesley went about his task of preaching, between noon and 1:00, "in a meadow to a numerous congregation. While we were singing, I observed a person in black on the far side of the meadow, who said, 'Come down; you have no business there.' Some boys who were on a wall, taking it for granted that he spoke to them, got down in all haste. I went on, and he walked away. I afterwards understood that he was the minister [John Reynolds] and the mayor of Grampound. Soon after, two constables came and said, 'Sir, the mayor says, you shall not preach within his borough.' I answered, 'The mayor has no authority to hinder me. But it is a point not worth contesting.' So I went about a musket shot farther and left the borough to Mr. Mayor's disposal" (21:125–126). The Methodist leader undertook one more visit to Grampound, that one on Saturday, 4 September 1762. He did preach there, but found nothing else of value to retain for inclusion into his journal extract.

Gulval

In the eighteenth century, the southwestern Cornish parish and tin-mining town of Gulval lay but two miles northeast of Penzance. The state of the place at mid-century might be best appreciated by examining a letter from Gulval, dated 30 January 1749, in which a local mining agent, George Borlase, informed one identified only as Lieutenant-General Onslow of the existence of heavy torrential rains that brought about heavy flooding of the mines, the result of which left thousands of tin miners out of work and starving.[1] More than four years earlier, during but a single recorded visit to Gulval, Charles Wesley had taken no notice of economic conditions there. On Friday, 27 July 1744, he delivered a sermon and, afterward, "admitted some new members [to an evangelical religious society], particularly one who had been the greatest persecutor in all this country" (*Manuscript Journal*, 2:413).

John Wesley initially came to Gulval on Monday afternoon, 9 April 1744, preaching at 4:00, and afterward, before departing, he "regulated the little society" (20:22)—meaning that he informed them of the rules under which a Methodist society should function. He returned there four days later, Friday, 13 April, preached at 3:00 in the afternoon, then left without entering further comment in his journal. Wesley managed to find "some life" (20:79) at Gulval on Friday, 12 July 1745; preached at an area known as Gulval Cross, midway between Penzance and Marazion on Friday, 10 July 1747, and did so again on Friday, 23 September 1745. Whether he made one last visit to Gulval in early September 1757 cannot be readily determined, but a remark in his journal for Thursday, 8 September 1757, relates clearly the state of Methodist affairs there: "In Gulval, not one class, not one member, remains" (21:123). Early in 1742, John Wesley divided Methodist societies into "classes," small groups of no more than a dozen members of the society, concerned primarily with the exercise of discipline among the entire society. Wesley, himself, appointed the leader for each class—that person being the spiritual overseer of the group and one with whom he felt comfortable in confiding.

Gunnislake

The town of Gunnislake lay eight miles due north of Saltash. On Saturday, 27 September 1760, in the midst of heavy rain and high wind, John Wesley and his companions found themselves unable to engage a boat across the River Tamar at Saltash, Cornwall, into Devonshire, and then south to Plymouth. Thus, "we determined to ride round by the *new bridge*. The rain still fell on either side, but for twenty miles we had not one drop and not a considerable shower all day. Soon after four o'clock in the afternoon, we came safe to Plymouth Dock" (21:282).

Nehemiah Curnock responded to Wesley's reference to "the new bridge" with his explanation that "ordinary passengers might count upon crossing the Tamar at Saltash on a big flat-bottomed boat. Horses required an education for this crossing—an education which Wesley's horses had no doubt received." The Rev. Curnock's assessment on the "education" of Wesley's horses amounts to pure speculation. Nonetheless, he proceeded to explain that "on the present occasion the ordinary ferry-boat was unavailable because of the storm. The travellers were compelled to take the road toward Callington [eight miles to the northwest from Saltash], turning eastward under Kithill to **Gunnislake**; this would be quite twelve miles from Saltash. One almost wonders that Wesley did not here insert a description of Gunnislake as it then was, and the graceful new bridge existing in 1760, which had become the one attractive feature of the scene. [The English watercolorist and landscaper painter, Joseph Mallord William] Turner's [1775–1851] painting, 'Crossing the Brook [1815],' now [c. 1912] hung in the National Gallery [London], refers to the Tamar at Newbridge. Mr. Henry Roseveare, to whom we are indebted for his interesting geographical description, knows the neighbourhood well and the painting. He adds: 'The graceful arches of the New Bridge are painted with great minuteness and faithfulness.' The journey across to Tavistock [Devonshire], thence by the high and exposed road to Plymouth Dock, would be nine or ten miles [more like fifteen]; this, with the twelve miles on the other side of the river would account for Wesley's twenty miles" (*Journal*, 4:414, note 1).

W. Reginald Ward paid no attention to Curnock's remarks, stating, simply, "The New Bridge at **Gunnislake**, built, in fact, c. 1520." He then cited a source, Charles Henderson and H. Coates, *Old Cornish Bridges and Streams* (London, 1928), 30—with a photograph at plate 26 (21:282, note 9). Professor Ward might have added a word or two as to why a bridge constructed in 1520 or so would have remained in a serviceable state 234 years later. Generally, in the fifteen and sixteenth centuries (and even before), after a bridge had been constructed, and it had fallen wholly or partly in disrepair, the responsibility for its restoration proved not an easy task to identify. Even after the identity of the person or corporation had been ascertained, there remained the consideration of obtaining the necessary funds for restoration or repair. In a number of instances, the construction or repair of English bridges became projects underwritten by individuals, the clergy being the most prominent. For example, Walter Skirlaw, Bishop of Durham, rebuilt, at his own expense, the old stone bridge which, until the time of Henry IV (1367–1413, reigned 1399–1413), had spanned the River Wear at Shincliffe, near Durham. He also bridged the Gaunless River at Auckland and the River Tees at Yarm, in the North Riding of Yorkshire. Further, J. R. Boyle in his *The County of Durham* (London, 1892) reported that Hugh de Pudsey (1125?-1195), Bishop of Durham (1153–1195), initially built the Elvet Bridge in the county of Durham. Those prove but two examples of what one historian of transportation labeled "the efforts of patriotic and self-sacrificing benefactors." Apparently, in the fourteenth and fifteenth centuries, the building of a bridge ranked especially high among the outward manifestations of piety. In addition, the maintaining of those bridges, as well as providing assistance in such projects, also came within the category of pious acts, as evidenced by instances of bequests of various amounts left for the maintenance and repair of bridges. For instance, in 1439, one William Neel, in his will, bequeathed, "for the repair of "the great bridge" at Market Harborough, Leicestershire, the sum of 3s. 4d. Thomas del Bothe (?-1338) had built a chapel on the old bridge at Salford, Lancashire, for "the repose" of its founder's soul, while in his will he directed a gift of £30 for the maintenance of the bridge. The repair of the bridges over the River Trent at Nottingham appeared to have been the object of a number of bequests: On 23 May 1501, Robert Poole emerged as one among a number of persons who provided a house and a portion of land; Thomas Willoughby, a Nottingham alderman, willed to Hethbeth Bridge four of his best pieces of timber; a chapel dedicated to St. James stood upon the High Bridge, and in 1535, it possessed lands valued at £2. 6s. 2d. per year; and the town of Burton-on-Trent had received various bequests for "charitable purposes," a number of which directed funds for the repair of bridges. Lastly, consider the act, in 1394, of Walter, Bishop of Durham, who granted release from penance "all Christian people" who would contribute toward the rebuilding of the Chollerford Bridge, in Durham, across the River Tyne.[1]

Gwennap

Located approximately two and one-half to three miles southeast of Redruth, in south-central Cornwall, eighteenth-century Gwennap has been identified, simply, as a copper-mining parish. Nonetheless, the Wesleys extended to the town a goodly proportion of their attentions during their visits to Cornwall—perhaps because of its proximity to the larger town of Redruth. Nonetheless, in c. 1725, the Cornish industrialist William Lemon[1] turned his attention to the Gwennap area and began copper mining on an extensive scale, utilizing a number of steam engines built on the principle developed by Thomas Newcomen and John Calley and erected by Joseph Hornblower. Newcomen (1663–1729), an English blacksmith, born at Dartmouth, Devonshire, in association with John Calley (or Cawley), invented, in 1705, an engine in which steam admitted to a cylinder became condensed by a jet of cold water, with the piston driven by atmospheric pressure. Newcomen then entered into partnership with Captain Thomas Savery (see Breage), and improved upon the latter's primitive steam engine for pumping water from mines (patented in 1698). He built Savery's device into a practical working engine that became, as early as 1712–1715, a common machine in English collieries. Thus, from those beginnings until the early nineteenth century, Gwennap stood as the richest copper mining area in the Western world.[2]

In the mid–1740s, the officials at Gwennap, both civil and ecclesiastical, tended to label Methodists as Dissenters. The incumbent there, Rev. Henry Phillips, reported (as recorded in vol. 225c. of the *Exeter Diocesan Visitation Returns*), "'Tis thought there are about a hundred families in the parish. As to any Dissenters, we had none till of late a certain sect, usually distinguished by the name of Methodists came among us, of which sort there may be about forty or fifty persons that follow them. They have a meetinghouse in the parish, but not licensed, in which there is a constant succession of teachers, that run up and down the country." In 1746, the Methodist Conference assigned its first itinerant preachers to the Cornwall circuit; thus, the Rev. Phillips' "runners" would have included Thomas Meyrick, J. R. Reeves, John Trembath, Francis Walker, and Charles Wesley.[3] "Three of their followers belonging to this parish," continued Phillips, "have of late set up for public teachers, viz.: James and Samuel Hitchins [*sic*], and Henry Youren."[4] James Hitchens the younger (fl. 1745–1760), a native of Busveal, Cornwall, and a Methodist itinerant preacher, accompanied his brother, William Hitchens, from Busveal to Bradford-upon-Avon, Wiltshire, for the former's appearance before the appeals commissioners there on his having been impressed into the Royal Army. William Hitchens (fl. 1740–1780) served the Methodist itinerancy between 1745 and 1758 and earned the reputation as "a sensible, pious, good man." Thus, when John Wesley came to Alpraham, Cheshire (after having been at Bilbrook, Somersetshire; Newport, Gloucestershire; and Whitechurch, Shropshire), on Thursday, 4 April 1751, "William Hitchens had not begun, so I took his place and felt no weakness or weariness." At Bradford-on-Avon, Wiltshire, on 30 January 1757, five soldiers impressed William Hitchens into the Royal Army, but the appeals commissioners released him. Hitchens eventually married, left the Methodist itinerancy, and settled in Bristol as a hatter and local preacher. As late as 1793, his wife continued to operate his business.[5]

Interestingly enough, the Rev. Samuel Walker, the evangelical occupant of the Church of England living at Truro,[6] provided additional (but abstract) insight into the ministry of Henry Phillips at Gwennap. His opinion of Phillips soared to favorable theological heights, as evidenced in a letter to Thomas Mitchell (?-1773), vicar of Veryan, Cornwall (1743–1773), in May 1754: "Let me tell you that I was, as proposed, at Gwennap, and surely I have never preached to a congregation where so many expressed an experience of the power of the Word, and all in a manner heard with a more than curious attention." The direct Scripture reference will be found in Hebrews 1:3: "Who [Jesus Christ] being the brightness of his [God the Father's] glory, and the express image of his person, and upholding all things by **the word of his power**, when he had by himself purged our sins, sat down on the right hand of the Majesty on high" (KJV). Further, declared Walker, "I was tempted to wish myself an assistant to my dear friend [Phillips] there, where the harvest is so plentiful and promising." In other words, according to Matthew 9:37, "Then saith he [Jesus Christ] unto hid disciples, **The harvest truly is plenteous**, but the labourers are few" (KJV). "May God direct his heart into the knowledge of all faith," concluded Walker. "He seems singularly fitted for his important trust by the more than ordinary measure of natural endowments which he is possessed of, and I am abundantly rejoiced in the proofs I see in him of a work of grace carrying on upon his soul."[7]

The first of Charles Wesley's seven recorded visits to Gwennap occurred on Saturday, 23 July 1743, when he preached at Gwennap Pit "to near 2,000 hungry souls, who devoured the word of reconciliation." Charles Wesley had turned to 2 Corinthians 5:18–19—"And all things are of God, who hath **reconciled** us to himself by Jesus Christ, and hath given to us the ministry of reconciliation;/To wit, that God was in Christ, **reconciling** the world unto himself, not imputing their trespasses unto them; and hath committed unto us **the word of reconciliation**" (KJV). He then returned to his narrative, seemingly admitting that "half my audience were tinners from about Redruth" (2:362). Throughout the major portion of the eighteenth century, Gwennap Pit had been an amphitheatre formed either by the natural sinking of the level of the surface of the area into the ground, or by surface mining, or by both. By 1799, Gwennap Methodists instituted the practice of all-day preaching on Gwennap Green as competition to a sporting event held in the Pit, and the sporting people soon abandoned their venue. Later, in 1806, workers repaired, reconstructed, and generally improved upon Gwennap Pit by leveling and cutting circular terraces of seats, tier above tier, forming twelve terraced steps four feet wide for seating. They also filled in the old mine shafts and redirected the previous road. The relatively new amphitheatre opened on 18 June 1807, Whit-Monday—according to the 1662 Book of Common Prayer (BCP), the first day following the Feast of Pentecost (Whitsunday/Whitsun). Beginning in that year, the Methodists established the practice of preaching and revival meetings on Whit-Monday for at least the remainder of the nineteenth century in the refurbished Pit.[8]

Charles Wesley next arrived "rejoicing" at Gwennap on Sunday, 7 August 1743, and "as soon as I went forth, I saw the end of my coming to Cornwall, and of Satan's opposition. Such a company assembled as I have not seen, excepting some few times at Kennington [Common, Surrey]. By their looks I perceived they all heard, while I lifted up my voice like a trumpet [Isaiah 58:1: "Cry aloud, spare not, **lift up thy voice like a trumpet**, and shew my people their transgression, and the house of Jacob their sins" (KJV)] and testified, 'God sent his Son to be the Saviour of the world'"—1 John 4:14. "And we have seen and do testify that **the Father sent the Son to be the Saviour of the world**" (KJV). "The convincing Spirit was in the midst as I have seldom, if ever, known. Most of the gentry [those possessed of rank by birth; the qualities or rank of gentlemen; those possessed of superior breeding, courtesy, and generosity; persons of gentle birth and breeding; the class immediately below the nobility] from Redruth were just before me, and so hemmed in that they could not escape. For an hour my voice was heard by all, and reached farther than their outward ears. I am inclined to think that most present were convinced of righteousness or of sin. God hath now set before us an open door, and who shall be able to shut it?" (2:368–369). Note, in that last sentence, the paraphrase of Revelation 3:8—"I [Jesus Christ] know thy [the angel of the church in Philadelphia, in Lydia] works: behold, **I have set before thee an open door**, and **no man can shut it**; for thou hast a little strength, and hast kept my word, and hast not denied my name" (KJV).

The third visit to (or "near") Gwennap came at 9:00 p.m. Tuesday, 17 July 1744, with Charles Wesley in company with the Rev. John Bennet (1670?-1750) of Tresmere, Cornwall, and Rev. John Meriton (1698–1753), and there they lodged at the home of an unnamed "host." Wesley's words echoed his high spirits: "Here a little one is become a thousand. What an amazing work of God done in one year! The whole country is alarmed, and gone forth after the sound of the gospel. In vain do the pulpits [of the established Church] ring of 'Popery, madness, enthusiasm.' Our preachers are daily pressed to new places, and enabled to preach five or six times a day. Persecution is kept off till the seed takes root. Societies are springing up everywhere, and still the cry from all sides is 'Come and help us.'" Wesley then reported that he "preached near Gwennap [Gwennap Pit?] to about a thousand followers of Christ on 'Fear not, little flock' [Luke 12:32. "**Fear not little flock**; for it is your Father's good pleasure to give you the kingdom" (KJV)]. Great love and joy appeared in their faces, such as the world knoweth not of." He then met with members of the Gwennap Methodist society, where he "found almost the whole congregation waiting quietly without the door, longing to be admitted with the rest. Stood at the window so as to be heard of all. I felt what manner of spirit they were of, and had sweet fellowship with them, and strong consolation" (2:408–409)—Hebrews 6:17–18: "Wherein God, willing more abundantly to shew unto the heirs of promise the immutability [unalterable course] of his counsel, confirmed it by an oath:/That by two immutable things, in which it was impossible for God to lie, we might have a **strong consolation**, who have fled for refuge to lay hold upon the hope set before us" (KJV).

Eighteen days later, on 4 August 1744, Charles Wesley came once again to Gwennap, preaching and observing (and generalizing) that "the awakening is general. Very many who have not courage to enter into the Society have yet broke off their sins by repentance, and are waiting for forgiveness. The whole country is[9] sensible of the change. For last assizes there was a gaol-delivery—not one felon to be found in their prisons, which has not been known before in the memory of man." Within the context of English law, the *Assizes* constituted a system, fully developed by the fourteenth century, of visitations to the English provinces by Royal justices. Justices of assize (the administration of justice and the law) rode six circuits, hearing both criminal and civil cases. In the nineteenth century, the number of circuits increased to eight for England and Wales, but the government abolished the Assizes in 1971. "At their last revel," continued Charles Wesley, "they had not men enough to make a wrestling match, all the Gwennap-men being struck off the devil's list, and found wrestling against him, not for him."

On the next day, Saturday, 5 August, he "preached my farewell sermon at Gwennap [Pit?] to an innumerable multitude. They stood mostly on the green plain before me, and on the hill that surrounded it. Many scoffers from Redruth placed themselves on the opposite hill, which looked like Mount Ebal. O that none of them may be found among the goats in that day!" A number of biblical references underscore the two preceding sentences—(1) Joshua 8:30: "Then Joshua built an altar unto the Lord God of Israel in **mount Ebal**" (KJV). Mt. Ebal proved conspicuous in the Samaritan highlands (now in Jordan), approximately 1,207 feet above the valley and 2,077 feet above sea level. In obedience to the instructions from Moses (Deuteronomy 27:13), Joshua built the altar on Ebal and erected stones inscribed with the Law, pronouncing to the assembled Israelites (Deuteronomy 11:29, 27:13; Joshua 8:33) the curses that would follow violations of those sacred statutes. Thereafter, Ebal became known as the Mount of Curses. (2) Matthew 25:32–33: "And before him [the Son of man] shall be gathered all nations: and he shall separate them one from another, as a shepherd divideth his sheep from the **goats**:/And he shall set the sheep on his right hand, but the **goats** on the left" (KJV). Wesley's narrative then proceeded with the determined declaration that "I warned and invited all by threatenings and promises. The adversary was wonderfully restrained, and I hope disturbed in many of his children. My Father's children were comforted on every side. They hung upon the word of life, and they shall find it able to save their souls. Spoke on for two hours. Yet knew not how to let them go. Such sorrow and love as they then expressed, the world will not believe, though a man declare it unto them. My brother [vicar of St. Gennys, Cornwall, the Rev. George] Thomson [1698–1782][10] was astonished, and confessed he had never seen the like among Germans, predestinarians, or any others." Thomson might have experienced contact with Germans during the decade 1722–1732, when he served as chaplain aboard H.M.S. *Tiger*, sailing to British North America, where he then attached himself as chaplain to the 40th Regiment of Foot. Insofar as concerns *Predestinarians*, those so called followed the doctrine according to which human free will and cooperation become totally eliminated from the process of salvation by a thorough-going application of the principle of *predestination*: the Divine decree according to which certain persons will be infallibly guided to eternal salvation. In Matthew 20:23, for instance, Jesus Christ tells the apostles, "Ye shall drink indeed of my cup, and be baptized with the baptism that I am baptized with: but to sit on my right hand, and on my left, is not mine to give, but shall be given to them for whom it is prepared of my Father" (KJV).[11] "With great difficulty," stated Wesley, "we got through them at last, and set out on our journey. Several men and women kept pace with our horses for two or three miles, then parted, in body, not in spirit" (2:412–413).

When Wesley came to Gwennap almost two years later, on Thursday, 26 June 1746, he "encouraged the poor persecuted sheep by that promise, Zechariah 13:7, 8, 9. The Lord smiled upon our first meeting." The full text of those verses reads, "Awake, O sword, against my shepherd, and against the man that is my fellow, saith the Lord of hosts: smite the shepherd, and the sheep shall be scattered: and I will turn mine hand upon the little ones./And it shall come to pass that in all the land, saith the Lord, two parts therein shall be cut off and die; but the third shall be left therein./And I will bring the third part through the fire, and will refine them as silver is refined, and will try [purify] them as gold is tried: they shall call on my name, and I will hear them: I will say, It is my people: and they shall say, The Lord is my God" (KJV). On the next day, he examined separately each member of the Methodist society and "found the Society in a prosperous way. Their sufferings have been for their furtherance, and the gospel's. The opposers behold and wonder at their steadfastness and goodly conversation" (2:464). He remained at Gwennap through Monday, 30 June. A month later (Monday, 28 July 1746), weakened, he claimed, by substituting a milk diet for the regular partaking of tea, which brought about frequent and "violent purging," Charles Wesley nonetheless returned to Gwennap, where he preached and met with members of the Methodist society. He hoped to eat there, "being very faint and weary, but could get nothing proper." Persistent, he spent the time from Sunday evening, 3 August, through most of Tuesday, 5 August, back at Gwennap. On Sunday, he had found, according to his exaggerated figures, "at least five thousand sinners" gathered in a valley near his lodging, "waiting for the glad tidings of salvation. I bade them to the Great Supper, in my Master's name and words, and even compelled them to come in." A slim parallel in sound and sense to the preceding sentence might well be found in portions of Luke 14:15–24—"And when one of them that sat at meat with him heard these things, he said unto him, Blessed is he that shall eat bread in the kingdom of God./...For I say unto you, That none of those men which were bidden shall taste of my supper" (KJV). Further, after preaching there on the 5th, Wesley came away rejoicing "over those blessed mourners. Some I heard were then filled with all joy in believing" (2:470–471)—Acts 16:34: "And when he had brought them into his house, he set meat before them, and rejoiced, believing in God with all his house" (KJV); Romans 15:13—"Now the God of hope fill you with all joy and peace in believing, that ye may abound in hope, through the power of the Holy Ghost" (KJV). Thus ends the extant written record of Charles Wesley's missionary labors in Gwennap.

As usual, John Wesley's recorded visits to Gwennap far exceed those of his younger brother, the former extending the work there from Saturday, 3 September 1743, to Monday, 10 September 1787. On that first visit, the elder Wesley indicated a gathering on the green of "four or five hundred" souls, and to them he preached on Luke 4:18, "He hath anointed me to preach the gospel to the poor."

The complete verse reads, "The Spirit of the Lord is upon me, because he hath anointed me to preach the gospel to the poor; he hath sent me to heal the brokenhearted, to preach deliverance to the captives, and recovering of sight to the blind, to set at liberty them that are bruised" (KJV). Afterward, a person who resided in or near Gwennap invited John Wesley to lodge at his house, and on the following morning, at dawn, he guided the Methodist leader back to the green, where the latter, in front of five or six hundred people, "applied those gracious words, 'I will heal their backsliding, I will love them freely'" (19:336–337)—Hosea 14:4. "I will heal their backsliding, I will love them freely: for mine anger is turned away from him" (KJV).

Ten days later, on Tuesday, 20 September 1743, Wesley returned to Gwennap, arriving slightly before 6:00 p.m. finding "the plain[12] covered from end to end. It **was supposed**[13] there were ten thousand people, to whom I preached Christ our 'wisdom, righteousness, sanctification, and redemption.'" The text of 1 Corinthians 1:30 reads, "But of him are ye in Christ Jesus, who of God is made unto us wisdom, and righteousness, and sanctification, and redemption" (KJV). The sermon continued until darkness, but the Methodist leader determined that "there was on all sides the deepest attention, none speaking, stirring, or scarce 'worshipped in the beauty of holiness'!" Wesley had anchored his observation to Psalms 29:2—"Give unto the Lord the glory due unto his name; worship the Lord in the beauty of holiness" and Psalms 96:9—"O worship the Lord in the beauty of holiness: fear before him, all the earth" (KJV). In citing from Psalms, the Wesleys tended to rely upon the 1662 Book of Common Prayer (BCP) version. Thus: 29:2—"Give the Lord the honour due unto his Name: worship the Lord with holy worship"; 96:9—"O worship the Lord in the beauty of holiness: let the whole earth stand in awe of him." Wesley then singled out a member of that throng, a "Mr. P., whom he identified as "once a violent adversary. Before sermon began he whispered [to] one of his acquaintance, 'Captain [a leader, one who stands at the head of others], stand by me; don't stir from me.' He soon burst out into a flood of tears, and quickly after, sunk down. His friend caught him and prevented his falling to the ground. O may the Friend of sinners lift him up!" The biblical parallels derive from (1) Matthew 11:19—"The Son of man came eating and drinking, and they say, Behold a man gluttonous and a winebibber, a friend of publicans and sinners. But wisdom is justified of her children." (2) Luke 7:34—"The Son of man is come eating and drinking; and ye say, Behold, a gluttonous man, and a winebibber, a friend of publicans and sinners!" (KJV). Hours later, between 3:00 a.m. and 4:00 a.m. on Wednesday, 21 September 1743, Wesley found himself rudely awakened by a group of tin miners who, "fearing they should be too late had gathered round the house and were singing and praising God." At 5:00 a.m., he preached on "Believe in the Lord Jesus Christ, and thou shalt be saved." The full text of Acts 16:31 reads, "And they said, Believe on the Lord Jesus Christ, and thou shalt be saved, and thy house" (KJV). The Methodist leader quickly reached the conclusion that his entire congregation "devoured the word. O may it be health to their soul and marrow unto their bones" (19:340–341). He provided variation on two verses from Proverbs: 3:8—(1) "It shall be health to thy navel and marrow to thy bones" (KJV) and 16:24—(2) "Pleasant words are as an honeycomb, sweet to the soul, and health to the bones" (KJV).

Seven months would pass before John Wesley found an opportunity to return to Gwennap, arriving there on Tuesday, 3 April 1744. That evening he preached to "a plain, simple-hearted people, and God comforted us by each other." Eight days later (11 April), in a "calm, still evening," Wesley stood on a wall in Gwennap, "with the sun setting behind me, and almost an innumerable multitude before, behind, and on either hand. Many likewise sat on the little hills, at some distance from the bulk of the congregation." He maintained, however, that "all could hear distinctly while I read, 'The disciple is not above his Master,' and the rest of those comfortable words [Matthew 10:25—"It is enough for the disciple that he be as his master, and the servant as his lord. If they have called the master of the house Beelzebub, how much more shall they call them of his household?" (KJV)] which are day by day fulfilled in our ears."—Luke 4:21— "And he began to say unto them, This day is this scripture fulfilled in your ears" (KJV). Continuing to maintain his efforts in Gwennap, Wesley returned on Saturday evening, 14 April 1744, remaining there to preach at 5:00 on the following morning and again at that same hour in the afternoon, "on a little hill near the usual place. It rained from the time I began till I concluded. I felt no pain while I spoke, but the instant I had done and all the time I was with the [Methodist] society, my teeth and head ached so violently that I had hardly any senses [awareness, clarity of thought]. I lay down as soon as I could and fell asleep. In the morning [Sunday, 15 April] (blessed be God) I ailed nothing" (20:20, 23, 25).

John Wesley next preached at Gwennap on Saturday evening, 22 June 1745, his sermon text derived from 2 Timothy 3:12, "All that will live godly in Christ Jesus shall suffer persecution." The biblical reference proved to have been especially appropriate, since the Methodist leader received word from Penzance of the arrest, incarceration, and military impressment of one of his itinerant preachers, Thomas Maxfield.[14] In any event, the Methodist leader spent the night in the town and preached again on the following morning at 5:00 (20:71–72). Returning there on late Wednesday afternoon, 3 July 1745, he found the assembled congregation far too numerous for the local preaching house, and thus proceeded to deliver his sermon while standing before the door of the building. Then followed, what *initially* appeared to have been, one of those incidents that would, in various modes, almost become common occurrence for those, including the Wesleys, who pursued the Methodist itinerancy throughout the British Isles: "I was reading my text when a man came, raging as if just broke out of their tombs, and riding into the thickest of the people, seized three or four, one after another, none lifting up a hand against him. A second (gentleman, so called) soon came after, if possible more furious than he, and ordered his men to seize on some others, Mr. Shepherd in particular." That person most likely would have been William Shepherd (fl. 1740–1750), a Methodist itinerant preacher who traveled occasionally with John Wesley. Shepherd's name appears in John Wesley's journal on a dozen occasions between Monday, 29 August 1743 and Sunday, 5 July 1747. Then he disappears from the narrative of Methodist history.[15] "Most of the people, however," continued Wesley, "stood still as they were before and began with all his might, 'Seize him, seize him. I say, seize the preacher for his Majesty's service.' But no one stirring, he rode up and struck several of his attendants, cursing them bitterly for not doing as they were bid. Perceiving still that they would not move, he leaped off his horse, swore he would do it himself, and caught hold of my cassock [a cloak, or long loose cloak or coat; a close-fitting garment with sleeves, fastened to the neck and reaching to the heels, worn under the surplice, alb, or gown by clerics or choristers—or worn as the ordinary clerical costume], crying, 'I take you to serve his Majesty.' A servant taking his horse, he took me by the arm, and we walked arm in arm for about three quarters of a mile. He entertained me all the time with the wickedness of the fellows belonging to the society. When he was taking breath I said, 'Sir, be they what *they* will, I apprehend it will not justify *you* in seizing me in this manner and violently carrying me away, as you said, to serve his Majesty.'" At that point the conversation, and indeed the incident itself, veered off onto a strange path. [John or

Francis] Beauchamp [of Pengreeb, Cornwall],[16] replied, "'I seize you! and violently carry you away! No, sir, no. Nothing like it. I asked you to go with me to my house. And you said you was willing. And if so, you are welcome. And if not, you are welcome to go as you please.' I answered, 'Sir, I know not if it would be safe for me to go back through this rabble.' 'Sir,' said he, 'I will go with you myself.' He then called for his horse and another for me, and rode back with me to the place from whence he took me" (20:74–75).

With that experience having concluded, John Wesley departed from Gwennap, returning, in company of William Shepherd, on Saturday, 6 July 1745, where they found the occupants of the town "in the utmost consternation. Word was brought that a great company of tinners, made drunk on purpose, were coming to do terrible things." Wesley declared that he "labored much to compose their minds. But fear had no ears, so that abundance of the people went away. I preached to the rest on 'Love your enemies.'" [Matthew 5:44—"But I say unto you, love your enemies, bless them that curse you, do good to them that hate you, and pray for them which despitefully use you, and persecute you" (KJV); Luke 6:27—"But I say unto you which hear, Love your enemies, do good to them which hate you" (KJV).] The event showed this also was a false alarm, an artifice of the devil, to hinder men from hearing the word of God." Shepherd and Wesley remained overnight in Gwennap, and on Sunday, 7 July, at 5:00 a.m., the latter preached to "a quiet congregation" before leaving for Stithians. Following six days of travel to various sites in Cornwall, John Wesley came back to Gwennap on Saturday, 13 July, preaching in the evening "without interruption" (20:78, 80).

Approximately one year later, at 7:00 p.m. Thursday, 4 September 1746, the elder Wesley reached Gwennap to find an awaiting congregation. He began his sermon "without delay and found no faintness or weariness while I expounded, 'We all, beholding, as in a glass, the glory of the Lord, are transformed into the same image, from glory to glory, as by the Spirit of the Lord'"—2 Corinthians 3:18: "But we all, with open face beholding as if an glass the glory of the Lord, are changed into the same image from glory to glory even as by the Spirit of the Lord" (KJV). Remaining at Gwennap through a portion of the following day, Friday, 5 September, Wesley inquired into the recent illness of John Trembath (?-1793?) a native of St. Gennys, Cornwall, who had joined the Methodist itinerancy in 1743, but whose record and effectiveness had proven, at best, inconsistent. He had suffered "a second relapse into the spotted fever [an infliction characterized by the appearance of spots on the skin, later to be identified as epidemic cerebro-spinal meningitis, typhus, tick fever, rickettsial fever, or petechial fever] in the height of which they [?] gave him sack [the general name for a class of white wines formerly imported from Spain and the Canary Islands; thus: Canary sack, malaga, sherry], cold milk, and apples, plums as much as he could swallow." Wesley concluded, "I can see no way to account for his recovery, but that he had not then finished his work." Less than a week later, Wednesday, 10 September, in company with, perhaps, an itinerant preacher by the name of William Tucker,[17] John Wesley returned to Gwennap, but the specifics of his brief stay do not appear in the journal extract. Finally, on Sunday, 14 September, at 4:30 p.m. the Methodist leader once again preached at Gwennap, "to an immense multitude of people," his text based upon the whole of Philippians 1:21, "To me to live is Christ, and to die is gain." Wesley initially feared that "my voice would not reach them all, but without cause, for it was so strengthened that I believe thousands more might have heard every word." Immediately following the sermon, Wesley read to the gathering a narrative relating to the death of Thomas Hitchens—a work that the Methodist leader would eventually publish under the title, *A Short Account of the Death of Thomas Hitchens. By James Hitchens, Tinner* (Bristol: Felix Farley, 1747)—four editions through 1747; six additional imprints of the fourth edition between 1748 and 1790. A native of Busveal, Cornwall, near Redruth, and one of the four sons of James Hitchens the elder of Gwennap, Thomas Hitchens (?-1746) served as one of John Wesley's preachers. Father and sons had constructed and maintained a large chapel, preached therein, and endured considerable persecution. Wesley would preach Thomas Hitchens' funeral sermon. Commenting upon his listeners' reaction, Wesley observed, "And the hearts of many burned within them, so that they could not conceal their desire to go to him and to be with Christ" (20:135, 139–141)—Philippians 1:23: "For I am in a strait between two, having a desire to depart, and to be with Christ; which is far better" (KJV).

John Wesley's work in Cornwall for the year 1747 took him to Gwennap on Sunday, 5 July, where he began to preach at 5:30 p.m. "I was afraid my voice would not suffice for such an immense multitude," he would note in his journal extract. "But my fear was groundless, as the evening was quite calm, and the people all attention." However, at a meeting of the Gwennap Methodist society later that evening, he found difficulty in being heard "amidst the cries of those on the one hand who were pierced through as with a sword, and of those on the other who were filled with joy unspeakable" (20:181). Two verses from Scriptures provide the sound and the sense of that sentence: (1) Luke 2:35—"(Yea, a sword shall pierce through thy own soul also) that the thoughts of many hearts may be revealed" (KJV); (2) 1 Peter 1:8—"Whom having not seen, ye love; in whom, though now ye see him not, yet believing, ye rejoice with joy unspeakable and full of glory" (KJV). Wesley remained at Gwennap for the night, but departed, without incident, at some point in mid-morning on Monday, 6 July (20:181).

Not until Thursday, 9 August 1750, did the elder Wesley return to preach at Gwennap, and, after that brief stop, waited until Wednesday, 11 September 1751 for his return. He preached that evening in the midst of hard winds and incessant rain, "but the congregation stood as if it had been a fair summer's evening." Two years later, on Monday, 6 August 1753, he preached there at 5:00 a.m., remarking on what he termed "a strange sight—a man that is *old* and *rich* and yet not covetous" (20:356, 401, 471). Did Wesley mean to imply all old and rich men to have been covetous? The observation, without benefit of identification and explanation, becomes almost meaningless. At any rate, the wild weather of Cornwall continued to harass John Wesley, even after the passage of four years, as indicated by his visit to Gwennap on Sunday, 31 August 1755. There, at 5:00 p.m. he preached "to several thousands—but not one of them light [unsteady in belief or commitment; of little concern; frivolous in action or concentration] or inattentive. After I had done, the storm arose, and the rain poured down till about four in the morning. Then the sky cleared, and many of them that feared God gladly assembled before him."[18] Again the waters poured down upon Wesley at Gwennap on the occasion of his next visit, Sunday evening, 18 September 1757: "It rained all the time I preached, but none went away," he claimed. "A shower of rain will not fright experienced soldiers"—possibly English troops who had been held prisoners in France, recently set ashore in Penzance, and who then traveled through Redruth and vicinity on their journeys to their homes. Not unexpectedly, "it rained all the time I was preaching at Gwennap," reads Wesley's journal entry for Sunday, 21 September 1760. "We concluded the day with a love-feast, at which James Roberts, a tinner of St. Ives, related how God hath dealt with his soul."[19] The Methodist form of the "love-feast" emerged as a deliberate revival on the part of John Wesley of the meal of Christian fellowship (or *agape*) practiced with varying degrees of success in and by the early Christian Church and revived in the early eighteenth century by the German Moravians. Wesley first experienced the ceremony in the Savannah, Georgia, settlement on 8 August 1737,[20] then encountered it again among the Moravians in Germany and London in 1738. When, in September 1738, Wesley returned to the Moravian religious society in Fetter Lane, London, he established, as one of the monthly rules, the conducting of a general love-feast from seven until ten in the evening. When Wesley and his followers left the Fetter Lane society in 1740, they retained the organization of the Moravian bands (inner circles, or "select societies"), and for those groups he promoted his quarterly-held love-feasts. Both men and women would assemble jointly, "that we might together eat bread," as had the early Christians, "with gladness and singleness of heart." The only food offered at those gatherings consisted of plain cake and water. However, continued Wesley, "we seldom return from them without being fed, not only with 'the meat which perisheth.' But with 'that which endureth to everlasting life.'"[21] Returning to Wesley's narrative of James Roberts, the Methodist leader explained that he [Roberts] became "one of the first society in St. Ives but soon relapsed into his old sin, drunkenness, and wallowed in it for two years, during which time he headed the mob which pulled down the preaching-house [on 5 April 1744]. Not long after, he was standing with his partner, at Edward May's shop, when the preacher went by. His partner said, 'I will tell him I am a Methodist.' 'Nay,' said Edward. 'your speech will bewray [reveal, divulge, make known] you.' James felt the word as a sword [Hebrews 4:12—"For the word of God is quick, and powerful, and sharper than any twoedged sword, piercing even to the dividing asunder of soul and spirit, and of the joints and marrow, and is a discerner of the thoughts and intents of the heart" (KJV)], thinking in himself, 'So does my speech now bewray *me!*'" [Matthew 26:73—"And after a while came unto him they that stood by, and said to Peter, Surely thou also art one of them; for thy speech bewrayeth thee" (KJV).] He turned and hastened home, fancying he heard the devil stepping after him all the way. For forty hours, he never closed his eyes nor tasted either meat or drink. He was then at his wit's end [Psalms 107:27—"They reel to and fro, and stagger like a drunken man, and they are at their wits [[wit's]] end" (BCP/KJV)] and went to the window, looking to drop into hell instantly, when he heard those words, 'I will be merciful to thy unrighteousness; thy sins and iniquities will I remember no more' [Hebrews 8:12]. All his load was gone, and he has now for many years walked worthy of the gospel" (21:25–26, 124–125, 281).

Two years later, on Sunday, 5 September 1762, the fifty-five-year-old Methodist leader reported that "the wind was so high at five [p.m.] that I could not stand in the usual place at Gwennap. But at a small distance was a hollow, capable of containing many thousand people." That area had come to be known as "Gwennap Pit," an amphitheater formed, most likely, from surface mining operations. Wesley stood on one side of the amphitheater, toward the top, while the listeners stood beneath and on all sides of it. He "enlarged on those words in the Gospel for the day [the thirteenth Sunday after Trinity] (Luke10:23[-24]), 'Blessed are the eyes which see the things that ye see, [...]²² and hear the things that ye hear'" (21:388). The complete text of Luke 10:23–24 reads, "And he turned him unto his disciples and said privately, Blessed are the eyes which see the things that ye see:/for I tell you, that many prophets and kings have desired to see those things which ye see, and have not seen them; and to hear those things which ye hear, and have not heard them" (KJV).²³

A large congregation awaited John Wesley when he next came to Gwennap from Redruth, on Sunday evening, 8 September 1765, a gathering "equal to any I have seen in Moorfields." Known later as Finsbury Circus and Finsbury Square, Moorfields existed, for the greater portion of the eighteenth century, as a large fen, or moor, on the north side of London. It stretched, approximately, from Bishopsgate to Cripplegate, and from London Wall to Finsbury Square. Londoners considered that marsh ground a favorite place for Sunday strolling, since it had been laid out in grass plots, intersected by broad, gravel walks. Beneath a row of well-grown elms lay what the promenaders designated "the city mall," which, because of the smartness of its company, often rivaled the mall of St. James's Park. "Here might be seen," noted Luke Tyerman, "wives and daughters flaunting in all their finery and displaying their charms to city maccaronis [male "dandies"], whose hats were cocked diagonally, and who gave themselves quite as many airs as the aristocratic coxcombs in the royal grounds. Under the trees were booths, whose fans, toys, trinkets, and confectionary found ready purchasers; while on the grass plots were erected mountybank [*sic*] diversions for the amusement of the people."²⁴ "Yet," proceeded Wesley with his narrative, "I think they all heard while I enforced, 'Why will ye die. O house of Israel?'" (22:19)—Ezekiel 18:31: "Cast away from you all of your transgressions, whereby ye have transgressed; and make you a new heart and a new spirit: for why will ye die, O house of Israel?" (KJV). Following the preaching, Wesley returned to Redruth.

At Gwennap Pit on Sunday, 14 September 1766, John Wesley added to the description of the Cornish ampthitheater: "It is a round, green hollow, gently shelving down, about fifty feet deep. But I suppose it is two hundred [feet] across one way and near three hundred the other. I believe there were twenty thousand people,²⁵ and the evening being calm, all could hear." Two years later, at five o'clock on Sunday afternoon, 11 September 1768, the Methodist leader "took my old stand at Gwennap in the natural ampthitheatre. I suppose no human voice could have commanded such an audience on plain ground. But the ground rising all round gave me such an advantage that I believe all could hear distinctly." In a note, Ward and Heitzenrater (*Journal*, 21:388), stated that Gwennap Pit had been improved, in 1806, by leveling and cutting circular terraces of seats. However, some sort of similar accommodation had been carried forth well in advance of that year, since, when John Wesley preached in Gwennap Pit at 5:00 p.m. on Sunday, 3 September 1769, "thousands ... were so commodiously placed, row above row, that I believe all could hear." Note, also, that in this journal entry, Wesley referred to Gwennap Pit as "our amphitheatre at Gwennap," assuming, symbolically, Methodist possession of, or entitlement to, the area. At any rate, at 5:00 on the "evening" of Sunday, 2 September 1770, John Wesley and the Methodists again occupied Gwennap Pit: "The people covered a circle of near fourscore [eighty] yards in diameter and could not be fewer than twenty thousand. Yet upon inquiry, I found they could all hear distinctly, it being a calm, still evening" (22:61, 157, 203, 249).

When John Wesley came once more to Gwennap Pit, at 5:00 p.m. on Sunday, 23 August 1773, in the seventieth year of his long life, he appeared to have found a method, albeit an imperfect means, by which to determine the size of his congregation. He began by declaring, "The people both filled it and covered the ground round about to a considerable distance. So that, supposing the space to be fourscore yards square [eighty square yards, or 2,880 square feet] and to contain five persons in a square yard [or one person occupying 5.76 feet], there must be above two and thirty thousand [80 x 80 x 5 = 32,000]—the largest assembly I had ever preached to." Nonetheless, concluded Wesley, "I found upon inquiry, all could hear, even to the skirts of the congregation! Perhaps the first time a man of seventy had been heard by thirty thousand persons at once!" Relative to the substance of that exclamation, the readers of Benjamin Franklin's *Autobiography* will recall, perhaps, the writer's analytical account of George Whitefield's early visit to Philadelphia (2 November 1739?), during which the Calvinist Methodist orator "preach'd one Evening from the Top of the Court House Steps, which are in the middle of Market Street, and on the West Side of Second Street which crosses it at right angles. Both Streets were fill'd with his Hearers to a considerable Distance. Being among the hindmost in Market Street, I had the Curiosity to learn how far he could be heard, by retiring backwards down the Street towards the [Delaware] River, and I found his Voice distinct till I came to Front-Street [c. 500 feet from the Court House], when some noise in that Street, obscur'd it. Imagining then a Semi-Circle, of which my Distance should be the Radius, and it were fill'd with Auditors, to each of whom I allow'd two square feet, I computed that he might well be heard by more than Thirty-Thousand. This reconcil'd me to the Newspaper Accounts of his having preach'd to 25000 People in the Fields, and to the antient Histories of Generals haranguing whole Armies, of which I had sometimes doubted." The editors of the Benjamin Franklin Papers argued that on the basis of the 500 feet between the Court House and Front Street, Franklin's calculation proved "faulty." However, those scholars maintained that "in *Poor Richard*, 1749, in discussing the same matter he pointed out more accurately that 45,000 persons might stand in a space 100 yards square or 21,780 on an acre of ground."[26]

The Methodist patriarch, confident of his calculations concerning the size of his outdoor congregations, continued to sound the same notes when next he came to Gwennap at 5:00 p.m. Sunday, 4 September 1774. Again in the Pit, he "judged" the assembly "to cover four square yards, and yet those farthest off could hear." Wesley approached his Gwennap Pit exercises from another perspective when he preached there at five o'clock in the "evening" of Sunday, 3 September 1775: "I think," he would note later in his journal extract, "this is the most magnificent spectacle which is to be seen on this side heaven. And no music is to be heard on earth comparable to the sound of many thousand voices when they are all harmoniously joined together, singing praises to God and the Lamb" (22:387, 428, 464).

Once again in Gwennap Pit, at the usual hour of 5:00 p.m. Sunday, 25 August 1776, John Wesley preached to "full twenty thousand persons. And they were so commodiously placed in the calm, still evening that everyone heard distinctly." A year later, on Sunday, 31 August 1777, after preaching at St. Agnes in the morning, he journeyed to Gwennap and addressed, in the evening, "a huge congregation" in Gwennap Pit, "larger (it was supposed) by fifteen hundred or two thousand than ever it had been before." There appeared no end to Wesley's ability to attract large numbers to Gwennap Pit, for upon his return there on Sunday, 30 August 1778, he stood before an estimated "four-and-twenty thousand," following which he spent "a solemn hour" with the Gwennap Methodist society before claiming to have "slept in peace." Although two years passed before John Wesley would once more appear in Gwennap Pit, the entry in his journal extract essentially echoed a number of entries that preceded it. Thus, on Sunday, 27 August 1780, "it was supposed twenty thousand people were assembled at the amphitheatre at Gwennap. And yet all, I was informed, could hear distinctly in the fair, calm evening." They assembled and heard yet again at 5:00 p.m., on Sunday, 2 September 1781, where he speculated that "two or three and twenty thousand were present. And I believed God enabled me so to speak that even those who stood farthest off could hear distinctly. I think this is my *ne plus ultra* [the point of highest achievement; nothing more beyond; the uttermost point attained or attainable; acme; culmination]. I shall scarce see a larger congregation till we meet in the air."—1 Thessalonians 4:17—"Then we which are alive and remain shall be caught up together with them in the clouds, to meet the Lord in the air: and so shall we ever be with the Lord" (KJV). On Sunday, 1 September 1782, Wesley, then approaching his eightieth year, "expounded on the parable of the sower[27] at Gwennap to how many thousands I know not—but all (I was informed) could hear distinctly. 'This is the Lord's doing.'"—Psalms 118:23—"This is the Lords [*sic*] doing: and it is marvelous in our eyes" (BCP) (23:30, 66, 104, 184, 222, 250).

Five years would lapse before Wesley found another opportunity to preach in Gwennap Pit—that occasion coming, as usual, at 5:00 p.m. on a Sunday, 9 September 1787. "I suppose," he commented, "we had a thousand more than ever were there before. But it was all one; my voice was strengthened accordingly, so that everyone could hear distinctly" his sermon on Isaiah 66. One might have noted that this marks the eighth appearance of the word "distinctly" in the journal extract entries related to Wesley's sermon addresses in Gwennap Pit. In any event, he remained at Gwennap, conducted a love-feast, preached to a "large congregation" on the morning of Monday, 10 September, then moved off to Kenwyn. When the Methodist patriarch next preached at Gwennap Pit, on Sunday evening, 23 August 1789, he speculated that it might be the last occasion upon which he might do so—"for my voice cannot now command the still increasing multitude. It was supposed they were now more than five and twenty thousand. I think it scarcely possible that all should hear." Indeed, Wesley proved correct; he had conducted his final visit to Gwennap (24:58, 151, 152, 220).

Gwithian

On Thursday, 8 September 1757, John Wesley and his traveling companion(s) rode from Camborne, Cornwall, to (and through) the parish of Gwithian, approximately 7.5 miles west of Redruth. A Mr. Harris, a resident of Camborne who had accompanied Wesley, pointed to the place where his father and a number of his relations had resided. "It is now only a mountain of sand," noted Wesley. "Within a few years this so increased as to bury both the church and the whole town" (21:123).

Hayle

John Wesley described the eighteenth-century industrial town of Hayle by "a small arm of the sea which runs up into the land, two or three miles [southeast] from St. Ives, and makes a tolerable harbor." He preached there, for the first time, at "about noon" on Saturday, 14 September 1765. For whatever his reasons, the Methodist leader did not return to Hayle until Saturday, 27 August 1785, but once there he preached at the new Methodist Copperhouse Chapel, which "I suppose such another is not in England nor in Europe nor in the world." Wesley had learned of the Copperhouse Chapel two years earlier, in a letter from Captain Richard Williams. Responding from London on 10 December 1783, the Methodist leader simply stated, "I know nothing ... of the Copper House at Hayle."[1] When the Methodist leader did learn, first hand, about that building, he described it as "round, and all the walls are brass, that is, brazen slugs. It seems nothing can destroy this till heaven and earth pass away." Nehemiah Curnock (7:110) and Professors Ward and Heitzenrater (23:374) add further details relative to the Copperhouse Chapel, namely its conical roof, windows at the top of the wall, and a single door facing the road. The principal building material for its construction appeared common to Hayle—blocks made from the molten dross (or "scoria") remaining after the extraction of copper from the ore. Each one of those blocks, rectangular in shape, measured not less than a cubic foot in size; they tended to function as bricks, being largely applied in the building of houses and boundary walls. Although brittle, they proved extremely hard and durable. "Tens of thousands of such 'bricks,'" stated Curnock, "may be seen in Hayle to-day"—meaning c. 1915. Apparently, smelting in Hayle did not thrive during the nineteenth century, the ore being shipped to South Wales, where there existed an abundance of coal. Another structure replaced Copperhouse Chapel in 1817, and that building claimed a brick-tiled floor. A second Methodist house of worship existed in Hayle, known as the Foundery (22:21; 23:374–375).

John Wesley came again—and for the final time—to Hayle on Sunday, 9 September 1787, where, at 9:00 a.m., he preached, on 2 Corinthians 5:19—"To wit, that God was in Christ, reconciling the world unto himself, not imputing their trespasses unto them; and hath committed unto us the word of reconciliation" (KJV). He delivered that sermon at the copper works "to a large congregation gathered from all parts, I believe 'with the demonstration of the Spirit.'"—1 Corinthians 2:4: "And my speech and my preaching was not with enticing words of man's wisdom, but in demonstration of the Spirit and of power" (KJV). Following the address, he met with the Methodist society at Hayle in the Copperhouse Chapel (22:21; 23:374–375; 24:58, 220).

Helston

Helston would have been found as one of the four "coinage towns" of Cornwall when the first list of those sites appeared in 1305.[1] Daniel Defoe, at the end of the seventeenth century, described Helston as lying approximately seven miles to the west from Penryn, in southeast Cornwall, lying upon "the little river Cober, which, however, admits the sea into its bosom as to make a desirable good harbor for ships a little below the town. It is the fifth town, allowed for the coining of TIN, and several of the ships called 'tin' ships are laden here" (*Tour*, 233).

Charles Wesley's manuscript journal records but two indirect references to Helston by the early Methodist itinerant, the initial one in the entry for Thursday, 3 July 1746, in which he refers to the place as "a town of rebels and persecutors." Nonetheless, a number of them who had attended the preaching at Stithney on that day had been "struck, and confessed their sin, and declared they would never more be found fighting against God." Again at Stithney on 19 July 1746, Charles Wesley reported that "the rebels of Helston threatened hard," accusing the Methodists of being Papists, supporters of the exiled young Pretender (the grandson of the exiled James II, Charles Edward Louis Philip Casimir Stuart [1720–1788]). The fragments of Charles Wesley's manuscript journal do not indicate his having set foot in the town itself (2:465, 467).

John Wesley, as had been the practice of his younger brother, did not, initially, put forth the effort toward regular visits to Helston. Instead, as had Charles Wesley, he viewed the town through the actions of certain of its citizenry. On Sunday, 14 September 1746, at 8:00 a.m., the elder Wesley preached at Stithney, with a number of persons from Helston in the congregation, most of whom, "in times past had signalized themselves by making riots. But the fear of God was upon them; they all stood uncovered, and calmly attended from the beginning to the end." However, seven years later, on Monday evening, 30 July 1753, Wesley began to preach at Helston, although he offered no additional comment or observation in his journal extract entry of that date. Returning to the town on Wednesday afternoon, 3 September 1755, the Methodist leader observed that the once turbulent atmosphere there had quieted considerably, and, therefore, he preached, at 6:00, "on a rising ground about a musket shot from the town."

Two drunkards attempted to interrupt him, but one walked away and the second leaned on the neck of his horse and fell asleep. Wesley pointed to the example of one identified only as "W.T." to underscore the "good" that had come to Helston. "He was utterly without God in the world when his father died and left him a little estate encumbered with huge debt. Seven or eight years ago he found peace with God. He afterward sold his estate, paid all his debts, and with what he had left furnished a little shop. Herein God has blessed him in an uncommon manner. Meantime, all his behavior is of peace. So that more and more of his neighbours say, 'Well, this is the work of God!'" The Methodist leader remained in Helston throughout the following day (Thursday, 4 September), and in the evening, a heavy rain fell as he announced the opening hymn. Then it ceased as he cited the biblical text for his sermon address. "I spoke very plain, and it seemed to sink into many hearts. As they showed by attending at five in the morning (5 September), when we had another happy and solemn hour" (20:141, 470; 21:26).

On the journey from St. Ives to Helston on Thursday, 15 September 1757, Wesley found an opportunity to express his interest in natural phenomena. He felt "the sun was near as hot as it was at midsummer. Yet all along the trees looked as in the depth of winter, that scorching wind having destroyed all it touched." Once settled in the town, he spent those moments free from preaching to peruse a volume, *Observations on the Antiquities, Historical and Monumental, of the County of Cornwall* (Oxford, 1754; 2nd ed. 1769), by William Borlase, LL.D. (1695–1772)— educated at Exeter College, Oxford (M.A. 1719); rector of Ludgvan, Cornwall (1722); vicar of St. Just, Cornwall (1732); and holder of both of those livings until his death. Although Borlase complained of the offensive conduct against temperance and violations of the Sabbath on the parts of his parishioners at St. Just, he proved to have been an effective minister and a competent antiquarian. On the basis of the *Observations*, Wesley thought of William Borlase as "a fine writer and quite master of his subject, who has distinguished with accuracy the ancient Saxon monument from the more ancient Roman and from those of the Druids,[2] the most ancient of all." Three years later, on Thursday, 18 September 1760, at approximately 6:00 p.m. Wesley preached near Helston. "The rain stopped till I had done," he noted, "and soon after it was as violent as before" (21:124, 280).

When John Wesley next journeyed near Helston, on Friday, 5 September 1766, he preached to "an exceeding large and serious congregation. What a surprising change is wrought here also (within a few years!), where a Methodist preacher could hardly go through the street without a shower of stones." He echoed that sentiment (as well as the language) seven years later, at 6:00 p.m. Tuesday, 17 August 1773, after preaching in the main street of Helston: "How changed is this town since a Methodist preacher could not ride through it without hazard of his life!" Three years later, on Tuesday evening, 20 August 1776, Wesley preached at Helston, again noting in his journal extract entry that "prejudice is at an end, and all the town, except a few gentry, willingly hear the word of salvation." That prospect gained substance when, at the Quarterly Meeting held at St. Ives on Saturday, 30 August 1777, he received the report of membership increases in the Cornish Methodist societies, particularly at St. Just, Penzance, and Helston. The Methodist leader preached again at Helston at some point between 24 and 26 August 1778; Tuesday evening 22 August 1780; and Tuesday evening, 28 August 1781. On the last occasion, he preached in the High Street and afterward declared, "I scarce know a town in the whole county which is so totally changed. Not a spark of that bitter enmity to the Methodists in which the people here for many years gloried above their fellows." The journal extract entry for Friday, 23 August 1782 indicates only that John Wesley preached "in the street" at Helston, and again on an unspecified day of the week of 22 August 1785. However, Wesley's diary reveals that on Wednesday, 24 August 1785, he drove his chaise from Penryn to Helston, arriving at 10:45 a.m., then engaging in "necessary talk (religious)" until noon, at which time he preached on 2 Timothy 3:5— "Having a form of godliness, but denying the power thereof: from such turn away" (KJV). Following more "religious talk" and prayer, he departed Helston in his chaise at 2:30 p.m. (22:60, 386; 23:29, 66, 103, 184, 220, 250, 374, 533).

On Wednesday, 19 August 1789, according to the journal extract, eighty-six-year-old John Wesley—again in his chaise from Penryn— preached at noon, and for the last time, in the High Street in Helston. There he stood before "the largest and most serious congregation which I ever remember to have seen there." That might well have been an accurate statement, but there appears a decided discrepancy between the diary and the entry in the journal extract, which neither Nehemiah Curnock (8:3) nor Ward and Heitzenrater (24:151–152, 291) bothered to reconcile. Simply, the journal extract in both editions, as indicated, reads that Wesley preached at Helston at noon; according to the diary entry in both editions, however, he did not leave Penryn until **2:15** p.m., arriving in Helston at 4:00, where he engaged in "necessary talk (religious) to many"; prayed, had tea, and then at **5:15** (not "noon"), he preached on Ecclesiastes 7:12— "For wisdom is a defence, and money is a defence: but the excellency of knowledge is, that wisdom giveth life to them that have it" (KJV). That issue aside, Wesley remained in Helston throughout the evening and night—involved in more religious conversation, writing "notes," supper, even further religious talk, prayer, and, finally, to bed at 9:30 p.m. One might note that on that final visit to Helston, John Wesley reportedly preached on a step at the entrance to the old Market House—a structure dating from 1576, partially reconstructed in 1793, and taken down c. 1840. It stood at the juncture of the four principal streets of the town and faced Coinage Hall Street, "in which the present [c. 1916] Wesleyan Methodist Church stands." A Mr. Richard Andrew, a retired Helston draper, served as John Wesley's host whenever the Methodist leader came to town (Curnock, *Journal*, 8:4).

Illogan

The copper mining parish of Illogan—also known as Three-Cornered Down and Illogan Downs (near the Illogan Highway)—lay, according to John Wesley's calculations, nine or ten miles east of St. Ives and two miles west of Gwennap. Ward and Heitzenrater (20:401) place it 2¾ miles northwest of Redruth. There, on Saturday, 3 September 1743, he "found two or three hundred tinners, who had been some time waiting for us. They all appeared pleased and unconcerned, and many of them ran after us to Gwennap." The elder Wesley noted, without comment, that he preached at Illogan on Tuesday, 10 September 1751, and reference to the town appears in the journal extract entry for Monday, 5 September 1757. On that day, he did not proceed to the house where he had preached previously, one owned by a Mr. P. Before he died, his wife promised him that she would always receive the preachers, but the woman soon changed her mind. "God had just taken her only son," explained Wesley, "suddenly killed by a pit falling upon him. And on Tuesday last [30 August] a young strong man riding to his burial, dropped off his horse, stone dead. The concurrence of these awful providences added considerably to our congregation" (19:335; 20:401; 21:122).

Three years passed before Wesley found another opportunity for a visit to Illogan. On Friday, 19 September 1760, a heavy rain came forth before he began his sermon, but its severity waned considerably during the preaching. He returned there again to preach at one o'clock in the afternoon of Friday, 17 September 1762, and, for the final time, on Saturday, 22 August 1773. Neither of the last two journal extract entries reveals observations and/or comments (21:280, 389; 22:387).

Kenneggy Downs

Kenneggy Downs, situated five miles west of Helston and five miles south of St. Ives, consisted of a flat chalky plain. Charles Wesley preached there initially on Monday, 18 July 1743, "to near a thousand tinners, who received the seed into honest and good hearts. While I pointed them to the Lamb of God [John 1:29—"The next day John seeth Jesus coming unto him, and saith, Behold the Lamb of God, which taketh away the sin of the world" (KJV)], many wept, and particularly the captain,[1] general of the sinners, a man famous in his generation for acts of valour and violence, and his usual challenge to fight any six men with his club. He is known through the west by the title of the Destroyer. This leopard will soon, I trust, lie down with the Lamb."—Isaiah 11:6—"The wolf also shall dwell with the lamb, and the leopard shall lie down with the kid; and the calf and the young lion and the fatling together; and a little child shall lead them" (KJV). Upon returning to Kenneggy Downs a week later, on Monday, 25 July 1743, the younger Wesley preached "to a multitude of simple-hearted tinners: 'Who is this that cometh from Edom, with dyed garments from Bozrah?' [Isaiah 63:1]. They received the word with gladness and gratitude." The final visit of Charles Wesley to Kenneggy Downs that one finds in the fragments of his manuscript journal occurred on Monday, 1 August 1743: "[I] Took my leave of Kenneggy Downs in, 'The blind receive their sight, and the lame walk,' etc." [Matthew 11:5—"The blind receive their sight, and the lame walk, the lepers are cleansed and the deaf hear, the dead are raised up, and the poor have the gospel preached to them" (KJV).] (2:359, 363, 367).

John Wesley's single recorded visit to Kenneggy Downs came on Thursday, 8 September 1743, shortly after his brother's last sermon there. He preached on "the resurrection of the dry bones" [Ezekiel 37:1–14], noting that "there is not yet so much as a shaking among them, much less is there any breath in them" (19:336).

Land's End

Known in ancient times as Bolerium, the rocky promontory and cape on the southwest coast of Cornwall, Land's End takes its name, of course, as the westernmost land of England. Of more than passing interest, perhaps, John Telford, for one, reported that John Edwards, one of John Wesley's itinerant preachers and a native of London, had conducted in 1747, at his own expense, an extensive preaching tour from Land's End, through the midland counties, and ending in the North Riding of Yorkshire.

John Wesley, himself, preached at Land's End on Saturday, 17 September 1743, and again on the following morning (Sunday, 18 September), at which time he "largely declared (what many shall witness in due time), 'By grace ye are saved through faith.'"—Ephesians 2:8—"For by grace are ye saved through faith; and that not of yourselves: it is the gift of God" (KJV). When next the leader of the Methodists came through that area, on Saturday, 10 September 1757, he took note of the unusual land formation comprising Land's End: "I know no natural curiosity like this. The vast, ragged stones rise on every side when you are near the point of land, with green turf between as level and smooth as if it were the effect of art. And the rocks which terminate the land are so torn by the sea that they appear like great heaps of ruins." When John Wesley came again to Land's End, twenty-eight years later, late Thursday morning, 25 August 1785, he and his companion(s) climbed down the rocks to the very edge of the water. "And I cannot think," exclaimed the eighty-two-year-old Wesley, "but the sea has gained some hundred yards since I was here forty years ago [on 11 September 1743]."[1] Ward and Heitzenrater raised the question as to why Wesley should have thought that "this imperious cliff was crumbling at such a rate is hard to imagine" (23:374). At any rate, this proved to have been Wesley's final visit to Land's End (19:337, 339–340; 21:133; 23:374, 533).

Laneast

In the first half of the eighteenth century, the village of Laneast would have been situated approximately eight miles west of Launceston and south of the Launceston-Camelford road. During the 1730s and 1740s, Church officials could identify thirty families who worshipped regularly there at fortnightly services; reportedly, however, no Protestant Dissenters resided there during those two decades.[1] During the same general period, a single curate tended to serve the Church of England parishes of Laneast, Tresmeer, and North Tamerton.

Charles Wesley noted, upon the pages of the fragments of his manuscript journal, only a single occasion when he preached at Laneast: On Friday night, 22 August 1746, he preached at Laneast church "to a people seeking the Lord" (2:408, 474).

John Wesley first came to Laneast on Tuesday, 18 May 1745, and upon that occasion, at Laneast church, the evangelically-minded curate, the Rev. John Bennet (1670?-1750)—B.A. (1697) and M.A. (1726) Queens' College, Cambridge, and an acquaintance of the Wesleys' father, the Rev.

Samuel Wesley the elder—read prayers, and Wesley preached on "The redemption that is in Jesus Christ"—Romans 3:24: "Being justified freely by his grace through the redemption that is in Christ Jesus" (KJV). The Methodist leader again preached, and also read prayers, at Laneast church between 4:00 and 5:00 p.m. Monday, 15 August 1745. He based his text upon Romans 8:1—"There is no condemnation in them that are in Christ Jesus"—and commented, "O how pleasant thing is even outward peace! What would not a man give for it but a good conscience!" The third visit to Laneast came a year later, on Monday, 15 September 1746; yet another one on Saturday, 25 July 1747—when, as Wesley and his companions walked through the town, "we had a large train to attend us. Only one stone struck me on the shoulder," reported Wesley. Finally, John Wesley preached at Laneast church on Tuesday evening, 28 August 1750, "to a large and attentive congregation. What can destroy the work of God in these parts," he asked, "but zeal for, and contending about, opinions?" (20:25, 69, 80, 142, 184, 359). One might assume that after John Bennet's death in 1750, opportunities for preaching and conducting the business of Methodism in Laneast became limited, and thus Wesley simply abandoned his own efforts there and, perhaps, turned the work over to his itinerant preachers.

Launceston

Launceston—in the eighteenth century a market town, Parliamentary borough, and parish—lay by the River Tamar, two miles from the Devonshire border, 25.5 miles northeast of Bodmin, and approximately 214 miles southwest from London. Among the historic sites within and directly around Launceston, one notes, particularly, Launceston Castle ("Castle Terrible"), a building noted for its strength, where a high ring wall of stone, six feet thick, dates from the late twelfth or early thirteenth century. Within that structure, Richard, Earl of Cornwall (1209–1271), the second son of King John and the brother of Henry III, erected, in the thirteenth century, a shell keep [a circular or polygonal stone wall surrounding a motte (a variation of "moat")] of considerable height. By the seventeenth century, Launceston Castle had gained a reputation for its filthy Doomsdale prison, and in 1656, Oliver Cromwell (1599–1658), Lord Protector of England, forced George Fox (1624–1691), the leader of the Society of Friends (Quakers), to be incarcerated there for his refusing to remove his hat in the presence of the chief judge of the Court of Assizes.[1] By the first decade of the nineteenth century, Launceston had reached a population of 2,460.[2]

Writing at some point within the opening decade of the eighteenth century, Daniel Defoe reported, through a negative eye, that he exited Cornwall "by passing the river Tamar at Launceston, the last, or rather the first, town in the county, the town shewing little else, but marks of its antiquity; for great part of it is so old, as it may, in a manner, pass for an old, ragged, decayed place, in general. In the time [thirteenth century] when Richard, Earl of Cornwall, had the absolute government of this county, and was, we might say, king of the country, it was a frontier town, walled about, and well fortified, and had, also a strong castle to defend it; but these are seen, now, only in their old clothes, and lie all in ruins and heaps of rubbish." Turning from the physical fragments of Launceston to issues economic, Defoe reported, "It is a principal gain to the people of this town, that they let lodgings to the gentlemen, who attend here in the time of the assizes,[3] and other public meetings; as particularly, that of electing knights of the shire, and at the county sessions, which are held here; for which purposes, the town's people have their rooms better furnished than in other places of this country, though their houses are but low [in quality; average or below] or do they fail to make a good price to their lodgers, for the conveniences they afford them."

Defoe then expanded the miscellaneous range of his seemingly jaundiced attention to include, at Launceston, "a fine image, or figure of Mary Magdalen [*sic*; one of the women who followed and supported Jesus Christ; a key witness to his death; the first to encounter the risen Christ], upon the tower of the church, which the Catholics fail not to pay their reverences to, as they pass by. There is no tin, or copper, or lead, found hereabouts, as I could find, nor any manufacture in the place; there are a pretty [considerable in number] many attorneys here, who manage business for the rest of their fraternity at the assizes. As to trade, it has not much to boast of, and yet there are people enough in it to excuse those who call it a populous place."[4]

John Wesley came to Launceston on Wednesday, 21 September 1743, but posted not a single word of that visit onto a page of his journal extract. Six months later, on Monday, 2 April 1744, he rode through the snow, rain, and hail, "as in the depth of winter," from Sticklepath, Devonshire, to Launceston, but again found nothing worthwhile to record or to comment upon the latter. Then, on Saturday, 31 August 1751, arriving at Launceston from Tiverton, Devonshire, the Methodist leader wrote, "The mob gathered immediately and attended us to the room. They made much noise while I was preaching, and threw all kind of things at the people as they came out, but no one was hurt." Wesley remained in the town for part of the following day (Sunday, 1 September), and "at the desire of many, he proceeded to the main street. There, a "large congregation of serious people" gathered before him, followed by "a mob of boys and gentlemen" who collected on the other side of the street, created such noise that Wesley could not be heard, and forced him to continue and to conclude his discourse indoors. Later, following attendance at Launceston church, he quickly retreated from the town. Apparently dissatisfied with that effort, John Wesley returned to Launceston on Tuesday, 17 September 1751, preaching, without incident, at noon.

In terms of the organization of Methodism in Launceston, Wesley's itinerant preachers must have achieved a certain degree of success, for when the Methodist leader again came to the town less than two years later, on Monday, 23 July 1753, he attended the first general meeting of the stewards of the Methodist societies for the eastern section of Cornwall. Also, he noted in his journal extract that in the evening of 23 July, "I preached in perfect peace—a great blessing, if it be not bought too dear, if the world does not begin to love *us* because we love the world."[5] A year later, again in Launceston (Wednesday, 4 September 1754), Wesley preached at 6:00 p.m. and met with the Methodist society there. The next day (Thursday the 5th) he preached in the town hall "to a very wild [enthusiastic?], yet civil congregation," followed by an afternoon (2:00) meeting of Methodist society stewards from the northern and western circuits of Cornwall. At 6:00 p.m. he returned to the town hall for another sermon. "For the sake of this hour only (had no other end been answered)," he recalled, "I should have thought all the labour of my journey well bestowed."

On Thursday, 18 September 1755, as Wesley and his traveling companion(s) entered Launceston, a heavy rain began, and thus, between five and six o'clock in the late afternoon, he preached in the dining room of an unnamed "gentleman"—the space provided accommodating "hundreds of people." At 5:00 on the following morning (Friday, the 19th), he preached in the town hall and departed almost immediately thereafter. The weather on the next visit, Tuesday, 30 August 1757, proved no better than the last, with Wesley having to ride from Tiverton, Devonshire, "through wind and many hard showers." Little wonder, then, that he suffered from "a violent fit of the toothache," but, nonetheless, managed to deliver his sermon. "Such a night I never remember to have passed before," he recalled, "but all is good which lies in the way of glory." The next morning, he carried his toothache with him to Camelford. He returned to the town again to preach on Saturday, 1 October 1757.

After an absence of almost three years, John Wesley reached Launceston on Wednesday, 3 September 1760, where he found "the small remains of a dead, scattered [Methodist] society. And no wonder, as they have had scarce any discipline, and only one sermon in a fortnight [fourteen days]." Wesley's notion of discipline meant strict adherence to the "Rules of the Band Societies," drafted as early as 25 December 1738. Wesley's two-sentence preface to those "Rules" read, "The design of our meeting is to obey the command of God, 'Confess your faults to one another, and pray one for another that ye may be healed.' [James 5:16]. To this end we intend": Then followed but six rules:

1. To meet once a week, at the least.
2. To come punctually at the hour appointed, without some extraordinary reason.
3. To begin (those of us who are present) exactly at the hour, with singing or prayer.
4. To speak, each of us in order, freely and plainly the true state of our souls, with the faults we have committed in thought, word, or deed, and the temptations we have felt since our last meeting.
5. To end every meeting with prayer, suited to the state of each person present.
6. To desire some person among us to speak *his* [*her* to be substituted as necessary] own state first, and then to ask the rest in order as many and as searching questions as may be concerning their state, sins, and temptations.[6]

Before leaving Launceston, Wesley, on 4 September 1760, wrote to the Rev. Samuel Furly (?-1795), then curate of Kippax, in the West Riding of Yorkshire, concluding, "I am now entering into Cornwall, which I have not visited these three years, and consequently all things in it are out of order. Several persons *talk* of sharing my burthen, but none *does*; so I must wear out one first." Such a statement appears to underscore Wesley's overall lack of confidence in a number of his itinerant preachers, which no doubt had convinced him that he could not administer and control the religious organization known as Methodism from a distant office building. He, too, had to become an active member of the Methodist itinerancy.

Conditions at Launceston appeared not to have changed upon Wesley's next visit, Sunday, 26 September 1762, when he described the spiritual state of the inhabitants as "dead." Nonetheless, he did not abandon hope that the people might "be quickened, by the voice that raiseth the dead"— citing from (1) Ruth 4:5: "Then said Boaz, What day thou buyest the field of the hand of Naomi, thou must buy it also of Ruth the Moabitess, the wife of the dead, to raise up the name of the dead upon his inheritance" (KJV) and (2) Ruth 4:10—"Moreover, Ruth the Moabitess, the wife of

Mahlon, have I purchased to be my wife, to raise up the name of the dead upon his inheritance, that the name of the dead be not cut off from among his brethren, and from the gate of his place: ye are witnesses this day" (KJV).

Conditions at Launceston appeared to have improved slightly when Wesley preached there on Wednesday evening, 17 September 1762, in a room "that would not near contain the congregation." There he "strongly applied the case of 'the impotent man' at the pool of Bethesda [John 5:6–7]. Many were much affected. But O how few are 'willing to be made whole.'" Six years would elapse before Wesley again came to Launceston, and there, on Wednesday, 24 August 1768, he found "both the seriousness and largeness of the congregation, evening and morning [Thursday the 25th], gave us reason to hope that all our labour will not be in vain." Preaching there a year later, on Tuesday, 29 August 1769, he "strongly applied, 'Hath God forgotten to be gracious?'"—Psalms 77:9. "Hath God forgotten to be gracious: and will he shut up his loving kindness and displeasure?" (BCP). Wesley concluded with a declaration of his belief that God "answered for himself in the hearts of several backsliders." The Methodist leader passed through Launceston on Tuesday, 21 August 1770, but offered, in his journal extract, nothing relative to his activities or observations. At some point during the week of 24 August 1773, he again passed through Launceston and again offered nothing specific of what occurred there.

Wesley proved a bit more informative when he visited Launceston on Tuesday, 30 August 1774, describing the gathering to whom he preached as an "elegant congregation" (whatever that meant), but, at the same time, "what is that unless they are alive to God?" [Romans 6:11—"Likewise reckon ye also yourselves to be dead indeed unto sin, but alive unto God through Jesus Christ our Lord" (KJV).] He returned to the town, to preach, a week later (Wednesday, 7 September) and again on Friday, 1 September 1775. At Launceston on Thursday, 15 August 1776, Wesley "found the plain reason why the work of God had gained no ground in this circuit all the year. The preachers had given up the Methodist testimony." For whatever the reasons, the circuit under criticism appears to have been that of East Cornwall (which included Launceston), served, in 1775, by the itinerant preachers John Roberts (?-1788), Richard Rodda (1743–1788), William Whitaker, and Richard Wright.[7] What clouds the issue focuses upon the fact that Methodist membership throughout Cornwall for 1775 had increased slightly (+67) over the previous year (2,149 from 2,082 in 1774).[8] Nonetheless, Wesley advanced the opinion that "either they [the Methodist preachers] did not speak of perfection at all (the peculiar doctrine committed to our trust), or they spoke of it only in general terms, without urging the believers to 'go on to perfection,' [Hebrews 6:1—"Therefore, leaving the principles of the doctrine of Christ, let us go on unto perfection; not laying again the foundation of repentance from dead works, and of faith toward God" (KJV)], and to expect it every moment. And wherever this is not earnestly done the work of God does not prosper." In the Sermon on the Mount, Jesus Christ commanded, "Be ye therefore perfect, even as your Father which is in heaven is perfect" (KJV). Thus, the *perfection* demanded of Christians comprises a condition of spiritual maturity, or completeness. In other words, Jesus Christ commanded his followers to strive toward a state of moral and spiritual Godliness in all aspects of their lives.

Wesley next preached, but without narrative or comment, at Launceston on Thursday, 20 August 1777, and again at 6:00 p.m. on Monday, 31 August 1778—on the latter occasion in "a town little troubled with religion." Yet another instance of preaching at Launceston, on Tuesday, 29 August 1780, passed without comment, as did one more occasion on Wednesday, 5 September 1781. One year later, on Tuesday, 3 September 1782, Wesley, on his way from Camelford to St. Gennys, came upon "a white-headed old man" who grasped his hand and said to him, "Sir, do you not know me?" Upon Wesley's immediate and negative response, the man announced, "My father, my father! I am poor John Trembath."[9] Wesley then arranged for a meeting with Trembath at Launceston that evening, during which he learned that his former itinerant preacher had been reduced to extreme poverty, so as to "hedge and ditch for bread [to divert from the straight or proper way; to shift, shuffle, dodge; to avoid]. But in his distress he cried to God, who sent him an answer of peace. He likewise enabled him to cure a gentleman that was desperately ill, and afterward several others, so that he grew into reputation and gained a competent livelihood." Trembath informed Wesley that at present, "I want for nothing. I am happier than ever I was in my life." One should know that Wesley had severely chastised Trembath following the Methodist leader's visit to Launceston on 18 September 1755. In a letter written from Tiverton, Devonshire, on 21 September 1755, he had informed the itinerant preacher, "The plain reason why I did not design to speak with you at Launceston was because I had no hope of doing you good. I observed long ago that you are not patient of reproof; and I fear you are less so now than ever. But since you desire it, I will tell you once more what I think, fear, or hear concerning you." Specifically, Wesley reproached Trembath for his vanity, tendency to lie, becoming "more and more dead to God," engaging in "miserable employment" (farming, fishing) to the neglect of his ministerial responsibilities, and even countenancing smuggling. In any event, with that matter settled, Wesley proceeded from Launceston to St. Gennys.

The eighty-two-year old Wesley next arrived at Launceston at 4:00 p.m. on Wednesday, 31 August 1785, in time for prayer, tea, and, at 6:00, a sermon on 1 Kings 19:9—"And he [Elijah] came thither [to or toward that place: Mt. Horeb] unto a cave, and lodged there; and, behold, the word of the Lord came to him, and he said unto him, What doest thou here, Elijah?" (KJV). Then followed "necessary" religious conversation, supper, more religious conversation, prayer, and, at 9:30, sleep. Arising at 3:30 a.m. the next day (Thursday, 1 September), Wesley prayed, took tea, and, one hour later, departed in his chaise for Okehampton, Devonshire.

A month prior to Wesley's final visit to Launceston, the Methodist patriarch, from Otley, in the West Riding of Yorkshire, on 21 July 1789, had written to Samuel Bardsley (?-1818), one of his itinerant preachers, informing him, "I should hardly have expected any increase of the work of God in Launceston; but probably it will be enlarged by your preaching in the Town Hall. For many will come thither [to that place] who would not come to our preaching house." The visit itself began at 1:00 p.m. Friday, 28 August 1789, at which hour he partook of dinner, wrote letters, drank tea (at 5:00 p.m.), prayed, and, at 6:00, preached "in the new house" on Ezekiel 37. Following that exercise, he met with the Methodist society at Launceston, prayed, took supper (8:00 p.m.), engaged in religious conversation followed by more prayer, and retired for the night at 9:30. Arising at 3:00 a.m. on Saturday, 29 August, the Methodist patriarch ingested more tea, engaged in more religious conversation, and departed from Launceston at 3:45 a.m. He concluded his decades of visitations to the Cornish town with the succinct observation that "there is a fair [bright, promising] prospect in Cornwall from Launceston to the Land's End."[10]

Lelant

In the short period of 1744–1745, prior to the Wesleys having establishing a consistent itinerancy in Cornwall, officials at Lelant—situated three miles east from St. Ives—claimed that 180 families resided in the town, with sixty of them communicants of the Church of England at Easter out of one hundred eligible. Further, during 1745–1746, with evangelical activity especially active in Cornwall, William Simonds, vicar of Lelant, stood as one of the most bitter opponents among Cornish clericals to Methodism, going so far as to encourage mobs to commit harmful acts against the Methodist leaders and their itinerant preachers.[1]

John Wesley preached at Lelant at 1:00 p.m. Monday, 12 September 1757, and again, five years later, at the same hour, on Tuesday, 14 September 1762. Seeming unwilling to deviate from the rigidity of his itinerary, Wesley on 15 September 1765, at 1:00 p.m. preached in a meadow at Lelant, and once more in the same area at 5:00 p.m. "to a larger congregation than before. Indeed, the whole town seems moved, the truths we preach being so confirmed by the lives of the people." In yet another September (1766), at the same hour (1:00 p.m.), the day being Wednesday the 10th, the Methodist leader attempted to preach outdoors at Lelant, but a hard rain drove both preacher and congregation into the Methodist preaching house. Wesley appeared not to have engaged in further activity in Lelant, perhaps leaving the work there entirely in the hands of his itinerant preachers (21:123, 389; 22:21, 61; *Letters*, ed. Telford, 2:99).

Liskeard

Liskeard, a village (or town) .75 miles south of St. Cleer, seven miles from Saltash, and four miles west of St. Austell, would have been found among the four "coinage towns" of Cornwall when the first list of those sites appeared in 1305. Daniel Defoe identified the place as "a considerable town," well constructed, inhabited by a number of "people of fashion," containing "a very great market," and sending two members to Parliament. He also noted Liskeard as one of the five "Stannary Towns, that is to say, where the blocks of TIN are brought to the coinage of which by it self. This coinage of tin is an article very much to the advantage of the towns where it is settled, though the money paid goes another way." The term "stannary" has been defined as those districts having comprised the tin mines and smelting works of Cornwall and Devonshire that lay under the administration and jurisdiction of the "Stannary Courts" of law. Further, by the phrase "another way," Defoe referred to a system of heavy duties paid to the English Crown, a system that would exist into the nineteenth century. From a general historical perspective, Defoe noted that Liskeard had once held the status of "eminent," with a "good" castle and a large residence where the ancient dukes of Cornwall maintained their court. However, Defoe did not mention—if, indeed he knew of, the existence of —two ancient sites at Liskeard: (1) The Hurlers, a Bronze Age[1] monument, the remains of which consisted of three stone circles in a line, with thirteen, seventeen, and nine stones that continued to stand out of an original number of twenty-five to thirty-five stones in each circle; (2) Trethevy Stone, originally a Neolithic entrance grave, this portal dolmen (or *cromlech*—a large flat unhewn stone resting horizontally on three or more stones set upright) consists of six standing stones supporting a capstone, one stone having fallen.[2]

According to Defoe's view of Liskeard, the only worthwhile public edifices within the town assumed the forms of the guild, or town hall; a :very good" free school; a "very fine" conduit in the market place; an ancient large church; and, "which is something rare, for the county of Cornwall, a large new built meeting-house for the Dissenters, which I name, because they assured me there was but three more, and those very inconsiderable in all the county of Cornwall." He thought, in addition, the town had been "remarkable" for considerable trade in all aspects of the manufacture of leather, and "some spinning of late years is set up here, encouraged by the woolen manufactures of Devonshire."[3]

In 1770, contractors began a new road from Torpoint, twelve miles northwest to Liskeard, identified as an engineering feat, since it must have involved a considerable commitment of public funds, owing to the hilly nature of the district. In a number of places along the route, cuttings had to be executed through more than twenty feet of solid rock.[4]

Apparently, by the early 1750s. those Methodists and other interested parties from Liskeard journeyed to St. Cleer if they wished to see John Wesley and hear him speak. Thus, he found no real need to visit the town itself during that period of his Cornish itinerancy. Not until Tuesday, 27 September 1757, did Wesley actually set his feet (or those of his horse) within Liskeard, which he believed to have been "one of the largest and pleasantest towns in Cornwall"—even though W. Reginald Ward referred to it as "a village."[5] Wesley preached in the middle of the town, "in a broad convenient place" to a silent congregation, repeating the exercise to an equally quiet gathering at 6:00 on the following morning (Wednesday, the 28th). Afterward he examined the Methodist society there, finding himself "agreeably surprised to hear that every one of them had found peace with God—and (what was still more remarkable) that none of them has left their first love, that at this day not one is in darkness!"

Three years later, at noon on Friday, 26 September 1760, Wesley preached at an unidentified site near Liskeard, and on Wednesday, 18 September 1765, on his way from Redruth to Plymouth Dock, Devonshire, the Methodist leader called upon one of his friends (name not cited) near Liskeard. The man's wife, "once strong in faith," had plunged into "the very depth of despair. I could not but admire the providence of God, which sent us so seasonably thither [timely, to that place]. We cried strongly to God in her behalf and left her not a little comforted." A full decade passed until Wesley found another opportunity to preach at Liskeard, at 11:00 a.m. on Thursday, 7 September 1775, in the town hall. There he addressed "a large and serious congregation." Yet another decade lapsed before the Methodist leader again visited Liskeard, on that occasion—Monday, 22 August 1785—arriving in the town at 9:00 a.m. and having tea before preaching on Acts 16:31—"And they said, Believe on the Lord Jesus Christ, and thou shalt be saved, and thy house" (KJV). He departed almost immediately thereafter.

Although John Wesley did pause at Liskeard on his itinerant journey on Tuesday morning, 11 September 1787, he had no intention of preaching there. However, finding "a few people" gathered there, he delivered a "short discourse," drank some tea, and met with the Methodist society before he moved on to Torpoint. The final visit of the eighty-six-year-old patriarch of Methodism came at 7:30 a.m., Monday, 17 August 1789, whereupon he remained only for a single hour for tea. Although Wesley noted that occasion in his diary, it did not find space in his journal extract for that day.[6]

Little Carharrack

John Wesley reported, in his journal extract for Wednesday, 6 September 1775, that having left St. Ives on his way to Cubert, he stopped at Little Carharrack (or, simply, Carharrack), where he preached at 9:00 a.m. Although the hamlet of Little Carharrack lay as but an inconsequential speck upon the Cornish map, its location proved convenient as a meeting center for surrounding townships. A local versifier, in c. 1845, tried to force his unsteady hand at establishing the everlasting insignificance of the place and its connection with eighteenth-century Methodism:

> A vast congregation of Carharrack presents
> On the Sabbath-day ev'ning, and former events
> It recalls to the mind, here, too, the wise zeal
> Of Wesley shone forth for the listener's **weal**,   [**weal** = well-being]
> The octagon chapel that was on this spot,
> With his sanction first built, will soon be forgot.[1]

Lizard Point

Identified as the most southerly point of mainland England, the peninsula of Lizard Point (also The Lizard, Lizard Head) extends south from the town of Helston, Cornwall, and the Helford River. On Monday, 29 November 1736, on board the *Hannah* from Boston, Massachusetts, to England, Charles Wesley recorded in his manuscript journal, "We were waked between six and seven by the captain crying out, 'Land.' It was the Lizard Point, about a league [three nautical miles] distant. What wind there was, was for us! I felt thankful for the divine mercies."[1]

Fourteen months later, on Sunday, 29 January 1738, John Wesley, aboard the *Samuel* from Charleston, in the Carolinas settlement, to England, recorded that "we saw English land once more, which about noon appeared to be the Lizard Point. We ran by it with a fair wind, and at noon the next day [Monday, the 30th] made the west end of the Isle of Wight."[2] For both Wesleys, the sighting of Lizard Point signified the end of their failed mission to Georgia.

Looe

East and West Looe comprised two small chapelries (the districts attached to a chapel; a chapel with its precincts) on opposite sides of the mouth of the River Looe, the eighteenth-century population of the settlements combined exceeding slightly more than 1,000–1,200 persons. The area functioned, in the eighteenth century, as one of the principal pilchard[3] fisheries in Cornwall.[2] Until the Reform Act of 1832, West Looe returned two members to Parliament, beginning with the reign of Edward VI (1537–1553), and East Looe sent two more members, beginning in the reign of Elizabeth I (1558–1603). John Wesley dined at Looe on Thursday, 4 September 1746, and nine years later, he recorded in his journal that on Monday, 25 August 1755, he "rode over the mountains close by the sea to Looe" (20:135; 21:24).

Lostwithiel

Lostwithiel would have been found among the four "coinage towns" of Cornwall when the first list of those sites appeared in 1305. Approximately one and one-half miles from the town lay the ruins of Restormel Castle, the outer wall of which had been constructed by Robert de Cardinan late in the twelfth century, while the interior buildings arose from the efforts of Richard, Earl of Cornwall and his son, Edmund, in the mid- to late-thirteenth century.[1]

John Wesley's only visit to that town occurred late in his long life and at the end of his work on the Methodist itinerancy—arriving by chaise on Monday, 17 August 1789, at 11:00 a.m. There he spent an hour engaged in "necessary" conversation before boarding his chaise at noon for St. Austell (24:290).

Ludgvan

The parish of Ludgvan lay approximately 2.5 miles (according to Kimbrough and Newport; four miles according to Ward and Heitzenrater) northeast of Penzance. As an interesting aside to the goings on in that town, consider an incident that not only relates to its rector, the Rev. William Borlase (1695–1772)—who, in addition, held, as a dual living, the vicarage of St. Just— but also casts a bit of light upon certain aspects of commerce in mid-eighteenth-century Cornwall. According to papers in the archives of the Penzance Library that reveal the twelve months' wine account, as well as the receipts for same, for Borlase, dated 1768, the rector purchased three deliveries of his wine from James Ma'Carmick and Son, of Truro—a ten-gallon cask of the best red port at 6s. per gallon (total £9). With the first cask, Borlase purchased four dozen bottles, and corks, priced at 3s. per dozen (total 12s.) The charge of the carriage from Truro to Ludgvan came to 3s. 6d. for each of the three shipments (total 10s. 6d.). Thus, the total cost for satisfying the Rev. Borlase's taste for the year came to £9. 11s. 6d.—no small sum by the economics of the time.[1] Place that figure beside the yearly stipends, in 1768, for two of the Rev. Borlase's Cornish Church of England colleagues: Robert Blatchford received £11 per annum as vicar of Tywardreath and £8 as vicar of St. Samson, neither appointment providing lodging. Samuel Gurney, vicar of both Warleggan and Colan, received, annually, £10 from the former and £20 from the latter. Having seven children to support, he assigned curates to Warleggan and Colan, assumed permanent residence at Tregony, served as master of the grammar school there, and ministered to the churches of Merther and Cornelly for an additional stipend of £38 per annum.[2]

Turning to matters spiritual within a different context, one notes that Charles Wesley appeared in Ludgvan on Thursday, 3 July 1746, where he preached "Christ crucified"—1 Corinthians 1:23: "But we preach Christ crucified, unto the Jews, a stumblingblock, and unto the Greeks foolishness" (KJV). He then engaged in conversation with members of the Methodist classes,[3] "who seem much in earnest." Some two weeks later, on Thursday, 24 July 1746, Wesley rode "with a merry heart"[4] to Ludgvan, and "called many sin-sick souls to their Physician" [Jeremiah 8:22—Is there no balm in Gilead; is there no physician there? why then is not the health of the daughter of my people recovered? (KJV).] (2:465, 469).

John Wesley preached at Ludgvan on Friday, 23 September 1748; at noon on Friday, 17 August 1750; and on Monday, 9 September 1751. In none of those instances did he include, in his journal extracts, comment concerning the town, its citizens, or the state of Methodism therein. He did indicate, on Monday, 30 July 1753, that because of severe headache and nausea, he had to send an unidentified person to Ludgvan to preach in his place. Finally, on Thursday, 8 September 1757, John Wesley preached, at 6:00 p.m. to a "numerous congregation" at Ludgvan, remarking that "some years since, when there was a flourishing [Methodist] society in Gulval (the parish adjoining), there was none at all here. But how is the scene changed! In Gulval not one class, not one member remains; in Ludgvan there is a lively society!" (20:249, 357, 401, 469–470; 21:123).

Luxulyan (Methrose)

The village of Luxulyan lay in south-central Cornwall, between Lostwithiel to the northeast and St. Austell to the southwest, with the English Channel approximately seven miles to the south. One mile south of the village stood Methrose, a Tudor style estate built by an affluent and respected person, Nicholas Kendall, and leased as a farm house in a considerably less stately condition, during the 1750s, to a Mr. Meager.[1]

On Monday, 25 August 1755, at Fowey, John Wesley and his party met "a little company" who guided them to Luxulyan, and between five and six o'clock in the evening, the Methodist leader preached outside Methrose, where a courtyard had once existed. Wesley remarked that the former owner of the house (Nicholas Kendall), whom he did not name, and "all his family are in the dust, and his very memory is almost perished. The congregation was large and deeply serious." In the journal extract for Monday, 26 September 1757, Wesley provided a description of Methrose: "I have not seen a room so stately in Cornwall as either this hall or the chamber opposite it. The place likewise where the gardens were, the remains of the terrace walk, the stately trees still left, with many other tokens, show that grand men lived here once. But they are vanished like smoke, their estate torn in pieces, and well-nigh their memory perished." John Wesley preached at Methrose on Wednesday evening, 1 September 1762, and, three years later, Tuesday, 17 September 1765, he presided, at Methrose, over the Quarterly Meeting of the Methodist circuit for east Cornwall. "Here ... we had an agreeable account," he reported, "of a still increasing work of God. This [Methodist] society has eighty-six members, and *all* rejoicing in the love of God. Fifty-five or fifty-six of these believe he has saved them from all sin. And their life no way contradicts their profession. But how many will endure to the end?"

Wesley found the answer to his question when he next visited Luxulyan, on Wednesday, 3 September 1766. "There was last year the most lively [Methodist] society in Cornwall," he recalled. "But they are decreased both in number and strength, many who were then strong in the Lord being now weak and faint. [Ephesians 6:10—"Finally, my brethren, be strong in the Lord and in the power of his might" (KJV).] However, we had a deeply serious congregation[2] in the evening and a remarkable blessing at the meeting of the [Methodist] society." Wesley next preached at Methrose on Wednesday, 14 September 1768, and on the day following (Thursday, the 15th) he held another Quarterly Meeting of the local Methodist societies. He lamented upon having found little change in the spiritual state of Luxulyan from that of two years earlier, "when the whole society was in a flame. 'The love of many' is now waxed cold."—Matthew 24:12: "And because iniquity shall abound, the love of many shall wax cold" (KJV). Upon Wesley's return to Luxulyan and Methrose a year later, on Monday, 4 September 1769, he viewed a similar scene. Again, at what had once been "the liveliest society in Cornwall, I found but a few, and most of those faint and weary" [Isaiah 40:30 —"Even the youths shall faint and be weary, and the young men shall utterly fall" (KJV)].

Wesley next visited Methrose on Tuesday, 4 September 1770, and again, after an absence of six years, on Thursday evening, 29 August 1776. During the latter stay, he found himself "pleased to see an old friend with his wife, his two sons and two daughters." Professors Ward and Heitzenrater suggest (*Works*, 23:30) the identity of the family as the Meagers, who had leased Methrose. In any event, Wesley advanced the belief that "God sent a message to their hearts, as they could not help showing by their tears" [Judges 3:20, Haggai 1:13]. Finally, in his journal extract entry for Monday, 24 August 1778, Wesley noted only that he had proceeded on his way from Plymouth Dock, Devonshire, to Methrose. One would assume that he eventually arrived (21:24, 127, 387; 22:22, 59, 158, 203, 249; 23:30, 103).

Madron

Identified as "the mother church of Penzance"—meaning a parish church, or the principal or original church of a region or city; or, the orig-

inal church from which all other churches in the district have sprung—
Madron proved to have been, at the time of John Wesley's visitation there,
the ecclesiastical responsibility of Dr. Walter Borlase (1694–1776), who
held the living for more than half a century. The third son of John Borlase
of Pendeed, Cornwall, and the older brother of William Borlase (1695–
1772),[1] Walter Borlase served as vicar of Madron (1720–1776); vicar of
Kenwyn, Cornwall (1731–1776); and prebendary[2] of Exeter (1757). He held
the LL.D. degree and served as justice of the peace of the St. Ives, Cornwall,
area, which allowed him to lend legal substance to his outspoken opposition to Wesleyan Methodism.

Related to the anecdotal or folk history of Madron, there emerged,
second hand, from the pen of Joseph Hall (1574–1656)—rector of Halstead, Essex; rector of Waltham Holy Cross, Hertfordshire; prebendary of
the Collegiate Church of Wolverhampton, Staffordshire; Bishop of Exeter,
Devonshire (1597–1641); Bishop of Norwich, Norfolk (1641–1649)—a narrative of "a marvelous cure which was wrote [Hall's source unknown] upon
a poor cripple, at St. Madern's, in Cornwall, whereof, besides the attentions
of many hundreds of neighbours, I took a strict examination in my late
visitation [Cornwall then in the see of Exeter]. The man for sixteen years
together, was obliged to walk upon his hands, by reason the sinews of his
legs were so contracted. Upon an admonition [counsel, advice, suggestion]
in his dream to wash in a certain well he was suddenly so restored to his
limbs that I saw him able to walk and get his own maintenance. The name
of this cripple was John Treble."[2]

John Wesley's one and only stop at Madron came when he preached
there at 1:00 p.m. on Monday, 15 September 1760 (21:277).

Marazion

Situated three miles east of Penzance, Marazion derived its modern
name from "Marghasiewe," or "Market Jew," having originated, supposedly,
from a market in the town frequented by Jews. From another perspective,
however, the name of the town emerged from "Market die Jou," a reference
to the market held there on Thursdays and a linguistic corruption of "Dies
Jovis"—the Latin name for that day.[1]

From Crowan on Friday, 21 June 1745, John Wesley and his compan-
ion(s) rode to Marazion "(vulgarly called Market-Jew)" in response to a
warrant issued earlier that month requiring constables of nearby parishes
to "apprehend all such able-bodied men as had no lawful calling or sufficient maintenance" and to bring them before the justices at Marazion on

21 June. Thomas Maxfield,[2] one of John Wesley's itinerant preachers, found himself included in that group—which, naturally enough, prompted Wesley's initial visit to Marazion. Upon arrival, the Methodist leader found that the justices had not yet assembled, and thus he turned his attention to a walk up St. Michael's Mount. "The house at the top," he observed, "is surprising large and pleasant. Sir John St. Aubyn had taken much pains and been at considerable expense, in repairing and beautifying the apartments. And when the seat was finished, the owner died!" Having been educated at Exeter College, Oxford (M.A. 1721), John St. Aubyn (1696–1744), eventually gained election as a Member of Parliament for Cornwall (1722–1744). An opponent of the administration of Robert Walpole, he had served, in 1744, as a member of the Parliamentary committee to investigate the ethical conduct of the Prime Minister. Following the outdoor excursion, Wesley returned, at 2:00 p.m. to the room where the justices and commissioners had assembled. Principal among them, Dr. John Borlase (1666–1754), former Member of Parliament for St. Ives (1705–1710), arose and inquired of John Wesley if he had any business before the justices. Wesley replied in the affirmative, stating, "We desired to be heard concerning one who has been apprehended at Crowan." Informed that "the business of Crowan" had yet to come before the justices, Wesley had to wait in another room for seven hours until Maxfield's case came before Borlase and his colleagues. Advised to wait a bit longer before entering the hearing, Wesley remained until he received notice that Maxfield had been sentenced to service with the Royal Army, and thus immediately transported to Penzance. Wesley then entered the commission chamber, only to discover that "the honourable gentlemen had departed." Wesley had no other recourse but to leave Marazion and proceed to St. Ives.[3]

John Wesley appeared not to have preached at Marazion until Thursday, 20 August 1773, and following that visit he waited eight years before he came there again. He wended his way through that town on Wednesday, 29 August 1781, and someone informed him that a large congregation awaited to receive the word. Thus, the Methodist leader descended from his chaise and "immediately" began to preach. "And we had a gracious shower"—a downpour of grace. "Some were cut to the heart, but more rejoiced with joy unspeakable"—1 Peter 1:8 "[Jesus Christ]. Whom having not seen, ye love; in whom, though now ye see him not, yet believing, ye rejoice with joy unspeakable and full of glory" (KJV). A year later, at 11:00 a.m., on Saturday, 24 August 1782, he preached at Marazion, perhaps the result of having heard positive news about the state of Methodism in that town. There exists a letter from Wesley, written from London on 26 January

1783, to one of his itinerant preachers, Joseph Taylor (1752–1830), then on the Cornwall circuit, beginning "I am glad to hear so good an account of Marazion." For whatever the reason, Wesley returned once more to that Cornish town on Wednesday, 23 August 1785, at 4:00 p.m. preaching on Job 28:28—"And unto man he said, Behold, the fear of the Lord, that is wisdom; and to depart from evil is understanding" (KJV). An hour later, he took to his chaise for Penzance.

On Monday, 24 August 1789, the aged Wesley, for the last time, paused at Marazion on his way from Redruth to Penzance, fulfilling a promise to preach there. Within several minutes following his 10:00 a.m. arrival, the preaching house had filled to capacity, "so that I could not refrain from preaching a short sermon. And God was there of a truth." He based his sermon text upon Numbers 23:10—"Who can count the dust of Jacob, and the number of the fourth part of Israel? Let me die the death of the righteous, and let my last end be like his!" (KJV). "We had a rainy afternoon," he continued, "so I was obliged to preach in the new preaching house, considerably the largest and in many respects far the best in Cornwall."[4] Interestingly enough, Wesley, in his chaise, required two hours to drive from Redruth to Marazion (8:00 a.m.-10:00 a.m.) and thirty minutes (noon to 12:30) to guide his vehicle from Marazion to Penzance.

Mevagissey

Mevagissey functioned, in the eighteenth century, as one of the principal pilchard[1] fisheries in Cornwall.[2] John Wesley recorded in his journal extract for Wednesday, 8 August 1753, that he had received an invitation to Megavissey, "a small town on the south sea [English Channel]"—opposite Port Isaac on the north. As soon as he and his companion(s) entered the town, "many ran together, crying, 'See, the *Methodes* are come.' But they only gaped and stared, so that we returned unmolested to the house I was to preach at, a mile from the town. Many serious people were waiting for us, but most of them deeply ignorant. While I was showing them the first principles of Christianity, many of the rabble from the town came up. They looked as fierce as lions, but in a few minutes changed their countenance and stood still. Toward the close some began to laugh and talk, who grew more boisterous after I had concluded. But I walked straight through the midst of them and took horse without any interruption."

Upon Wesley's next visit to Mevagissey, on Thursday, 22 September 1757, the Methodist leader noted that the absence of a preaching house, as well as loud opposition to his presence, had forced him, four years previously, to preach about a half-mile outside of the town. "But things are altered now," he claimed. "I preached just over the town to almost all the inhabitants. And all were still as night." Remaining in Mevagissey to preach on Friday night, the 23rd, he noted a drunkard standing behind him "made some noise.... But after a few words were spoken to him, he quietly listened to the rest of the discourse." Wesley then, in his extract journal, entered his observation that "on the south side of the town there is an extremely fine walk, broad and smooth, over the top of high rocks, from whence is a view of the main sea at a vast distance below and all the coast, east and west." According to Nehemiah Curnock, the view described by John Wesley extended from the Ram's Head in the east to the Dead Man in the west. At any rate, the Methodist leader remained in Mevagissey to preach, at 12:30 on Saturday afternoon, 24 September, after which he prepared to leave. However, "All the time that I stayed the wind blew from the sea, so that no boat could stir out. By this means all the fishermen (who are the chief part of the town), had opportunity of hearing"—the warnings of an angry God filtered through the sounds of Nature or of Wesley's sermon?

Wesley had another opportunity to preach at Mevagissey on Friday, 3 September 1762, and again, six years later, on Tuesday evening, 13 September 1768. On the latter occasion, he proclaimed "a season of solemn joy," declaring, "I have not often found the like. Surely God's thoughts are not as our thoughts!"—Isaiah 55:8—"For my thoughts are not your thoughts, neither are your ways my ways, saith the Lord (KJV). Wesley then posed the question, "Can any good be done in Mevagissey?" On the next visit to Mevagissey by the Methodist leader, at noon on Monday, 3 September 1770, he preached "in a vacant space" near the center of the town "and strongly applied those words [from Ezekiel 33:11, beginning, "Say unto them, As I live, saith the Lord God, I have no pleasure in the death of the wicked; but that the wicked turn from his way and live:], 'Turn ye, turn ye from your evil ways; for why will ye die, O house of Israel?'" (KJV). When he preached in the town on Tuesday evening, 27 August 1776, in that familiar open space and to "most" of the townspeople, he "saw a very rare thing—men swiftly increasing in substance, and yet not decreasing in holiness."[3] Compare with/contrast to John's statement (John 3:30),"He must increase, but I must decrease," as well as Wesley's 1755 commentary on that verse: "So they who are now like John, burning and shining lights [John 5:35] must (if not suddenly eclipsed) like him gradually decrease, while others are increasing about them; as they in their turns grew up, amidst the decays of the former generation. Let us know how to set, as well as how to rise; and let it comfort our declining days to trace, in those who are likely to succeed us in our work, the openings of yet greater usefulness."[4] John Wesley last preached at Mevagissey on Tuesday evening, 22 August 1780, entering and leaving that town without comment (20:471; 21:126, 387; 22:158, 249; 23:30, 184).

Mitchell

A village on the main road from Redruth to Bodmin, Mitchell lay six miles north of Truro and five miles southeast of Newquay. Charles Wesley managed three visits to Mitchell, the first of which, on Friday, 15 July 1743, required a four-hour ride from Bodmin. Suffering acutely from the cholic, he found that he could not stand, and thus, almost immediately, found a bed upon which to lie. He then rose with "fresh strength" and proceeded on to Redruth. A month later, Charles Wesley came a second time to Mitchell at 4:00 p.m. Sunday, 7 August 1743, having been called by John Wesley to return to London for conferences. He remained overnight but left on the following day—presumably early in the morning. Finally, the younger Wesley reported that on Sunday, 5 August 1744, after having preached at Gwennap, he and his companion(s) lodged at an unidentified place three miles "short" of Mitchell (2:357, 369, 415).

As for John Wesley, Gerald Cragg speculated that the Methodist leader "had *probably*[1] passed through Mitchell during the week beginning 19 July 1747,"[2] but the published journal extract does not include an entry for that date.[3] Instead, Wesley's single *recorded* visit to Mitchell, on Saturday, 25 August 1750, focused hard upon a visit to a Mrs. Morgan, the proprietress, with her husband, of the Plume and Feathers tavern and a resident of that village—a person involved in the ongoing game of hearsay and rumor concerning the Wesleys and Methodism. To begin, at some point in 1750, George Lavington (1684–1762), Bishop of Exeter, initiated before a gathering of clergy from Cornwall and Devonshire, and caused to be spread by them, a story against John Wesley and his itinerant preachers. According to Lavington's version, Wesley and his Methodist itinerants tended to enter public houses (more specifically the Morgans' Plume and Feathers), and instructed the landlords that they would be damned if they demanded anything from those itinerants in return[4]; Bishop Lavington then published that report in a tract titled *The Enthusiasm of Methodist and Papist Compar'd* (London, 1751). Cragg further speculated that the Bishop had received the account of the incident from Mrs. Morgan in the summer of 1748.[5] When John Wesley confronted Mrs. Morgan at Mitchell on 25 July 1750, she "readily" told him, "and that over and over again, that she 'never saw or knew any harm by me.' Yet I am not sure that she has not just said the contrary to others. If so, she, not I, must give account for it to God" (20:358). Wesley would expand upon that journal entry of the confrontation and conversation with Mrs. Morgan in *A Second Letter to the Author of the Enthusiasm of Methodists and Papists Compar'd* (1751; 2nd edition 1752).[6]

Morvah

Identified as a "cliff-top" parish, Morvah lay on the North Sea, six miles northwest of Penzance, eight miles west of St. Ives, and three to four miles east of St. Just. When Charles Wesley rode in the rain to Morvah on Friday, 22 July 1743, he termed the town "a settlement of tinners, to whom I could preach nothing but gospel." He returned a week later, on Friday, 29 July, "invited the whole nation of tinners to Christ, and recorded the names of several of them who appeared desirous of forming a Methodist society. Although the adversaries have labored with all their might to hinder this good work, ... we doubt not of our seeing a glorious church in this place." Yet but another week passed before Charles Wesley again set his feet upon the ground at Morvah (Friday, 5 August), preaching, there, "my farewell sermon to our sorrowful brethren." He expressed, in his manuscript journal for that day, the belief, "I shall think it long till I see them again, but my comfort is that I leave them following after God." Charles Wesley also bid his farewell to the "friendly" mayor of Morvah, whom he acknowledged as "our deliverer from the unrighteous and cruel men"—Romans 1:18. "For the wrath of God is revealed from heaven against all ungodliness and unrighteousness of men, who hold the truth in unrighteousness" (KJV). According to Wesley, that unnamed mayor "expressed the same affection for us as from the beginning; listened to our report, for which our Lord gave us a fair opportunity; ordered his servant to light [guide, conduct] us home; in a word, received and sent away the messengers in peace."

On Sunday, 22 July 1744, the younger Wesley, denied access to the church at Morvah, preached out of doors at Morvah. There he told a person who spoke out against him that he would converse with him later. After a "visible blessing confirmed the word,"[1] Charles Wesley engaged his antagonist and led him to the Methodist preaching house. There he "begged" the man "to accept of a book. He was won, excused his rudeness, and left me hugely pleased." Later that day, Wesley, having rushed off to Zennor, returned to Morvah and "rejoiced over many who were lost and are found"—Luke 15:32. "It was meet [proper, right] we should make merry, and be glad: for this thy brother was dead, and is alive again; and was lost, and is found" (KJV). One might also recall the opening lines from the Rev. John Newton's classic hymn from 1 Chronicles, "Faith's Review and Expectation" (1779):

> Amazing grace! (how sweet the sound)
> That sav'd a wretch like me!
> I once was lost, but now am found,
> Was blind, but now I see.[2]

At any rate, Wesley claimed that 150 persons had joined the Morvah Methodist society, and those individuals "continue steadfastly in the Apostles' doctrine, and in fellowship, and in breaking of bread and prayers" [Acts 2:42] (KJV)]. On the following morning, Monday, 23 July, he breakfasted at the home of one identified only as Mr. L., "a poor slave of Satan, till, at the sound of the gospel, his chains fell off and left him waiting for the seal of his pardon. I pointed many sinners to the Lamb of God, which taketh away the sin of the world [John 1:29]. All were in tears at the remembrance of His sufferings."

Continuing his movements back and forth to the towns and villages in the area, Charles Wesley found, on Wednesday, 25 July 1744, "the brethren at Morvah beginning to build a Society-house. We knelt down upon the place, and prayed for a blessing." Then, after attending Church services at St. Ives on Sunday, 29 July, he rushed off to Morvah and preached "to a vast congregation on 'Blessed are they that hear the word of God, and keep it' [Luke 11:28]." Returning to Morvah two years later, on Saturday, 12 July 1746, Wesley demonstrated to those "(who were growing rich) the farter rest for the people of God, and inculcated [instilled, taught] the first great lesson of humility"—Hebrews 4:10 (KJV). "For he that is entered into his rest, he also hath ceased from his own works, as God did from his" (2:360, 366–368, 411–413, 466).

John Wesley's associations with the people of Morvah began on Friday, 2 September 1743, when he preached on "'The land of Zebulon [between the Sea of Galilee and Mount Carmel] and the land of Nephthalim [north of the Sea of Galilee], by the way of the sea.... The people which sat in the darkness saw great light, and to them which sat in the region and shadow of death light is sprung up'" [Matthew 4:15–16]. Within the gathering, the Methodist leader observed "an earnest, stupid [deadened, dulled, stunned] attention ... many of whom appeared to have good desires, but I did not find one who was *convinced of sin*, much less who knew the pardoning love of God"—John 8:46. "Which of you convinceth me [Jesus Christ] of sin? And if I say the truth, why do ye not believe me?" (KJV). On this first visit to Morvah, Wesley met Alice Daniel, a widow, in her garden collecting honey and asked her for a cup of water. She invited him into her home and fed him bread and honey, and Wesley reciprocated by offering her the words of "truth." In future visits to Morvah, Wesley normally lodged in her house. Alice Daniel's sons had departed (left their home or had died); a daughter, continually ill, remained with her; and by 1766 Alice Daniel had become totally blind.

Wesley preached at Morvah again four days later (Tuesday, 6 September 1743) on "Righteousness and peace and joy in the Holy Ghost [Romans 14:17]," but admitted that "still I could not find the way into the hearts of the hearers, although they were earnest to hear what they understood not." Less than a week later (Sunday, 11 September), at 1:00 p.m. Wesley stood beside the north wall of Morvah church, where the "Spirit of the Great King was in the midst. And I was filled with both matter and words.... 'My strength will I ascribe unto thee' [Psalms 59:9 (BCP)]." A week later (Sunday, 18 September), Wesley returned to Morvah at 1:00 p.m. and preached on Romans 8:15—"For ye have not received the spirit of bondage again to fear; but ye have received the Spirit of adoption, whereby we cry, Abba, Father" (KJV). He claimed to have stood before "the largest congregation I had seen in Cornwall." Afterward he met with the Methodist society at Morvah, which he estimated to number one hundred members. "Which of these will endure to the end," he asked.

Consistent rain and wind literally dampened Wesley's next two visits to Morvah, on Saturday, 7 April and again on Thursday, 12 April 1744. However, on the latter day, at 6:00 p.m. he managed to preach to "a little company" on "Ask and it shall be given to you" (Matthew 7:7; Luke 11:9 [KJV]). A year later, he preached there on Thursday, 27 June 1745, and again on Sunday, the 30th—but on neither day did he enter a comment or reaction in his journal extract. Wesley cast not much more light upon his activities in Morvah when he came there on Sunday, 7 September 1746, noting only that he "preached to a large congregation." The Methodist leader broadened the range of his observation ever so slightly when he preached at Morvah at noon, Sunday, 12 July 1747, to the largest crowd he had ever seen in that town, but his visit a year later, at 8:00 a.m., Sunday, 25 September 1748, elicited only the usual utterance of "I preached." At 1:00 p.m. Sunday, 19 August 1750, Wesley preached to "a great multitude" at Morvah, while on Sunday, 8 September 1751, at noon, he "made shift to stand on the lee side of a house at Morvah and preach Christ to a listening multitude." Two weeks later, Sunday, 22 September, he preached at Morvah, returning to that town at 8:00 Sunday morning, 29 July 1753, to preach to a "large congregation, and again at 1:00 p.m. "to near the same number. How many backsliders were among them, to whom I cried, 'How shall I give thee up, Ephraim?' [Hosea 11:8] Few of the congregation were unmoved. And when we wrestled with God in prayer, we had a strong hope he would not cast them off for ever."

While at St. Just on Friday, 2 September 1768, John Wesley received word that Alice Daniel had become terribly decrepit and had not heard a sermon within a number of years. Thus, on Saturday, the 3rd, he went to see her at Morvah and preached near her house on "They who should be accounted worthy to obtain that world, and the resurrection from the dead ... are equal unto the angels; and are the children of God, being the children of the resurrection" (Luke 20:35–36). The sixty-five-year-old Wesley then recorded his long-held notion about the emergence of "something venerable in persons worn out with age, especially when they retain their understanding and walk in the ways of God." With the passing of Alice Daniel, John Wesley appeared to have lost his interest in further visits to Morvah.

Mount Edgecumbe

Situated within St. Anthony's parish, Cornwall, the estate of Mount Edgecumbe had earned a reputation both for the aesthetics of its structure and the magnificence of the view that it offered. John Wesley visited the place on Wednesday morning, 12 September 1787, and "walked through all the improvements. The situation is fine indeed. The lofty hill, nearly surrounded by the sea and sufficiently adorned with trees, but not crowded, is uncommonly pleasant." At the end of his tour, Wesley, as though possessed of visions into the future, exclaimed, "And are all these things to be burned up!" At some point during World War II, Mount Edgecumbe burned to the ground! (24:59, 221).

Mousehole

John Wesley, when he preached initially at Mousehole at 8:00 a.m., Sunday, 7 September 1766, described the place as "a large village southwest from Newlyn." He did not return there until Sunday, 25 August 1782, at 9:00 a.m., preaching to "a large congregation." Returning at 8:30 a.m. on Thursday, 25 August 1785, the Methodist patriarch partook of tea and found "one of the liveliest societies in Cornwall." He based his sermon on Hebrews 6:1—"Therefore leaving the principles of the doctrine of Christ, let us go on unto perfection; not laying again the foundation of repentance from dead works, and of faith toward God" (KJV). By 10:30 a.m. he had boarded his chaise for Land's End (22:60; 23:250, 374, 533).

Mullion

The village of Mullion, near the Lizard's Point, lay five miles south of Helston. John Wesley arrived there for his first and only visit on Monday afternoon, 6 September 1762, received "gladly" by "a man who *was* a sinner." The unnamed individual, according to Wesley, "knew God had received him [Romans 14:3, Galatians 4:14], having been deeply convinced of sin the last time I preached near Helston and, not long after, filled with peace and joy in the Holy Ghost" [Romans 14:17]. At the beginning of Wesley's sermon, "a flame was kindled [Isaiah 43:2] ... which increased more and more all the time I was preaching, as well as during the meeting of the [Methodist] society. How tender are the hearts of these people! Such is the advantage of true, Christian simplicity!" [2 Corinthians 11:3] (21:388).

Newlyn

Identified as a hamlet with a harbor, Newlyn, situated in the parish of Paul, lay approximately one-half mile from Penzance. At 5:00 p.m. Sunday, 12 July 1747, John Wesley walked to an elevated area near the shore, where he stood on "a smooth white" stretch of sand before an "immense multitude of people ... but their voice was as the roaring of the sea. I began to speak and the noise died away. But before I had ended my prayer some poor wretches of Penzance began cursing and swearing, and thrusting the people off the bank. In two minutes I was thrown into the midst of them, when one of Newlyn [Peter Jaco (1729–1781), who had converted to Methodism in 1746 and would begin to preach in 1751], a bitter opposer till then, turned about and swore, 'None shall meddle with the man; I will lose life first.' Many others were of his mind." Thus, Wesley walked "a hundred yards forward" and completed his sermon without further interruption. A year later, shortly after 4:00 p.m. on Sunday, 25 September 1748, Wesley returned to Newlyn, where he had to confront "a rude, gaping, staring, rabble-rout" of a congregation, a number of whom threw stones and dirt continually. However, before he had completed his sermon, the crowd had quieted, and a number among them "looked as if they felt what was spoken."

Having preached at Newlyn on Friday evening, 17 August 1750, John Wesley concluded, "Through all Cornwall I find the [Methodist] societies have suffered great loss from want of discipline.[1] Wisely said the ancients, 'The soul and body make a man; the spirit and discipline make a Christian.'" The student of John Wesley's sermon literature will see those words again almost three decades later, in *Some Account of the Late Work of God in North America, in a Sermon on Ezekiel i.16*[2] (London: R. Hawes, 1778): ¶7[3]—"It was a true saying, which was common in the ancient church, 'The soul and the body make a man, and the spirit and discipline make a Christian.'" Three years later, at 5:00 p.m. Sunday, 29 July 1753, Wesley preached at Newlyn on that portion of the Gospel prescribed for that day, Matthew 5:20: "Except your righteousness shall exceed the righteousness of the scribes and Pharisees [members of the largest and most influential political party during the period of the New Testament], ye shall in no wise [manner, means] enter into the kingdom of heaven." Here, however, he found himself forced to deal with the physical hazards to which eighteenth-century travelers found themselves exposed. He awoke on the following morning (Monday the 30th), between 2:00 and 3:00, continuing to endure a "looseness" (diarrhea) that had been plaguing him for several days and increasing "every hour." However, he determined, "with God's help," to preach at the appointed time and place. "I had now, with the flux [dysentery], a continual headache, violent vomitings, and, several times in an hour, the cramp in my feet and legs—sometimes in both legs and both thighs together. But God enabled me to be thoroughly content and thankfully resigned to him." According to John Telford, Wesley's wife, Mary (Molly) Goldhawk Vazeille Wesley (1710–1781), accompanied her husband on this round of the Cornish circuits, the editor of Wesley's correspondence citing the journal entries of 12 and 18 July 1753, both of which begin with "We."[4] Telford also notes, as evidence that Molly Wesley attended to her husband's illness at Newlyn, Wesley's comments in his letter of 5 September 1768 (see below).

When John Wesley next visited Newlyn, on Friday (late afternoon or evening), 5 September 1755, he received word that a strong, healthy man had been found dead in his bed on the previous morning (Thursday, the 4th)—an event that had "startled" a number of townspeople. Thus, Wesley "endeavoured to deepen the impression by preaching on those words, 'There is no work, nor device, nor knowledge, nor wisdom, in the grave whither thou goest'" [Ecclesiastes 9:10]. With that problem out of mind, Wesley departed from Newlyn, not to return until 5:00 p.m. Sunday, 11 September 1757, at which time he preached to "a huge multitude." Only one person among that gathering appeared "offended—a 'very good sort of woman' who took great pains to get away, crying aloud, 'Nay, if going to church and Sacrament will not *put us to heaven*, I know not what will.'" Again at Newlyn on Wednesday and Thursday, 17–18 September 1760, the Methodist leader had to deal with a rainstorm that forced him to speak indoors, while during an overnight stay there on Saturday evening–Sunday morning, 11–12 September 1762, he found "God in the midst, and many hearts were broken in pieces." Another slight disruption occurred at Newlyn on Wednesday evening, 11 September 1765. Despite a hoarseness of voice, Wesley preached "in a little ground ... to a numerous congregation. None behaved amiss but a young gentleman, who seemed to understand nothing of the matter."

Three years later, John Wesley came to Newlyn at c. 5:00 p.m. Sunday, 4 September 1768, preached, and remained there overnight. Early the next morning (5 September), he wrote to his wife, Mary (Molly) Goldhawk Vazeille Wesley, who, in mid–August of that year, at London, had suffered from a serious attack of fever. Thus, after three weeks had passed, he addressed Molly Wesley: "My Dear Love—I can make allowances for faintness and weakness and pain. I remember when it was my own case at this very place [Newlyn, July 1753; see above], and when you spared no pains in nursing and waiting upon me, till it pleased God to make you the chief instrument of restoring my strength. I am glad you have the advice of a skillful [*sic*] physician. But you must not be surprised or discouraged if you do not recover your strength so soon as one might wish, especially at this time of the year. What is chiefly to be desired is that God may sanctify all his dispensations to you: that all may be means of your being more entirely devoted to Him whose favour is better than strength or health or life itself. I am, dear Molly, Your ever affectionate Husband."[5] The Wesleys had been married since 18 February 1751, but that union, which ended in separation, proved an unfortunate experience for both, and probably should never have occurred.[6]

Wesley next preached at Newlyn on Wednesday, 29 August 1770, and did not return to the town until 11:00 a.m. on Friday, 21 August 1789. On that final visit, he engaged in the usual religious conversation before preaching on Hosea 14:4—"I will heal their backsliding, I will love them freely; for mine anger is turned away from him" (KJV).[7]

North Tamerton

North Tamerton, in the eighteenth century recognized as a small perpetual curacy, lay approximately two miles from Tetcott, five miles southwest of Holsworthy, twelve miles from St. Gennys, and twenty-four miles from Bideford. Since the church there lacked a parsonage house, the incumbent had to seek lodgings elsewhere. Further, the parish housed sixty families, with 140 eligible communicants, and the minister held a weekly service and four administrations of the Sacraments each year. Reportedly, no Protestant Dissenters resided in the town.[1]

John Wesley managed three visits to North Tamerton, the initial one occurring on Tuesday evening, 16 July 1743. Between 6:00 and 7:00, he read prayers and preached on John 4:24—"God is a Spirit: and they that worship him must worship him in spirit and in truth" (KJV). He returned on Sunday morning, 26 July 1747, preaching in North Tamerton church, and for the final time on Tuesday, 28 August 1750, at the invitation of the curate, John Bennet (1670?-1750). However, upon arrival, Wesley discovered that notice had not been posted as to his preaching in the church, and that the key to the building had been stored "a mile off." Therefore, he delivered his sermon in a large room adjoining the church (20:80, 184, 359).

Penhale

On Thursday, 18 September 1760, John Wesley, in southern Cornwall, rode through heavy rain from Newlyn to Penhale (near Breage), but when he came to the latter village, the rain had ceased. "The people flocking from all parts, we had a comfortable opportunity together." The Methodist leader preached there again, but for the final time, on Thursday evening, 9 September 1762 (21:280, 388). There exists little doubt that the death of his evangelical-minded friend, John Bennet, in October 1750 dampened Wesley's interest in Penhale.

Penryn

Penryn, a seaport, parliamentary borough (one that sent members to Parliament), and market town, would have been found two miles northwest of Falmouth. According to Daniel Defoe, the town lay upon "the same branch of the haven [a recess or inlet of the sea] as Falmouth, but stands four miles higher towards the west, ye ships come to it of great size...; it is a very pleasant agreeable town, and for that reason has many merchants in it, who would perhaps otherwise live at Falmouth." Defoe identified pilchard[1] and Newfoundland fishing as the principal and profitable commerce of Penryn. The town, continued Defoe, "had formerly a conventional church, with a chantry [a chapel with an endowment for the maintenance of Catholic priests who would sing (or chant) during mass], and a religious house, a cell to Kirton,[2] but they are all demolished, and scarce the ruins of them distinguishable enough to know one part from another."[3]

The extant fragments from Charles Wesley's manuscript journal yield but the narrative of a single visit to "a large gentleman's seat near Penryn" on Thursday, 2 August 1744. Whether the adjective "large" referred to the unidentified gentleman, to a specific section of the gentleman's torso, or to the size of the gentleman's landed estate ("seat") remain linguistic problems yet to be solved. In any event, Wesley noted, "The people come pouring in from Falmouth and all parts. "The court-yard which might contain 2000, was quickly full." Charles Wesley stood in a gallery above the gathering and preached upon a text from Isaiah 1:16—"Wash ye, make you clean" (KJV). Those gathered before him "eagerly listened to the word of life—even the gentlemen and ladies listened—while I preached repentance towards God, and faith in Jesus Christ'" [Acts 20:21]. "I exhorted them in many words," concluded Wesley, "to attend the ordinances of the Church, to submit to every ordinance of man for the Lord's sake, to stop the mouths of gainsayers [those who contradict, oppose, reject] by fearing God and honoring the King [1 Peter 2:17. "Honour all men. Love the brotherhood. Fear God. Honour the King" (KJV)], and to prevent the judgments hanging over our heads by a general reformation" (2:414).

John Wesley's first recorded visit to Penryn occurred at 1:00 p.m. Tuesday, 27 September 1748, where he preached, "in a convenient place, encompassed with houses," to a rowdy gathering that soon "softened" to attentiveness. Returning there on Wednesday evening, 8 August 1750, the Methodist leader observed the presence of a collection of gentry, a number of whom "I permitted to stay when I met the [Methodist] society. They seemed much moved. It *may* last more than a night, for 'with God all things are possible' [Matthew 19:26; Mark 10:27]." A year later, on Thursday, 12 September 1751, he rode to Penryn, where he gained access to the works of "that odd writer, William Dell [1604–1670]." Having gained admittance as a sizar (holder of a partial grant) at Emmanuel College, Cambridge (1624), Dell graduated B.A. in 1628. Following ordination into the Church of England, Dell received a fellowship at Emmanuel College, then served Archbishop William Laud (1573–1645) as a secretary and also acted as chaplain to the Parliamentary troops of Baron Thomas Fairfax (1612–1671) and performed the marriage between Bridget Cromwell and Henry Ireton (1611–1651). Dell succeeded, in 1649, as Master of Gonvil and Caius College, Cambridge—the occupant having been ejected—serving there until 1660. Two years later, the Church ejected Dell, himself, from his ecclesiastical living at Yeldon, Bedfordshire. Philosophically, he opposed the then current notion of a classical education as the substantial preparation for a clerical calling, maintaining that "the Gospel of Christ understood according to Aristotle, hath begun, continued and affected the mysteries of iniquity in the outward Church." Dell maintained further that "as long as the Spirit of God dwells in the flesh, it will still be reforming the flesh to the Spirit ... till all be perfected." To the surprise of few, Dell became popular among the Quakers. Dell's sermons and theological treatises reached the press between 1645 and 1697, and an edition of his *Selected Works* would come forth at London in 1773 and 1817, while John Wesley included extracts of his tracts in *The Christian Library* (1751–1768).[4] "From his [Dell's] whole manner," commented Wesley, "one may learn that he was not very patient of reproof or contradiction, so that it is no wonder there is generally so much error mixed with the great truths which he delivers."

At Penryn once more, on Monday evening, 6 August 1753, Wesley "found my strength so restored that I could speak loud enough to be heard by a numerous congregation." He remained there overnight and preached on the following morning (Tuesday, the 7th) before departing for Besore. Two years later at Penryn, on Monday, 1 September 1755, Wesley preached "to abundantly more than the house could contain," and two years after that, on Monday evening, 19 September 1757, he found "both the house and court ... more than filled." At some point during the day, he wrote at length to the Church of England evangelical cleric the Rev. Samuel Walker,[5] in response to the latter's suggestion that Wesley submit to the care of a group of evangelical Church clergymen those societies that the Methodist leader had formed within their parishes. The basis for Walker's argument rested upon his belief that control of Wesley's societies by parish ministers would prevent society members from leaving the Church. Wesley countered that notion, in part, with the reasoning that members of his societies belonged to the Church, to the parish, and to the parish minister by "legal establishment." If those members of his (Wesley's) societies "receive the Sacrament from him [the parish minister] thrice a year and attend his ministrations on the Lord's Day, I see no more which the law requires. But (to go a little deeper into this matter of legal establishment)" do "you think that the King and Parliament have the right to prescribe to me what pastor I shall use? If they prescribe one to whom I know God never sent, am I obliged to receive him? If he be sent of God, can I receive him with a clear conscience till I *know* he is? And even when I do, if I believe my former pastor is more profitable to my soul, can I leave him without sin? Or has any man living a right to require this of me? I extend this to every gospel minister in England. Before I could with a clear conscience leave a Methodist Society even to such an one, all these considerations must come in."[6] Having completed that task, Wesley continued his stay at Penryn and "willingly embraced" an invitation by one identified only as "Mr. H." to preach before the door of his house at noon on Tuesday, the 20th—finding that site "a most pleasant place, on the side of an hill, commanding a fruitful vale, the opposite hills, and Falmouth harbour. Tall trees hung over me and surrounded a bowling-green which was behind me. A wide door is now open at Penryn also. O that none may shut it."—Revelation 3:8: "I [Jesus Christ] know thy works: behold I have set before thee an open door, and no man can shut it; for thou hast a little strength, and hast kept my word, and hast not denied my name" (KJV).

Five years would pass before the Methodist leader would again come to Penryn—Monday evening, 22 September 1760. Rain came both before and after his sermon, but none fell while he spoke. During the prayer, "a sheet of light seemed to fill the yard, and *the voice of the Lord* was heard over our heads. This fixed the impression they had received upon the minds of many—as if it had said in express terms, 'Prepare to meet thy God!' [Amos 4:12]." Wesley returned to preach at Penryn on Monday, 6 September 1762, and again on Thursday evening, 4 September 1766—on the latter occasion in the main street and at the door of one of "the chief gentlemen in the town. I never saw such a congregation here before. And all seemed to hear as for life." On Thursday evening, 30 August 1770, he preached at Penryn, after which there appears a lengthy lapse of fifteen years before his next visit, that occurring on Tuesday, 23 August 1785. Arriving by chaise at 4:30 p.m. the eighty-two-year-old Wesley partook of tea at 5:00, engaged in the usual religious talk and prayer, and at 6:00 preached on Job 22:21—"Acquaint now thyself with him, and be at peace: thereby good shall come unto thee" (KJV). Afterward, he met with the Methodist society, had supper, engaged in more religious talk and prayer, and then retired for the night at 9:30. On the day following (Wednesday the 24th), he began the day at 4:00 a.m. with prayer, followed by a sermon at 6:00 a.m. on Job 6:18—"The paths of their way are turned aside; they go to nothing, and perish" (KJV). Then came the writing of a letter, tea, and religious talk at 8:00, and boarding his chaise and departure at 8:45 a.m. Wesley's final visit to Penryn, on Wednesday, 19 August 1789, proved a bit shorter, his activities beginning there at 11:15 a.m., at which time he again based his sermon text upon Job 22:21. At 1:00 p.m. he paused for

his dinner, executed the usual prayer, and by 2:15 he had boarded his chaise
for Helston.

Penzance

At some point during the reign of Charles II (1660–1685), to accommodate the tin manufacturers of western Cornwall, Penzance had been
added to the original list of "coinage towns" of Cornwall, those sites so
designated in 1305. Daniel Defoe claimed Penzance to have been the farthest town "of any note west, being 254 miles from London,[1] and about
ten miles of the promontory, called Lands End." He viewed the town pos-
itively, if not in the most general of terms, as "a place of good business,
well built and populous, has a good trade, and a great many ships belonging to it, notwithstanding it is so remote. Here are also a great many good
families of gentlemen, though in this utmost angle of the nation; and,
which is yet more strange, the veins of lead, tin, and copper ore, are said
to be seen, even to the utmost extent of land at low water mark, and in
the very sea; so rich, so valuable a treasure is contained in these parts of
Great Britain, though they are supposed to be so poor, because so very
remote from London, which is the centre of our wealth."[2]

Interestingly enough, eighteenth-century Penzance claimed a local
literary society; an assembly room for music and dancing, at which place
participants met fortnightly; a theater and cockpit (i.e., the pit of the theater); a ladies' book club (founded in 1770); and a grammar school established by 1789.[3] Insofar as concerned the Church of England during the
periods of the Wesleys' visitations to Cornwall, records reveal that in 1779,
255 persons presented themselves as candidates for Confirmation.[4]

Charles Wesley indicated in his journal for Tuesday, 24 July 1744,
that he preached "*near*" *[my italics]* Penzance, to the "little flock encompassed by ravening wolves" [Matthew 7:15: "Beware of false prophets,
which come to you in sheep's clothing, but inwardly they are ravening
wolves" (KJV)]. "Their minister [Walter Borlase?][5] rages above measure
against this new sect," continued Wesley, "who are spread throughout his
four livings. His reverend brethren follow his example. The grossest lies
which are brought them they swallow without examination, and retail
[recount or tell over again; repeat] the following Sunday. One of the
[Methodist] society (James Dale) went lately to the Worshipful and Reverend Dr. [Walter] Borlase for justice against a rioter, who had broke open
his house and stole his goods. The Doctor's answer was, 'Thou conceited
fellow, art thou too turned religious? They may burn thy house if they

will. Thou shalt have no justice.' With these words he drove him from the judgment-seat" [Acts 18:16].

Six days later (Monday, 30 July), Charles Wesley returned to another (the same?) place *near* Penzance and "cried to a mixed multitude ... 'Is it nothing to you, all ye that pass by?'" (Lamentations 1:12). He then engaged in prayer with "the still increasing flock, whose greatest persecutor is their minister [Walter Borlase?]. He and the clergy of these parts are much enraged at our people's being so ready [prepared, knowledgeable] in the Scriptures. One fairly told Jonathan Reeves [(?-1787) among the earliest of Methodist itinerant preachers][6] he wished the Bible were in Latin only, that none of the vulgar [the common] might be able to read it. Yet these are the men that rail at us as Papists!" The next day (Tuesday, the 31st), either near or actually in Penzance, Wesley preached on "the Woman of Canaan [Matthew 15:22–28] to a house-full of sincere souls, who had sat up all night to hear the word in the morning." He spoke with a number of attendees "who have tasted the good word of grace, though they live in Penzance, where Satan keeps his seat [Revelation 2:13]." Before departing, he visited, for the second time, "a poor dying sinner, who now gives up his own filthy rags for the best robe [Isaiah 64:6, Luke 15:22]. His daughter, upon her request, I admitted into the [Methodist] Society" (2:411, 413).

John Wesley's visits to or near Penzance began at 1:00 on Saturday afternoon, 11 September 1762, when he preached on a cliff near the town, followed, four years later on Saturday, 6 September 1766, at 1:00 p.m. when he preached in a nearby meadow. "The whole congregation behaved well," he observed. "The old bitterness is gone. And perhaps, had it not been market-day, I might have had a quiet hearing in the market-place." Returning to Penzance two years later, at 9:00 a.m., Monday, 5 September 1768, he exclaimed, "Surely God will have a people even in this place, where we have so long seemed only to beat the air."—1 Corinthians 9:26: "I [Paul] therefore so run, not as uncertainly; so fight I, not as one that beateth the air" (KJV). Five years would pass before Wesley found another opportunity to apply the work at Penzance, preaching in the town hall on Wednesday, 18 August 1773, the room there fully occupied. In addition, according to Wesley, "it was filled with the power of God. One would have thought every soul must have bowed down before him." At Penzance a year later, on Thursday afternoon, 1 September 1774, the Methodist leader noted at least one principal change in the spiritual state of the town: "When the people here were as roaring lions, we had all the ground to ourselves. Now they are become lambs."

John Wesley then turned his attention to an individual and his friends who had taken "true pains" to create divisions within the Methodist society at Penzance. Attempts to determine the name of the leader of that group prove extremely difficult because (1) Wesley did not, in his journal extract, provide a complete spelling of the surname, and (2) the principal editors of Wesley's journal offered various versions of what Wesley (or his printers) had actually inscribed upon the page. Thomas Jackson, in the third edition of Wesley's *Works* (1872), identified the person as "Mr. S——**b**" [my **bold** in all instances], but without any attempt to speculate, by way of a notation, who that person might have been.[7] Nehemiah Curnock apparently followed Jackson's lead by repeating "Mr. S——**b**," but, in addition, submitted an explanation of sorts: "Neither Secumb nor Slocumb, who both have been suggested [by whom?], is at all probable. They were brave and devoted men whose stories are worth preserving."[8] In that same note, Curnock directed the reader to Charles Wesley's journal entry for Friday, 13 July 1744, which begins, "Set out [from Middlezoy, Cornwall] with our guide, John Slocombe [?-1776], a poor baker's boy, whom God has raised up to help these sincere souls, and not only to labour [on the Methodist itinerancy],[9] but also to suffer, for them."[10] Yet more editorial confusion arises here, brought about by a series of different spellings for Charles Wesley's guide and Methodist itinerant preacher: (1) "Slocum," in Thomas Jackson's edition of Charles Wesley's *Journal* (1:368); (2) "Slocombe" in Jackson's edition of *The Works of John Wesley* (8:281); (3) "Slocomb" in Luke Tyerman's *Life and Times of John Wesley* (1:440); (4) "Slocumb," in Curnock's edition of John Wesley's *Journal* (6:38); (5) "Slocomb," again in Curnock's edition of John Wesley's *Journal* (8:159); (6) "Slocomb" in *Works of John Wesley: Journal* (1991, 20:251); (7) "Slocomb," in Heitzenrater, *Wesley and the People Called Methodists*, 2nd ed. (297); (8) "Slocombe" in *Works of John Wesley: Methodist Societies* (2011, 10:147). Finally, to add to the confusion and discomfort, Ward and Heitzenrater, in their edition of John Wesley's *Journal and Diaries* (1993), interpret Wesley's autograph copy of the journal extract entry for 1 September 1774 as "Mr. S——**h**," accompanied by a note of extremely fragile substance: "The identity of this person is unknown, though the name might be Smith" (22:417). The discussion of such editorial inconsistencies aside, Wesley continued the narrative by informing his readers that the majority of the members of the Penzance Methodist society "(blessed be God!)...stand firm in one mind and in one judgment. Only a few, whom we had expelled, they have gleaned [gathered, recruited] up. If they can do them good, I shall rejoice." That evening, Wesley proceeded to the end of the town and preached "the whole gospel to a listening multitude," after which he "exhorted" the Methodist society "to 'follow after peace and holiness'" [Hebrews 12:14].

When Wesley returned to Penzance on Wednesday, 21 August 1776, he preached "in a gentleman's balcony, which commanded the market-place." Reportedly, that balcony belonged to the Star Inn at Penzance, and it would eventually become the site of Methodist societies' quarterly meetings. The leader of the Methodists addressed a "large" congregation on the text, "'Without holiness no man shall see the Lord' [Hebrews 12:14]. The word fell heavy, upon high and low, rich and poor. Such an opportunity I never had at Penzance before." He preached again at Penzance on Wednesday, 26 August 1778, and, two years later, on Wednesday, 23 August 1780, when he paused to consider his visit "a pleasure" because of the "little flock being united together in love." He preached not far from the Methodist preaching house, noting the presence of a company of British soldiers quartered in the town. Toward the end of the sermon, the "good" commanding officer ordered his troops to march through the congregation, but as the attendees "opened and closed again," the maneuver created "little disturbance." On Wednesday evening, 29 August 1781, Wesley planted his pulpit in the Penzance marketplace, intending to meet with members of the Methodist society following his sermon. However, "the people were so eager to hear all they could that they quickly filled the house from end to end. This is another of the towns wherein the whole stream of the people is turned, as it were, from east to west" [Ezekiel 48]. A year later, he arrived at Penzance on Saturday evening, and on the next morning "prayed that God would 'stay the bottles of heaven' [Job 38:37], and he heard our prayer."

The visit to Penzance on Wednesday–Thursday, 24–25 August 1785 proved generally uneventful, yet the eighty-two-year-old Wesley, in his diary, indicated a crowded itinerary of the usual activities. He arrived after 5:00 p.m. on Wednesday, and after tea at 6:00, he preached on Daniel 9:24—"Seventy weeks are determined upon thy people and upon thy holy city, to finish the transgression, and to make an end of sins, and to make reconciliation for iniquity, and to bring in everlasting righteousness, and to seal up the vision and prophecy, and to anoint the most Holy" (KJV). Wesley then met with members of the Methodist society, partook of supper, engaged in religious conversation, led prayers, and, at 9:30, took to his bed. He arose at 4:00 a.m. on Thursday, prayed, and then preached on 2 John 8—"Look to yourselves, that we lose not those things which we have wrought [worked, brought about], but that we receive a full reward" (KJV). After writing a letter and drinking tea, he boarded his chaise at 8:30 a.m., bound for Mousehole.

However, Wesley's next visit to Penzance, on Thursday, 6 September 1787, contained significant elements of frustration and a slight dose of drama. Three weeks earlier, on Tuesday, 14 August, the aged Wesley, in company with the Rev. Dr. Thomas Coke (1747–1814), then Wesley's principal assistant and legal advisor, sailed from Southampton aboard *The Queen* to begin a preaching tour of the (English) Channel Islands—Jersey, Guernsey, Alderney, Sark, and a number of smaller islands, all of them ten to thirty miles off the west coast of France. Wesley had hoped to return to England by late August, but heavy storms, highlighted by strong contrary winds, prevented the ship's passage. By Wednesday, 4 September, he continued to linger and wait at St. Peter Port, on the Isle of Guernsey, when he received word that a French vessel had recently landed at Guernsey and that the captain proposed to sail for Penzance the next morning. Thus, on Thursday, 6 September, Wesley boarded that vessel, the *Commerce*, which faced but "a fair, moderate wind." However, the wind quickly died away. According to Wesley, "We cried to God for help, and it [the wind] presently sprung up, exactly fair, and did not cease until it brought us into Penzance Bay." Once in Penzance at 10:00 a.m. on Friday, the 7th, "We appeared to our friends here as men risen from the dead. Great was their rejoicing over us, and great was the power of God in the midst of the congregation while I explained and applied those words, 'Whosoever doth the will of God, the same is my brother and sister and mother'" [Mark 3:35]. At 6:00 a.m., on Saturday, the 8th, Thomas Coke preached to a capacity crowd in the Methodist preaching house, and four hours later, Wesley found himself "obliged to take to the field by the multitude of people that flooded together. I found a very uncommon liberty of speech among them and cannot doubt that the work of God will flourish in this place" [Psalms 92:11–12: "The righteous shall flourish like a palm-tree: and shall spread abroad like a cedar from Libanus ([Lebanon])./Such as are planted in the house of the Lord: shall flourish in the courts of the house of our God" (BCP)]. He had based his sermon for that morning upon 1 Samuel 20:3—"And David sware moreover, and said, Thy father certainly knoweth that I have found grace in thine eyes; and he [the Lord] saith, Let not Jonathan know this, lest he be grieved: but truly as the Lord liveth, and as thy soul liveth, there is but a step between me and death" (KJV).

John Wesley would undertake three more visits to Penzance, all of them within a short span of one another. On Thursday, 20 August 1789, he arrived at 8:30 a.m. and proceeded to the home of William Carne (?-1836), an active and devoted Methodist, where he engaged in religious conversation. Some eighteen months earlier, on 26 January 1787, Wesley had written to Carne from London, relative to the construction of a preaching house at Penzance: "Fifty by thirty-two or thirty-four I suppose will do," suggested Wesley. "I think Biscoval House[11] is of the best form I have seen in Cornwall. I beg you will employ no lawyer to settle it when built, but transcribe the Conference Form verbatim, and observe the little Rules laid down in the Minutes.[12] You may consider whether the Preachers' house should not be two rooms of a floor and two stories high. It seems a good thought to add a week, which will ruin nobody. Certainly you ought to keep the writings in your hands, giving a bond to settle the house on Trustees when the debt is paid."[13] The discussion at Carne's home, or with Carne himself, concluded, Wesley, at 1:45 p.m. boarded his chaise for St. Just. He returned to Penzance the next day, Friday, 21 August, at or slightly prior to noon; wrote "notes"; took dinner at 1:15, followed by religious conversation, prayer, and the continued reading (begun earlier that day at St. Just) of Georg Forster's *A Voyage Round the World on His Britannic Majesty's Sloop, Resolution, Commanded by Captain James Cook [1728–1779], during the Years 1772, 1773, 1774, and 1775,* 2 vols. (London, 1777). Johann Georg Adam Forster (1754–1794), German traveler and writer, had accompanied James Cook on his voyage around the world beginning in 1772. At any rate, from 4:15 until 5:00, the Methodist leader "visited," after which he took tea and engaged in religious conversation prior to his 6:00 sermon on Romans 1:16—"For I [Paul] am not ashamed of the gospel of Christ: for it is the power of God unto salvation to every one that believeth; to the Jew first, and also to the Greek" (KJV). He then met with members of the Penzance Methodist society, prayed, ate supper at 7:45, engaged in more religious conversation and prayer, and went to bed at 9:15. Rising at 5:00 the following morning (Saturday the 22nd), Wesley prayed, wrote a letter (not published), and at 7:00 preached on Hebrews 6:1—"Therefore, leaving the principles of the doctrine of Christ, let us go on unto perfection; not laying again the foundation of repentance from dead works, and of faith toward God" (KJV). After taking tea, at 8:30 he boarded his chaise for Redruth.

Two days later, at 12:30 p.m. Monday, 24 August 1789, the Methodist patriarch came to Penzance. At 1:00, he sat for an hour for dinner and religious conversation; spent two hours writing "notes"; and drank tea and engaged in more religious conversation between 5:00 and 6:00. He then preached on Isaiah 51:6—"Lift up your eyes to the heavens, and look upon the earth beneath: for the heavens shall vanish away like smoke, and the earth shall wax old like a garment, and they that dwell therein shall die in like manner: but my salvation shall be for ever, and my righteousness shall not be abolished" (KJV). Wesley then met with the Methodist society of Penzance, partook of supper, religious conversation, and prayer, and retired for the night at his usual hour of 9:30. On Tuesday morning, the 25th, he arose at 5:00, worked on the *Arminian Magazine*, and, at 7:00, preached on Isaiah 57:1–2—"The righteous perisheth, and no man layeth it to heart: and merciful men are taken away, none considering that the righteous is taken away from the evil to come./He shall enter into peace: they shall rest in their beds, each one walking in his uprightness" (KJV). After the sermon, Wesley christened a child; drank tea; and engaged in religious conversation and prayer. At 9:30, he wrote in his diary, after which he boarded his chaise for the drive to St. Ives.[14]

Perranwell

John Wesley's sole visit to Perranwell, between three and four miles southwest of Truro, occurred on Monday, 29 June 1747, he having arrived there at approximately 6:00 a.m. An hour later he preached to "a very large congregation," and "the word was as the rain on the tender herb"— Deuteronomy 32:2—"My doctrine shall drop as the rain, my speech shall distil as the dew, as the small rain upon the tender herb, and as the showers upon the grass" (KJV) (20:180).

Polperro

Polperro, a fishing village and market town five miles east of Fowey, on the English Channel coast, functioned, in the eighteenth century, as one of the principal pilchard fisheries in Cornwall. Although Cornwall generally proved a Royalist stronghold during the Civil War of 1642–1649, a number of the residents of Polperro fought in the ranks of the Parliament Army, and upon the restoration of Charles II in 1660, they returned to the obscurity of their village homes. A segment of those former followers of Oliver Cromwell continued to live, worship, and maintain their piety as Puritans by forming their own religious society. Further, three of those persons supposedly became regular attendants of the Polperro parish church and combined their efforts to defray the cost of the Sacrament of the Lord's Supper so that they might partake of that rite more often than the parish church provided it.[1]

John Wesley came to Polperro at 2:00 p.m. Wednesday, 1 September 1762, describing the place as "a little village four hours' ride from Plymouth

Passage, surrounded with huge mountains. However, abundance of people had found their way thither. And so had Satan too. For an old, grey-headed sinner was bitterly cursing *all the Methodists* just as we came into the town. However, God gave his blessing both to us and the congregation." Six years later, on Friday, 16 September 1768, Wesley rode through heavy rain for his second and final visit to Polperro, where he encountered even a more uncomfortable condition. "Here the room over which we were to lodge being filled with pilchards and conger-eels, the perfume was too potent for me; so that I was not sorry when one of our friends invited me to lodge at her house." Further discomfort came in the form of additional heavy rain as Wesley began his sermon, but the gathering remained throughout the entire service (21:387; 22:158).

Pool

The first of Charles Wesley's three visits to Pool, a village of tin miners situated two miles northeast of Camborne, occurred on Tuesday, 10 July 1743. Immediately prior to the sermon, a drunkard attempted a bodily assault upon Wesley, at which moment the latter had "to break off my prayer and warn the fellow to take care of himself." When the besotted one tried to grab hold of Wesley, "a sinner cried, 'Down with him!' In a moment the Philistines were upon him [Judges 16:9]." Wesley tried to rescue his attacker, pleading with the "Philistines" not to hurt him, or else he [Wesley] would leave. The incident came to an end when friendly members of the gathering grabbed hold of the assailant and "taking him by the legs and arms, quietly handed him down from one to another, till they had put him without the congregation, and he was heard no more." Wesley then noted in his manuscript journal, "I published [broadcast, announced] the faithful, acceptable saying, and their hearts seemed all bowed and opened to receive it. God, I nothing doubt, will call these people who were not a people [Hosea 2:23]. Our prayers for the opposers also began to be answered, for the fiercest of them came in the evening to the room, and behaved with great decency."

More than two weeks later, on Tuesday, 26 July 1743, Charles Wesley returned to Pool, where a local church warden stopped him and demanded his "letters of orders"—the documents verifying his ordination. Wesley then produced a copy of his sermon on Ephesians 5:14, *A Sermon Preach'd on Sunday, April 4, 1742; before the University of Oxford* (London: Strahan, 1742),[1] and rode away. However, the warden and another person followed him, with the former declaring that Wesley would not preach in his parish.

When, later, Wesley did begin to preach, the churchwarden "shouted and hallooed, and put his hat to my mouth." Wesley then moved to another site to resume his sermon, but his assailant followed "like Shimei" [2 Samuel 16:5–6]. "I told him," noted Wesley, "I should surely deliver my message, unless his master was stronger than my mine." Accompanied by nearly two thousand persons (by Wesley's calculations), mostly tin miners, Wesley moved on to the next parish to continue his sermon. Finally, on 2 August 1743, Charles Wesley again appeared in Pool, but only to guide "my tinners" to the next parish (2:359, 364, 367).

Porkellis

Porkellis lay 4.5 miles north of Helston and approximately two miles from Wendron. John Wesley preached there on Wednesday, 10 September 1746, to more persons than the building could accommodate. He returned four days later (Sunday, the 14th), to preach, at a site *near* the town, to a large congregation. The Methodist leader would have preached at Porkellis on Tuesday, 31 July 1753, but, because of headaches, violent vomiting, and cramps in his feet and legs, he had to appoint someone else to perform that task. Thus, he did not preach there again until 1:00 p.m. Saturday, 17 September 1752, returning, a decade later, to deliver yet another sermon at the same hour on Tuesday, 7 September 1762. John Wesley's final preaching opportunity at Porkellis came—once more at 1:00 p.m.—on Monday, 9 September 1765 (20:139, 141, 470; 21:124, 388; 22:20).

Port Isaac

The town of Port Isaac lay due north of Trelights, in northwestern Cornwall, between Port Quin and Port Gaverne, and between Port Quin Bay and Port Isaac Bay. Although John Wesley's journal extract initially contains reference to Port Isaac in the entry for Saturday, 25 July 1747, the language of that narrative indicates a possible earlier visit. The lack of clarity derives from a gap in the journal extract for the ten-day period of 15–24 July. In any event, on the 25th, Wesley received a welcome of sorts to Port Isaac by a larger "company" than he had expected, headed by the leader of the mob that, earlier in the month, had left Edward Greenfield for dead. Greenfield (1699-?), a tin miner from St. Just, with a wife and seven children, had been converted to Methodism in c. 1742 and arrested three years later. To return to the narrative, the head of the anti–Methodist mob and his cohorts followed Wesley to the house of Richard

Scantlebury, who, supposedly, had invited the Methodist leader to lodge there—that invitation conveyed to Wesley by (perhaps) William Tucker, a native of Sithney, Cornwall, and a member of the Methodist itinerancy. After Wesley's knocking at length at Scantlebury's door and receiving no answer, the owner appeared—"an hoary, venerable old man," according to Wesley, who asked him the whereabouts of Tucker. Scantlebury pled ignorance, the two men exchanged names, and since Wesley perceived that the old man had nothing more to say, left to find another house. The mob followed him, "hallowing and shouting," but none among them laid a hand upon Wesley or threw any object at him. The aforementioned leader of the mob raised his stick as though to strike Wesley, but a companion "interposed," and the man "went quietly away." Wesley spent thirty minutes in the town, then rode on to Camelford.

Returning to Port Isaac on Monday, 19 September 1748, John Wesley preached, at 5:00 p.m. in the street to "near the whole town," no one speaking an unkind word. Although he preached during a steady rain, apparently no one left the congregation. On the following morning (20 September) he preached, at 4:00, in a room filled to capacity before he departed. Two years later, on Saturday evening, 25 August 1750, Wesley again preached in the street at Port Isaac, the preaching house unable to contain the gathering. His next visits occurred on Thursday, 9 August 1753; at 6:00 p.m. Monday evening, 15 September 1755; and on Wednesday, 31 August 1757. "This was long a barren soil," he declared, "but is at length likely to bring forth much fruit." Three years later, on Sunday morning, 7 September 1760, Wesley rode to Port Isaac to attend service at the collegiate church of St. Endellion, the rector being Mydhope Wallis. However, W. Reginald Ward speculated that William Buckingham, the curate (1759–1764), who embraced Methodist sympathies, might have actually preached the sermon. After the service, Wesley stated that he had the "satisfaction of hearing an excellent sermon," and then went on to deliver his own address at a small distance from St. Endellion to a "numerous" congregation, and later, at 5:00, to an even larger gathering at another site in the town. In examining the state of the Methodist society at Port Isaac, Wesley "found much reason to bless God on their behalf. They diligently observe all the rules of the society, with or without a preacher. They constantly attend the church and Sacrament, and meet together at the times appointed. The consequence is that thirty out of thirty-five, their whole number, continue to walk in the light of God's countenance [Psalms 89:15]."

Wesley's itinerary for Tuesday, 21 September 1762 took him to Port Isaac for a meeting of the Methodist society stewards for the eastern circuit. "What a change is wrought in one year's time!" he exclaimed. "That detestable practice of cheating the king [smuggling] is no more found in our societies. And since that accursed thing has been out away, the work of God has everywhere increased. This society, in particular, is more than doubled, and they are all alive to God." An interesting sidelight appears at this point concerning the preparation of Wesley's itinerary. From Limerick, Ireland, on 9 June 1765, he wrote an open letter to the leaders and stewards of the Methodist societies in Devonshire, Cornwall, and Bristol, informing them of his travels between 3 and 21 September 1765. Friday, 6 September 1765 would find him in Port Isaac.[1] He missed the mark by a single day! In any event, the positive conditions remained in Port Isaac when Wesley came again on Thursday, 5 September 1765, finding that he had to preach indoors because of the rain to a crowd that stood both within and outside of the building. "It was a glorious opportunity," exclaimed Wesley, "God showering down his blessing on many souls." The "blessing" continued, apparently, for the next twelve months, for when Wesley came to Port Isaac on Tuesday, 16 September 1766, he found "one of the liveliest places in Cornwall." The uncertainty of the weather caused him to speak near the preaching house, but the rain held while he preached—"except the gracious rain which God sent upon his inheritance [Psalms 68:9, BCP]." William Buckingham, the curate of St. Endellion Church, met with Wesley and informed him that he had to sever his connections with the Methodists for fear of reprisals from his bishop, Frederick Keppel (?-1777), Bishop of Exeter. Keppel, in turn, immediately removed Buckingham from his curacy. Insofar as concerned Wesley's own personal well-being, on the next day, Wednesday the 17th, he suffered a severe cut that bled "violently," which he managed to stop before he reached Launceston—his remedy being the application of a "brier-leaf," or the leaf of a wild rose.

"Port Isaac, now the liveliest place in the circuit," announced John Wesley, as he came to the town on Saturday, 27 August 1768. He then preached from a balcony in the center of the town, which caused him to recall his experience at the house of Richard Scantlebury, when the old man shut his door to Wesley once he saw the mob that had followed him there. Ironically, on this 1768 visit to Port Isaac, Wesley lodged in the very house once occupied by Scantlebury, that man "being gone to his fathers." Wesley's host and at that time the proprietor of the house, Richard Wood, a Port Isaac merchant, belonged to the Methodist society in that town. During this visit, Wesley wrote a lengthy letter to Lawrence Coughlan (?-1785), an Irish Methodist itinerant preacher and, reportedly, a converted Roman Catholic. Wesley maintained that Coughlan possessed no learning at all and had him removed from the Methodist connexion in 1764 when the Greek bishop Erasmus ordained him. Coughlan managed another ordination in 1765 from Richard Terrick, Bishop of London, after which he and his wife served (1776–1773) the Society for the Propagation of the Gospel in Newfoundland. Nonetheless, Wesley and Coughlan maintained their friendship and correspondence. Coughlan died in the Methodist leader's presence, having been seized with a paralytic stroke while the two conversed in the Irish minister's study. In that letter of (or about) 27 August 1768, Wesley underscored the point that "I told you it was love: the love of God and our neighbor; the image of God stamped on the heart, the life of God in the soul of man, the mind that was in Christ, enabling us to walk as Christ also walked."[2]

Wesley paused briefly at Port Isaac on Tuesday, 21 August 1770; one day in the week of 24 August 1773; and Wednesday, 7 September 1774. On Friday evening, 16 August 1776, he preached in Richard Wood's yard "to most of the inhabitants of the town," recognizing the "spirit ... that seemed to move upon every heart. And we had all a good hope that the days of faintness and weariness are over and that the work of God will revive and flourish." He would come again to Port Isaac on Monday, 28 August 1780; Monday, 2 September 1782; and Monday, 29 August 1785— on which occasion he arrived at 2:00 p.m. sat for dinner, wrote letters, and attended to prayer. At 6:00 he preached on Hebrews 2:3, after which he met with the Methodist society, ate supper, attended to "necessary business," prayed, and retired at 9:15. Arising at his usual hour of 4:00 a.m. on Tuesday the 30th, Wesley prayed, preached on Luke 20:34, wrote more letters, took tea at 7:30, engaged in religious conversation, wrote another letter, worked on the *Arminian Magazine*, and at 11:00 a.m. boarded his chaise (destination not indicated; he might even have remained in and around Port Isaac, visiting various persons).

On Thursday evening, 27 August 1789, eighty-six-year-old John Wesley preached in "an open part" of Port Isaac to "almost all" of the inhabitants of the town. "How changed," he remarked, on this his final visit to the town, "when he [Richard Scantlebury] that invited me durst not take me in for fear his house should be pulled down!" The Methodist patriarch had arrived in Port Isaac at 12:45 p.m. read until 1:15; sat down to dinner; engaged in religious conversation; wrote letters from 2:30 until 4:30; drank tea; and engaged in more religious conversation and prayer. At 6:00 he preached on Hebrews 10:31, after which he led prayers, ate supper at 7:30, engaged in still more religious conversation and prayer, and retired at 9:15. Arising at 4:00 on Friday morning, the 28th, Wesley led prayers, preached on Hebrews 2:1, took tea, engaged in religious conversation and prayer, and boarded his chaise for Camelford at 6:15 a.m.[3]

Redruth

Two historical landmarks near the eighteenth-century market town of Redruth, in south-central Cornwall, northeast of Camborne and south-west of Truro, deserve mention: (1) Carn Brae, 2.5 miles southwest of the town, comprised an Iron Age defensive hill fort of thirty-six acres, with ramparts to the north and south. Its interior houses the foundations of a number of Iron Age huts, as well as the remains of guard chambers; (2) the two-hundred-year-old Tolgus tin streaming mill, one mile to the north, operated from c. 1730 until 1928 and functioned for the separation of tin from ore mostly extracted from the wastes deposited by larger mills up river. The largest part of the machinery dates from the nineteenth century, although the operation of the mill began in the century previous. What remains provides an excellent introduction to the technological history of the Cornish tin industry.[1]

For Daniel Defoe's commercial eye and mind, Redruth, at the end of the seventeenth century, proved to have been of "no consideration," and thus nothing will be gained from the page of his *Tour*.[2] One detail concerning the eighteenth-century commercial history of Redruth might deserve consideration, however: In 1766, a party of unemployed and underpaid tin miners at Redruth combined their numbers and rioted against farmers, forcing them to lower their prices for corn, barley, butter, and potatoes.[3]

Unfortunately, the fragmentary state of Charles Wesley's manuscript journal does not allow for an accurate chronicle of his visits to that town. Thus, he could only comment, concerning his initial visit to Redruth, on Friday, 15 July 1743, that "I left it at four [p.m.]." He provided a bit more substance eight days later (Friday, 23 July) at Gwennap when, according to his usually inflated figures, he addressed a throng of two thousand souls, half of them "tinners from about Redruth, which, I hear is *taken*. God has given us their hearts." Further comment from Charles Wesley relative to Redruth came on Sunday, 6 July 1746, when he noted in his journal that "Redruth ... seems on the point of surrendering to the Prince of Peace." However, on Sunday, 20 July 1746, he "crossed the country to Redruth" and walked a mile through the town to the church, being "surprised by the general civility." Followed by "a congregation," he proceeded to an open field and addressed a gathering of "more than 8,000" (!) on the subject of the Good Samaritan (Luke 10:29–37). "Surely he has a multitude of patients here," he exclaimed. Finally, Wesley attended services at Redruth church on Saturday evening, 2 August 1746, following which he rode off to Gwennap (2:357, 362, 465, 467, 471).

John Wesley had intended an initial visit to Redruth on Thursday, 29 June 1745, but that item on his itinerary had to be canceled because of the impressment of Thomas Maxfield.[4] Therefore, the Methodist leader's first *recorded* visit to Redruth did not come about until Saturday, 4 July 1747, when he preached in the street before a large and attentive gathering. "Indeed," he remarked, "there are now scarce any in the town (but gentlemen) who are not convinced of the truth." On Sunday morning, 12 August 1750, Wesley attended services at Redruth church, where the rector, John Collins (1708?-1775), who served there from 1734 until his death and had known both Wesleys while at Oxford University, delivered "an exceeding useful sermon ... upon the General Judgment [the Last Judgment on humankind after the resurrection of the dead; God's final sentence on humanity]. At 1:00 p.m. Wesley preached in the street "to thrice as many" as the preaching house would have contained. Afterward, he visited with a poor old woman who lived a mile from the town. "Her trials had been uncommon; inexpressible agonies of mind, joined with all sorts of bodily pain, not (it seemed) from any natural cause, but the direct operation of Satan. Her joys were now as uncommon; she had little time to sleep, having for several months last past seen as it were the unclouded face of God, and praised him day and night." Wesley returned to Redruth to preach at noon, Tuesday, 10 September 1751, and again on Sunday afternoon, 5 August 1753, preaching to a "large" gathering in an open part of the street. Although he experienced problems with his voice, the day proved calm and, apparently, all could hear him. He wrote, "I felt myself considerably stronger than I was when I began."

At 5:00 p.m. Saturday, 30 August 1755, John Wesley, extremely tired from a full day of preaching and traveling, found a congregation awaiting him in a "broad, convenient" part of the street in Redruth. Apparently, his friends there, so pleased to see him, neglected to offer him food or drink. However, the Methodist leader's weariness vanished when he began his sermon, which prompted him to conclude that "surely God is in this place [Genesis 28:16]." Two weeks later, at 10:00 Sunday morning, 14 September, he again attended Redruth church, where he noticed a young gentlewoman in the next pew laughing and talking. Then, during the reading of the Confession, she appeared "very uneasy," uttered several screams, dropped down, and had to be carried from the church. Wesley offered no comment upon the incident, remarking only that the Rev. John Collins read prayers "admirably well" and preached "an excellent sermon" on 1 Peter 2:21. Later, Wesley preached on "faith, hope, and love," expressing surprise at the behavior of those who had gathered to listen to him. "At length," he declared, "God seems to be moving on all their hearts."

Before proceeding further with the narrative, one needs to recall that in May 1756, Britain had declared war on France, and in August 1756, Frederick the Great had attacked Saxony, thus beginning the Seven Years War (1756–1763). With that in mind, John Wesley arrived in Redruth on Saturday evening, 17 September 1757. At 8:00 the following morning (Sunday the 18th), he reported that a number of French military prisoners had joined with those who usually gathered to hear him speak, with more in attendance at 1:00. He learned, later, that several days previously, "some hundred" English soldiers who had been imprisoned in France had been landed at Penzance, and a number of them had passed through Redruth on the way to their homes—"but in a most forlorn condition." At Redruth, the French prisoners extended to those men extreme compassion for their states, giving them food, clothes, and even money, telling them, "We wish we could do more. But we have little for ourselves here." Apparently, according to what Wesley heard, several French soldiers who possessed but two shirts gave naked English counterparts one.

Three years later, the Methodist leader again preached in the main street of Redruth—on Saturday evening, 20 September 1760—before a calm gathering of both rich and poor. "So is the roughest become one of the quietest towns in England," observed Wesley. He went to the same site at 8:00 on the following morning (Sunday the 21st). At Redruth church, young Rev. Samuel Cooper (1736-?), curate of Cubert (1759–1760), preached at both morning and afternoon services and "strongly confirmed" what Wesley had spoken. At 1:00 p.m. "the day being mild and calm," Wesley spoke before a large congregation. Back again, on the same street and at the same time, on Sunday, 5 September 1762, Wesley found the people of Redruth, both the affluent and the poor, equally attentive to his message, and he returned to that town on Saturday, the 18th. Three years later, Sunday, 8 September 1785, he again spoke to his congregation at 1:00 p.m. on the street in Redruth, and later that day listened to an emotional story of spiritual transformation from Grace Paddy (?-1767), a member of the Redruth Methodist society and described as a well-bred and sensible young woman. Essentially, she had traveled the path of one "convinced of sin, converted to God, and renewed in love within twelve hours! Yet it is by no means incredible," proclaimed Wesley, "seeing one day is with God as a thousand years [2 Peter 3:8]." Grace Paddy married William Terril on 8 September 1766, and died eight months later, with burial in Redruth on 18 May 1767. Wesley remained in Redruth throughout Monday morning, 9 May, preaching at 5:00 before a capacity crowd in the preaching house and exclaiming, "How is this town changed! Some years since, a Methodist preacher could not ride safely through it. Now high and low, few excepted, say, 'Blessed is he that cometh in the name of the Lord!'" [Psalms 18:26; Matthew 23:39]. A week later, Monday, 16 September, the Methodists of the area held their Quarterly Meeting at Redruth, "and it appeared," asserted Wesley, "by the accounts from all parts that the flame which was kindled[5] the last year, though abated, is not extinguished." At 6:00, Wesley began his service on the steps of the market house before a large gathering, and in the middle of the opening hymn, the Rev. John Collins, rector of Redruth church, interrupted and began to read "the Act against riots"— the Parliamentary statute passed in 1715 arising during the first Jacobite rebellion and declaring that if twelve persons continued for one hour following a proclamation bidding them to disperse had been issued to them by local magistrates, they stood guilty of a felony. Obviously upset, Wesley addressed Collins: "I did not expect this from *you*; I really thought you had more understanding." Collins did not respond, "but stood like one astonished, neither moving hand nor foot." Wesley and his congregation removed themselves "two or three hundred yards" from the site and "quietly" completed his discourse. A year later, Saturday evening, 13 September 1766, Wesley confronted a different problem at Redruth—the weather. The preaching house proved too small to contain the crowd, but exceedingly high winds, combined with frequent and heavy rain, created a dilemma. Nonetheless, Wesley selected "the most convenient" part of the street and managed to deliver his sermon, interrupted but by a single short shower. Returning the next afternoon (Sunday, the 14th) at 1:00, he stood before one of the largest congregations he had ever seen in that town.

At Redruth on Tuesday, 20 August 1768, Wesley found people from all parts of the area who had come to listen to him, "and God gave a loud call to the backsliders." There had arisen a need to call upon the Deity, for when Wesley transferred the itinerant preacher Thomas Rankin (1738–1810) from the Cornwall circuit to Epworth, Lincolnshire, in 1766, the latter had left behind between three and four hundred members in the Redruth Methodist society. Now, two years later, Wesley found but 110 persons in that organization. He returned to Redruth on Saturday, 2 September 1769, to participate in the Quarterly Meeting, and that evening he preached to "eleven or twelve hundred people. But there was no trifler, much less mocker, among them. They heard as for eternity" [Job 17:2, Jeremiah 15:17]. On the next day (Sunday the 3rd) he sat among a large congregation at Redruth church and heard a "useful" sermon, after which, between 1:00 and 2:00 p.m. he preached to "some thousands in the main street." Wesley preached again at Redruth on Tuesday, 21 August 1770; on Saturday, 21 August 1773; Sunday afternoon, 22 August 1773; Wednesday evening, 31 August 1774; and Saturday, 3 September 1774—that being the time of the Quarterly Meeting. "This is frequently a dull, heavy meeting," admitted Wesley, "but it was so lively an one today that we hardly knew how to part." He came back to the town the next day, Sunday the 4th, to preach in the street, the weather having turned from rain to fair skies. One year later, Saturday, 2 September 1775, he preached, as usual, in the main street of Redruth, his sermon text based upon Psalms 144:15 (BCP), returning on Sunday (the 5th) at 11:00 a.m.

On horseback from St. Agnes to Redruth on Sunday, 18 August 1776, Wesley encountered heavy rain that saturated his clothes and added to his fatigue as he entered the town. However, after sleeping for fifteen minutes, "all my weariness was gone." Wesley spent the next day (Monday, the 19th) at Redruth, attending to organizational issues, beginning with reuniting the *select society*, whose members had been "flying asunder, though they all acknowledge the loss they have sustained thereby." The *select* Methodist societies had been formed by John Wesley at London in 1743 to advise "all those who ... continued in the light of God's countenance, which the rest of their brethren did not want, and probably could not receive. So I desired a small number of such as appeared to be in this state to spend an hour with me every Monday morning ... not only to direct them ... to *press after perfection*; to exercise their every grace, and improve every talent they had received; and to incite them to love one another more, and to watch more carefully after each other; but also to have a *select company* to whom I might unbosom myself on all occasions, without reserve, and whom I could propose to all their brethren as a pattern of love, of holiness, and of all good works."[6] At 11:00 a.m., Wesley met with fifty or sixty children, which brought to mind an obvious question—"How much depends upon these? All the hope of the rising generation."

At noon on Saturday, 23 August 1777, the Methodist leader again preached at Redruth, as well as on Tuesday, 25 August 1778; then he attended the Quarterly Meeting on Saturday, 26 August 1780, "where all was love and harmony." Another Quarterly Meeting convened at Redruth on Saturday, 1 September 1781, after which Wesley preached in the market place on Ephesians 2:8. A year later, Saturday, 31 August 1782, he preached that evening and again at noon on Sunday, 1 September. Three years later, at 2:00 p.m. Saturday, 27 August 1785, the stewards (trustees, leaders) of the forty-five Methodist societies in the Redruth circuit met at Redruth, representing a membership of 2,517—an average of fifty-six persons for each society. The meeting combined matters of business and spiritual concerns, and, as W. Reginald Ward noted, records of that gathering "cast interesting light on the cost of itinerancy." Each preacher received £3. 3s. per quarter; house rent came to £3. 2.s. 3d. for three quarters; horseshoeing at Redruth cost £5. 16s., and horses and a driver for John Wesley amounted to £5. 0s. 6d. From a spiritual perspective, Wesley noted that "nothing but peace and love [existed] among them [the stewards] and among the societies from whence they came, and yet no great increase!" That evening, during a love-feast,[7] several of "our friends declared how God had saved them from inbred sin, with such exactness both of sentiment and language as clearly showed they were taught of God." Returning to the open street at Redruth between 1:00 and 2:00 p.m. the following day, Sunday, the 28th, the aged Methodist patriarch preached on Luke 10:42 to "thousands upon thousands [?]. And my strength was as my need. Yet I was afraid, lest I should not be able to make all those hear that assembled in the evening. But though it was supposed there were two or three thousand more than ever were there before, yet they heard (I was afterwards informed) to the very skirts of the congregation."[8]

Of particular interest, one should note that on 1 November 1786, Wesley received a letter from Francis Wrigley, a native of Cork, Ireland, and one of Wesley's long-time itinerant preachers, who wrote to the Methodist patriarch from Penryhn, providing a detailed account of the revival in Redruth and the surrounding neighborhood. That prompted Wesley's response from London on 26 November 1786, beginning, "Now is the very time wherein you should earnestly exhort the believers to go on to perfection [Hebrews 6:1]. Those of them that hunger and thirst after righteousness [Ezekiel 5:6] will keep their ground; the others will lose what God has wrought [Numbers 23:23]."

Two years passed before Wesley once more preached in Redruth, between 1:00 and 2:00, Sunday afternoon, 9 September 1787, in the market place. He claimed to have addressed the largest congregation that he had seen there, with a number of people sitting on the rooftops. Two months following that visit, Wesley received word from an itinerant preacher, Benjamin Rhodes (1743–1815), then in his first year in Cornwall (he would serve there from 1788 to 1791). Wesley wrote to him from London on 6 November 1788, acknowledging that "it has been observed for many years that some at Redruth were apt to *despise* and very willing to *govern* their preachers. But I commend you for standing in your place, and changing both general and particular stewards." Nine months later, Wesley would ascend the steps of the Redruth market house at 6:00 p.m. Saturday, 22 August 1789. "The word seemed to sink deep into every heart," he claimed. During that visit, Wesley lodged in the home of Andrew Harper, a cooper (maker and repairer of casks and barrels) and a shopkeeper at Redruth, and a member of the Methodist society. Wesley preached there again the next morning (Sunday the 23rd), and once more on Wednesday, 26 August, on 2 Corinthians 5:19. Meeting with the Methodist society, he explained the nature and rise of Methodism. "I have never read or heard of, either in ancient or modern history" he added, "any other church which builds on so broad a foundation as the Methodists do; which requires of its members no conformity either in *opinions* or *modes* of worship, but barely this one thing, to 'fear God and work righteousness' [Ephesians 5:14]." That proved to have been his final appearance at Redruth.[9]

Roche

The journal extract of John Wesley reveals only a single visit to Roche, a village than lay 4.5 miles north of St. Austell and seven miles southwest of Bodmin. On Wednesday, 14 September 1768, he drove there and spent a "comfortable" visit with his "old acquaintance" Samuel Furly (1722–1795), the evangelical vicar of Roche, from 1765 until his death (22:158). Although Furley and John Wesley differed on certain theological issues (the doctrine of assurance being one), the two became and remained close friends—that connection beginning in late 1743 or early 1754, while Furley still pursued his undergraduate studies at Queens' College, Cambridge. The voluminous correspondence between the two began at that time, also.

Rosemergy

The far southwestern Cornish hamlet of Rosemergy would have been found, in the eighteenth century, 1.5 miles from Zennor and fairly close to Morvah. A miner by the name of John Daniel held a small plot of land there, and when he went off to Bristol in 1744, his wife, Alice Daniel, added two rooms to their cottage to host the early Methodist itinerant preachers (including John Wesley). Wesley's sole visit to Rosemergy came on Satur-day, 7 April 1744, when he rode through hard wind and heavy rain, to be met by "some of our brethren." Wesley learned of their concern, "occasioned by the confident assertions of some that they had seen Mr. Wesley a week or two ago with the Pretender [Charles Edward Stuart (1729–1788), "the Young Pretender"] in France; and others, that he was in prison in London. Yet the main body still stood firm together and were not removed from the hope of the gospel" (20:22, 23).

Rosewarne

Rosewarne has been identified as the home of a local Methodist, a Mr. Harris, located outside of the town of Camborne and that functioned, on occasion, as a Methodist preaching house (20:40).

St. Agnes

John Wesley's initial visit to St. Agnes, a market town and parish 8.5 miles northwest of Truro, occurred on Sunday, 5 July 1747. At 2:00 p.m. he preached to "a large multitude of quiet hearers," a number of whom appeared "deeply affected." However, soon after he had completed his discourse, a group among them began to throw dirt and clumps of earth at Wesley and his companions. The horse of William Shepherd—the Yorkshire stonemason and itinerant preacher—became frightened from that disruption and leaped over one of the throwers as he bent down to grab more dirt. The man screamed but arose unhurt, and he and his companions engaged in throwing stones after the horse. Unaware of the disruption, Wesley later rode through the midst of the unruly ones, and "none lifted up a hand or opened his mouth." The Methodist leader preached again at St. Agnes at 1:00 p.m. Tuesday, 20 September 1748, and two years later on Friday evening, 24 August 1750, when he addressed "a multitude, not of curious hearers, but of men that had 'tasted of the good word' [Hebrews 6:5]." One more opportunity came about on Tuesday evening, 24 July 1753.

At 5:00 p.m. Sunday, 14 September 1755, John Wesley preached at St. Agnes, "where all received the truth in love, except two or three, who soon walked away." During his next visit to that town, on Friday, 2 September 1757, he learned that "the great man," Joseph Donnithorne (?-1757), a member of the St. Agnes Methodist society, had died. Wesley, following the sermon, responded to an invitation from Donnithorne's mother and sister to come to their house, and there he found himself "received into a comfortable lodging with the most free and cordial affection. So in this place," he observed, "the knowledge of God has already travelled, 'from the least unto the greatest' [Acts 8:10]." The next day (Saturday the 2nd), Wesley heard an account of the earthquake that had struck St. Agnes on 15 July of that year. It began with a rumbling noise beneath the ground, "hoarser and deeper than common thunder," followed by common thunder and a trembling of the earth, which waved back and forth violently once or twice. On that morning, Wesley also spoke with "old" Mrs. Donnithorne, who possessed command of all her senses, read without spectacles, walked without a staff, and, at age ninety, evidenced "scarce a wrinkle." More importantly, observed Wesley, "she is teachable as a child and groaning for salvation." Later that afternoon, he conversed with the Rev. James Vowler (1728?-1758), curate of St. Agnes parish, "who rejoices in the love of God and both preaches and lives the gospel." On Sunday the 4th, one of Wesley's itinerant preachers, John Turnough, who served various Methodist circuits from 1755 to c. 1763, preached at 5:00 a.m., to which the Methodist leader responded, "I could scarce have believed it if I had not heard it, that few men of learning *write* so correctly as an unlearned tinner speaks *extempore.*" In addition, Wesley heard James Vowler preach two "thundering" sermons at church "as I have scarce heard these twenty years. O how gracious God is [2 Chronicles 30:9; Jonah 4:2] to the poor sinners of St. Agnes! In the church and out of the church, they hear the same great truths of the wrath of God against sin and his love to those that are in Christ Jesus [1 Corinthians 16:24; 1 Timothy 1:14; 2 Timothy 1:13]."

Wesley's next visit to St. Agnes came on Monday evening, 8 September 1760, and he preached there again at 5:00 on the following morning (the 9th). Afterward, he examined the Methodist society at St. Agnes, disturbed to discover that of the ninety-eight members, all but three or four had neglected the rite of the Lord's Supper. "I told them my thoughts very plain," wrote Wesley; "they seemed convinced, and promised no more to give place to the devil" [Ephesians 4:27]. On Wednesday, 10 September, he engaged in an extensive conversation with William Philp (1727?-1762), who had succeeded James Vowler (who had died of fever in 1758) as curate of St. Agnes. Wesley identified Philp as "a man of an humble, loving, tender spirit. Between him on the one hand and the Methodists on the other, most in the parish are now awakened. Let but our brethren have 'zeal according to knowledge' [Romans 10:2], and few will escape them both."

On Saturday evening, 18 September 1762, Wesley returned to St. Agnes. He preached at 8:00 on Sunday morning, the 19th, and afterward listened to an "excellent" sermon by James Walker (1712?-1794), vicar of Perranzabuloe and St. Agnes (1739–1793), as well as of Lanlivery (1752–1793). Walker announced his intention to preach, that afternoon, a funeral service for his late curate, William Philp, "a man eminently humble, serious, and zealous for God [Numbers 25:13; Acts 22:3]. He was snatched away by a fever three weeks since, as was his successor, Mr. Vowler, three or four years before—another upright, zealous servant of God, and indefatigable in his labour. How strange a providence is this!" exclaimed Wesley. "Who can account for it? Did the God of love take them away that they might not out of zeal for him continue to oppose their fellow-labourers in the gospel?" In his "strong and pathetic" sermon—"well wrote and well pronounced," commented Wesley—the Rev. Walker extended to Philp due praise, concluding with, "God grant *me* (and I believe you will join in the petition) like him to live, like him to die." As the service came to a close, the rain began to fall, bringing with it exceedingly high winds. Wesley had intended to execute his sermon in the Methodist preaching house, but the gathering proved too large. Because of the weather, he could not preach atop a nearby hill, so he removed to the bottom of it, being sheltered somewhat from the winds. Fortunately, the rain ceased before he had finished. In his discourse, Wesley "particularly advised all that feared God to confirm their love to each other, and to provoke each other, not to doubtful disputations, but to love and to good works."

The next visit to St. Agnes by John Wesley occurred at 8:00 a.m., Sunday, 8 September 1765—a date that had been determined three months earlier. On 9 June 1765, from Limerick, Ireland, Wesley sent an open letter to Methodist society leaders and stewards, stating, "I shall have little time to spare this autumn; yet I will endeavor (with God's leave) to spend a few days in Cornwall. I hope to be ... on Sunday morning and afternoon [8 September 1765] at St. Agnes." Given the inconsistencies of weather, road conditions, and the susceptibility of the human body to all manner of misfortunes, one stands in awe of Wesley's ability to meet the commitments of his travel schedule. In any event, the Methodist leader followed with another stop at St. Agnes, again to preach at 8:00 a.m., on Sunday, 14 September 1766. Two years later, on Tuesday, 30 August 1768, he found a "large" congregation at St. Agnes, returning there to preach at 9:00 a.m., Sunday, 11 September, and later between 1:00 and 2:00 p.m. On Thursday, 23 August 1770, Wesley preached at St. Agnes, as well as on Sunday, 23 August 1773; on a rainy Sunday morning, 4 September 1774; at 8:00 a.m., 3 September 1775 on Acts 16:31; in the Methodist preaching house, because of the rain, on Sunday, 18 August 1776; Sunday morning, 31 August 1777; and, finally, at 8:30 a.m., Sunday, 28 August 1785, preaching "to the largest congregation I ever saw there" on Matthew 8:13, and again at 1:30 p.m. on Matthew 22:21.[1]

St. Austell

St. Austell, "a neat little town," according to John Wesley, lay in east-central Cornwall, three miles west of the English Channel and twenty-eight miles west of Plymouth, Devonshire. At 5:00 a.m., Friday, 29 August 1755, Wesley preached there to more persons than the room in the Methodist preaching house could contain, and when he returned there on Saturday, 24 September 1757, he held forth at 6:00 p.m. on the side of "a fruitful" hill. The next day, Sunday the 25th, the Methodist leaders attended church service conducted by the Rev. Stephen Hewgoe (1666?–1758), who had been the vicar of St. Austell, according to Wesley, for between sixty and seventy years. "O what might a man full of faith and zeal," mused Wesley, "have done for God in such a course of time!" Five years passed before Wesley thought to include St. Austell upon his itinerary, preaching there on Thursday evening, 2 September 1762. He waited another six years, Wednesday, 14 September 1768, before his next visit, but arrived there the following year near noon on Monday, 4 September 1769, preaching in Lower Street to a "very numerous and very serious congregation." At 6:00 p.m. Monday, 3 September 1770, Wesley stood "at the head of the street" and exhorted before "a large and quiet congregation" upon Matthew 4:10. His next visit came on Monday evening, 16 August 1773, followed by another stay on Wednesday, 28 August 1776, when the rain forced him into the preaching house and where, he believed, "some of the stout-hearted [Psalms 76:5; Isaiah 46:12] trembled [1 Samuel 28:5]."

Again in the main street of St. Austell, Wesley, on Monday, 21 August 1780, preached before "a large and very quiet congregation," and a year later, on Monday, 27 August 1781, after having traveled over a road "ready to break our wheels to pieces." Once there, he delivered his discourse, and "God greatly comforted the hearts of his people." He preached at St. Austell on Thursday, 22 August 1782. Prior to his next visit, Wesley had to confront a serious theological issue that had arisen in St. Austell. Writing from London on 11 June 1785, he instructed Francis Wrigley,[1] "You that are on the spot are the best judge concerning William Ellis"—then on the Methodist itinerancy in the Cornwall West circuit. I refer it wholly to you whether he should preach or no till I come to Cornwall myself. You cannot suffer [allow] any one to preach either at St. Austell or elsewhere that is tainted with Calvinism or Antinomianism [the notion of Christians, by grace, having been set free from the need of observing any form of moral law]. 'Tis far easier to prevent the plague than to cure it." When Wesley arrived at St. Austell on Monday, 22 August 1785 to preach on Galatians 6:15, he offered no further comment on that issue.

On Monday, 10 September 1787, the Methodist leader preached in the still uncompleted preaching house on 2 Corinthians 5:19 to "a crowded audience who seemed all sensible that God was there." At some point in late 1784, George Flamank, then a resident of Fore Street, St. Austell, had donated the site for the new preaching house, for on 2 February 1785, from London, John Wesley wrote to young Adam Clarke (1762–1832), then serving the Methodist itinerancy in the Cornwall East circuit: "If you build at St. Austell, take care that you do not make the house too small." Also, on 26 January 1787, in writing from London to William Carne, then stationed in the Penzance circuit, Wesley added a postscript to the effect that "St. Austell is on the list of 'houses to be built' in the *Minutes* [of the Methodist Conference] of 1786." However, on the day following, Tuesday the 11th, Wesley preached at 5:00 a.m. on Hebrews 13:22, preferring the "well filled" *old* preaching house. Apparently, the new house failed to solve the inadequate accommodations at St. Austell, for when Wesley arrived there "by dinner time," 1:45 p.m. on Monday, 17 August 1789—his final recorded visit to the town—he remarked, "I knew not where to preach, the street being so dirty and the preaching house so small." He then determined "to squeeze as many as we could into the preaching house, and truly God was there."[2]

St. Buryan

Located approximately 5.5 miles southwest of Penzance, St. Buryan witnessed the arrival of John Wesley on Sunday, 7 September 1766, when he worshipped at the local church. Following the conclusion of the service, he began to preach near the churchyard to "a numerous congregation." However, Wesley immediately observed "a gentleman" confronting him, shaking his whip violently, and attempting to speak—being unable to do so intelligibly because of his temper. After walking a bit, back and forth, the man simply mounted his horse and rode away. The Methodist leader did not appear for his second and final visit to St. Buryan until sixteen years later, at 2:00 p.m. Sunday, 15 August 1782. There, without incident, he preached to a "large" gathering (22:60; 23:250).

St. Cleer

John Wesley preached but once at St. Cleer, a parish town situated two and three-quarters miles north of Liskeard, on Saturday afternoon,

14 September 1751, returning there ten days later (Tuesday the 24th). He discovered that the Methodist preaching house would not contain even half of the people who had gathered to hear him, so he stood on the porch of that building, allowing those both inside and outside to hear him. "A solemn awe" converged "upon the whole assembly," he recorded (20:402).

St. Columb Major

The parish town of St. Columb Major, in central Cornwall, lay approximately twenty miles southwest of Bodmin, twelve miles from St. Ewe, and approximately five miles east of the Bristol Channel coast. Riding from Gwennap for three hours in bright moonlight, John Wesley arrived at St. Columb at 9:00 p.m. Sunday, 14 September 1746, but recorded nothing in the way of his activities there. Fourteen years later, Monday, 8 September 1760, Wesley intended to lodge at an inn in St. Columb, but a "gentleman" followed him there and conveyed him to his house, where he found three or four more individuals "as friendly as himself." W. Reginald Ward speculated the "gentleman" to have been William Rawlings, a friend of the evangelical vicar of Truro, Samuel Walker, and a merchant of St. Columb. Rawlings would move to Padstow, Cornwall, in 1770.

Wesley waited another six years before returning to St. Columb, arriving on Tuesday morning, 16 September 1766, having been "desired to break the ice here." He began to preach in the yard of "a gentleman," adjoining the main street, having chosen that site as "neither too public nor too private." Although concerned that the larger portion of the hearers understood little of what he said, he did extend to the audience credit for having behaved with seriousness and proper manners. When Wesley next came to St. Columb on Monday, 29 August 1768, he intended to preach there, but upon failing to find a site agreeable to him, he prepared to leave. When an unidentified person offered him his meadow close to the town, a crowd quickly gathered there, to whom Wesley "explained the nature and pleasantness of religion. I have seldom seen a people behave so well the first time I have preached to them," he noted. Not until Thursday morning, 27 August 1789 did Wesley return to St. Columb Major, but his diary entry for that date contains nothing to reveal the activities of his brief stay. Indeed, the journal extract does not even indicate the presence of Wesley at St. Columb on that day.[1]

St. Ewe

St. Ewe proved to have been a parish town with ample supplies of tin and copper, situated five miles west of St. Austell. A portion of John Wesley's journal extract entry for Monday, 26 September 1748, reads, "About four [p.m.] I came to ————, examined the leaders of the [Methodist] classes[1] for two hours, preached to the largest congregation I had seen in Cornwall,[2] met the [Methodist] society and earnestly charged them to 'beware of covetousness' [Luke 12:15]. All this time I was not asked either to eat or drink. After the society, some bread and cheese were set before me. I think verily ———— will not be ruined by entertaining me once a year!" The preceding paragraph had been omitted from the 1774 edition and beyond of John Wesley's *Works,* Nehemiah Curnock suggesting that the omissions occurring during Wesley's lifetime came about "because of a desire to avoid offence." W. Reginald Ward speculated that St. Ewe would have been the location in question—although he never cited evidence to support that, nor did he connect his reasoning with that of Curnock.[3]

John Wesley did identify the town of St. Ewe in his journal extract after he had visited there on Tuesday, 7 August 1750. "There was much struggling here at first," he noted, "but the two gentlemen [unidentified by name] who occasioned it are now removed, one to London, the other into eternity." He preached there on Tuesday, 7 August 1753, and again on Thursday evening, 28 August 1755, when he claimed that one or two persons "felt the edge of God's sword and sunk to the ground. And indeed it seemed as if God would suffer none to escape him, as if he both heard and answered our prayer, 'Dart into the melting flame/Of love, and make the mountains flow.'"[4] Wesley's final recorded visit to St. Ewe came on Wednesday evening, 21 September 1757, when he preached before a "large congregation," a number of whom had come from a distance, and "they did not come in vain. The flame of love ran from heart to heart, and scarce any remained unmoved" (20:250 + note, 355, 471; 21:25, 126).

St. Gennys

Eighteenth-century St. Gennys, in northwestern Cornwall, has been described as a bleak, windswept village ten miles north of Camelford, on the summit of the cliffs overlooking the Atlantic Ocean. In 1727, a former vicar there described the vicarage in a sad state of repair, having been constructed of stone, mud, and rags, containing six rooms and a large entry. One of the rooms revealed a deal floor,[1] but none of the rooms appeared to have been wainscoted[2] or ceiled (having lined the roof, or the walls of a room,. with woodwork or plaster). Thus, the Rev. George Thomson, appointed vicar of St. Gennys in early September 1732, rebuilt the house, a project that he began in 1734. A decade later, the population of St. Gennys stood at eighty families, none of whom belonged to a Dissenting sect. The usual number of communicants averaged approximately seventy, but upon one Whit-Sunday, the attendance had risen to 103. The church offered five Sacramental services per year. George Thomson reported, "I preach constantly every Lord's Day, twice when on the spot and often on other days when I can get my people together.... In Lent, I catechise all that are sent. But alas! few come." By 1771, a considerable decline in the population of St. Gennys had occurred, the number of families there having decreased from eighty to fifty, and thus occurred a corresponding reduction in the number of communicants. The aged Thomson continued to catechize the young people in the summer months, but he also admitted the existence of a number of Dissenters from the Church, although those persons had not yet constructed their own meeting-house. In 1779, the average number of communicants at St. Gennys had declined to forty; the summer catechizing of children continued—whenever the youngsters could be persuaded to attend. In a word, even the scattered and fragmented statistics relative to St. Gennys mirrored the gradual and uniform decline in religious observance of the Church of England in Cornwall during the second half of the eighteenth century—a portion of it the result of the Wesleys' and their itinerants' evangelical efforts.[3]

On Sunday, 15 July 1744, the Rev. John Bennet (1670?-1750)[4] guided Charles Wesley and his traveling companion, John Slocombe,[5] from Sticklepath, Devonshire, to St. Gennys, there to be met by "our loving brother," the Rev. George Thomson (1698–1782), vicar of St. Gennys since 1732. Wesley preached from St. Gennys church on Isaiah 40:1 and later on Mark 10:46–52. "The word took place in some hearts, I cannot doubt," he noted, "though I am nothing [1 Corinthians 13:2]." Returning to the town on Wednesday, 8 August 1744, Charles Wesley read prayers and preached, noticing a "neighbouring" clergyman in the pews—a contemporary of his at Christ Church, Oxford, unidentified by name, "who came in much love to invite me to his house." Wesley's last visit to St. Gennys—"recorded" in the fragments of his manuscript journal—came on Sunday, 24 August 1746, when he preached there morning and evening, but "not my own words" (2:408, 416, 472). Could he have read a sermon written by brother John Wesley?—a practice associated with him on more than one occasion.

John Wesley first reached St. Gennys on Sunday morning, 16 June

1745, finding the church there "moderately filled with serious hearers, but few of them appeared to *feel* what they heard." He preached both morning and afternoon, as well as on Monday evening, the 17th. "Many *assented* to and *approved* of the truth," he noted. Wesley preached in the town again on Sunday evening, 26 July 1747, and returned on Sunday, September 1748. On the latter occasion, John Bennet read prayers and Wesley preached on Mark 12:34, after which he questioned whether "there were more than two persons in the congregation who did not take it to themselves." The Rev. George Thomson's mother and the Rev. John Bennet found themselves in tears during the major portion of the sermon, while the latter "afterwards spoke of himself in such a manner as I rejoiced to hear." Two years later, after Wesley had preached at St. Gennys both morning and evening, on Sunday, 26 August 1750, he expressed the fear that his words had "little effect." A year later, on Tuesday evening, 17 September 1751, he preached once more at St. Gennys, and two years after that, he rode through heavy rain to arrive on Saturday, 11 August 1753. Attending church services the next day, Sunday the 12th, and then delivering the sermon, Wesley noted that never had he seen such a crowd in St. Gennys church, nor "did I ever before speak so plainly to them. They *hear*, but when will they *feel*? O what can a man do toward raising either dead bodies or dead souls!"

Finally, at Camelford on Tuesday, 3 September 1782, John Wesley learned that the Wesleys' friend, the Rev. George Thomson, lay near death and desired to see him. Thus, the aged Wesley borrowed a horse and rode immediately to St. Gennys, finding the vicar barely alive, but lucid. The Methodist patriarch sensed that the dying Thomson appeared to have been the only person in the house pleased by his arrival—the reason(s) for that conclusion not discussed in the journal extract. At any rate, the dying cleric "had many doubts," according to Wesley, "concerning his final state and rather feared than desired to die. So that my whole business was to comfort him and to increase and confirm his confidence in God. He desired me to administer the Lord's Supper, which I willingly did; and I left him much happier than I found him, calmly waiting until his change should come" (20:69, 184, 248, 359, 402, 471–472; 23:251). With the death of George Thomson, Wesley apparently saw no further need for visits to St. Gennys.

St. Hilary

In 1720, twenty-four-year-old industrialist-to-be William Lemon formed a partnership with two men from Marazion and installed, at St.

Hilary—a parish five miles east of Penzance and between ten and twelve miles southeast of St. Ives—the first successful steam-pumping engine in Cornwall.[1] Also catalogued among the "firsts" at St. Hilary, one unfortunate woman had aroused the displeasure of the vicar of that town, who wrote, "We have only one Methodist in the parish, an infamous woman of Marazion, fit only to associate with such a sect."[2]

Charles Wesley's only recorded contact with this area occurred on Thursday, 28 July 1743, when he rode from St. Ives to St. Hilary Downs, described as an "open chalk upland" [high ground]. "Here," wrote Wesley, "the careless hearers were kept away by the enemy's threatenings. But near a thousand well-disposed tinners listened to the joyful tidings" sounded in Isaiah 40:1. "That word of grace," continued Wesley, citing Isaiah 6:7, "quite melted them down into tears, on all sides" (2:365).

On Friday, 9 September 1743, John Wesley rode in search of St. Hilary Downs, which he found—but without an expected congregation. However, by the time he donned his clerical garb, approximately one hundred persons had gathered, to whom he "earnestly called 'to repent and believe the gospel' [Mark 1:15]. And if but one heard, it was worth all the labour." Almost three decades later, on Friday, 10 September 1762, John Wesley preached on St. Hilary Downs to a congregation "gathered from all parts. Abundance of them were athirst for God [Psalms 42:2], and did not deceive their hope. The cry of mourners went up before him [Ezekiel 24:17], and he sent down an answer of peace" [Genesis 41:16, Deuteronomy 20:11]. Wesley initially preached in St. Hilary proper on Friday evening, 12 September 1766, near the new Methodist preaching house, on Ephesians 5:14. On riding back to his lodging in the darkness, he escaped serious injury when his horse almost stepped into "a tin-pit." Fortunately, "an honest man" caught the horse by the bridle and turned the animal's head away from the pit. The Methodist leader's final visit to St. Hilary came about when he preached there at noon, Monday, 5 September 1768.

St. Ives

On the Bristol Channel, along the northwest coast of Cornwall and on the west side of St. Ives Bay, the town of St. Ives lay nine miles northeast by north of Penzance, twelve miles from Morvah, and sixty miles west of Plymouth, Devonshire. The area near the town claimed at least two distinct prehistoric sites: (1) The remnants of Chysauster, an Iron Age village consisting of the substantial foundations of four pairs of circular houses with inner courtyards, set on either side of what appears to have been a street. A short distance from there one would have found the ruins of a *fougou*—a prehistoric underground chamber, its function not clear, but it proved peculiar to Cornwall; (2) Men Scrypha, a solitary standing stone with a nearly illegible inscription memorializes a Dark Age Cornish chieftain and his son.[1]

Daniel Defoe, in 1722, identified St. Ives as "a pretty good town" that had achieved affluence from the fishing trade. He described the town as providing a "pleasant" view of Madern Hills and the plain adjacent to them. On the way from Land's End to St. Ives, he wrote, one can grasp in a single sight "a prospect of the ocean at the Land's-End west; of the British Channel at Mount's Bay south; and the Bristol Channel, or Severn Sea, north." At St. Ives, continued Defoe, neither of the two seas lay more than three miles away, and could be clearly seen—as well as, on a clear day, the Scilly Isles, more than thirty miles distant.[2]

To expand upon Defoe's observations, St. Ives functioned, in the eighteenth century, as one of the principal pilchard[3] fisheries in Cornwall,[4] while, at the same time, providing a haven of sorts for Protestant Dissent. One report came forward in 1745 that "twenty families are Dissenters (Presbyterians) and have a meeting house. Mr. Jasper How is the minister. There are likewise many people in this town called Methodists, who frequently assemble at the house of John Nance[5] at unseasonable hours." One or two years earlier, a report had surfaced concerning the formation of a religious society at St. Ives, with a dozen men and women meeting together "to pray and read Burkitt's Notes on the New Testament.[6] When Captain [Joseph] Turner,[7] a member of the Methodist society in Bristol, put in at St. Ives, and informed them of Mr. Wesley and his proceedings, they immediately applied to him, and a preacher was appointed to visit Cornwall, who formed a [religious] society in St. Ives.... In 1743, Mr. [Charles] Wesley visited them, at which time the Society had increased to 120."[8]

Charles Wesley's often stormy visits to St. Ives began between 7:00 p.m. and 8:00 p.m. on Saturday, 16 July 1743, with shouts and general harassment from the local rowdies, who pursued him to the home of John Nance. "But," noted Wesley, "I was too weary to regard them." On Sunday morning, the 17th, he engaged with a number of "this loving, simple people, who are as sheep in the midst of wolves" [Matthew 10:16]. He complained that the local clerics agitated the people, poisoning their minds against the Methodists. Although John Stephens, the mayor of St. Ives, "an honest Presbyterian [according to Wesley] whom the Lord hath raised up," had attempted to check the violence, he had achieved only moderate success. On that day, Wesley preached indoors at 8:00 a.m. on Matthew

1:21 and "found his presence sensibly among us. So did the opposers themselves." Later, at church, he heard the rector preach from Matthew 5:20. "His application," wrote Charles Wesley, "was downright railing at the new sect, as he calls us, those enemies to the Church, seducers, troublers, scribes and pharisees, hypocrites, etc. I had prayed for a quiet heart, and a steady countenance, and my prayer was answered. My calmness was succeeded with strong consolation." Later in the day he met with the Methodist society of St. Ives, remarking that "the enemies of the Lord melt away like wax, more and more being convinced that we speak as the oracles of God [Hebrews 5:12, 1 Peter 4:11]." On Monday the 18th, Wesley went to the market-house to preach, beginning with Psalms 100. The anti–Methodist mob gathered there beat upon a drum and shouted, while Wesley simply stood silent. He offered to speak with the most violent among them, but they simply assaulted him, demanding that he not preach and grabbing on him. "They had no power to touch me," recalled Wesley. "My soul was calm and fearless. I shook off the dust of my feet [Matthew 10:14], and walked leisurely through the thickest of them, who followed like ramping [storming and raging with violent gestures] and roaring lions—but their mouth was shut [Daniel 6:22]." He then met the mayor, who "saluted" him and threatened the rioters, leaving Wesley to return to his lodgings and rejoice "in our Almighty Jesus." A final sermon for that day at St. Ives derived from Mark 10:46–52, and the first sermon for Tuesday, the 19th, came from Isaiah 45:24, in which Wesley demonstrated that "the two inseparable marks of justification are peace, and power over all sin."

On Friday, 22 July 1743, Charles Wesley, preparing to speak in the Methodist preaching house at St. Ives, had just named the text (Isaiah 40:1) for his sermon when the gang of anti–Methodist rioters broke in upon the congregation, threatening to murder people if they did not leave the building. They proceeded to break the candlesticks, smash the windows, tear away the shutters, and break the benches and the collection box for the poor. Wesley "stood silently looking on, but my eyes were unto the Lord." The rioters swore bitterly, demanding that Wesley not preach there again, to which the latter responded that "Christ died for them all." On a number of instances the rioters raised their hands and clubs as though to strike Wesley, but "a stronger arm restrained them." They then dragged the women about the room, particularly one "of great age, and trampled on them without mercy." The longer the mob remained and the more they raged, "the more power I found from above," related Wesley. "I bade the people stand still and see the salvation of God [Exodus 14:13], resolving to continue with them, and see the end." An hour passed "before the word came, 'Hitherto shalt thou come, and no farther' [Job 38:11]." The rioters began to quarrel among themselves, one striking the head of the town clerk, their leader, and stormed from the building. Wesley then led those who had remained in giving thanks "for the victory, and in prayer the Spirit of glory rested upon us." On the way to their lodgings, Wesley and his companions met Mayor Stephens and another justice and thus returned to the preaching house to show them the destruction created by the mob. The mayor commended the Methodists, according to Charles Wesley, "as the most quiet, inoffensive subjects; encouraged us to sue for justice; said he was no more secure from lawless violence than we; wished us success, and left us rejoicing in our strong Helper [Hebrews 13:6]."

Charles Wesley continued to note, in the entry to his manuscript journal of Saturday, 23 July, the events of the evening immediately preceding. He began with the thesis, "I cannot find one of this people who fears those that can fear the body only [Luke 12:4]." Claiming as miraculous that additional "mischief" had not been committed during that incident, he identified the leader of the mob as Mayor Stephens' son, reporting, "I laid my hand upon him and said, 'Sir, you appear like a gentleman, I desire you would show it by restraining these of the baser sort. Let them strike the men, or me, if they please, but not hurt poor helpless women and children.'" Not surprisingly, the young man "turned into a friend immediately, and laboured the whole time to quiet his associates." A number of attendees, although not members of the St. Ives Methodist society, arose in defense of the Methodists and stood between the attackers and their intended victims, while another of that group physically engaged the villains of the piece. Wesley also identified a group of "our bitterest enemies who had been brought over by the meekness of the sufferers, and malice of the persecutors." The incident having come to an end, Wesley preached in that same room at 5:00 a.m. on Isaiah 54:3–17.

Back in St. Ives on Tuesday, 26 July 1743, quiet reigned, Wesley having learned of Mayor Stephens' determination to swear twenty new constables and to suppress the rioters by force of arms. Throughout Wesley's sermon, the mayor stood off to the side, his very presence deterring potential rioters. Although Stephens' actions served only to turn the town against him, he informed the Rev. William Hoblyn, one of the outspoken and enthusiastic anti–Methodist clergymen of St. Ives, that he (Stephens) "would not be perjured to gratify any man's malice." Hoblyn had reportedly declared that "they [the authorities] ought to drive us [the Methodists] away by blows, not arguments." Wesley continued to remain at St. Ives throughout Wednesday the 27th and Thursday morning, the 28th, returning later that day to explicate, without interruptions, the Beatitudes (Matthew 5:12, Luke 6:20–23). Nine days later, Saturday, 6 August, Wesley again preached at St. Ives, on Acts 20:32, giving no thought to the rioters, although Mayor Stephens had informed him of the latter's intention that they would exercise "a parting blow" at the Methodists. True to their word, as Wesley and the Methodist society met at the home of John Nance, the mob stormed the room. Nance rushed forward and stood in the middle of them "till our King scattered the evil with his eyes [Proverbs 20:8], and turned them back to the way that they came. The great power of God was, meantime, among us, overturning all before it, and melting our hearts into contrite, joyful love." At 4:00 a.m., Sunday, the 7th, Wesley bid farewell to members of the Methodist society, noting that "great peace was upon them all. Their prayers and tears of love I shall never forget. I nothing doubt, if I follow their faith, that I shall meet them in the new Jerusalem [Revelation 3:12, 21:2]." Two hours later, he and his companions "left the lion's den." Although a number of them wanted to exit St. Ives by a back way, Charles Wesley would not proceed in haste or in the appearance of flight, but rode through the largest street of the town, "in the face of our enemies."

Interestingly enough, at Newcastle-upon-Tyne, Northumberland, on Sunday, 4 March 1744, Charles Wesley received word that the anti–Methodist mob, with the blessing of certain ministers, had destroyed the Methodist preaching house at St. Ives. Nonetheless, four months later, on late Thursday afternoon, 19 July 1744, he and his companions "set our faces against the world" and rode to St. Ives. He received word that two weeks earlier, at night, the mob had broken the windows of "all that were only suspected of Christianity." Having lodged once again at the home of John Nance, Wesley found an opportunity to be alone for an hour in the garden, where he "suffered to feel my own great weakness. Without were fightings, within fears. But my fears were all scattered by the sight of my dear brethren and children. I rejoiced over them with singing, but their joy and love exceeded. We all rejoiced in hope of receiving him in the air [1 Thessalonians 4:17]." The next day, Friday, the 20th, he preached on John 14:1, and later, in company with the Rev. John Meriton,[9] he walked through the town to church. The Rev. William Hoblyn, the anti–Methodist curate, "saluted us courteously," while no one shouted against them—principally out of respect for Meriton's reputation. Afterward, Wesley preached at 1:00 p.m. confident that "God may deal with this sinful nation, but our prayers for Jerusalem will one day be answered." On Saturday, 21 July, while Wesley and his friends were walking near St. Ives quay, the mob formed and shouted against them; demonstrating "plain marks of their Cornish disposition." However, they cast but a single stone; Wesley and friends walked through the middle of them and left the town.

Four days later, Wednesday, 25 July 1744, Wesley preached at St. Ives, where he learned of a Methodist woman complaining to Mayor Stephens of heavy stones having been thrown into the house where she lodged, a number of which fell on the pillow within inches of her infant child. The local magistrate, who owned the house, "damned her" and said, "You shall have no justice here. You see there is none for you at London, or you would have got in before now." He then evicted the woman and her child from his house. Despite the continued harassment at St. Ives, Charles Wesley managed to conduct the first love-feast[10] there on Sunday, 29 July 1744, during which several participants became "overpowered with love." Wesley returned to St. Ives on Wednesday, 1 August, and found "our beloved brother," the Rev. George Thomson,[11] who had come to see him and "the children whom God had given us." His presence alarmed the anti–Methodists and gave confidence to the society members, and that night Wesley preached on Acts 2:42.

Charles Wesley permitted himself a respite from the traumas of St. Ives before returning to that town on Monday evening, 30 June 1746, where he preached on Isaiah 35:9–10. Three weeks later at St. Ives on Thursday, 17 July 1746, no one attempted the least disturbance against the Methodists, and Wesley maintained that the attitude of the entire town had become outwardly changed. He walked the streets "with astonishment, scarce believing it St. Ives." From another view, however, Wesley had to expel "a disorderly walker, the first of the kind," from the Methodist society there. Three days later, Sunday the 20th, Wesley found that nearly one hundred of those men hired by the ministers of St. Ives to attack him and his followers had now sworn to lose their lives in defense of the Methodists. However, he had no need for their services; all appeared quiet throughout the town. Wesley then began his final visit to St. Ives on Sunday, the 27th, by preaching on Luke 13:11–17 and the next day (Monday the 28th) began his "experiment" of ceasing to drink tea and proceeding with a milk diet—resulting in extreme tiredness, increase in headaches, violent "purging," and general weakness. He remained largely in the town through Friday, 1 August 1746, on which day he removed two or three members from the Methodist society "of doubtful character … not daring to trust them with the honour of God and his people." In the end, he joined with the St. Ives society in desiring "to return to God in weeping, and fasting, and mourning." The members promised, from that time forward, "to meet the true membership of the Church of England at the throne of grace on this day."[12]

When John Wesley initially arrived in St. Ives, on Tuesday evening, 30 August 1743, he issued an invitation for a 7:00 gathering to "all guilty, helpless sinners who were conscious they 'had nothing to pay' [Luke 7:42], to accept of free forgiveness." The preaching house filled to capacity and others collected outside, but all persons remained quiet and attentive. The next day, Wednesday the 31st, he spoke with individuals and Methodist society members, the latter numbering close to 120—nearly one hundred of those having "found peace with God." At 11:00 a.m. as Wesley and his companions proceeded to church, a large group in the marketplace greeted them with "a loud huzza [a shout of acclaim—but in this case, one of derision]—wit as harmless as the ditty sung under my window (composed, one assured me, by a gentlewoman of *their own town*): 'Charley Wesley is come to town,/To try if he can pull the churches down.'" The wit and the church service done with, Wesley that evening explicated Acts 1:4. Following the preaching, a number in attendance began to cause trouble, but John Nelson[13] walked into the midst of them and addressed the loudest, who then departed from the scene. On Thursday, 1 September, Wesley noted, tersely, "We had a day of peace."

At 7:00 p.m. Monday, 5 September 1743, Wesley met the Methodist society at St. Ives, at which time and place two women from Penzance "fell down as dead and soon after cried out in the bitterness of their souls. But we continued crying to God in their behalf, till he put a new song in their mouths [Psalms 40:3]." During the same time, a young man, also from Penzance, who had "once known the peace of God but had sinned it away, had a fresh and clear manifestation of the love of God." From Zennor on Saturday evening, 10 September, Wesley "hastened" to St. Ives, where he and his flock "concluded the day in praising God with joyful lips." Two days later, Monday evening the 12th, he preached at St. Ives, remarking, "The dread of God fell upon us while I was speaking, so that I could hardly utter a word; but most of all in prayer, wherein I was so carried out as scarce ever before in my life." However, problems arose for Wesley at St. Ives on Friday evening, 16 September, in the midst of his sermon. A mob burst into the room, shouting and striking those who stood in their way. A combination of fear and zeal on the part of the assemblage only increased the pandemonium, and thus Wesley waded into the mass of humanity, managed to find the leader of the mob, and conveyed him to the speaker's desk. Although Wesley received a blow to the head in the process, he and the mob leader eventually reached an agreement, causing the latter to quiet his colleagues. He then departed the town for other parts of that area of Cornwall before returning to St. Ives on Sunday evening, the 18th, concluding the day "with our brethren" and "rejoicing and praising God."

When John Wesley again came to St. Ives at 11:00 a.m. on Wednesday, 4 April 1744, he expressed surprise upon entering the house of John Nance and finding a number of persons waiting for him, and he joined them as "we poured out our souls together in praises and thanksgiving." As soon as the group exited the house, the usual "huzzas," stones, and clumps of dirt saluted them, but that evening, all assembled remained quiet as Wesley preached on Psalms 18:1, 3. The next day, April 5, the Methodist leader viewed the ruins of a Methodist's house that a mob had destroyed in February 1744 while celebrating the victory of Admiral Thomas Matthews (1676–1751) over a combined French and Spanish fleet near Toulon. "Such is the Cornish method of thanksgiving!" sarcastically mused Wesley. "I suppose if Admiral [Richard] Lestock [1689?-1746] had fought, too, they would have knocked all the Methodists on the head." Lestock, not on speaking terms with Admiral Matthews, had been accused of not supporting Matthews during the engagement at Toulon. That comment aside, Wesley preached both morning and evening on 5 April to a room filled to capacity. In the Methodist society, "God did indeed sit upon his people, as a refiner's fire [Malachi 3:2–3]. He darted into all (I believe hardly one excepted) the melting flame of love,[14] so that their heads were as water and their eyes as fountains of tears [Jeremiah 9:1]." On Friday the 6th, he spoke, individually and collectively, with members of the Methodist society at St. Ives, observing, "with great satisfaction," that persecutors had caused only three or four members to defect, but had given strength to the remainder. Wesley placed the blame for such persecution directly upon the Rev. William Hoblyn (1723–1759), lecturer at St. Ives (1744–1758) and the Rev. William Symonds (1686–1776), vicar of St. Ives (1735–1768), whom he labeled "gentlemen worthy to be had in everlasting remembrance for their unwearied efforts to destroy heresy." The next day (Saturday, 7 April) Wesley recorded portions of the recent anti–Methodist riots at St. Ives as evidence of the rioters' disregard for George II's 1744 proclamation that reinforced the Riot Act of 1715.[15] Nonetheless, the Methodist leader thought that "much good" had been realized from the King's action, "particularly the great peace we now enjoy." Wesley returned to St. Ives on Wednesday, 8 April, noting, on Wednesday the 11th—a public fast day proclaimed by a threatened invasion from France by the Young Pretender, Charles Edward Stuart (1729–1788)[16]—the church being "well filled." The Rev. Hoblyn preached from Matthew 10:25, and then fulfilled that passage by "vehemently declaiming against the 'new sect' as enemies of the Church,

Jacobites, Papists, and what not!" After church, Wesley met with the society and spent an hour in prayer, "not forgetting the poor sinner against his own soul." Following an absence of two days, Wesley returned to St. Ives on Friday evening, 13 April, only to depart before noon on the next day.

Although John Wesley did not conduct further visits to St. Ives for the remainder of 1744, he did manage to gather news of events in that town. Henry Millard, a young resident of St. Ives and a member of the Methodist society there, who eventually died of the smallpox, wrote to Wesley at least twice during August-September 1744, informing him of the actions of anti–Methodist mobs in St. Ives. "They now triumph over us more and more, saying nothing can be done against them," lamented Millard. Wesley did return to St. Ives on Wednesday, 3 July 1745, but only for two or three hours of rest before moving on. When he came to St. Ives again on Monday, 8 July, he identified conditions there as "the most still and honourable post (so are the times changes) which we have in Cornwall." Five days later, Saturday the 13th, he met with the stewards of the St. Ives Methodist societies. He did not preach there again until Friday evening, 5 September 1746; at 5:00 Sunday evening, 7 September, to "an understanding people" on Mark 12:34; and on Friday and Saturday, 12–13 September—all without incident or comment.

When Wesley's next tour of Cornwall took him to St. Ives on Tuesday, 30 June 1747, prior to morning prayers, he walked to church "without so much as one huzzah. How strangely," he reflected, "has one year changed the scene in Cornwall. This is now a peaceable, nay, honourable station. They give us good words almost in every place. What have we done that the world should be so civil to us?" The issue of politics replaced matters of civility the next day, Wednesday, 1 July, when Wesley spoke with a number of eligible voters in the forthcoming Parliamentary election. The particular interest in St. Ives, according to Professor W. Reginald Ward, focused upon the control of one of the two Parliamentary seats for St. Ives that had been held by John Hobart and his followers from 1715 to 1734 and, with assistance from Mackworth Praed, two seats in the general elections of 1741 and 1747. However, in 1747, Hobart determined to seek a seat for Norwich, which necessitated a by-election to replace him. In his conversations with an unspecified number of voters, Wesley discovered that not a single one of them would accept either food or drink from the person for whom he had voted. One individual identified only as "T. C.," received five guineas (£5. 5s.), but he returned the money immediately, while another, "T. M."—believed to have been either Captain Timothy Major or Thomas Matthews—refused to accept any gift. When he heard that his mother had received three guineas (£3. 3s.) for her vote, he forced her to hand the money to him, and he quickly returned it. The election occurred the next day, Tuesday, 2 July, and, according to Wesley, the event went forward "without any hurry at all." He preached that evening to "a large congregation, among whom two or three roared for the disquietness of their heart [Psalms 38:8], as did many at the [society] meeting which followed, particularly those who had lost their first love [1 John 4:19]." He preached again at St. Ives on Tuesday, 7 July, and on 18 July 1747, he wrote from St. Ives to his friend and legal and financial advisor in London, Ebenezer Blackwell (1711–1782), "A great door and effectual [that which produces its intended effect or answers its purpose] is opened [1 Corinthians 16:9] now, almost in every corner of this country. Here is such a change within these two years as has hardly been seen in any other part of England. Wherever we went we used not carry our lives in our hands; and now there is not a dog to wag his tongue."

More than a year later, at 7:00 p.m. Sunday, 25 September 1748, Wesley arrived in St. Ives, only to find, once more, that the preaching house would not contain all who had come to hear him speak. Those who could not gain access to the room stood in the adjacent orchard, and Wesley discovered, during his sermon on 2 Corinthians 5:20, that "God *can* wound by the gospel as well as by the law (although the instances of this are exceeding rare, nor have we any Scripture ground to expect them)." As he spoke, a young woman, "cut by the heart," fell to the ground; afterward, she could not provide a clear, rational reason why she had done so. Wesley remained in St. Ives, departing on the next day (Monday the 26th) at noon. He would not return until Sunday evening, 19 August 1750, in preparation for the Quarterly Meeting to be held on Wednesday the 22nd, at which the stewards of all the Cornish societies would be present. The gathering held the first watch-night in Cornwall, and "great was the Holy One of Israel in the midst of us" [Isaiah 12:6]. John Wesley had instituted the solemn watch-night service in London on 9 April 1742—a worship vigil that extended for four hours and assigned, by Wesley, on the Friday night nearest the full moon, so that those who resided a far distance would have the light of the moon to find the way to their homes after midnight.[17] On Thursday, the 23rd, continuing at St. Ives, Wesley received permission from John Edwards, the mayor, to preach in the evening, not far from the marketplace; he did so before "a vast concourse of people" that included the majority of the adult residents of the town. He had managed his way through two-thirds of his discourse when (most likely) John Stephens, a political agent, dispatched one of his servants to ride his horse through the midst of Wesley's congregation. A number of the influential men of St. Ives urged the Methodist leader to continue, but Wesley determined to stop speaking and to leave the scene. Nonetheless, the people followed him to the preaching house, filling the room and all of the space near the door and windows, and there he completed his sermon.

After settling in at St. Ives on Thursday afternoon, 19 September 1751, Wesley spent a portion of the following day (Saturday, the 20th) reading, "with great prejudice in their favour," *Law-Death, Gospel-Life; or, The Death of Legal Righteousness, the Life of Gospel Holiness; Being the Substance of Several Sermons upon Galatians 2:19* (Edinburgh, Scotland, 1724), by Ralph Erskine (1685–1752), minister of the Associate Presbyterian church in Queen Anne Street, Dunfermline, Scotland. "But how was I disappointed!" bemoaned the Methodist leader. "I not only found many things [?] odd and unscriptural but some [?] that were dangerously false, and the leaven of antinomianism[18] spread from end to end [1 Corinthians 5:8]." However, the business of Methodism left little time for specifics. Almost two years later, on Wednesday, 25 July 1753, Wesley met the stewards from western Cornwall at St. Ives, and on Thursday the 26th, he began an examination of individuals of the St. Ives society. He had to delay that exercise upon discovering "an accursed thing among them—wellnigh one and all bought or sold uncustomed [smuggled] goods," and thus he called for a meeting of the entire society that evening. He told them that they must cease "this abomination" or they would see him no more. On Friday the 27th, he reported that the members had promised to halt the practice, "so I trust this plague is stayed."[19]

Arriving at St. Ives late Sunday night, 7 September 1755, Wesley had to wait until the next morning for an arranged meeting with a young solicitor, John Krill (1733–1811)—he would become collector of customs at St. Ives (1762–1782) and mayor of that town (1767). Krill had attended a number of Methodist preachings, but on Saturday, 6 September, he had fallen "raving mad." When Wesley saw him, he "sung, and swore, and screamed, and cursed, and blasphemed, as if possessed by Legion [Mark 5:9]." However, as soon as Wesley approached Krill, the twenty-two-year-old called the Methodist leader by name and began to speak. Wesley sat down on the bed, and Krill became quiet, soon shedding tears and engaging in prayer. Wesley joined in the prayer and left Krill in a state of calm. On Tuesday, 9 September, Wesley called for Wednesday, the 10th, as a day of fasting and prayer on behalf of John Krill, and as the prayers began, he received word that Krill had ceased his raving and had begun to utter a series of biblical phrases.[20] After thirty minutes he ceased those recitations and resumed his raving. By Thursday, 11 September, Krill had become more "outrageous," but Wesley and his followers continued their prayers into the evening, after which the young man sunk into a deep ten-hour sleep. His strange behavior eventually ceased, "although [wrote Wesley] the time of deliverance was not come."

Further, on Monday, 12 September 1755, during a respite at St. Ives, John Wesley wrote to Ebenezer Blackwell concerning one of his itinerant preachers, Michael Fenwick (?-1797), reportedly possessed of a weak head but a good heart. Wesley extended credit to a "remarkable providence" that Fenwick had been "so often hindered from settling in business because God had other work for him to do. He is just made to travel with me, being an excellent groom, valet de chambre, nurse, and upon occasion a tolerable preacher. We have hitherto had an extremely prosperous journey—almost everything has been just as we desired. And so I have no care upon my mind but what properly belongs to me—to feed and guide the flock of Christ." The Methodist leader further informed, briefly, Blackwell of the "odd circumstance" of John Krill. He then wrote another letter on 12 September, to Christopher Hopper (1722–1802), among the significant figures to engage upon the Methodist itinerancy, a short note calling upon him to understand the design of God's "gracious wisdom, and to answer and fulfill that design."

During his next visit to St. Ives, on Monday, 12 September 1757, Wesley learned that Robert Swindells (?-1782), one of his itinerant preachers, had attempted, unsuccessfully, to preach in the street of that town, but received an offer to do so at a "more convenient" meadow near the town. Wesley quickly proceeded to that site, arriving by 6:00 p.m. and standing at the bottom of it—"the people rising higher and higher before me." On Tuesday evening, the 13th, the gathering increased, due to the arrival of persons from the country, and that number increased on Wednesday the 14th. When he returned to St. Ives three years later, on Wednesday, 10 September 1760, John Wesley determined to preach in the street, but high winds caused him to seek a small enclosure nearby, one end of which comprised native rock "rising ten or twelve feet perpendicular, from which the ground fell with an easy descent. A jetting [projection] out of the rock, about four feet from the ground, gave me a very convenient pulpit." On that site, Wesley conjectured, the entire town—"high and low, rich and poor"—gathered, quiet and serious. He repeated the exercise in that natural setting for the next three evenings, even during the roaring of the sea and extremely high wind on Saturday, 13 September. "God gave me so clear and strong a voice," he claimed, "that I believe scarce one word was lost." At 8:00 a.m., Sunday, the 14th, he returned to the same meadow where he had preached three years earlier, the congregation standing row above row, where one could see and hear. "It was a beautiful sight," he exclaimed. "Everyone seemed to take to himself what was spoken. I believe every backslider in the town was there. And surely God was there to 'heal their backslidings' [Hosea 14:4]." At 5:00 p.m. Wesley went "once more into the ground" at St. Ives to preach to "such a congregation as I think was never seen in any place before (Gwennap [pit] excepted) in this county." He noted the attendance of a number of the principal persons of St. Ives, they not standing on the edges of the crowd, but placed themselves in the midst of them. "The clear sky, the setting sun, the smooth still water, all agreed with the state of the audience. Is anything too hard for God?" The scene turned his poetic eye to the ninth stanza of the paraphrase of Psalms 89:9 in *A New Version of the Psalms of David, Fitted to the Tunes Used in the Churches* (1696), by Nahum Tate (1652–1715) and Nicholas Brady (1659–1726),

> Thou didst the lawless sea control,
> And smooth [change] the prospect of the deep.
> Thou mak'st the sleeping billows roll;
> Thou mak'st the rolling billows sleep.

Continuing at St. Ives on Monday, 15 September 1760, Wesley inquired concerning the violent "uncommon" storm that occurred in the area on 9 March 1759 (he having been in Norwich, Norfolk). Heavy wind and rain began near Land's End between 9:00 p.m. and 10:00 p.m. and proceeded eastward, approximately one mile in width, and passed over St. Just, Morvah, Zennor, St. Ives, and Gwinear (3¼ miles southwest of Camborne), then turned northward over the Bristol Channel. About a mile southeast of St. Ives, the storm uprooted a rock weighing approximately twelve or fourteen tons [!] from the top of a rising ground and "whirled" it down upon another rock, which it split through while, at the same time, dashing it to pieces. The storm destroyed the pinnacles of Gwinear church, and those pieces forced their way through the roof of the building. The rain that accompanied the wind proved to have been "as salt as any sea water."

Two years later, on Tuesday evening, 14 September 1762, John Wesley came to St. Ives, where "two or three pretty butterflies came and looked and smiled and went away. But all the rest of the numerous congregation behaved with the utmost seriousness." The day following (Wednesday the 15th) witnessed the Quarterly Meeting, and on Thursday, Wesley "appointed the children to meet." He expected twenty to appear, but he estimated that eighty actually came, with all of them "wanting" and a number of them "desiring" doctrinal instruction. In his open letter from Limerick, Ireland, on 9 June 1765, to the leaders and stewards of the Methodist societies within the Cornwall circuits, Wesley informed them that he would be in St. Ives on Tuesday, 10 September 1765. However, he did not manage to reach that town until Friday evening, 13 September 1765, where he preached on the seashore. Although little wind arose, the noise of the waves prevented a number of the gathering from hearing him. Thus, when he prepared to preach again on Saturday, the 14th, he did so on a meadow on the side of a hill, and on Sunday morning, at seven o'clock, he based his discourse on 1 John 1:3. A year later, on Tuesday evening, 9 September 1766, he preached a short distance from St. Ives "to the largest congregation I ever saw there. Indeed," he proclaimed, "the whole town seems convinced of the truth, yea, and almost persuaded to be Christians" [Acts 26:28]. Although on the next day, the rain forced him into the St. Ives preaching house, a lull in the weather allowed him to return to the meadow on Thursday, the 11th, there to deliver an oration on Revelation 22:20.

That same meadow at St. Ives housed Wesley and his congregation on Tuesday evening, 30 August 1768, and on Wednesday he "met with the children, a work which will exercise all the talents of the most able preachers in England." On Thursday, 1 September, the grass in the meadow became too wet for people to stand, but Wesley found an open area where he preached on Psalms 77:9. He addressed another large congregation at St. Ives on Friday evening, 1 September 1769, after which he met with the Methodist society. Upon his return on Saturday, 25 August 1770, he found that "God has made all our enemies to be at peace with us, so that I might have preached at any part of the town." He selected a meadow where persons could sit, either on the grass or in the hedges—"(so the Cornish term their broad stone walls, which are usually covered with grass)"—and preached on Ecclesiastes 12:13. A number of persons who could not negotiate the hill to the meadow requested that Wesley preach in the town proper, which he did on Sunday, the 26th, near the marketplace at 8:00 a.m., basing his text upon Hebrews 12:14. He listened to a "useful" sermon at St. Ives church later that morning and another in the afternoon, delivered "in a strong and earnest manner," before preaching again at 5:00—addressing "all the town" and "thousands from all parts of the country" on 1 John 3:8. Remaining at St. Ives through most of Monday, the 27th, Wesley expressed surprise in discovering that the select society[21] among the Methodists had been totally neglected. After consulting several members of that group, he could not find "so much as one who had not 'given up his confidence' [Hebrews 10:35]." Turning his attention to the children, who had not recently received attention, he declared, "So dead a company have I seldom seen. I found scarce one spark of even the fear of God among them."

Wesley preached again in the marketplace at St. Ives on Thursday evening, 19 August 1773; at the same site on Friday, 2 September 1774; and Monday, 4 September 1775—noting, lastly, that a number of his friends there appear "grey-headed, as well as me." In the evening, he preached in the small meadow above the town where he had done so a number of years earlier, noting that "the people in general here (excepting the rich) seem 'almost persuaded to be Christians' [Acts 26:28]. Perhaps the prayer of their old pastor, Mr. [Thomas] Tregosse [(?-1671), a native of St. Ives and curate there, but in Presbyterian orders], is answered even to the fourth generation." A year later, on Saturday evening, 24 August 1776, he preached in the meadow at St. Ives, then met the children on Sunday—repeating his view of that task as the most difficult part of the ministerial office. On Saturday evening, 23 August 1777, he preached on the cliff of St. Ives, and when he visited there again on Friday, 28 August 1778, he met with the stewards of the Cornish Methodist societies, they being "a company of pious, sensible men." Wesley expressed his pleasure in finding that "peace and love prevailed through the whole circuit," principally the result of the Calvinist Methodist itinerant preachers under the sponsorship of Selina Shirley Hastings, Countess of Huntingdon (1707–1791), "who screamed and railed and threatened to swallow us up" having left the field. "I cannot learn," wrote Wesley, "that they have made one convert—a plain proof that God did not send them."

When Wesley preached at the market house at St. Ives on Friday, 25 August 1780, he observed "no oppose now. Rich and poor *see*, and very many *feel* the truth." During his stay there, he "looked over" the two volumes of *Essays, Moral and Literary* (London, 1778), by Vicesimus Knox (1752–1821), master of the school at Tonbridge, Kent; rector of Runwell and Ramsden Crays, Essex; and minister of the chapelry at Shipton, Kent. According to Wesley, Knox had emerged as "a lively writer of middling understanding," his *Essays* being "prim, affected, and highly frenchified. I object to the beginning so many sentences with participles. This does well in French, but not in English. I cannot admire his judgment in many particulars. To instance in one or two. He depresses[22] [the metaphysical English poet Abraham] Cowley [1618–1667] beyond all reason, who was far from being a mean [poor, lowly, incompetent]. Full as unreasonable does he depress modern eloquence. I believe I have heard *speakers* at

Oxford, to say nothing of Westminster, who were not inferior to either Demosthenes or Cicero." Wesley continued his literary criticism at St. Ives after preaching in the marketplace there on Friday, 31 August 1781. The next day, he completed his reading of "that curious book," *Remains of Japhet*[23]; *Being Historical Inquiries into the Affinity and Origin of the European Languages* (London, 1767), by James Parsons, M.D. (1705–1770)— physician, antiquary, assistant foreign corresponding secretary of the Royal Society, and knowledgeable in ancient Irish and Welsh. In Wesley's view, Parsons, a "very ingenious author [,] has struck much light into some of the darkest parts of ancient history. And although I cannot entirely subscribe to every proposition which he advances, yet I apprehend he has sufficiently proved the main of his hypothesis." Wesley then went on to outline ten major points of that hypothesis, concluding his précis of the work by stating, "The foregoing particulars this fine writer has made highly probable. And these may be admitted though we do not agree to his vehement panegyric [elaborate praise of] on the Irish language—much less receive all the stories told by the Irish poets or chroniclers as genuine, authentic history."

Prior to his next visit to Cornwall, John Wesley wrote briefly, from London on 25 February 1783, to Joseph Taylor (1752–1830), who had ridden upon the Methodist itinerancy since 1777 and participated in the religious revival in Cornwall during 1782–1784. If nothing else, Wesley's letter casts light upon the responsibilities of the Methodist itinerant beyond the task of preaching. "I make no doubt," encouraged the Methodist patriarch, "but you will be able to collect enough in the circuit to enlarge the house at St. Ives. And the sooner you begin the better. Only see that you have good workmen and a good plan! Remember, light enough and air enough; and do not make a bungling but a neat work." Yet again at the St. Ives market place on Friday evening, 26 August 1785, Wesley recollected that "this was the first place in Cornwall where we preached and where Satan fought fiercely for his kingdom. But now all is peace." He learned, on this day, that "old John Nance had rested from his labours. Some months since, sitting behind the preacher in the pulpit, he sunk down, was carried out, and fell asleep." The Methodist patriarch returned to the town in 1787, carrying forth his missionary labors from 1:00 p.m. Saturday, 8 September until 6:30 a.m. on the following morning. Eighty-six-year-old John Wesley's final visit to St. Ives extended from 11:00 a.m., Tuesday, 25 August 1789, to 9:00 a.m., Wednesday the 26th, when he preached on one side of the marketplace. "Surely," he reflected, "forty years labour has not been in vain here."[24]

St. John's

According to the "Sermon Register" included in Nehemiah Curnock's edition of John Wesley's *Journal*, the Methodist leader first visited the village of St. John's, located in southwestern Cornwall, near Helston, on Friday, 19 September 1760, at which time he preached on Romans 12:20.[1] Further, Curnock, again in his edition of Wesley's *Journal*, cited from an article in the *Methodist Magazine* (1835, p. 37), stating that c. 1760, one Peter Quintrel formed a Methodist society in St. John's, in the home of a Mrs. Warren, consisting of five persons. That number increased, within a short time, to fourteen men and "several" women. Curnock added that the society eventually built a Methodist chapel not long after John Wesley's 1765 visit, and that structure continued as such throughout the nineteenth century. Following the construction of a new chapel in Helston, the stewards of the Methodist society ceded or sold the St. John's house to a Mr. R. Andrew, John Wesley's host in Helston, but by some point between 1909 and 1916 it had been converted into a warehouse.[2]

Two years following John Wesley's initial visit to St. John's, the Methodist leader returned on Wednesday, 8 September 1762, declaring that the congregation had trebled in size since he had last preached there. After a passage of three years, Wesley managed another visit to St. John's, at 6:00 p.m. Monday, 9 September 1765, "once as furious a town as Redruth. Now almost all the gentry of the town were present and heard with the deepest attention"—although Wesley noticed, the next morning, his voice beginning to fail, causing him to reduce, temporarily, his preaching engagements to two per day. One should note that on 11 September 1765, while still at St. John's, Wesley wrote to Thomas Rankin,[3] underscoring his belief that "there is a good work in Cornwall. But where the great work goes on well we should take care to be exact in little things." Specifically, the Methodist leader voiced his concerns about gaudy dress among certain women in the select societies; the singing of hymns with repetitions and flourishes that obscure the sounds of legitimate devotion; lack of essential books supplied to the societies (the vast majority written and published by Wesley himself); and the "miserable" conditions of a number of Methodist preaching houses.

When Wesley did preach again at St. John's, on Monday and Tuesday evenings, 5–6 September 1768, he concluded that even "the most senseless then felt the Word of God, sharp as a two-edged sword" [Hebrews 4:12]. On Wednesday the 7th, he preached early in the morning, then met with the select society[4]—"such a company of lively believers, full of faith and love, as I never found in this county before." Wesley's attitude toward St. John's and its inhabitants remained firmly positive, as witnessed by his visit there at 5:00 p.m. Wednesday, 30 August 1769, when he preached an hour later, being "comforted among a loving earnest people." His final visit to St. John's on Wednesday, 29 August 1770 prompted no comment other than the fact that he preached there.[5]

St. Just

Situated four miles north of Land's End, between six and seven miles northwest of Penzance, twelve miles from St. Ives, and four miles from Morvah, the town and large tin-mining parish of St. Just (or, St. Just-in-Penwith) yielded at least two ancient sites within the immediate surrounding area: (1) the small Brane chambered Neolithic tomb, 2.5 miles to the southeast and a variety of the entrance grave, covered by a round barrow (a grave mound) twenty feet across and 6.5 feet high; (2) Tregeseal stone circles, 1.5 miles to the northeast, the remaining two of three circles of a Bronze Age monument, one with sixteen stones that survived, and one with only two stones.[1] Beyond those sites, within the town proper, one could have found an amphitheater for the production and performance of miracle plays during the medieval period (1000 A.D.-1500 A.D.).

In 1732, William Borlase (1695–1772)[2] received the appointment as vicar of St. Just, and shortly thereafter he reported that the average church attendance "in the forenoon on Sundays was 1,000, and in the afternoon 500." If, in the least, generally accurate, those figures demonstrate that Church life in that part of Cornwall had not descended to the low levels usually attributed to that period.[3] Further data reveals that in c. 1744, Borlase held three celebrations of the Sacrament each year at St. Just, with an average of 120 communicants[4]—the large majority of them tin miners.

Charles Wesley first preached at St. Just on Saturday, 20 July 1743, his text being Matthew 11:5, with emphasis also upon Isaiah 6:7 and Ephesians 4:32. "The hearts of thousands," he exclaimed in a poetic-like voice, "seemed moved as the trees of the forest, by the wind which bloweth as it listeth [John 3:8]. The door stood wide open, and a multitude are just entering in. Here it is that I expect the largest harvest." The next day, Sunday the 21st, Wesley rode back to St. Just from Land's End, attended the evening church service, and then proceeded to a plain by the town, "*made for field preaching.*" There he stood on a green bank and discoursed on Isaiah 53:6. "About 2,000, mostly tinners, attending," he noted, "no one offering to stir or move an hand or tongue. The fields are white unto harvest [John 4:35]. Lord, send forth labourers!" Wesley returned to preach on that plain on Saturday, 21 July 1744, visualizing that "our Lord rides triumphant through this place," with more than "two hundred" persons involved in Methodist society classes,[5] "most of whom have tasted the pardoning grace of God." On Sunday the 22nd, Charles Wesley preached in the street at St. Just on Isaiah 55:1, asserting, "The word of God ran very swiftly. When God gives it, who can hinder its course?" He then found opportunity of communicating with "a sick brother," after which he attended church service, "crowded with those schismatical Methodists, who have not all, it seems, left it through our means." The curate, he concluded, had been viewed by his parishioners as "half a Methodist, only because he does not rail at us like them." Wesley preached once more at St. Just on Tuesday, 24 July to "the largest company that had ever been seen there," then met with the Methodist society to warn its members against "spiritual pride." Again at St. Just on Sunday, 29 July, he expounded upon Isaiah 35, where he viewed "just as many hands that hung down" being "lifted up." He then went off to church service. Two days later, Tuesday, 31 July, he preached from late afternoon to nightfall from Luke 21:34, attracting "a larger congregation than ever," claiming that "the Spirit of love was poured out abundantly, and great grace was upon all." After meeting with the Methodist society, Wesley walked to a nearby hill, where he led singing, prayer, and a general rejoicing. Wesley concluded the day and the month "as I would wish to conclude my life."

Charles Wesley addressed, "with great charity and love," the St. Just Methodist society on Sunday, 13 July 1746 from John 6:67, encouraging members to "cast up the stumbling block of sin [Ezekiel 14:4, 7], to turn unto the Lord with weeping and fasting and mourning, that the gospel door might be again opened among them." With considerable tears and emotion, members promised "amendment," and requested that Wesley return. At Redruth on Sunday, 21 July 1746, Wesley received "sad" accounts of people at St. Just having been "scattered" by persecution and thus wandered into "by-paths of error and sin." A week later, Sunday, the 27th, Charles Wesley attended church at St. Just, then proceeded to "my old pulpit, the large stone by brother Chinhall's house." There he preached from Matthew 22:1 and beyond. Those in attendance remained quiet until he uttered, "And the remnant took his servants, and entreated them spitefully, and slew them" [Matthew 22:6]. At that point, someone began to throw stones, an act that did not prevent Wesley from continuing his exhortation for persons "to save themselves from this untoward generation." He described his sermon as being as "mixed as the multitude—law, gospel, threatenings, promises, which I trust the Spirit applied to their several cases." Unfortunately, the fragmented state of Charles Wesley's manuscript journal does not allow one to provide a clear beginning, middle, or end to Charles Wesley's total experience in St. Just (2:366–367, 410–414, 466–470).

John Wesley's initial mention of St. Just in his journal extract occurred in the entry for Saturday, 10 September 1743, in which he noted afternoon prayers that extended until 4:00 p.m. He then preached at the "cross" (intersection, crossroad) to an estimated one thousand persons, all of them quiet and serious. He preached there again the next morning, Sunday the 11th, between 8:00 and 9:00, on the green plain near the town, "to the largest congregation (I was informed) that had ever been seen in these parts," and he "cried out, with all the authority of love," a sermon derived from Job 4:31–32. "The people trembled and were still," Wesley noted, he not having experienced "such an hour before in Cornwall." Returning to St. Just on Saturday, 17 September, he preached, but without comment, waiting another seven months before walking, on Saturday, 7 April 1744, through heavy wind and rain from Morvah to St. Just. Although the weather limited his congregation to "hundreds," he nonetheless preached on Luke 7:42, recording what he thought as "remarkable that those of St. Just were the chief of the whole country for hurling,[6] fighting, drinking, and all manner of wickedness. But many of the lions have become lambs, are continually praising God and calling their old companions in sin to come and magnify the Lord together." Wesley remained at St. Just on Sunday the 8th to preach at 5:00 a.m. and noon.

After arriving at St. Just on Tuesday, 25 June 1745, Wesley preached at 7:00 a.m. to "the largest congregation since my coming," after which he met with the "earnest, loving" Methodist society, where "our hearts were all in a flame." At 5:00 a.m., Wednesday the 26th, he explicated for those members Romans 8:1, and when he had finished, a constable entered with a warrant, issued by the Rev. Dr. Walter Borlase,[7] for the arrest of Edward Greenfield, a tin-miner, age forty-six, with a wife and seven children. Three years earlier, Greenfield had earned a reputation for "cursing, swearing, and all manner of wickedness," but he had undergone reformation of sorts and currently had proved himself "remarkable for a quite contrary behavior." Wesley inquired of "a little gentleman" at St. Just concerning the objections to Greenfield, and the man answered, "Why, the man is well enough in other things, but his impudence the gentlemen cannot bear. Why, sir, he knows his sins are forgiven!" Obviously upset, Wesley wrote, "And *for this cause* he [Greenfield] is adjudged to banishment or death!" Two weeks later, Tuesday, 9 July 1745, Wesley came again to St. Just, and as he began his sermon, William Eustick (or "Ustick"),[8] a justice of the peace whose district included St. Just, approached him, took him by the hand, and said that he must go with him. To avoid a scene, Wesley did so. Eustick told the Methodist leader that he (Wesley) had recently promised not to return to St. Just for a month—a statement that Wesley denied. After holding Wesley for thirty minutes or so, Eustick returned him to his inn.

Two years later, on Saturday, 11 July 1747, Wesley examined the Methodist society at St. Just—a group "established and settled in the grace of God"—then preached at 5:00 a.m. the next day. When he returned on Saturday, 24 September 1748, he "rejoiced over the society here; their hearts are so simple and right toward God." Of the more than 150 members, more than one hundred of them walked "in the light of his countenance" [Psalms 44:3, 89:15, 90:8; Matthew 28:3; Revelation 1:16]. On Sunday, the 25th, believing "my strength would not allow my preaching five times in the day," Wesley "desired" that John Whitford, one of his itinerant preachers since 1745 (who would leave the itinerancy in 1754), preach the 5:00 a.m. sermon at St. Just. Wesley claimed, when next he came to St. Just on Saturday, 18 August 1750, that the Methodist society there remained the largest in Cornwall and housed "so great a proportion of believers I have not found in all the nation beside." He spoke with forty-five of those members, all of them "walking in the light of God's countenance." The next morning, 18 August, he preached at 8:00 to "a great multitude," departing that day and not returning until Saturday, 21 September 1751. At 6:00 p.m. on Saturday, 28 July 1753, Wesley found, at St. Just, "such a congregation ... as we used to have ten years since." Again, he emphasized, "I did not find any society in the county so much alive to God as this." He claimed the addition of between fifty and sixty new members, as well as "many [?] children filled with peace and joy in believing" [Romans 15:13]. On Sunday, the 29th, Wesley preached at 8:00 a.m. to another "large" gathering. Once again, after having preached at St. Just on Saturday evening, he noted the size of his audience in the superlative degree: "Except at Gwennap [pit][9] I have seen no such congregation in Cornwall." He also sought a connection between his outdoor service and the elements of Divine Nature: "The *sun* (nor could we contrive it otherwise) shone full in my face when I began the hymn. But just as I ended it a cloud arose, which covered it till I had done preaching. Is anything too small for the providence of him whom our 'very hairs are numbered?'" [Matthew 10:30].

In the journal extract entry for Sunday, 7 September 1755, is mentioned a "strange" letter written at some point in 1754 at Penzance and published in the "Historical Chronicle" (31 October 1754) of the *Gentleman's Magazine*, (1754), 24:482. The writer of the piece described an event wherein two residents of St. Just witnessed, at 10:00 p.m. a large fleet of ships in the sky; soon after a cloud fixed in front of that image, and the scene shifted to an army seemingly engaged in battle. The scene lasted some fifteen minutes, allowing a number of additional persons to view the scene. John Wesley, on this day at St. Just, spoke with the original two witnesses to the nocturnal phenomenon, James Tregear and Thomas Sackerly—both of them from St. Just parish, both "sensible" men, and neither one affiliated with the Methodists. In Wesley's middle-road view, the meaning of what those men saw, "if it was real (which I do not affirm), time only can show." With that, Wesley went on with his schedule, which found him back in St. Just on Saturday, 13 September 1755, preaching on the first stone of the new Methodist society house—the second Methodist chapel in that town, described as almost twice the size of the first one. Wesley preached in that building on his next visit to St. Just on Friday, 9 September 1757, styling it "the largest and the most commodious in the county." He went back to the town at 9:00 a.m., Sunday, the 11th, not returning until Monday, 15 September 1760, where, yet again, he proclaimed that "I have not seen such a congregation here for twice seven years. Abundance of backsliders being present, I chiefly applied to them. Some of them smiled at first, but it was not long before their mirth was turned into mourning. And I believe few, if any, went away without a witness from God that he 'willeth not the death of a sinner.'"—See, in the Book of Common Prayer (1662), "The Order for Morning and Evening Prayer," "The Absolution or Remission of Sins" (as pronounced by the priest alone) beginning, "Almighty God, the Father of our Lord Jesus Christ, who desireth not the death of a sinner, but rather, that he may turn from his wickedness and live."[10] Two days later, Wednesday the 17th, at 5:00 a.m., in a room filled to capacity, "God gave us a parting blessing," and on Monday and Tuesday, 13–14 September 1762, he spent "two comfortable nights" at St. Just, the congregations being "very large" both evening and morning.

When John Wesley came to St. Just on Thursday, 12 September 1765 (he had intended to be there on Monday the 9th), he learned of the death of John Bennetts, a resident near the town and a member of the Methodist society there. "He was a wise and good man," noted Wesley, "who had been above twenty years a father to that society." Shortly before his death, Bennetts had examined, with satisfaction, each of the society members concerning "their abiding in the faith," remarking, "Now I have no doubt we shall meet again at the right hand of our Lord" [Habakkuk 2:6; Psalms 110:5, 118:15–16]. Bennetts then, according to Wesley, "cheerfully committed his soul to Him and fell asleep." One should not ignore W. Reginald Ward's dénouement to this entry from Wesley's journal extract, noting "a John Bennetts was still in receipt of sums from the St. Just Society in 1767 and 1768."[11] In any event, that evening, before "a numerous congregation," Wesley preached on Ecclesiastes 9:10. A year later, Monday, 8 September 1766, the size of the assembled at St. Just forced Wesley to preach outdoors, in the rain. However, the elements appeared not to have discouraged that gathering, who remained throughout the sermon and even lingered after Wesley had finished. On Friday evening, 2 September 1768, he preached to yet another large audience at St. Just, while on Thursday, 31 August 1769, a violent wind prevented him from preaching out of doors. "However, God spoke to many hearts, both evening and the morning, September 1." During his time there, Wesley read a work by John Erskine (1721?-1803)—then minister of the Scottish Kirk at New Greyfriars Church, Edinburgh, and not especially on friendly terms with the Wesleyan Methodists—*The Nature of Saving Faith*, being the third of his *Theological Dissertations* (1765). In Wesley's view, Erskine claimed "(if I comprehend him right), 'It is in general an assent to the Word of God, in which there is a light, a glory, a brightness, which believers, and they only, perceive. In particular, it is an assent of the understanding to the gospel method of salvation, in which there is an excellency and a glory which only believers see. A supernatural conviction of this is faith.' But if this be his judgment, why does he quarrel with *me*? For how marvellously small is the difference between us! Only change the word *assent* for conviction ... and do we not come within a hair's breadth of each other? I do not quarrel with the definition of faith in general, 'a supernatural *assent* to the Word of God,' though I think a *supernatural conviction* of the truths contained in the Word of God is clearer. I allow, too, that the Holy Spirit enables us to perceive a peculiar light and glory in the Word of God, and particularly in the gospel method of salvation. But I doubt whether saving faith be properly 'an assent to its light and glory.' Is it not, rather, 'an assent (if we retain the word), to *the truths* which God has revealed? Or, more particularly, a divine conviction that 'God was in Christ, reconciling the world unto himself' [2 Corinthians 5:19]?"

Wesley's next visit to St. Just occurred on Monday, 27 August 1770, when he delivered his sermon from Revelation 20:12 in front of the Methodist preaching house. He declared "a glorious hour," both there and at the meeting of the Methodist society. "At such a season," he maintained, "who does not feel that nothing is too hard for God?" He returned to preach once more on Wednesday evening, 18 August 1771, as well as on Thursday, 22 August 1776, at 6:00 p.m. in the marketplace, where two or three "well-dressed" persons "walked by, stopped a little, and then went on." They repeated the exercise two or three times, causing Wesley to remark, "Had it not been for shame, they might have heard that which is able to save their souls." On Friday the 23rd, both morning and afternoon sermons attracted "large" gatherings, "and great was our rejoicing in the Lord." When Wesley next preached at St. Just, in the marketplace on Thursday evening, 27 August 1778, he noticed that "very few of our old society are now left; the far greater part of them are in Abraham's bosom [Luke 16:22], but the new generation are of the same spirit, serious, earnest, devoted to God, and particularly remarkable for simplicity and Christian sincerity." Near the preaching house at St. Just on Thursday, 24 August 1780, Wesley reported that "God applied his word with power, especially at the meeting of the society, when all our hearts were as melting wax [Psalms 22:14]." A year later, on Thursday, evening, 30 August 1781, he proclaimed "a happy season" at St. Just, and in late March or early April 1782, at Oldham, Lancashire, he received a letter from Christopher Watkins (1750–1805), then superintendent of the West Cornwall circuit, informing the Methodist patriarch, in part, "The last time I was at St. Just the leaders [of the Methodist society] gave me an account of seventy persons who had found either pardon or perfect love within the last fortnight [two weeks]. And the night and morning I was there, twenty more were delivered. One and twenty likewise were added to the society, most of whom have found peace with God."

On Sunday evening, 25 August 1787, Wesley preached at St. Just to a congregation that exceeded those at Mousehole and St. Buryan combined during the previous two days, and when there again on Thursday evening, 25 August 1785, he repeated an earlier assessment that although "many of our eldest brethren" remain, "many are gone to Abraham's bosom." At 6:00 p.m. he preached on John 5:8. John Wesley's final visit to St. Just came on Thursday evening, 20 August 1789, where the eighty-six-year-old patriarch of Wesleyan Methodism preached to "a lovely congregation, many of whom have not left their first love."[12]

St. Lawrence

When John Wesley came to preach at St. Lawrence, near Bodmin, in central Cornwall, on Friday, 13 September 1751, he described the place as "a little ugly, dirty village, eminent for nothing but an hospital for lepers, founded and endowed by Queen Anne [1665–1714; Queen of Great Britain and Ireland (1702–1714)]." Actually, Wesley proved off the mark in terms of the history of that institution. It dates from a deed of "29 Henry VIII" (1537–1538), later incorporated by Elizabeth I in 1582. Upon its closure in 1810, the trustees transferred the revenues of the St. Lawrence facility to the Royal Cornwall Infirmary at Truro.[1] Aside from that and despite his description, Wesley found that "God was there, even before I opened my mouth to a small loving congregation, one of whom had been sensible of his acceptance with God for above six and fifty years" (20:402).

St. Mewan

John Wesley initially visited St. Mewan, a parish one mile west of St. Austell, at 8:00 a.m., Wednesday, 28 September 1748. He walked through a continual rain to the village green, the usual site for the preaching, but the moment he began to speak, the rain ceased and did not resume until Wesley had finished his discourse. Returning to St. Mewan on Monday, 6 August 1750, again in the rain, he found "a large congregation" awaiting his arrival. As Wesley exited his lodging, a "huge" man fell against him twice and began to "curse and swear," at which point Wesley changed the course of his direction. However, the man pursued him through the crowd and "planted" himself close to Wesley. Toward the close of the sermon, the man's demeanor changed; he removed his hat, and at the conclusion he squeezed Wesley's hand in earnest and "went away, as quiet as a lamb." Wesley returned but one more time to St. Mewan, preaching there on Friday, 13 September 1751 (20:250, 355, 401).

St. Stephen's Down

John Wesley preached on St. Stephen's Down, in northeast Cornwall, near Launceston, at noon on Wednesday, 29 July 1747, and again "a little before six [p.m.]" on Sunday, 18 September 1748. On the latter occasion, all in attendance stood silent during his sermon, but the moment he ceased, "the chain fell off their tongues. I was really surprised. Surely was never such a cackling made on the banks of the Cayster, or the common of Sedgemoor." Wesley's analogies demonstrate his awareness of ancient literature and of fairly recent English history: The eighty-five-mile long Cayster River, in southwestern Asia Minor (now western Turkey in Asia), north of the Menderes River, flows west to the Aegean Sea, near Ephesus.

Homer celebrates the Cayster in the *Iliad*, as perceived by Alexander Pope in his edition of that epic (1715–1720):

> Not less their number than th' embody'd cranes,
> Or milk-white swans in *Asius'* watry plains,
> That o'er the windings of *Cayster's* springs,
> Stretch their long necks, and clap their rustling wings,
> Now tow'r aloft, and course in airy rounds;
> Now light with noise; with noise the field resounds [2:540–545].

Sedgemoor exists as a tract of moorland in Somersetshire, near Bridgewater, in southwestern England. There, on 6 July 1685, the forces of King James II defeated those of James Scott, Duke of Monmouth.

Wesley's third and final recorded visit to St. Stephen's Down came on 28 August 1750, where he preached at 8:00 p.m. "to such a congregation as I had not seen there for several years. The night overtook us soon after we had begun, but the moon gave us all the light we wanted." One man in the crowd "at first bawled out for the *church*," but he departed ashamed. Everyone else, observed Wesley, "seemed to be such as really desired 'to worship God in spirit and in truth' [John 4:23–24]" (20:184, 248, 359).

St. Stephen's–in-Bramwell

John Wesley preached but once in the village of St. Stephen's-in-Bramwell, four miles west of St. Austell, first attempting the exercise in a lone house on the side of a barren mountain, at 2:00 p.m. Sunday, 25 September 1757. He reported that neither the house nor its court could contain the people, so he led his congregation to a nearby meadow, "where all might kneel (which they generally do in Cornwall) as well as stand and hear. And they did hear and sing and pray as for life. I saw none careless or inattentive among them" (21:127).

St. Teath

The parish of St. Teath lay four miles southwest of Camelford, and John Wesley's lone visit came when he preached there on Wednesday evening, 19 June 1745. He offered no reaction (20:69).

St. Tudy

In first half of the eighteenth century, St. Tudy would have been situated five miles northeast of Wadebridge. Charles Wesley preached there but once, on Monday, 11 August 1746, on Mark 1:15, and as he concluded his discourse, a "gentleman," a drunken lawyer, rode up to him "fiercely" and ordered him to come forward. The two exchanged words and proceeded into the preaching house to extend the conversation. The lawyer then became less belligerent and left the scene, only to be accosted by John Adams, a mentally unstable resident of Tresemeer, who spent his time traveling about the county as "Overseer of all the Ministers" (2:472).

Saltash

In spring or early summer of 1722, Daniel Defoe, at Plymouth, Devonshire, crossed the Tamar River by ferry to Saltash, which he labeled "a little poor shattered town." He speculated that Saltash seemed to have been the ruins of a larger town, and he viewed a number of the houses in various stages of collapse. Undoubtedly, suspected Defoe, in an effort to underscore his point, "the rats and mice have abandoned many more." Nonetheless, he found the town governed by a mayor and an alderman, endowed with a number of "privileges," sent members to Parliament, collected tolls from vessels that passed by on the river, and controlled the considerable oyster-fishing industry over the entire river. Defoe also recorded that he had heard of merchants beginning to trade at Saltash, as well as ships involved in the Newfoundland fishing industry, but such activities proceeded only on a minor scale.[1]

One and one-half miles south of Saltash lies Trematon Castle, a ruined shell keep (a circular or polygonal stone wall surrounding a *motte*— a variation of "moat") built by Reginald de Valletort in the late twelfth century. The attached curtain wall surrounding the *bailey*—the external wall— and the gatehouse appear to have been added at a later date.[2]

On Friday afternoon, 26 September 1760, John Wesley endured heavy wind and steady rain as he paused at Saltash on his way to Plymouth. However, no boat could manage over the Tamar River because of those conditions, thus forcing him to lodge in the town. Realizing, on Saturday, the 27th, that he would not be able to cross the river from Saltash, Wesley headed for the bridge at Gunnislake. However, fifteen years later, on Thursday, 7 September 1775, the Methodist leader arrived at Saltash for the same purpose, but on that occasion, a number of Methodists met him there with a boat, and they safely crossed the Tamar to Plymouth Dock (21:282; 22:465).

Sancreed

Situated southwest of Penzance and west of Newlyn, in extreme southwest Cornwall, Sancreed had been the scene of Methodist preaching since 1750, particularly in the home of the father of one of Wesley's itinerant preachers, Richard Rodda (1743–1815). John Wesley first preached there on Sunday afternoon, 12 September 1762, between 1:00 and 2:00, observing an abundance of strangers who "came from every side, and I believe not many went empty away." His second and final recorded visit to Sancreed occurred on Sunday, 4 September 1768, when he attended church service and heard an "excellent" sermon. Later that afternoon, again between 1:00 and 2:00, he explained "that happy religion which our Lord describes in the eight Beatitudes" [Matthew 5:2–12] (21:388–389; 22:157).

Scilly, Isles of

The Isles of Scilly comprise a group of 140 small islands, totaling approximately six square miles and lying between twenty-five and thirty-five miles off the western extremity of Land's End, Cornwall. The five inhabited group of isles includes St. Mary's (the principal island), St. Martin's, Tresco, St. Agnes, and Bryher. On St. Mary's, one would have found, (1) on the northwest coast, Bant's Cairn, a small Neolithic entrance grave chambered tomb covered by a mound; (2) Innisdgen, a Neolithic chambered tomb, partially covered, on the northeast coast; (3) Porth Hellick Down, yet another small, partially covered, Neolithic entrance grave; (4) Star Castle (1593), an Elizabethan fort built by the court engineer Robert Adams in the shape of an eight-pointed star to defend the southwest coast of England against the return of the Spanish following the defeat of the armada in 1588 (eventually converted to a hotel). Tresco houses (1) a tall round tower, being the remains of Cromwell's Castle, a fort built by Admiral Robert Blake (1599–1657) during 1651–1652 to guard the west coast of England against royalist privateers and landing parties; (2) Tresco Abbey, a lush subtropical garden with a large variety of exotic plants from Africa, grown on the island because of its proximity to the Gulf Stream.[1]

On Thursday afternoon, 26 January 1738, aboard the *Samuel*, from Charleston, in the Carolinas settlement, to England, John Wesley reported that Captain Percy, because of difficulty in sighting, "began to be uneasy, fearing we might either get unawares into the Bristol Channel, or strike in the night on the rocks of Scilly." However, by noon Saturday, 28 January, "we had an exact observation, and by this we found we were as well as we could desire, about eleven leagues [thirty-three miles] south of Scilly."

More than five years later, Wesley openly expressed his "desire to go and publish the love of God our Saviour [Titus 2:10, 13; Jude 25], if it were but for one day, in the Isles of Scilly." On Monday evening, 12 September 1743, three members of the Methodist society at St. Ives volunteered to transport him there, providing that he obtain the mayor's boat—reportedly the best vessel available. Having done that, on Tuesday morning, 13 September, Wesley and six others sailed from St. Ives—the itinerant preachers John Nelson and William Shepherd, three unidentified men, and one pilot. Wesley expressed a sense of discomfort in attempting to negotiate more than thirty miles of open sea in a fishing boat, "especially when the waves began to swell and hang over our heads." Relying upon what he knew best, Wesley summoned his companions to sing "lustily and with a good courage," a verse (slightly altered from the original) from Charles Wesley's 1739 hymn, "Peace, doubting heart, my God's I am":

> When passing through the watery deep,
>   I ask in faith his promised aid,
> The waves an awful distance keep,
>   And shrink from my devoted head.
> Fearless their violence I dare:
>   They cannot harm, for God is there.

At 1:30 p.m. the boat landed at St. Mary's, and the group appeared before Lord Francis Godolphin (1678–1766), governor of the Scilly Isles, Wesley presenting him with a newspaper and a copy of his *An Earnest Appeal to Men of Reason and Religion* (1743). However, the minister of St. Mary's, Ralph Hathaway, refused Wesley his church, and thus the Methodist leader took to the street at 6:00 p.m. preaching to "almost all the town, and many soldiers, sailors and workmen" on Ezekiel 18:31, 33:11. "It was a blessed time," intoned Wesley, "so that I scarce knew how to conclude." Following the sermon, Wesley distributed "some little books" and hymns, "which they were so eager to receive that they were ready to tear both them and me to pieces." Wesley also noted that he could not understand the "*political reason*" why such a large number of workmen had been gathered, at so large an expense, "to fortify a few barren rocks, which whosoever would take deserves to have them for his pains." He resolved the question by declaring the presence of a "*providential reason*," that being "God might call them together to hear the gospel [Acts 15:17], which perhaps otherwise they might never have thought of." The next morning, Wednesday the 14th, at 5:00, Wesley preached again [Hosea 14:4], and between 9:00 and 10:00 spoke with a number of persons in private, distributing among them an additional two to three hundred hymns and more "little books." That task completed, "we left this barren, dreary place" and set sail for St. Ives (18:212; 19:338–339).

Although Wesley did not return to the Scilly Isles, he had to concern himself with one minor issue there. At some point in early Fall 1771, an evangelical Church of England cleric identified only as "Rev. S. L." had consulted with John Floyd (1749–1798), then a Methodist itinerant preacher in the Cornwall West circuit, as to the state of the work in Scilly. On 14 October 1771, the Rev. L. responded to a letter from Wesley, the former requesting that the Methodist leader send a preacher to assist him with the work. He informed Wesley that if he could not succeed in enacting changes, he would leave Scilly as soon as possible to converse with him concerning a solution to the problem. The exact nature of the changes or the problem have not yet come directly to light. Wesley responded to the Rev. L. from the London borough of Lewisham on 14 December 1771, informing him, frankly, that he had been wasting his talents. "A dispensation of the gospel is committed to you," chastised Wesley, "and yet you preach not the gospel, or but now and then, instead of continually stirring up the gift of God that is in you. Is this inactivity, this losing so many precious opportunities, owing to any temporal views? Do you expect to get more money by delay? I hope not. Do you want to avoid labour, shame, or censure? I would fain [gladly, willingly] think better things of you. Surely you have not so learned Christ [Ephesians 4:20]!"[2]

Sennen

Charles Wesley's manuscript journal reveals only a single visit to Sennen, located one mile east from the tip of Land's End and four miles south from St. Just. There, on Saturday, 30 July 1743, he lodged with a "hospitable" farmer, and from there walked to Land's End (2:366). John Wesley also managed but a single visit to Sennen, following closely that of his younger brother. At 6:00 p.m. Saturday, 10 September 1743, John Wesley preached at Sennen and "appointed the little congregation (consisting chiefly of old grey-headed men) to meet me again at five in the morning." However, on Sunday, the 11th, the larger part of that group had gathered between 3:00 and 4:00 a.m. Nonetheless, Wesley spoke at 4:00. "We began praising God," noted Wesley, and he then explicated Hosea 14:4.

Sithney

The "substantial" country parish of Sithney, two miles northwest of Helston, in the eighteenth century, generally demonstrated its inhabitants' theological loyalty to the Church of England. For example, in c. 1744, the local church there reported forty Easter communicants, two Sacramental services at Whit-Sunday and Trinity Sunday, and a total of seven such services throughout the year.

Charles Wesley appeared at Sithney on Thursday, 3 July 1746, where he demonstrated to more than "a thousand sinners" the love and compassion that Jesus Christ had extended to them. More than two weeks later, on Saturday, 19 July, he came again to Sithney, "where the word begins to take root," and on Saturday, 2 August, he spoke with a resident of the town "who had been set at liberty from the guilt of sin the first time he heard me, I think, as soon as I had named my text." That evening he preached on 1 Corinthians 1:23, and on Sunday morning, the 3rd, to a gathering that "seemed truly desirous to know him" (2:465, 467, 471, 570).

John Wesley first preached at Sithney at 6:00 p.m. on Saturday, 13 September 1746, but darkness descended upon the gathering and he would finish his sermon beneath the light of the moon. He had intended to meet with members of the Methodist society only, but he continued, instead, to speak to his congregation, exhorting them "not to leave their first love." On Sunday morning, the 14th, he delayed his sermon until 8:00 to accommodate those who had come from the surrounding area. He preached again at Sithney on Wednesday, 8 July 1747; on Monday, 26 September 1748, at noon; Monday evening, 13 August 1750; and, for the final time, on Tuesday, 10 September 1751 (20:141, 182, 250, 356, 401).

Sticker

A village three miles southwest of St. Austell, Sticker lay on the main road to Truro. John Wesley's only visit came when he preached there on Wednesday, 24 August 1785. He did not record his comments or observations.

Stithians

Charles Wesley "preached the gospel to the poor" at Stithians, three to four miles northwest of Penryn, on Sunday afternoon, 29 June 1746. Returning on Sunday 6 July, he sharply rebuked the Methodist society, allowing them two weeks "to know their own mind whether they will serve God or Mammon [Luke 16:13]." Wesley then reported on a woman who maintained the preaching house at Stithians who could not cease telling him "how rich and strong she was in grace, that she could not be proud, could not be deceived, could not fall, etc." Although Wesley assured her that a common harlot stood in a considerably better spiritual condition than she, "she was above all reproof, or conviction" (2:464, 465).

John Wesley first came to Stithians at 8:00 a.m., Sunday, 15 April 1744, where he preached on a green triangular plat capable, according to his estimate, "of holding eight to ten thousand men." Wesley stood on one of the walls that enclosed the site, while a number of persons sat on the other two. "Some thousands stood between" he observed, "and received the word with all readiness of mind." He returned the next year, at 8:00 a.m., Sunday, 23 June 1745, preaching to a "large, quiet congregation"; again at 8:00 a.m., Sunday, 7 July; and once again at that same hour on Sunday, 14 July. On the last cited date, Wesley exhorted the Methodist society "not to think of pleasing men but to count all things loss, so that they might win Christ." Before he completed that task, the constables and church-wardens came and pressed one of the members into the Royal Army. Two years later, Saturday, 4 July 1747, Wesley preached at Stithians at 7:00 p.m. and again at 5:00 a.m. on Sunday the 5th. He preached for the last time at Stithians at noon on Monday, 13 August 1750 (20:25, 72, 78, 80, 181, 356).

Tolcarn

Tolcarn, in Wendron parish, southern Cornwall, exemplifies anti–Methodist attempts to silence John Wesley and to reduce the effects of Methodism in Cornwall, as witnessed by the Methodist leader's appearance there on Thursday, 4 July 1745. He had expected to preach that evening, but a crowd halted him as he arrived, pleading with him not to proceed, explaining that the churchwardens, constables, and parish leaders awaited with a warrant for his arrest and conveyance before the justices at Helston. Wesley then rode forward to confront his accusers, who informed him that the warrant claimed his having spent considerable time in France and Spain and named him as an agent of the Pretender[1] sent to convince members of the Methodist societies to join the Jacobite cause. In the end, because of the sudden intercession of the Rev. John Collins,[2] Wesley left Tolcarn and rode to the house of a friend, "some miles off, and found the sleep of a laboring man is sweet" (20:77–78).

Torpoint

The village of Torpoint, a chapelry (the district or precinct attached to a chapel) in the parish of St. Anthony, three miles west of Plymouth Dock, Devonshire, had been connected to the latter by a ferry. According to John Wesley's journal extract, the Methodist patriarch had never preached there prior to 1787, and thus his initial visit, by invitation, did not occur until Friday, 2 March of that year, when he preached on Isaiah 55:7. Among his listeners on that day numbered "a large company from the Dock and a great multitude from all quarters. I suppose a great part of these had never heard this sort of preaching before. They now heard with inexpressible attention. And, I believe, not in vain. God opened, as it were, the windows of heaven and sent a gracious rain upon his inheritance. I am in hopes a plentiful harvest will spring from the seed which was sown this hour." Wesley returned once more to Torpoint on Tuesday, 11 September 1787, but only to pause for less than an hour before boarding the ferry for Plymouth Dock (24:6. 59, 202, 221).

Towednack

Towednack, in the eighteenth century, lay two miles southwest of St. Ives. In the early 1740s, official Church of England reports from Towednack indicated a population of approximately forty families, with the same number of eligible communicants—or an estimate, on the average, of one communicant for each family.[1]

Charles Wesley attended church services at Towednack on Sunday, 17 July 1743, where William Hoblyn,[2] the curate to the Rev. William Symonds (1684?-1776), vicar of St. Ives and Towednack, "entertained us with a curious discourse" on Matthew 7:15. Wesley stood near the pulpit and "heard such a hodge-podge of railing, foolish lies which Satan himself might have been ashamed of. I had asked that my countenance might not alter, and was kept in perfect peace. The poor people behaved very decently, and all followed me to hear the true word of God." Wesley later told the Rev. Hoblyn that he had been misinformed concerning the Methodists, to which the latter responded that he had spoken only the truth. Wesley countered with "if you believe what you preach, you believe a lie." "You are a liar," Hoblyn replied, and Wesley responded by reminding him "of the great day, testified my good will, and left him for the congregation." At his own service, Wesley "opened the door of utterance to preach the gospel of Christ Jesus. I know they found the difference between the chaff and the wheat."

Wesley encountered problems when he returned to Towednack a week later, Sunday, 24 July. He preached in the afternoon from Isaiah 53, attended evening church service, and would have continued his text from Isaiah, had not the mob assaulted the gathering, seeking revenge on the Methodists for creating a disturbance on the Sabbath and causing people to leave the Church. The mob attacked with sticks and stones and attempted harm upon Wesley, who pleaded that they strike him and spare the people. "Many lifted up their hands and weapons, but were not permitted to touch me. My time is not yet come [John 7:6]," he announced. Surrounded by the mob, Wesley escaped harm by the intervention of two men who underwent sudden changes of heart and led him safely from the scene. In the process, Wesley observed ten cowardly ruffians attacking one unarmed man, beating him with their clubs until he fell to the ground. Also, the mob continued to purse Wesley to the home of John Nance,[3] where he lodged. On the next day, Monday 25 July, the mayor of Towednack told Charles Wesley that Revs. Symonds and Hoblyn had sponsored the mob's actions, principally by representing Methodists, in their sermons, as emissaries of the Pope and encouraging their parishioners to riot against them. "Yesterday we were stoned as popish incendiaries," exclaimed Wesley. "Today it is our turn to have favour with the people" (2:358, 360, 363–363).

Tredinney

On Monday, 13 July 1747, John Wesley preached at Tredinney, a hamlet two miles northwest of St. Buryan, to "a large and earnest congregation, notwithstanding the wonderful [false, fictional] stories they have frequently heard related to the pulpit for certain truths." The next day, Tuesday the 14th, from Tredinney, he addressed a letter to the Rev. Robert Corker (1708?-?),[1] a native of Falmouth and curate of St. Buryan, in response to Corker having informed his congregation that Wesley had ordered that £100 be raised immediately for an undetermined purpose. "Can it be," inquired Wesley, "that you should be so totally void (I will not say conscious, of religion, but) of good nature, as to credit such a tale? And of good manners and common sense as *thus* to repeat it." The Methodist leader demanded a retraction, but Corker never responded (20:183).

Tregavarah Downs

Located in the parish of Madron, Tregavarah Downs lay between 2 and 2.5 miles west of Penzance. John Wesley preached there at noon, Monday, 9 April 1744, to a "great" congregation that proved deeply attentive, deriving his text from Acts 28:22. He preached there again at noon on Friday, 13 April (20:22, 24–25).

Trenouth

On Monday, 27 August 1781, John Wesley wrote that he had been requested to preach at Trenouth at noon, "*a little way* (they [?] said)" out of the road from St. John's (?) to St. Austell. "The 'little way,'" bemoaned Wesley, "proved six or seven miles, through road ready to break our wheels [of his chaise] in pieces." A purely geographical problem arises because, as stated by W. Reginald Ward and Richard P. Heitzenrater, "No satisfactory identification of this place has been made." Those editors suspect that the site might have been "Trenouth, a mile east of St. Cleer, not far from Liskeard" and approximately "half way between Plymouth and St. Austell."[1] Nehemiah Curnock complicated the issue by deferring to Richard Green, Wesley's late nineteenth-century bibliographer, who suggested "Trenode" as the place visited by Wesley. However, Curnock argued that Wesley, traveling from Plymouth to St. Austell, and going out of his way to preach at a place so little known appeared improbable. He then offered the possibility of Tywardreath as Wesley's destination, that village having been marked on the map of Cornwall prepared by John (?) Cary[2] as lying nineteen miles from Truro, and appears in the Postal Guide as "Twyardreath," near the "present" [1909–1916] Par station.[3] With all of that having been noted, there exists no recorded evidence that John Wesley paused or preached at Trenouth.

Tresmeer

The village of Tresmeer, by the end of the seventeenth century a curacy and an extremely small parish, lay approximately four miles north of Trewint, seven to eight miles west of Launceston, north of the road from Launceston to Camelford, and twenty miles from North Tamerton. Prior to the Wesleys' visits to Cornwall, Tresmeer housed twenty families; ministers of the Church of England held four administrations of the Sacrament per year and fortnightly services, and claimed forty-six eligible communicants and thirty-eight recipients of that rite. Further, the village church officials declared the parish free of Protestant Dissenters—Congregationalists, Baptists, Presbyterians, et al.[1]

The Rev. John Bennet (1670?-1750),[2] the evangelical curate of the churches at Laneast, Tresmeer, and North Tamerton, invited Charles Wesley to read prayers and to preach on Luke 12:32 at Tresmeer on Monday, 16 July 1744, and Wesley preached there again on Tuesday afternoon, 7 August, where he expounded on the Good Samaritan (Luke 10:29–37) before a "thronged" congregation. A number of gentry had traveled, according to Wesley, eighteen miles "to hear the word, and received it with joy [Matthew 13:20; Luke 8:13]. We have not had a more generous season," he concluded, "since we came into the country." Charles Wesley returned to Tresmeer church on Wednesday, 25 June 1746, reading prayers and preaching to a gathering that "seemed to feel the word of reconciliation." Less than two months later, Tuesday evening, 12 August, Tresmeer church housed a crowded congregation that listened to Wesley's sermon on Mark 2:17, and nine days later, Thursday, 21 August, he proclaimed "the dying love of Jesus" in Tresmeer church (2:408, 415–416, 464, 472, 474).

John Wesley also found a friendly pulpit in Tresmeer church, and there, on Wednesday afternoon, 19 June 1745, before a crowded gathering, "both within and without," he preached on Romans 4:7. Following the service, Wesley "took leave of poor, mad, original enthusiast [John Adams[3]], who had been scattering abroad lies in every quarter." One month later, at 5:00 a.m., 16 July, Wesley read prayers and preached at Tresmeer church; preached there on Monday evening, 27 July 1747, and at 5:00 a.m. on both the 28th and 29th; again on Saturday evening, 17 September 1748; and between 3:00 and 4:00 Sunday the 18th, before a "large congregation. There was no need of speaking terrible things to these people ready prepared for the Lord," declared Wesley. Thus he began his sermon on 2 Corinthians immediately following prayers. On Monday evening, 27 August 1750, John Bennet "(now full of days and by swift steps removing into eternity)," read prayers at Tresmeer church, and John Wesley preached on Hebrews 4:14. Finally, on Sunday afternoon, 1 September 1751, as usual at Tresmeer church, Wesley read prayers and preached on Luke 10:23–24. "We 'sang praises lustily and with a good courage' [Psalms 33:3 (BCP)], till (in a manner I never remember before), 'A **solemn** reverence **checked** our songs,/And praise **sat** silent on our tongues'"—Wesley's variation of the final lines (6:3–4) of Isaac Watts' "Eternal Power! Whose high abode," the concluding piece of Book I, *Horae Lyricae: Poems, Chiefly of the Lyric Kind. In Three Books* (1706): "A **sacred** rev'rence **checks** our songs,/And praise **sits** silent on our tongues" (20:69, 80, 184, 248, 359, 400).

Treswithian Downs

The village of Treswithian lay one mile west of Camborne and five miles from St. Ives, and at Treswithian Downs on Sunday, 4 September 1743, John Wesley discovered "seven or eight hundred" persons gathered there to hear him preach on Ezekiel 18:31. Pausing for dinner, he preached again to a gathering of "about a thousand" people on Acts 5:31. In the end, he observed "a little impression made on two or three of the hearers; the rest (as usual) showing huge approbation and absolute unconcern." Undaunted, Wesley returned to Treswithian Downs a week later, at 1:00 on Monday the 12th, and again on Tuesday afternoon, the 20th, Wesley addressed "two or three thousand" persons from Isaiah 35:8—thus concluding his contact with Treswithian (19:336, 338, 340).

Trevowhan

John Wesley's only opportunity at Trevowhan, a hamlet one-half mile east of Morvah, came on Wednesday evening, 10 July 1745, at which time he preached on Isaiah 55:1. In less than fifteen minutes into that discourse, a constable and his "companions" approached and read the proclamation against riots.[1] When the man had finished his task, Wesley responded, "We will do as you require; we will disperse within an hour," and he continued his sermon. After preaching, Wesley had intended to meet alone with the Methodist society at Trevowhan, but a number of persons from the congregation followed him "with such earnestness" that he included them in the meeting. After exhorting the gathering "to love their enemies, as Christ loved us," the crowd became extremely emotional, and Wesley saw fit to respond to (and record) the event in verse:

> Even now the Lord doth pour
> The blessing from above;
> A kindly, gracious shower
> Of heart-reviving love [9:1–4],[2] [20:19].

Trewalder

Trewalder, a hamlet two miles west of Camelford, furnished the site for John Wesley's sermon on John 11:25, at approximately noon on Monday, 27 August 1750. A number of those gathered had "dissolved into gracious tears," with an equal number "filled with strong consolation." On Friday, 10 August 1753, the Methodist leader found there "a little"

Methodist society that met each night and morning, with or without a preacher's presence. "And whoever comes among them," wrote Wesley, "quickly feels what spirit they are of." He came there again at noon on Wednesday, 31 August 1757, and, three years later, on Saturday evening, 6 September 1760, preached at Trewalder before an "exceeding lively congregation." He proclaimed that "indeed, all the [Methodist] society stands well and 'adorns the doctrine of God our Saviour' [Titus 2:10]." Finally, about 2:00 p.m. on Friday, 24 September 1762, John Wesley preached at Trewalder "and found God there" (20:359, 471; 21:121, 274, 390).

Trewellard

The village (or hamlet) of Trewellard, situated two miles north of St. Just and belonging to that parish, proved to have been the home of the Methodist exhorter John Bennetts.[1] There Charles Wesley, at noon, Wednesday, 23 July 1746, found "about a dozen of the shattered [Methodist] Society, which quickly increased to fifty or sixty." He immediately perceived "a blessing in the remnant. We wrestled with God in his own strength"[2] from 1:00 until 9:00, pausing only for the preaching. After the "little flock" had been spiritually "comforted and refreshed abundantly," Wesley spoke with each society member, "amazed to find them just the reverse of what they had been represented.... Their exhorter appeared a solid, humble Christian; raised up to stand in the gap, and keep the trembling sheep together." Weary, but unable to sleep, Wesley left his bed at 4:00 a.m. (Thursday, the 24th) and spoke with a number of society members and "adored the miracle of grace, which has kept these sheep in the midst of wolves." Returning to Trewellard on Thursday, 7 August 1746, Charles Wesley spoke with the society and, before the preaching, read to those who had gathered a tract, *An Act More Effectively to Prevent Profane Cursing and Swearing* (London: Thomas Baskett, 1746)—a hundred copies of which had been sent to John Wesley by an unidentified justice of the peace. At that last recorded visit to Trewellard, Charles Wesley "rejoiced over this steady people. Near 150 are gathered again, and knit together in the love of Jesus" (2:467–469, 471).

When John Wesley entered Trewellard on Saturday, 6 September 1746, he found no Methodist society in Cornwall so "lively." Nonetheless, he felt obliged to reprove a number of its members for negligence in attending society meetings, which he termed always "the forerunner of greater evils." That evening, he preached in Green Court, "well filled with earnest hearers," and he held forth at 5:00 the following morning (Sunday the 7th) in the preaching house that would not contain the entire congregation (20:135–136). He would not return to Trewellard.

Trewergy

John Wesley undertook two visits to the village of Trewergy, near Redruth, in southern Cornwall. The first occurred on Friday evening, 31 August 1770, at which time he came across "an ingenious book"—either *Dialogues of the Dead* (1760) or *New Dialogues of the Dead* (1762), both by George, Lord Lyttleton (1709–1773). "A great part I could heartily subscribe to," he wrote, "though not to every word. I believe Madam Guyon [the French mystic Jeanne Marie Bouvier de la Motte-Guyon (1648–1717)] was in several mistakes, speculative and practical too. Yet I would no more dare to call her than her friend Archbishop Fenelon [Francois de Savignac de la Mothe Fenelon (1651–1715)], 'a distracted enthusiast.' She was understandably a woman of very uncommon understanding and of excellent piety. Nor was she any more 'a lunatic' than she was an *heretic*." Wesley argued further against Lyttleton's attacks upon the Methodists, asking, "Why should a good-natured and a thinking man ... condemn whole bodies of men by the lump? In this I can neither read the gentleman, the scholar, nor the Christian." In his journal extract for that day, Wesley noted that "since this writing, Lord Lyttleton is no more; he is mingled with common dust. But as his book survives, there still needs an answer to the just reflections [on the Methodists] contained therein."

Wesley's second and last visit to Trewergy began at 6:00 p.m. Saturday, 3 September 1774, when he preached "and applied closely to the Methodists, 'What do ye more than others?' [Matthew 5:47]." One member of the congregation cried out, "*Damnable* doctrine!"—to which Wesley responded, "True; it *condemns* all those who hear and do not obey it" (245–247, 428).

Trewint

The hamlet of Trewint, in northeastern Cornwall, lay four miles south of Tresmeer and seven miles southwest of Launceston. John Wesley arrived there at 2:00 p.m., Monday, 2 April 1744, "wet and weary enough, by the rain and hail for some hours." He preached indoors that evening to a gathering that exceeded the capacity of the preaching house. Two weeks later, Tuesday morning, 17 April, he preached at 5:00, and prior to his departure received word of the continued accusations against him of being associated with the Pretender,[1] as well as parading as the true John Wesley, who had since died. Still very much alive, Wesley appeared at Trewint more than a year later, preaching between 4:00 a.m. and 5:00 a.m., Monday, 15 July 1745. The Methodist leader's final visit to that village did not occur until fifteen years later, when he preached, near noon, on Sunday, 26 July 1762. He recorded that fact without substantive comment (20:19–20, 25, 80; 21:390).

Trezelah

Located in Gulval parish, the village of Trezelah claimed little of note or attention. John Wesley preached there but once, on Friday, 5 July 1745, although his appearance presented the potential of disruption and even danger. As he approached the village limits, several persons, "in great consternation," met him and reported that constables and churchwardens awaited his arrival. Nonetheless, he rode forward to meet "a serious congregation," but found neither churchwardens nor constables to molest him, his worship service, or the Methodist society meeting that followed. "After so many storms," remarked Wesley, "we now enjoyed the calm and praised God from the ground of the heart" (20:78).

Truro

Truro, "a very considerable town," according to Daniel Defoe, would have been noted as one of the four "coinage towns" of Cornwall when the first list of those sites appeared in 1305.[1] By the late seventeenth century, the town, situated up the river north by northeast of Falmouth and six miles from Gwennap, housed a long wharf in the front of the town and provided and functioned as a substantial port for *small* ships only. Defoe observed that "the Lord Warden of the Stannaries[2] always holds his famous Parliament of Miners," and that the town had achieved modest recognition for the stamping of tin. "There are at least three churches in it," he concluded, "but no Dissenter's meeting house, that I could hear of."[3]

Also, by mid-eighteenth century, Truro had become a center of popular culture and known for its affluent residents who lived in considerable comfort in fine houses on Princes Street[4] and indulged in such fashionable amusements as the theater, assembly rooms, the county library, a literary society, and the cockpit. Nonetheless, in a mining town in which various degrees of accidental occupational injuries would have been expected, a hospital for the treatment of injured miners did not come into being until

1799. Equally expected, the citizens of eighteenth-century Truro stood firmly in line with the Church of England, although, prior to the visitations from the Wesleys and their itinerant preachers, the Rev. Joseph Jane reported the existence of six or seven families of Presbyterian, or Independent, allegiance, but they had not, as yet, constructed a meeting house. When the Rev. Samuel Walker came to Truro as curate in July 1746, the population of the town had reached 1,600 persons, and its town officials boasted of its fine houses, its status as the center of the tin trade, and the presence of its "considerable social amenities." Truro also had achieved a reputation for "dissipation ... worldliness, and frivolity."

The shadows of concern quickly descended upon Walker's optimism at having received the Truro appointment within the initial year of his tenure there, principally as concerned his compensation. According to the historian William Hals,[5] "As when [c. 1700] it [Truro] was a free chapel [independent of the Established Church], the minister subsisted on the oblations [subsidies to persons who served the Church] and subventions [subsidies, grants] of the altar, so now [c. 1747] comparatively, on the piety and charity of his hearers by voluntary subscriptions: from whence it may be presumed that the rector must demean himself well, and labour hard in his vocation, to get a competent maintenance, at least he must walk with upright and wary conduct as he that went barefoot upon the edge of a very sharp knife, and did not hurt his feet: since he must converse with, and have to do with, men of divers principles and opinions in religion in this place ... as of old his predecessors had with monks, Dominican and Franciscan friars, who were sharers or pealers [those intent upon removing all or parts of the whole] of his profits."[6] Thus, once each year, Samuel Walker had to engage in an ordeal of "collecting the town" in order to increase his inadequate compensation. Fortunately, an order issued by the Truro Corporation dated 3 April 1747 provided £22 for "a year's gift sermons and town donation ... that is to say the sum of ten pounds will, it is apprehended, be about the amount for gift sermons, and the twelve pounds be a donation from the borough." That proved not to have been an especially large stipend, since, as late as 1787, the reputed value of the Truro living stood at only £120, and the certified value at but £30.[7]

Another problem confronting Walker focused upon St. Mary's Church, Truro, the earliest form of the structure described by a visitor to the town in 1750 as "a most elegant building of about Henry VIII's time [reigned 1509–1547], with some old painted glass in it and curious sculpture on the south and east fronts, and the letter which King Charles the first [1600–1649, reigned 1625–1649] writ to the people of Cornwall on their loyalty towards him is put up in the church."[8] Speculation had arisen that the monuments and glass had been damaged during the Commonwealth period (1649–1660), and a ruthless clearance had been executed during an incompetent attempt at restoration of the church in 1747. Further, the windows had been "modernized" at some point and a large portion of the painted glass supposedly given to children for toys. In addition, cartloads of dilapidated tombstones had been deposited on the river bank, and practically all of the tablets and memorials on the north wall had been subjected to destruction. All that work, reportedly, had been carried forth by the Truro Corporation, after which that body constructed, in c. 1750, "Corporation seats" for themselves and at their own expense.[9]

John Wesley rode through Truro on Saturday, 30 August 1755, at which point a person stopped his horse and insisted upon his alighting therefrom. Then, three or more of Samuel Walker's society approached and conveyed the appearance of a lengthy acquaintance with the Methodist leader. However, Wesley had to break away from the meeting for a preaching engagement at Redruth. Two years later, on 20 September 1757, Wesley received an invitation from a grocer and maltster by the name of Painter (?-1789) to lodge in his house at Truro. He found in that town and among the Methodist society, "a season of uncommon refreshment." Another five years passed before Wesley managed a visit to Truro, riding there from Grampound on market-day, Saturday, 4 September 1762, expecting a disturbance. He stood in a street at "a small distance" from the market, but he found nothing but quiet, concluding that "both persecution and popular tumult seem to be forgotten in Cornwall." On the day following, Sunday morning, the 5th, he occupied the same place and preached on Galatians 6:14, when "a poor man" began a disturbance, but the constables quickly rushed him from the scene.

After John Wesley had preached at Truro at noon, Thursday, 4 September 1766, he conveyed the hope that following the death of Samuel Walker in 1761, certain among the former vicar's followers would have ceased their "enmity" against the Methodists. "But not so," he noted. After five years, those persons "still look upon us as rank heretics and will have no fellowship with us." Nonetheless, Wesley continued his visits to Truro, riding there through the rain on Wednesday, 30 August 1769, where he learned that his former host, Mr. Painter, lay ill. He went directly to the grocer's house, but his recording of events in the journal extract ends abruptly. The record at Truro resumes on Monday morning, 3 September 1770, when, between 8:00 and 9:00, he preached during "a few" light showers. On Tuesday, 17 August 1773, Wesley preached in the Coinage Hall at

Truro, specifically in the upper lecture room of a building at the east end of Boscawen Street.[10] The next opportunity to preach at Truro came on Friday, 1 September 1775, in the piazza adjoining Coinage Hall and speaking on Ephesians 2:8—to which he added, "I doubt the antinomians[11] gnashed on me with their teeth; but I *must* declare 'the whole counsel of God' [Acts 20:27]." Then on Tuesday, 28 August 1781, in the midst of an extremely heavy rainstorm, Wesley arrived in Truro, where he found a congregation "seriously affected. One would have imagined, everyone that was present had a desire to save his soul." He returned on Friday, 23 August 1782. In the interim between that visit and the next, the Methodist leader wrote from London on 23 January 1783 to Joseph Taylor,[12] "You must endeavor to hire a larger room at Truro. We shall not build any more [preaching houses] in haste. I often preach abroad in winter as well as summer." Wesley rode again to Truro on Monday morning, 10 September 1787, but paused, first, at the home of the Rev. Richard Milles (1754?-1823), rector of Kenwyn, one-half mile from Truro—"a house fit for a nobleman," he observed, "and the most beautifully situated of any I have seen in the country."[13] At noon, he spoke in the preaching house at Truro, it being "well filled with deeply attentive hearers."

Wesley's next visit proved fortunate despite immediate circumstance. On Tuesday, 18 August 1789, expecting to preach at noon, he could not negotiate the main street of Truro to the Methodist preaching house—it being blocked by soldiers to the east and "numberless" tin miners to the west. The latter had come to beg or to demand an increase in their wages, "without which they could not live." Thus, Wesley had to retire to the other end of town where he preached by the Coinage Hall, where he preached on Acts 17:31 "to twice as many people, rich and poor, as the preaching-house would have contained. And many of them would not have come thither at all. How wise are all the ways of God!" Ten days later, Thursday, 27 August, Wesley reached Truro soon after 5:00 a.m. and preached, for the final time there, at 6:00 a.m. "to a house full of serious people" on Ephesians 5:14. "The congregation seemed to be awake."[14]

Velling-Varine

According to the editors of the most recent edition of Charles Wesley's *Manuscript Journal*, "Verine" refers to a family name in Cornwall, while "vellan" translates to "mill"—thus the locale to which the younger Wesley referred might have been a local mill at some point, in southern Cornwall, along the eleven- to thirteen-mile route between St. Ives and

Gwennap, or, perhaps, a hamlet close to that mill. Nonetheless, neither of those sites has come to light. In any event, Charles Wesley, at 8:00 a.m., Sunday, 8 August 1743, preached "faith in Christ to many listening souls in Velling-Varine"—the preposition *in* suggesting a town or village, rather than a mill. Wesley appeared convinced that the gathering "received the word with surprising readiness," their "tears and hearty expressions of love" evidencing "a work begun in their hearts" (2:368 + note 88).

Wadebridge

At 7:00 a.m., Tuesday, 20 September 1748, John Wesley breakfasted at Wadebridge, east of Port Isaac and six miles northwest of Bodmin, in west-central Cornwall, his companion being a "Dr. W."—"for many years a steady, rational infidel." However, "it pleased God to touch his heart"; he read Wesley's *An Earnest Appeal to Men of Reason and Religion* (1743), a tract that caused him to work toward becoming an "altogether Christian." After an absence of thirty-two years, Wesley returned for his second and final visit to Wadebridge to preach on Monday, 28 August 1780 (20:249; 23:185).

Week St. Mary

The small parish of Week St. Mary lay seven miles east of St. Gennys and seven miles south of Stratton. John Wesley had been invited to the town by the Rev. John Turner (1690?-1772), the rector there from 1716 until his death, and thus the Methodist leader arrived there on Tuesday afternoon, 18 June 1745. He "had not seen in these parts of Cornwall either so large a church or so large a congregation." A month later, he preached in that church again, at 3:00 p.m. Tuesday, 16 July, on Mark 1:15; again on Monday, 13 September, at which time he "spoke very plain"; and Sunday afternoon, 26 July 1747. When he next preached at Week St. Mary on Sunday, 2 October 1757, a "large" congregation had gathered, a number of whom had traveled "seven or eight miles" to attend. "The [Methodist preaching] house stands in the midst of orchards and meadows," reported Wesley, "surrounded by gently rising hills." He preached "on the side of a meadow, newly mown, to a deeply attentive people." Throughout his career on the evangelical itinerancy, once he had accepted the values and the advantages of outdoor preaching, John Wesley eagerly embraced the image of the pastoral scene as the ideal background for the drama of his Methodist mission.

The Rev. John Turner issued another invitation to Wesley to preach in his church, and the Methodist leader arrived at Week St. Mary at 4:00 p.m. Monday, 29 September 1760. Considering the weather (?), there assembled a "large" congregation, "quite attentive and unconcerned." On Wesley's final visit to the town, Monday, 27 September 1762, he found himself in the midst of "a kind of fair-day, and the people were come [from][1] far and near for wrestling and other diversions. But they found a better way of employing their time," as "young and old flocked to church from all quarters."[2]

Wendron

Charles Wesley's initial visit to Wendron (at least the one recorded in the fragments of his manuscript journal), situated between 2.5 and 3 miles north of Helston, in south-central Cornwall, occurred on Friday, 4 July 1746. There "a huge multitude" listened to his sermon on Isaiah 55:1, and afterward he explained to the newly organized Methodist society "the design of their meeting." Two weeks later, Friday the 18th, he preached there again "with much freedom." However, a drunkard, an alehouse keeper, caused a momentary disturbance, prompting Wesley's comment, "Men of his craft are generally our sworn enemies" (2:465–466).

Zennor

Zennor village, a mining parish, lay on the northern coast of Cornwall, approximately four to five miles west-southwest of St. Ives. Historically, a quarter-mile to the north would have been found Zennor Quoit (quoit = a flat stone disc), the remains of a Neolithic entrance grave consisting of five uprights comprising the size of the burial chamber, as well as two additional slabs forming the antechamber. The capstone, 18' x 19 1/2,' had partially slid off the uprights that originally supported it.[1] From an ecclesiastical perspective, during the early years of the Wesleys' visits to Zennor, the anti–Methodist Church of England priest the Rev. William Symonds (1684?-1776) and his young curate, the Rev. William Hoblyn (1723–1759), served the parish of Zennor.

Charles Wesley initially preached at Zennor on Wednesday, 20 July 1743, and expressed, with unqualified optimism, the belief that the parish had "come in, to a man, at the joyful news. Some hundreds of the poor people, with sincerity in their faces," received him. At 8:00 a.m. the next morning, Thursday the 21st, he preached on the subject of the Good

Samaritan (Luke 10:29–37), but he "could not proceed for pity to the poor mockers." Wesley "urged and besought, and with tears even compelled, them to come in. The Spirit made intercession for them, that God might grant them repentance unto life." Two weeks later, Wednesday, 3 August, he preached to "the dear people of Zennor" on Revelation 2:10, and with tears they begged him to return, demonstrating that "our labour had not been in vain in the Lord."

Indeed, Charles Wesley did return to Zennor, on Sunday, 22 July 1744, "where very few hold out against the truth," despite the Rev. Symonds' "pains to pervert the ways of the Lord." Wesley accused both the minister and "his drunken companions, whom he secures against the Methodists, and warns at the alehouse not to forsake the Church." Again at Zennor on Saturday, 29 July, he explained the parable of the Sower (Matthew 13:3–23) and concluded by exhorting his listeners "to meet God in the way of his judgments." Two years later, on Sunday, 13 July 1746, Charles Wesley attended church at Zennor, after which he addressed his own congregation, demonstrating the "twofold rest of pardon and holiness [Hebrews 4:10]." He then spoke with a young exhorter of Zennor, John Maddern (who would join the Methodist itinerancy in 1747), and advised him "to practise, before he preached, the gospel." A year after that, on Thursday, 24 July 1746, Wesley met the Methodist society at Zennor, "rebuked them sharply," and "silenced one of their exhorters"—all of that a fitting end to his final visit to the town (2:360, 367, 411, 413, 466, 469).

When John Wesley initially came to Zennor on Wednesday, 7 September 1743, he preached to "two or three hundred people ... and found much goodwill in them, but no life." He appeared there again on Sunday, the 11th, at 5:00 p.m. as well as a week later, Sunday the 18th, preaching on Isaiah 53 and "feeling no weariness at all." Seven months later, Tuesday afternoon, 10 April 1744, Wesley walked to Zennor from St. Ives, and after preaching, "settled the infant [Methodist] society" according to his own rules. He preached there again on Wednesday, 27 June 1745; on Saturday, the 29th; and "found some life there" on Thursday, 11 July. After attending church services at Zennor on Sunday, 12 July 1747, he preached under the wall of the churchyard. Two days earlier, Friday, 10 July 1747, from St. Ives, John Wesley had written a letter—comprising one of the twelve pieces of correspondence, dating from May 1745 and continuing over the next three years, between a devout and scholarly churchman known only as "John Smith" and him. "Smith" had challenged Wesley's belief that Methodist doctrine and practice belonged within the sphere of the Bible and the Church of England. In any event, in that letter of 10 July 1747, written from St. Ives, Cornwall, Wesley expressed his wish that "all the clergy throughout the land [quoting an earlier letter] 'were zealous for inward, solid virtue.' But I dare not say one in ten of those I have known are so in any degree. The two clergymen [William Symonds and William Hoblyn] of this place [St. Ives and Zennor], on a late public occasion, were led home at one or two in the morning in such a condition as I care not to describe. One of them [Symonds] is rector of Lelant also (a parish east of St. Ives), of Towednack to the south, and Zennor to the west. At Zennor he keeps another assistant, and one who is just as sober as himself, and near as zealous——not indeed for inward or outward virtue, but against these 'scoundrels [the Wesleys and their itinerant preachers] that pretend to preach in his parish.'"[2]

Wesley once more attended church service at Zennor on Sunday, 25 September 1748, and after listening to "a close, awakening sermon," he sought to enforce that message by his own words on Mark 12:34. Two years later, on Sunday, 19 August 1750, following the evening church service, he addressed "a great multitude" at Zennor, and a year after that, he preached there on Sunday, 23 September 1751 and, on the day following (Monday the 24th) conducted a general meeting of the Methodist society stewards and held "a solemn watch-night."[3]

The "great multitude" of 1750 turned to "the little flock" when Wesley next entered Zennor on Saturday, 28 July 1753, and on Sunday, 14 September 1760, he began to preach there as soon as the church service concluded, noting that "scarce six persons went away" and focusing his attention on those individuals in particular. "The spirit of mourning was soon poured out," Wesley recalled, "and some of them wept bitterly. O may the Lord yet return unto them and 'leave a blessing behind him' [Joel 2:14]!" John Wesley's final visit to Zennor occurred at noon on Friday, 2 September 1768, when he preached to "an earnest company."[4] Wesley never appeared to have a developed deep commitment to or involvement with the people of Zennor, even after a dozen or so visits to the place.[5]

• 4 •

Summary, Conclusion
and Assessment

*How strangely has one year changed the scene in Cornwall. This
is now a peaceable, nay, honourable station. They give us good
words almost in every place. What have we done that the world
should be so civil to us?*
                                —John Wesley, Tuesday, 30 June 1747

In attempting to assess the results of the Wesleys' overall mission to
Cornwall, a number of obvious problems, and two of them obviously
related to each other, immediately arise. Both of those relate directly to
the sources from which the details of the brothers' mission to Cornwall
necessarily derive. As has been indicated throughout the principal section
of this discussion, the manuscript journal of Charles Wesley, never seriously considered for publication, lies upon the printed page in fragments,
and thus one cannot determine specifically the number and names of Cornish towns, villages, hamlets, or even fields that the younger Wesley actually visited, let alone the extent of his activities therein. Charles Wesley's
extant correspondence lies in much the same disjointed state—even less
so, perhaps—than the journal entries.

As for John Wesley, one might be impressed by, and even content
with, the eight volumes of his journals—the first set edited by Nehemiah
Curnock (and "others") from 1909 to 1916, the later edition of W. Reginald
Ward and Richard P. Heitzenrater produced from 1988 through 2013.
However, one must remember that those publications exist as journal
extracts, meaning that Wesley edited carefully the entries, including and
omitting details that he did or did not want his readers to visualize, and

then publishing the volumes three or four years (or more) beyond the actual occurrences. Rather than a narrative journal in the purest sense of the word, John Wesley's extracts provide a lengthy series of morality lessons and moral caveats for his Methodist constituency. Charles Wesley's journals evolved into even more extensive examples of meditative and spiritual syrup. As far as concerns John Wesley's correspondence, John Telford's eight-volume 1931 edition will always remain incomplete, expurgated, and "standard by default" as long as the two extant volumes of the now-deceased Frank Baker's edition (1980, 1982) remain alone on the shelves, a reminder of a project that might never achieve completion during the lifetimes of current scholars.

Another problem relating to the Wesleys' visits to Cornwall arose from the location and situation of the county itself. Although considered, in the eighteenth century, as a remote province of the nation, isolated and sparsely populated, Cornwall contained a sufficient number of hamlets, villages, and towns from which to satisfy the demands, desires, and promises of any religious missionary endeavor. However, the Wesleys ought not to bear all of the blame of neglect simply because they could not completely satisfy those demands—potential, promised, or actual. John Wesley did not gush forth unseasoned rhetorical pudding when he declared that "all the world is my parish"—or at least the island-kingdom of England, Scotland, Wales, and Ireland part of that sphere. Indeed, Charles Wesley, until some two decades before his death, and John Wesley, almost to the very end of his long life, committed themselves to the Methodist itinerancy throughout what now has become the United Kingdom. Cornwall stood as but one item on the brothers' crowded itineraries, and the ninety-nine hamlets, villages, towns, and plains that they managed to visit and in which they preached during a combined period of forty-six years proved no small contribution to the eighteenth-century evangelical campaign. Nonetheless, despite the efforts of several studies that have reached the presses,[1] the narrative of Methodism in eighteenth-century Cornwall remains incomplete. Between 1746 and 1791, John Wesley, by way of the Wesleyan Methodist Conference, appointed no less than 147 itinerant preachers to serve the Cornwall circuits. Had at least 10 percent of those men maintained journals of their observations, reactions, and experiences in Cornwall, and had those journals reached publication, then the record of Methodism in Cornwall would have assumed broader perspective and a variety of view, and would have served, potentially and hopefully, to provide more measureable capacity and depth to the Wesleys' essentially incomplete narratives. Such narratives from those itinerants would have (again, hopefully and potentially) injected clear specifics into the repeated generalizations that continually plague the entries of the Wesleys' journals.

Another issue that continued to create problems for the Wesleys' labors in Cornwall—in addition to (perhaps even more so than) the obvious physical and legal assaults by anti–Methodist clerics, magistrates, mobs, municipal authorities and constabularies—assumed forms in the persons of the evangelical Church of England clergy, whom one might believe would have offered immediate and open assistance to the Wesleyan Methodist evangelical mission. Those clergy had been at work in their parishes prior to the arrival of the Wesleys in Cornwall, attempting to encourage their congregants toward religious conversion and permanent religious practices, while, at the same time, asking them to hold fast to the forms and traditions of the Church of England. Such clergy, Samuel Walker of Truro being the most distinguished and reputable among them, had gone so far as to form religious societies within their own parishes. Therefore, when the Wesleys entered the parishes of those evangelical clergy, although they might allow the brothers to preach in their churches, they resented the organization of Methodist societies there, viewing them as rivals to their own evangelical organizations. Even though the Methodist itinerant preachers had been instructed by John Wesley *never* to preach during the hours of church services, and to carry their congregations outside and away from church buildings and into Methodist preaching houses or onto the open fields, tensions between the Wesleys and the evangelical Church clergy developed and grew. What irritated the clergy, of course, focused on their realization that a significant number of their parishioners attended the Methodist preachings, and that the size of the latter's congregations largely and significantly outnumbered their own. Also, the evangelical clergy viewed with suspicion and distaste the Methodists' reliance upon unordained lay persons as preachers, as opposed to ordained deacons and priests of the Church of England.

Certainly Walker and his evangelical colleagues approved of the Methodists' emphasis upon religious conversion, religious experience, and charity. However, they balked at recognizing the legitimacy of the charisma and emotionalism of Methodist prayer meetings, the employment of extemporaneous prayer, the unorthodox substance of Methodist sermons, and the entire concept of the itinerancy—all of which they believed challenged the orthodoxy and the formality of the Church of England liturgy. In a word, Walker and his colleagues viewed the Wesleys not as Dissenters, but as unwelcome radical reformers to areas of Church doctrine and practice that, in their views, did not require reform.[2]

However, within the most general contexts, given the issues and problems confronting the evangelical work in Cornwall, the Wesleys could claim significant measures of success in that county. Once the brothers embraced George Whitefield's belief (appropriated from the Franciscan friars from five centuries earlier) in the advantages of preaching in the streets, the meadows, the marketplaces, and the open fields and meadows over the limits and restrictions of the church and the preaching house, they could address large crowds and varieties of Cornish men and women and even children. The poor, the miners, the merchants, the gentry—all of them came to listen. Not all of those persons, upon the closing words of a Wesley address, walked the path to conversion, followed by membership in local Methodist societies, but at least they heard the voices of practical religion and ecclesiastical reform. In the beginning of the mission to Cornwall, John Wesley had described the human scene in that county as comprised of those who "before neither feared God nor regarded man," but, in early 1743, a number of them "began to inquire what they must do to be saved." However, continued Wesley, there had arisen in Cornwall a certain "imprudence" that had established a foundation for disturbance, turning "many of our friends into bitter and implacable enemies," and "violent persecution" became "a natural consequence." The hope for the future, of course, derived from the firm belief that God would triumph over all such conditions (19:325–326).

Whether that hope would bear fruition depended upon John Wesley's mood on a particular day. Nearing the end of his Cornish mission, at Falmouth on Monday, 17 August 1789, the eighty-six-year-old Methodist patriarch declared, "The first time [4 July 1745] I was here above forty years ago, I was taken prisoner by an immense mob, gaping and roaring like lions. But how is the tide turned; both high and low lined the street from one end of the town to the other out of stark love and kindness, gaping and staring as if the King were going by." That evening, he preached on the top of Pike's Hill, outside of Falmouth and a short distance from the sea. There he surveyed "the largest congregation I have ever seen in Cornwall, except in or near Redruth [referring to Gwennap Pit]. And such a time I have not known before since I returned from Ireland." Indeed, God had "moved wonderfully, on the hearts of the people, who all seem to know the day of their visitation." Eleven days later, at 9:00 a.m., Friday, 28 August, John Wesley preached in the new Methodist preaching house in Camelford, Cornwall, where the room had filled to capacity, and again at 6:00 p.m. in another new Methodist house in Launceston, "still too small for the congregation who seemed exceedingly lively." Nonetheless the heat of the old man's emotions had cooled a bit, and he responded, at the end of that final day in that county, "So there is a fair prospect in Cornwall from Land's End to Launceston" (24:151, 153). Indeed, the Methodist experience in eighteenth-century Cornwall existed throughout as a series of rising and ebbing tides. It resulted as neither a complete success nor a total failure, but emerged as a sustained effort as part of, and on behalf of, historically significant religious and social revival.

Appendices

Table 1.

Preachers,
Cornwall Circuit (1746–1791)

PREACHER	YEAR(S)	LENGTH OF TERM
Acutt, John	1784	Twelve months
Algar, Joseph	1783	Twelve months
	1784	Twelve months
Ashman, William (?-1818)[1]	1769	Twelve months
	1770	Twelve months
	1778	Twelve months
	1789	Twelve months
Bardsley, Samuel (?-1818)	1788	Twelve months
	1791	Twelve months
Barker, William (1736–1786)	1766	Twelve months
	1767	Twelve months
Blade, John	1776	Twelve months
Blake, Robert	1779	Twelve months
Bland, Charles	1790	Twelve months
Bond, Charles	1785[2]	Twelve months
Booth, John (?-1820)	1780	Twelve months
Boyle, John	1790	Twelve months
	1791	Twelve months
Bradford, Joseph (?-1808)	1772	Twelve months
Brammah, William (?-1780)	1769	Twelve months
	1770	Twelve months
	1771	Twelve months
Brettel, Jeremiah (?-1828)	1780	Twelve months
Brettel, John	1774	Twelve months

Preacher	Year(s)	Length of Term
Bryant, Thomas (?-1798)	1760	Twelve months
Button, George	1786	Twelve months
Byron, James	1791	Twelve months
Carlill, Thomas (?-1801)	1765[3]	Twelve months
	1767	Twelve months
	1773	Twelve months
Church, William (1749–1830)	1784	Twelve months
Clarke, Adam (1762–1832)	1784	Twelve months
Condy, Richard (?-1800)	1778	Twelve months
	1779	Twelve months
Cornish, Richard (1758–1796)	1784	Twelve months
	1785	Twelve months
	1786	Twelve months
Cotty, James (?-1780)	1765	Twelve months
	1773	Twelve months
	1778	Twelve months
Coussins, Jonathan	1786	Twelve months
	1787	Twelve months
Cowmeadow, John (?-1786)	1783	Twelve months
	1784	Twelve months
Cricket, John (?-1806)	1786	Twelve months
Crowle, Jonathan	1770	Twelve months
	1774	Twelve months
Crowther, Jonathan	1790	Twelve months
	1791	Twelve months
Crowther, Timothy	1790	Twelve months
	1791	Twelve months
Davis, John (?-1786?)	1766	Twelve months
	1767	Twelve months
Day, Simon (?-1832)	1766	Twelve months
	1780	Twelve months
	1781	Twelve months
	1782	Twelve months
Dempster, James	1772	Twelve months
	1773	Twelve months
Dobson, Thomas	1789	Twelve months
	1790	Twelve months
Easton, John	1768[4]	Twelve months
Ellis, William	1765	Twelve months
	1771	Twelve months
	1772	Twelve months
Empringham, Robert (?-1792)	1790	Twelve months
Evans, James	1787	Twelve months
Fenwick, John (?-1787)	1754	Twelve months
Fish, William (1763–1843)	1788	Twelve months
Fisher, John	1754	Twelve months
	1780	Twelve months

PREACHER	YEAR(S)	LENGTH OF TERM
Floyd, Henry	1756	Twelve months
Floyd, John (1749–1798)	1770	Twelve months
Foster, Henry (?-1787)	1780	Twelve months
Furz, John (1717–1800)	1760	Twelve months
	1765	Twelve months
	1766	Twelve months
	1774	Twelve months
	1778	Twelve months
Gamble, Robert	1785	Twelve months
Gates, Samuel	1788	Twelve months
Gibbs, John	1760	Twelve months
Gilbert, Nicholas (?-1763)	1756	Twelve months
Goodwin, John (1739?-1808)	1768	Twelve months
	1769	Twelve months
Gore, James (?-1790)	1787	Twelve months
	1788	Twelve months
Green, William	1782	Twelve months
	1784	Twelve months
	1785	Twelve months
Greenwood, Paul (?-1767)	1756	Twelve months
Guilford, Joseph (?-1777)	1774	Twelve months
Hall, James	1782	Twelve months
Hanby, Thomas (1733-?)	1760	Twelve months
Hanson, Thomas (?-1804)	1769	Twelve months
	1770	
	1775	Twelve months
	1776	Twelve months
	1779	Twelve months
Harper, Joseph (1729–1813)	1767	Twelve months
Harrison, Lancelot (?-1806)	1768	Twelve months
Haughton, John (?-1781)	1748	July-August
Hitchens, William[5]	1760	Twelve months
Holmes, William (1752?-1833)	1783	Twelve months
	1789	Twelve months
Hosmer, John (?-1780)	1760	Twelve months
Hudson, George	1771	Twelve months
Hudson, James	1769	Twelve months
Jerom, Joseph	1785	Twelve months
Jones, John (1721–1785)	1748	Nov.-Dec.
	1751[6]	Twelve months
Jones, Joseph	1778	Twelve months
Leech, John (?-1810)	1775	Twelve months
Leggatt, Benjamin	1789	Twelve months
	1790	Twelve months
Lessey, Theophilus (1757-?)	1786	Twelve months
	1787	Twelve months
	1788	Twelve months

Preacher	Year(s)	Length of Term
Levick, Samuel (?-1771)	1767	Twelve months
	1768	Twelve months
Maddern, John[7]	1748	Nov.-Dec.
Magor, John	1767	Twelve months
Manners, Nicholas	1781	Twelve months
Mason, John (?-1810)	1765	Twelve months
	1766	Twelve months
	1777	Twelve months
	1778	Twelve months
	1788	Twelve months
	1789	Twelve months
McGreary, John	1789	Twelve months
Meyrick, Thomas (?-1770)[8]	1746	June
Mitchell, Thomas (1726–1785)	1755	Twelve months
Moon, John (?-1801)	1775	Twelve months
	1786	Twelve months
	1787	Twelve months
Moore, Joseph	1773	Twelve months
Moore, William	1783	Twelve months
Moseley, Abraham	1791	Twelve months
Mowat, George	1777	Twelve months
Myles, William (1756–1828)	1785	Twelve months
Newall, Thomas	1774	Twelve months
Palmer, W.	1787	Twelve months
Payne, Thomas	1781	Twelve months
Pearce, Benjamin (?-1794)	1785	Twelve months
Perfect, James	1776	Twelve months
Pescod, Joseph (1751–1805)	1789	Twelve months
Phillips, Richard	1788	Twelve months
Pilmore, Joseph (1739–1825)	1766	Twelve months
Poole, John (?-1801)[9]	1776	Twelve months
	1777	Twelve months
	1778	Twelve months
	1779	Twelve months
Proctor, Stephen	1780	Twelve months
Rankin, Thomas (1738–1810)	1768	Twelve months
	1771	Twelve months
Reeves, J[onathan?]. R.	1746	August
Rhodes, Benjamin (1743–1815)	1788	Twelve months
	1789	Twelve months
	1790	Twelve months
	1791	Twelve months
Roberts, John (?-1788)	1772	Twelve months
	1775	Twelve months
Robins, H,	1777	Twelve months
Rodd, W. (?-1760)[10]	1760	?[11]
Rodda, Martin	1773	Twelve months

PREACHER	YEAR(S)	LENGTH OF TERM
	1780	Twelve months
Rodda, Richard (1743–1815)[12]	1771	Twelve months
	1772	Twelve months
	1774	Twelve months
	1778	Twelve months
	1779	Twelve months
Rogers, James (1749–1807)	1777	Twelve months
Sandoe, John	1787	Twelve months
	1789	Twelve months
Saunders, William	1781	Twelve months
	1782	Twelve months
Shadford, George (1739–1816)	1768	Twelve months
	1787	Twelve months
	1788	Twelve months
Shaw, Thomas (?-1801)	1782	Twelve months
Shearing, Isaac (?-1778)	1777	Twelve months
Shorter, George	1773	Twelve months
Simpson, William	1779	Twelve months
Skinner, James	1776	Twelve months
Smith, John	1791	Twelve months
Stephens, James	1770	Twelve months
Story, George (1738–1818)	1765	Twelve months
Sutcliffe, Joseph (1762–1856)	1786	Twelve months
	1787	Twelve months
	1788	Twelve months
Suter, Alexander	1782	Twelve months
	1789	Twelve months
Swindels, Robert (?-1782)	1748	July-August
Taylor, Joseph (1752–1830)	1782	Twelve months
	1783	
Thom, James	1783	Twelve months
Tobias, Thomas (?-1767?)	1756	Twelve months
Tooth, Samuel	1771	Twelve months
Townsend, John	1786	Twelve months
Trembath, John (?-1793)[13]	1746	June-July
	1748	Nov.-Dec.
Tretheway, Thomas	1790	Twelve months
	1791	Twelve months
Tunney, William	1779	Twelve months
Turnough, John	1754	Twelve months
Vasey, Thomas (1745–1826)	1777	Twelve months
Wadsworth, George	1779	Twelve months
	1781	Twelve months
	1782	Twelve months
Waldron, Isaac	1774	Twelve months
Walker, Francis	1746	August
Walker, Peter	1785	Twelve months

Preacher	Year(s)	Length of Term
Watkins, Christopher (1750–1805)	1781	Twelve months
Watkinson, Richard (?-1793)	1790	Twelve months
	1791	Twelve months
Watson, James (1747–1813)	1775	Twelve months
	1776	Twelve months
Wells, Samuel (?-1779)	1770	Twelve months
Wesley, Charles (1707–1788)	1746	June
Westell, Thomas (1719?-1794)	1748	Sept.-Oct.
	1768	Twelve months
	1769	Twelve months
Whatcoat, Richard (1736–1806)	1776	Twelve months
	1777	Twelve months
Whitaker, William	1772	Twelve months
Wilkinson, Robert (1745–1780)	1772	Twelve months
	1773	Twelve months
Wittam, John (?-1818)	1781	Twelve months
	1783	Twelve months
Wolf, Francis	1771	Twelve months
	1780	Twelve months
	1781	Twelve months
Woodcock, Samuel	1767	Twelve months
Wright, Richard	1774	Twelve months
	1775	Twelve months
	1776	Twelve months
Wrigley, Francis	1784	Twelve months
	1785	Twelve months
	1786	Twelve months

Table 2.

Membership, Cornwall Methodist Societies (1765–1791)[14]

Year	Total Methodist Membership	Members in Cornwall Societies	% of Total	+/- over Previous Year (#/%)
1765	20,434	2321	11.4	— — — —
1766	19,753[15]	2235	11.3	-86/-0.1
1767	25,911	2160	8.3	-75/-3.0
1768	27,341	2038	7.5	-122/-0.8
1769	28,263	2230	7.9	+192/+0.4
1770	29,181	2311	8.0	+81/+0.1
1771[16]	31,338	2497	8.0	+186/=
1772	31,984	2453	7.7	-44/-0.3
1773	33,274	1994	6.0	-459/-1.7

Year	Total Methodist Membership	Members in Cornwall/ Societies	% of Total	+/- over Previous Year (#/%)
1774	35,672	2082	5.8	+88/-0.2
1775	38,145	2149	5.6	+67/-0.2
1776	39,826	2150	5.4	+1/-0.2
1777	38,274	2128	5.5	-22/+0.1
1778	47,057	2148	4.6	+20/-0.9
1779	42,486[17]	2130	5.0	-18/+0.4
1780	43,830	1971	4.5	-159/-0.5
1781	44,461	2151	4.8	+180/+0.3
1782	45,723	2569	5.6	+418/+0.8
1783	45,995	2543	5.5	-26/-0.1
1784	64,155	3043	4.7	+500/-0.8
1785	70,466	3515	5.0	+472/+0.3
1786	79,506	3512	4.4	-3/-0.6
1787	90, 386	3727	4.1	+215/-0.3
1788	96,843	3825	3.9	+98/-0.2
1789	118,887	3179	2.7	-646/-1.2
1790	120,183	3993	3.3	+814/+0.6
1791	136, 622	4192	3.1	+199/-0.2

Note: (1) The reason for the sudden rise in Methodist membership from 1783 to 1784 would have been due to the expansion of Methodism in North America, particularly following the formal end of the American Revolutionary War. The Congress of the United States had proclaimed the end of hostilities against Great Britain on 11 April 1783 and then, on 13 April, ratified the preliminary peace treaty negotiated in Paris. One must also recall that in September 1784, John Wesley would ordain preachers for North America. From 1784 to 1791, the *total* figures for the year reflect the total number of Methodists in both Britain and North America. (2) The Conference *Minutes* for 1789 lists only the circuits of Redruth and St. Ives (perhaps an editorial omission?); numbers for the St. Austell circuit will return in the *Minutes* for 1790 and 1791.

Table 3.

Funds Allocated to Cornwall (1766–1791)

Year	Total Subscription	Amount to Cornwall	+/- from Previous Year
1766	£ 695. 2 s. 11d.	— — — —	— — — —
1769[18]	2647. 4s. 5d.[19]	£137. 0s. 0d.	— — — —
1770	2176. 14s. 7d.	73. 17s. 10d.	£–63. 3s. 2d.
1771	1875. 18s. 4 1/2d.	25. 10s. 0d.[20]	-48. 7s. 10d
1772	3304. 15s. 18d.	31. 3s. 0d.	+ 5. 13s. 0d.
1773	2443. 6s. 3d.	0. 0s. 0d.	-31. 3s. 0d.[21]
1774	848. 8s. 5d.	7. 7s. 0d.	+ 7. 7s. 0d.
1775	847. 10s, 4d.	0. 0s. 0d.	–7. 7s. 0d.
1776	967. 13s. 2 1/2d.	13. 12s. 0d.	+13. 12s. 0d.

Year	Total Subscription	Amount to Cornwall	+/- from Previous Year
1777	380. 8s. 2d.[22]	————	————
1778	733. 9s. 10d.[23]	5. 0s. 0d.	+5. 0s. 0d.
1779	842. 4s. 2d.	10. 0s. 0d.	+5. 0s. 0d.
1780	1031. 3s. 6d.	0. 0s. 0d.	-5. 0s. 0d.
1781	440 1s. 1d.[24]	————	————
1782	1118. 18s. 8 1/2d.[25]	————	————
1783	1181. 0s. 4 1/2d.	————	————
1784	1310. 12s. 2d.	————	————
1785	1549. 11s. 1d.	————	————
1786	1603. 1s. 6d.	————[26]	————
1787	1774. 17s. 1d.	————	————
1788	£1985. 3s. 8d.	————[27]	————
1789	1948. 1s. 3d.	————	————
1790	2133. 4s. 9d.	————	————
1791	2373. 19s. 10d.	————	————

Table 4.

Places in Cornwall Visited by
Charles Wesley/ John Wesley (1743–1789)

Bodmin CW/JW
Brea JW
Breage JW
Callestick/Callestock JW
Camborne CW/JW
Camelford JW
Cape Cornwall CW
Carn Brae JW
Crowan CW/JW
Cubert JW
Falmouth CW/JW
Fowey JW
Goldstithney JW
Grampound JW
Gulval CW/JW
Gunnislake JW
Gwennap CW/JW
Gwithian JW
Hayle JW
Helston JW
Illogan JW
Kenneggy Downs CW/JW
Land's End JW
Laneast CW/JW

Launceston JW
Lelant JW
Liskeard JW
Little Carharrack JW
Lizard Point CW/JW
Looe JW
Lostwithiel JW
Ludgvan CW/JW
Luxulyan JW
Madron JW
Marazion JW
Mevagissey JW
Mitchell CW/JW
Morvah CW/JW
Mount Edgecumbe JW
Mousehole JW
Mullion JW
Newlyn JW
North Tamerton JW
Penhale JW
Penryn CW/JW
Penzance CW/JW
Perranwell JW
Polperro JW

Pool **CW**
Porkellis **JW**
Port Isaac **JW**
Redruth **CW/JW**
Roche **JW**
Rosemergy **JW**
Rosewarne **JW**
St. Agnes **JW**
St. Austell **JW**
St. Buryan **JW**
St. Cleer **JW**
St. Columb Major **JW**
St. Ewe **JW**
St. Gennys **CW/JW**
St. Hilary **CW/JW**
St. Ives **CW/JW**
St. John's **JW**
St. Just **CW/JW**
St. Lawrence **JW**
St. Mewan **JW**
St. Stephen's in Bramwell **JW**
St. Stephen's Down **JW**
St. Teath **JW**
St. Tudy **CW**
Saltash **JW**
Sancreed **JW**

Scilly Isles **JW**
Sennen **CW/JW**
Sithney **CW/JW**
Sticker **JW**
Stithians **CW/JW**
Tolcarn **JW**
Torpoint **JW**
Towednack **CW**
Tredinney **JW**
Tregavarah Downs **JW**
Trenouth **JW**
Tresmeer **CW/JW**
Treswithian Downs **JW**
Trevowhan **JW**
Trewalder **JW**
Trewellard **CW/JW**
Trewergy **JW**
Trewint **JW**
Trezelah **JW**
Truro **JW**
Velling-Varine **CW**
Wadebridge **JW**
Week St. Mary **JW**
Wendron **CW**
Zennor **CW/JW**

Chapter Notes

Chapter 1

1. "Cornwall," in *The Oxford Companion to the English Language*, ed. Tom McArthur (Oxford and New York: Oxford University Press, 1992): 265.

2. For a reproduction and description of Opie's piece, see Asa Briggs, *A Social History of England* (New York: The Viking Press, 1984): 180. For John Opie, see Erika Langmuir and Norbert Lynton, *The Yale Dictionary of Art and Artists* (New Haven and London: Yale University Press, 2000): 506.

3. See Thomas Moule, *The County Maps of Old England*. intr. Roderick Baron (London: Studio Editions, 1990): 32–33; Frederick Boase, *Modern English Biography* (1897; rpt. London: Frank Cass and Company, Ltd., 1965), 2:1004.

4. *Oxford Companion to the English Language*, 265.

5. See Charles Robert Leslie Fletcher, *An Introductory History of England* (London: John Murray, 1920–1921), 1:42.

6. Alvin Redmond, *The House of Hanover*, rev. ed. (London: Alvin Redman, 1968): 393.

7. Reprinted as *A Catalogue of Books (1841). Henry G. Bohn*, intro. Francesco Cordasco, 2 parts (vols.), (New York: AMS Press, 1974), 2:1939.

8. Glossography = the writing of glosses or commentaries; the compiling of glossaries; descriptions and/or groupings of languages.

9. Folio = a leaf of paper or parchment numbered only on the front; the page number of a printed book; a full-sized sheet folded once; a volume comprised of sheets of paper folded once; a volume of the largest size.

10. Calf = leather produced from the skin of a calf.

11. Armoric/Armorica = the ancient identity of that section of Gaul currently known as Bretagne, or Brittany.

12. William Prideaux Courtney and David Nichol Smith, *A Bibliography of Johnson* (Oxford: At the Clarendon Press, 1915, 1925): 76; [James] Boswell, *Life of Johnson*, ed. R.W. Chapman; new ed., rev. J.D. Fleeman (London and Oxford: Oxford University Press, 1970): 13, 219.

13. Quoted from Maynard Mack, *The Garden and the City: Retirement and Politics in the Later Poetry of Pope, 1731–1743* (Toronto: University of Toronto Press, 1969): 260–261.

14. Bohn, in his 1841 *Catalogue* spells the name "Price" on 1:400, No. 4831, and "Pryce" on 2:1712, No. 20497; Samuel Austin Allibone, in his *Critical Dictionary of English Literature* (Philadelphia: J.B. Lippincott and Company, 1872–1877), 2:1698, spells the name as "Pryce" for both titles in this listing.

15. See below. The six volumes of *Magnus Britannia* (1806) originally sold for £27. 4s, and in large paper for £46.10. See Allibone, *Critical Dictionary* 1:1150.

16. See note 9.

17. See, also, in Bohn's 1841 *Catalogue*, pp. 1571–1572, Nos. 18886–18895, partic-

ularly the commentary from *Portraits of Literature*.

18. For a listing, commentary, and bibliographical details of Whitaker's publications, see Allibone, *Critical Dictionary*, 3:2678–2679, as well as Bohn's 1841 *Catalogue*, 2:1900–1901, Nos. 22869–22874.

19. Viz. = the abbreviation of *Videlicet*, meaning "that is to say," "namely"; or "to wit"; the introduction of an amplification or a more precise explanation of a previous statement or word.

20. For listings of and commentaries upon Polwhele's publications, see Allibone, *Critical Dictionary*, 2:1618–1619; Bohn's 1841 *Catalogue*, 2:1690, Nos. 20355–20358.

21. See Boase, *Modern English Biography*, 1:1185.

Chapter 2

1. *Dictionary of the Christian Church*, 3rd ed., F.L. Cross and E.A. Livingstone (Peabody, Massachusetts: Hendrickson Publishers, Inc., 1997):1286.

2. Richard P. Heitzenrater, *Wesley and the People Called Methodists*, 2nd ed. (Nashville, Abingdon Press, 2013): 107.

3. See Boase, *Modern English Biography*, 3:1059.

4. See John Wesley's *Modern Christianity Exemplified at Wednesbury and Other Places in Staffordshire* (1745), in *Works of John Wesley* (1989), 9:133–158.

5. Luke Tyerman, *The Life and Times of the Rev. John Wesley, M.A., Founder of the Methodists* (New York: Harper and Brothers, Publishers, 1872), 1:415–416.

6. John Wesley, *A Short History of the People Called Methodists* (1781), in *Works of John Wesley* (1989), 9:343.

7. See *Who Was Who, 1929–1940*, 1331–1332; Betty M. Jarboe, *John and Charles Wesley: A Bibliography* (Metuchen, New Jersey, and London: The American Theological Library Association and The Scarecrow Press, Inc., 1987): 142–143, 301–302.

8. See above, pp. 14–16, 18–19.

9. John Telford, *The Life of the Rev. Charles Wesley, M.A.* (London: Wesleyan Methodist Book Room, 1900): 143–144.

10. See an article in *The Wesleyan Methodist Magazine* (1823): 204.

11. See Henry D. Rack, *Reasonable*

Enthusiast, 3rd ed. (London: Epworth Press, 2002): 221–222, 597 (note 156); Tyerman, *Life of John Wesley*, 1:416.

12. The names of the preachers assigned to Cornwall and the figures related to membership and finances will be found in *Works of John Wesley. Volume 10. The Methodist Societies*. I have extracted the data from that source relating to Cornwall and organized it into tables.

13. *Works of John Wesley. Volume 10. The Methodist Societies*, 122. My **bold** throughout this discussion.

14. *Works of John Wesley. Volume 10. The Methodist Societies*, 138.

15. See Robert Currie, *et al*, *Churches and Churchgoers* (Oxford: Clarendon Press, 1977): 139.

16. *Works of John Wesley. Volume 10. The Methodist Societies*, 308.

17. See references to Captain Joseph Turner on pp. 34–35.

18. John Wesley, "A Short History of the People Called Methodists" (1781), in *Works of John Wesley. Volume 9* (1989), 438.

Chapter 3

BODMIN

1. Defoe, *Tour through the Whole Island of Great Britain* (1724–1726), ed. Rogers, 243.

2. Quoted in Moule, *County Maps of Old England*, 32.

3. See, for example, the case of Thomas Westell in *Works of John Wesley* (1991), 20:40–41.

4. See Moule, *County Maps of Old England*, 32; *Merriam-Webster's Geographical Dictionary*, 3rd ed., 152.

5. *Dictionary of the Christian Church*, 3rd ed., 1270.

6. Davies, *Early Cornish Evangelicals*, 26.

7. *Manuscript Journal*, ed. Kimbrough and Newport, 2:357. All references in my text to this edition and will be noted by volume and page number, in parentheses, in the text itself.

8. See *Works of John Wesley* (1990), 19:334. Unless noted otherwise, all references in my text to John Wesley's *Journal* derive from this most recent edition of his *Works* and will be noted, parenthetically, by volume and page number(s).

9. Essentially the same note concerning that window appears in the *Journal of John Wesley*, ed. Curnock, 6:37, and in *Works*, 22:427.

BREAGE

1. *County Maps of Old England*, 33.
2. Davies, *The Early Cornish Evangelicals*, 20–21.
3. Actually, "*eleven* years ago" might be more accurate. See the discussions on Gulval and Tregavarah Downs.

CALLESTICK/ CALLESTOCK/CALSTOCK

1. See p. 43 above.

CAMBORNE

1. Davies, *The Early Cornish Evangelicals*, 24–25.
2. Rogal, *Biographical Dictionary of Eighteenth-Century Methodism*, 4:89.
3. See pp. 55–56, 59 above.

CAMELFORD

1. See *Journal, Volume IV*, ed. Ward and Heitzenrater, in *Works*, 21:2–3.
2. *Letters*, ed. Telford, 4:104; all references to John Wesley's letters in my text to this edition, with volume and page numbers in parentheses following quotations or paraphrases.
3. Davies, *The Early Cornish Evangelicals*, 12.

CARN BRAE

1. See Crowl, *Intelligent Traveller's Guide to Great Britain*, 47, 595.

CROWAN

1. See *Dictionary of the Christian Church*, 3rd ed., 1611.
2. Boswell, *Life of Johnson*, ed. Chapman-Fleeman, 22.
3. See *Works of John* Wesley (2011), 10: 298, 309.

CUBERT

1. Parochial = of, belonging, or in reference to various parishes; pertaining or confined to a narrow area or domain; narrow, provincial. The editors of the *Oxford English Dictionary (OED)* cite the example of a parish church council, consisting of the incumbent, churchwarden, and elected parishioners.

2. See Blackburn and Holford-Strevens, *Oxford Companion to the Year*, 440.

FALMOUTH

1. See Crowl, *Intelligent Traveller's Guide to Historic Britain*, 285–286, 299, 591. The castles of Pendennis and St. Mawes remain in tolerable condition and rank high on the list of attractions for those who tour Falmouth.
2. Trevelyan, *England under Queen Anne: Blenheim*, 310.
3. See Defoe, *Tour through Great Britain*, ed. Rogers, 231–232, 696.
4. *Autobiography*, ed. Labaree *et al*, 179.
5. See Rogal, *Biographical Dictionary*, 4:20; also below, and in the entry for "St. Ives." Further, Nehemiah Curnock cited from an article by H. Arthur Smith, "Footprints of the Wesleys in Cornwall," *Cornish Magazine*, 1 (1898): 241–251: "The house into which he [John Wesley] was assisted has been removed, but I am told that in the village of Buck's Head, near Truro, the door is still preserved, indented with stones which were hurled against it" (*Journal*, 3:190, note 1).
6. Rogal, *Biographical Dictionary*, 9:21–26.

FOWEY

1. See Crowl, *Guide to Historic Britain*, 97, 111, 591.
2. See Allibone, *Critical Dictionary*, 2:1741; Bonn's *Catalogue of Books*, 2:1721, no. 20600.
3. At 121 words, this sentence certainly proves worthy of some form of award or recognition for its length.
4. For "an ancient ... for pilchards," see Defoe, *Tour through Great Britain*, ed. Rogers, 229.
5. Davies, *The Early Cornish Evangelicals*, 13.
6. Davies, *The Early Cornish Evangelicals*, 23, 26.

GRAMPOUND

1. See above, p. 59.
2. Pope did not acknowledge authorship of *The Dunciad* (1728) or of *The Dunciad Variorum* (1729) until 1735.
3. See Allibone, *Dictionary of English Literature*, 1:795.
4. Davies, *The Early Cornish Evangelicals*, 12.

GULVAL

1. Davies, *The Early Cornish Evangel-icals*, 16–17.

GUNNISLAKE

1. See Jackson, *Development of Transportation in Modern England*, 14–22.

GWENNAP

1. See p. 50.
2. Davies, *The Early Cornish Evangel-icals*, 21.
3. See "Appendices," Table 1.
4. Davies, *Early Cornish Evangelicals*, 26. The name of "Henry Youren" does not appear in the published versions of the extant journals and correspondence of either of the Wesleys.
5. For the principal males in the Hitchens family, with sources at the end of each entry, see Rogal, *Biographical Dictionary*, 2:428–429.
6. See pp. 102–103.
7. Quoted in Davies, *Early Cornish Evangelicals*, 82. Davies, in turn, had extracted Walker's letter from an article—without reference to author or title—from *Christian Guardian* 2 (1810): 442 ff.
8. See Curnock, *Journal*, 5:387, note 1; *Proceedings of the Wesley Historical Society*, 4:56; S.W. Jones, "John Wesley and Gwennap Pit," *Old Cornwall*, 3 (1941): 402–406; and John Wesley's own descriptions of Gwennap Pit cited below.
9. See p. 121, line 1.
10. See Rogal, *Biographical Dictionary*, 8:141–143 (including sources).
11. See *Dictionary of the Christian Church*, 3rd ed., 1319–1320.
12. *Journal*, ed. Curnock (3:94), identified the "plain" as "Probably the comparatively level ground in front of the chapel at Carharrack [or Carrick]."
13. My **bold**.
14. See pp. 56, 57, 74.
15. See *Journal*, ed. Ward and Heitzenrater, 19: 334, 338; 20:69, 74–75, 78, 94, 116, 118, 181.
16. *Journal*, ed. Ward and Heitzenrater, 20:75.
17. Wesley's journal (20:139) reads "W—T—"; Ward and Heitzenrater (note 16) offered the name of "William Tucker."
18. See 1 Kings 8:5; Ezekiel 38:7; Acts 15:25.

19. See Psalms 13:6, 116:7; Joel 2:26; Revelation 12:3.
20. See *Journal*, ed. Ward and Heitzenrater, 18:537.
21. See Frank Baker, "Love Feast," in *Historical Dictionary of Methodism*, 131–132.
22. The two sets of brackets inserted by Ward and Heitzenrater, *Journal*, 21:388.
23. See, also, *The Book of Common Prayer* (1662), ed. Cummings, 353–354.
24. See Tyerman, *Life of John Wesley*, 1:214.
25. See Samuel J. Rogal, "Counting the Congregation: Wishful Thinking Versus Hard Reality in the Journals of John Wesley." *Methodist History*, 30:1 (October 1991): 3–9.
26. See *Autobiography of Franklin*, 179.
27. Matthew 13:3–9; Mark 4:3–9; Luke 8:4–8.

HAYLE

1. *Letters*, ed. Telford, 7:201.
2. See, also, *Letters*, ed. Telford, 7:201.

HELSTON

1. See Davies, *Early Cornish Evangelicals*, 13.

KENNEGY DOWNS

1. See pp. 75, 98.

LAND'S END

1. See, also, *Letters*, ed. Telford, 8:102, 103.

LANEAST

1. Davies, *Early Cornish Evangelicals*, 35, 37, 39–45.

LAUNCESTON

1. See p. 122; Crowl *Intelligent Traveller's Guide*, 141, 348, 593; Defoe, *Tour*, 244, 697.
2. Moule, *County Maps of Old England*, 32.
3. See pp. 122, 157.
4. Defoe, *Tour*, 244.
5. See John 3:16, 13:1, 15:19; 1 John 2:15.
6. *Works of John Wesley: Methodist Societies*, ed. Davies, 9:77.
7. See Appendices, Table 1.
8. *Works of John Wesley. Journal and Diaries (1776–1786)*, 23:28 + note 21.

9. See pp. 117, 132, + "Appendices," Table 1 (+note 13).

10. See *Works of John Wesley. Journal and Diaries*, 19:341; 20:19, 400; 20:402, 468, 490–491; 21:30–31, 121, 127, 273–274, 390–391; 22:62, 154, 202, 244, 287, 427, 428, 464; 23: 28, 66114, 185, 222, 250–251; 375, 534; 24:59, 221, 290; *Letters of John Wesley*, ed. Telford, 3:142, 194; 4:104; 8:155.

LELANT

1. Davies, *Early Cornish Evangelicals*, 23, 28.

LISKEARD

1. See p. 71.

2. Crowl, *Intelligent Traveller's Guide to Great Britain*, 593.

3. Defoe, *Tour through the Whole Island of Great Britain* (1724–1726), ed. Rogers, 228–229, 243.

4. Davies, *Early Cornish Evangelicals*, 12–13.

5. *Works of John Wesley. Journal and Diaries*, 21:127, note 96.

6. *Works of John Wesley. Journal and Diaries*, 20:42; 21:127, 282; 22:22, 465; 23:374, 533; 24:59, 221, 290.

LITTLE CARHARRACK

1. Quoted in *Works of John Wesley. Journal and Diaries*, 22:465.

LIZARD POINT

1. *Manuscript Journal of Charles Wesley*, 1:65.

2. *Works of John Wesley. Journal and Diaries*, 18:213.

LOOE

1. See pp. 107–108.

2. Davies, *Early Cornish Evangelicals*, 13.

LOSTWITHIEL

1. Crowl, *Guide to Historic Britain*, 593.

LUDGVAN

1. Davies, *Early Cornish Evangelicals*, 19.

2. Davies, *Early Cornish Evangelicals*, 24.

3. See p. 112.

4. See Judges 19:6, 19:9, 19:22; Ruth 3:7; 1 Samuel 25:36; 2 Samuel 13:28; 1 Kings 21:7; 2 Chronicles 7:10; Esther 1:10; Proverbs 15:7, 15:15, 17:22; Ecclesiastes 9:7; Isaiah 24:7.

LUXULYAN

1. *Works of John Wesley. Journal and Diaries*, 21:24.

2. See pp. 47, 87, 149, 150, 171.

MADRON

1. See pp. 73, 148–149, 174.

2. See p. 61.

3. Quoted in *Works of John Wesley. Journal and Diaries*, 21:277. John Wesley would eventually insert Bishop Hall's narrative into his *Arminian Magazine*.

MARAZION

1. See *Works of John Wesley. Journal and Diaries*, *Works of John Wesley. Journal and Diaries*, 20:70.

2. See pp. 56–57, 74, 129.

3. To continue John Wesley's narrative of Maxfield's impressment, see under "Penzance."

4. See *Works of John Wesley. Journal and Diaries*, 20:70–71; 22:387; 23:220, 250, 374, 533; 24:152, 291; *Letters of John Wesley*, ed. Telford, 7:163.

MEVAGISSEY

1. See pp. 107–108, 173.

2. Davies, *Early Cornish Evangelicals*, 13.

3. *Journal of John Wesley*, ed. Curnock, 4:239.

4. *Parallel Commentary on the New Testament*, 282.

MITCHELL

1. My *italics*.

2. *Works of John Wesley, Appeals*, 11:379.

3. *Works of John Wesley. Journal and Diaries*, 20:183.

4. *Works of John Wesley, Appeals*, 11:372

5. *Works of John Wesley, Appeals*, 11:379.

6. *Works of John Wesley, Appeals*, 11:379–380, 433–435.

MORVAH

1. The word visible occurs but once in the KJV, in Colossians 1:16—"For by him

were all things created, that are in heaven, and that are in earth **visible** and invisible, whether they be thrones, or dominions, or principalities, or powers: all things were created by him and for him:"
2. [Newton, Cowper] *Olney Hymns in Three* Books, 53.
3. See *Works of John Wesley. Journal and Diaries*, 19:335–337, 340; 20:22, 24, 73, 79, 136, 182, 249, 357, 401–402, 469; 22: 50, 156–157.

NEWLYN

1. See p. 161.
2. Ezekiel 1:16—"The appearance of the wheels and their work was like unto the colour of a beryl[a]: and they four had one likeness: and their appearance and their work was as it were a wheel in the middle of a wheel:": (KJV) Beryl = a transparent precious stone of a pale green color, passing into light blue, then yellow.
3. *Works of John Wesley. Sermons III*, 3:593, 598.
4. See *Works of John Wesley. Journal and Diaries*, 20:468.
5. *Letters of John Wesley*, ed. Telford, *Letters of John Wesley*, ed. Telford, 5:105.
6. See Coe, *John Wesley and* Marriage, 118–125, 128–130.
7. *Works of John Wesley. Journal and Diaries*, 20:182–183, 249, 357, 469; 21:27, 123, 280, 388; 22:20, 157, 245; 24:152, 291.

NORTH TAMERTON

1. Church officials finally erected a parsonage house in 1855. See Davies, *Early Cornish Evangelicals*, 37, 40.

PENRYN

1. See pp. 107–108.
2. Kirton—in Lincolnshire? Nottinghamshire? Suffolk?
3. Defoe, *Tour*, 233.
4. *Works of John Wesley. Journal and Diaries*, 20:401; Watts, *Dissenters*, 110, 112, 181, 189–190.
5. See pp. 102–103.
6. *Letters of John Wesley*, ed. Telford, 3:221–226.

PENZANCE

1. The *AA Road Atlas [of] Great Britain* (1999):vi, computed the distance from London to Penzance at 310 miles.
2. Defoe, *Tour*, 233.

3. Davies, *Early Cornish Evangelicals*, 20. Davies cited from a work by G.B. Millet, *Penzance*.
4. Davies, *Early Cornish Evangelicals*, 24.
5. See p. 179.
6. See (perhaps) "Appendices," Table 1.
7. *Works*, 4:27.
8. *Journal of John Wesley*, ed. Curnock, 6:38.
9. The name of John Slocomb (or any of the variant spellings of that name) does not appear upon the lists of Methodist itinerant preachers assigned to the Cornwall circuit, beginning in 1746. Of course, he might well have been on the Cornwall itinerancy prior to 1746.
10. *Manuscript Journal*, ed. Kimbrough and Newport, 2:408.
11. Neither the name nor the identity of Boscoval House appears in the standard editions of Wesley's journal, diary, correspondence, or works.
12. See *Works of John Wesley: Methodist Societies*, 10:868–870.
13. *Letters of John Wesley*, ed. Telford, 7:366.
14. *Works of John Wesley. Journal and Diaries*, 21:388; 22:60, 157, 386–387, 427; 23:29, 103, 184, 220, 250, 374, 523; 24:57–58, 152, 220, 291.

POLPERRO

1. Davies, *Early Cornish Evangelicals*, 13, 218; Davies identified his source as J. Couch, *The History of Polperro* (1871): 194.

POOL

1. *Sermons of Charles Wesley*, 209–224.

PORT ISAAC

1. *Letters of John Wesley*, ed. Telford, 4:306. One might also be interested to know that the letter of 9 June 1765 begins, "Yours of March evening, 28th, I received yesterday [8 June]." In other words, the letter from the leaders and stewards reached Wesley *seventy-two days* after it had been written and/or posted, or had been forwarded to the Methodist leader by other means.
2. See *Works of John Wesley. Journal and Diaries*, 21:175; 22:154–156; *Letters of John Wesley*, ed. Telford, 4:56, 204, 290; 5:109; 7:260.

3. See *Works of John Wesley. Journal and Diaries*, 20:183–184, 249, 359, 471; 21:30, 121, 274, 390; 22:18, 62, 154–156, 244, 387, 428; 23:28, 185, 250, 534; 24:152–153, 291–292.

REDRUTH

1. Crowl, *Traveller's Guide to Historic Britain*, 47, 432, 595.
2. Defoe, *Tour through Great Britain*, 242.
3. Davies, *Early Cornish Evangelicals*, 17.
4. See pp. 57, 180–181.
5. See pp. 67, 194.
6. *Works of John Wesley. Methodist Societies*, 9:269–270.
7. See pp. 135–136.
8. See pp. 97–98, 140–141.
9. See *Works of John Wesley. Journal and Diaries*, 20:69, 189, 356, 401, 471; 21:25, 29–30, 124, 281, 388, 389; 22:19–21, 61, 156, 203, 244, 387, 427–428, 464; 23:29, 66, 103, 184, 222, 250, 375, 533; 24:58, 152, 220, 291; *Letters of John Wesley*, ed. Telford, 7:335, 353; 8:102, 162.

SALTASH

1. Defoe, *Tour through Great Britain*, 227–228.
2. Crowl, *Traveller's Guide to Historic Britain*, 597.

SCILLY, ISLES OF

1. Crowl, *Traveller's Guide to Historic Britain*, 592.
2. *Letters of John Wesley*, ed. Telford, 5:292–293.

SITHNEY

1. Davies, *Early Cornish Evangelicals*, 23. Davies cites his sources as G.H. Doble, *Two Cornish Parishes in the Eighteenth Century* (1930): 8, 44; and *The Exeter Diocesan Visitation Returns*, vol. 225c.

ST. AGNES

1. See *Works of John Wesley. Journal and Diaries*, 20:181, 249, 358, 469; 21:30, 121–122, 275, 389–390; 22:19, 61, 156–157, 244, 387, 428, 464; 23:29, 66, 375, 534; *Letters of John Wesley*, ed. Telford, 4:306.

ST. AUSTELL

1. See p. 234.
2. See *Works of John Wesley. Journal and Diaries*, 21:24–25, 126–127, 387; 22:158, 203, 249, 386; 23:30, 184, 220, 250, 374, 533; 24: 58–59, 150–151, 220, 290; *Letters of John Wesley*, ed. Telford, 7:255, 273, 366.

ST. COLUMB MAJOR

1. *Works of John Wesley. Journal and Diaries*, 20:142; 21:126, 274; 22:61, 156; 24:291.

ST. EWE

1. See p. 112.
2. See pp. 55, 150, 150, 170, 191, 231, 248.
3. *Journal of John Wesley*, ed. Curnock, 3:379 + note 1; *Works of John Wesley. Journal and Diaries*, 20:250 + note 77.
4. See Isaiah 64:1–2 and a poetic paraphrase of Isaiah 64, beginning "O that thou wouldst the heavens rend," from the Wesleys' *Hymns and Sacred Poems* (1740).

ST. GENNYS

1. Deal = a slice of wood, most likely fir or pine, sawn from a log or timber; in England, that slice measuring nine inches wide and not more than three inches thick, and at least six feet in length.
2. See p. 95.
3. Davies, *Early Cornish Evangelicals*, 30–31, 40, 49.
4. See pp. 120, 155–156, 199.
5. See p. 209.

ST. HILARY

1. See pp. 50, 116.
2. Davies, *Early Cornish Evangelicals*, 26.

ST. IVES

1. Crowl, *Traveller's Guide to Historic Britain*, 50, 593.
2. Defoe, *Tour through Great Britain*, 241–242.
3. See pp. 107–108.
4. Davies, *Early Cornish Evangelicals*, 13.
5. See p. 35.
6. See p. 35.
7. See p. 35.
8. Davies, *Early Cornish Evangelicals*, 26–27.
9. See pp. 70, 74, 120.
10. See pp. 135–136, 143, 233.
11. See pp. 68, 123, 154–258.

12. See 2:357–363, 365–368, 392, 409–410, 412–414, 465–467, 470–471.
13. See pp. 45, 63, 240.
14. See, in the Wesleys' *Hymns and Sacred Poems*, Part II (1740), lines from "Isaiah LXIV," beginning "O that Thou would'st the heavens rend"—

Now let the heathens fear Thy Name;
Now let the world Thy Nature know;
Dart into all the melting flame,
Of love, and make the mountains flow.
(2:1–4)—

in *New and Critical Edition of Osborn's Works*, 1:508.
15. For the Riot Act, see. p. 230.
16. See pp. 146, 236.
17. Heitzenrater, *Wesley and the People Called Methodists*, 2nd ed., 136–137.
18. See p. 250.
19. See John Wesley's *A Word to a Smuggler* (Bristol: Printed by William Pine, 1767); *Works of John Wesley*, ed. Jackson, 11:174–178; Lecky, *History of England*, 3rd ed., 5:28–29.
20. Deuteronomy 31:17–18, 20; Lamentations 3:4; Numbers 24:8; Psalms 51:8; 89:46; Isaiah 38:13; Jeremiah 50:17; Ezekiel 3929; Habakkuk 2:6.
21. See pp. 136, 232.
22. Depresses = humbles, humiliates, castigates, disparages, depreciates, renders as dull.
23. See Genesis 5:32, 6:10, 9:27; 1 Chronicles 1:5.
24. See pp. 260–261, 265–266, 270.
25. *Works of John Wesley. Journal and Diaries*, 19:230, 333–340; 20:25, 40–41, 71–74, 79–80, 135, 136, 141, 180–182, 2490250, 357–358, 402, 469; 21: 28–29, 123, 275–277, 389; 22:21, 60–61, 156, 203, 244–245, 387, 427–428, 464; 23:30, 66, 103–104, 184, 221, 374, 533; 24:58, 152, 220, 291; *Letters of John Wesley*, ed. Telford, 1:116, 358; 2:99, 107; 3:139–141; 4:306; 7:168; 8:246; *Works of John Wesley. Letters*, 26:253, 586–588.

ST. JOHN'S

1. 8:245.
2. 4:412; 5:144.
3. See pp. 80, 86, 231.
4. See pp. 136, 232, 281.
5. *Works of John Wesley. Journal and Diaries*, 21:388, 463; 22:20, 157, 202, 245, 427; *Letters of John Wesley*, ed. Telford, 4:311–312.

ST. JUST

1. Crowl, *Traveller's Guide to Historic Britain*, Crowl, *Traveller's Guide to Historic Britain*, 596.
2. See pp. 73, 148–149, 174, 179.
3. Davies, *Early Cornish Evangelicals*, 20. Davies cited as his source an article in the *Quarterly Review*, 139 (1875): 394.
4. Davies, *Early Cornish Evangelicals*, 23.
5. See pp. 112, 120, 175–176, 253.
6. See pp. 32–33.
7. See pp. 73, 179, 206.
8. See Rogal, *Biographical Dictionary*, 8:300–301.
9. See p. 278.
10. *Book of Common Prayer*, 241.
11. Ward cited from an article in *The Proceedings of the Wesley Historical Society*, 18 (1931): 32.
12. See *Works of John Wesley. Journal and Diaries*, 19:337, 339; 20:22, 72–73, 79, 182, 249, 357, 402, 469; 21:28–29, 122–123, 276–277, 280, 389; 22:20–21, 60, 156, 202–203, 245, 387; 23:29–30, 66, 103, 184, 221, 235, 250, 374, 533; 24: 152; *Letters of John Wesley*, ed. Telford, 3:194; 4:306.

ST. LAWRENCE

1. Both Curnock (*Journal*, 3:538, note 4) and Ward and Heitzenrater (*Works: Journal and Diaries*, 20:402, note 40) cite as the source an article in *The Proceedings of the Wesley Historical Society*, 4 (1904): 190.

ST. STEPHEN DOWN

1. *Iliad* 1:2:117–118.

TOLCARN

1. See pp. 146, 236, 271.
2. See pp. 227–228, 230.

TOWEDNACK

1. Davies, *Early Cornish Evangelicals*, 23.
2. See pp. 264, 266, 271.
3. See pp. 260–261, 165–266, 284.

TREDINNEY

1. Telford (*Letters*, 2:106) identified the recipient of the letter as "To the Clergyman at Tredinney"; Ward and Heitzenrater (*Works: Journal and Diaries*, 20:183)

and Baker (*Works: Letters,* 26:252) *named* Corker.

TRENOUTH

1. *Works: Journal and Diaries,* 23:220, note 9.
2. Perhaps, but not certain, the map in question had been published in Cary's *New Itinerary through England, Wales, Scotland, and Ireland* (London, 1798; 10 eds. through 1821).
3. *Journal,* ed. Curnock, 6:332, note 1.

TRESMEER

1. Davies, *Early Cornish Evangelicals,* 35–36, 39–45.
2. See pp. 120, 155–156, 199, 255–256, 294–295.
3. See p. 301.

TREVOWHAN

1. See p. 271 + note 15.
2. From Charles Wesley's paraphrase of Psalms 133, in eleven verses of six lines each, beginning, "Behold how good a thing," first published in the Wesleys' *Hymns and Sacred Poems* (1742). See *New and Critical Edition of Poetical Works,* 8:1:370–374.

TREWELLARD

1. See pp. 294–295.
2. Genesis 30:8, 32:24–25; Ephesians 6:12.

TREWINT

1. See pp. 146–147, 236, 271, 303.

TRURO

1. Davies, *Early Cornish Evangelicals,* 13.
2. See p. 168.
3. Defoe, *Tour through Great Britain,* 231–232.
4. Those houses of the affluent on Princess Street eventually became offices and shops.
5. See p. 84.
6. See Davies, *Early Cornish Evangelicals,* 57. Davies did not quote Hals directly, but cited from Ashley Rowe, *Some Chapters in the History of Truro* (1943).
7. Davies, *Early Cornish Evangelicals,* 57. Davies cited as his source *Thesaurus Ecclesiasticus Provincialis* (1787): 102.

8. Davies, *Early Cornish Evangelicals,* 58. Davies cited from R.P. Chope, *Early Tours in Devon and Cornwall* (1918): 191.
9. Davies, *Early Cornish Evangelicals,* 58.
10. Authorities ordered the destruction of the building in 1848—Ward and Heitzenrater citing an article from the *Proceedings of the Wesley Historical Society,* 4 (1904): 193.
11. See pp. 250, 275.
12. See pp. 182, 284.
13. The house became, in 1877, the residence of the bishops of Truro and continued in that capacity until 1952. See *Works: Journal and Diaries,* 24:58, note 1.
14. See *Works: Journal and Diaries,* 21:25, 125,387–388; 22:59, 158, 202, 249, 386, 464; 23:30, 220, 250; 24:48, 151–152, 291; *Letters,* ed. Telford, 3:143; 7:163, 257.

WEEK ST. MARY

1. Brackets supplied by Ward and Heitzenrater.
2. See *Works: Journal and Diaries,* 20:69, 80, 142, 184; 21:127–128, 282, 291.

ZENNOR

1. Crowl, *Intelligent Traveller's Guide,* 20, 595–596.
2. *Works: Letters,* ed. Baker, 26:138, 245–246.
3. See p. 274.
4. See pp. 175, 190, 234, 240, 258, 281, 291, 305, 310, 312, 321.
5. See *Works: Journal and Diaries,* 19:336–337, 340; 20:23, 73, 79, 182, 249, 357, 402, 469; 21:276; 22:156.

Chapter 4

1. For example: John J. Beckerlegge, *Two Hundred Years of Methodism in Mousehole, Penzance, St. Clements Methodist Church* (n.p.: n.p., 1954; Oliver A Beckerlegge, *Free Methodism in Cornwall.* Occasional Publications, No. 2 (Truro: Cornish Methodist Historical Association, 1961); G.C.B. Davies, *The Early Cornish Evangelicals, 1735–1760: A Study of Walker of Truro and Others* (London: The Society for the Promotion of Christian Knowledge, 1951); Gilbert Hunter Doble, *John Wesley and His Work in Cornwall* (Liskeard, Cornwall: Philp and Sons, 1935); Lawrence Maker, *Cob*

and Moorstone: The Curious History of Some Cornish Methodist Churches (London: Epworth Press, 1935); John Pearce, ed., *The Wesleys in Cornwall: Extracts from the Journals of John and Charles Wesley and John Nelson* (Truro, Cornwall: D.B. Barton, 1964); John Charles Cripps Probert, *Methodism in Redruth until the Death of John Wesley* (Redruth, Cornwall: n.p., 1965); Probert, *The Sociology of Cornish Methodism to the Present Day.* Occasional Publication of the Cornish Methodist Historical Association, No. 17 (Redruth, Cornwall: Cornish Methodist Historical Association, 1971); Thomas Shaw, *A History of Cornish Methodism* (Truro, Cornwall: Barton, 1967); Shaw, *Methodism in the Camelford and Wadebridge Circuit, 1743–1963* (Camelford, Cornwall: n.p., 1963); Symons, R., *The Rev. John Wesley's Ministerial Itineraries in Cornwall: Commenced in 1743 and Concluded in 1789* (Truro, Cornwall: Symons, 1879).

2. H. Davies, *Worship and Theology*, 3:214–217.

Appendices

1. The dates of births and deaths, as well as the places of birth for natives of Cornwall, have derived from the appropriate entries in Rogal, *Biographical Dictionary of Eighteenth-Century Methodism.*

2. Beginning in 1785, John Wesley reorganized Methodism in Cornwall, replacing the circuits of Cornwall East and Cornwall West with those of St. Austell, Redruth, and St. Ives—each circuit to be supplied by three preachers.

3. Beginning in 1765, John Wesley divided the work in Cornwall into Cornwall *East* and *West*, but the county remained a single circuit.

4. Beginning in 1768, Cornwall East and Cornwall West each became a separate circuit.

5. A native of Busveal, Cornwall.

6. John Wesley appointed Jones, in 1749, as **assistant** in the Cornwall and Bristol circuits. The **Assistant** stood as the head of the circuit and in charge of the societies within that circuit, as well as the leader of his fellow preachers in that circuit. Later, the Conference added to the assistant's responsibilities, "To hold Quar-

terly Meetings, and therein diligently to inquire both into the spiritual and temporal state of each Society." See Heitzenrater, *Wesley and the People Called Methodists*, 2nd ed., 194–195.

7. A native of Cornwall.

8. Born in Cornwall.

9. Ill-health forced Poole, in the fall of 1789, to retire to Redruth, Cornwall, where he died in 1801. See *Letters of John Wesley*, ed. Telford, 8:75, 181; Joseph Beaumont Wakeley, *Anecdotes of the Wesleys: Illustrative of Their Character and Personal History* (New York: Carlton and Lanahan, 1869; London: Hodder and Stoughton, 1900): 141–142.

10. See *Works of John Wesley. Volume 10. The Methodist Societies*, 286, + note 1009.

11. Should the date of Rodd's death be correct, then he could not have completed his full term in the Cornwall circuit.

12. Born at Sancreed, Cornwall.

13. A native of St. Gennys, Cornwall.

14. I have determined the figures for columns 4 and five; the numbers in the remaining columns have been extracted from the *Works of John Wesley. Volume 10. The Methodist Societies*, beginning p. 306.

15. The *Minutes* for 1766 do not provide a total of all members; it includes in the list, but does not provide figures for, the circuits of London, Canterbury, Norwich, Oxfordshire, Devonshire, Dunbar, Wales, or Ireland.

16. This marks the first year in which the membership list includes the number of Methodists in British North America.

17. The membership figure for British North America has been omitted for 1779.

18. Figures not provided in the Conference *Minutes* for 1767 and 1768.

19. The total includes £187. 13.s. 10d. from the Kingswood School collection. Unless noted, subscription totals in future entries will include the Kingswood contribution.

20. This amount went to Cornwall West; the Cornwall East circuit received nothing from the Conference, most likely the result of steadily declining membership in the Methodist societies therein.

21. Apparently, the Conference did not allocate funds for Cornwall in 1773.

22. This figure represents the amount received from the Kingswood School con-

tribution. In response to the question, "What is contributed to the yearly expenses?" John Wesley replied, "Nothing. There is only one contribution this year, namely for the New Chapel [in City Road] in London." *Works of John Wesley. Volume 10* (2011), 469–470.

23. For this year, the Kingswood School contribution and the contributions for yearly expenses came to the exact same total of £366. 14. 11d. Coincidence? Error in transcription onto the *Minutes*?

24. This figure represents the amount received from the Kingswood School collection. The text of the Conference *Minutes* does not indicate receipts from the general collection nor does it list allocations of funds to the circuits or the societies.

25. During 1782–1791, the Methodist Conference did not distribute any money to the circuits or to the societies.

26. Although, the Conference *Minutes* for 1786 indicates the planning of a preaching house at St. Austell, Cornwall, one cannot be certain whether the Conference did or did not commit funds for that purpose.

27. The list of proposed preaching houses to be constructed within the year included buildings at Penryn and Penzance.

Bibliography

Primary Sources

Autobiography of Benjamin Franklin, The. 2nd ed. ed. Leonard W. Labaree, Ralph L. Ketcham, Helen C. Boatfield, and Helene H. Fineman. New Haven and London: Yale University Press/Yale Nota Bene, 2003.

Book of Common Prayer, The: The Texts of 1540, 1559, and 1662. ed. Brian Cummings. Oxford: Oxford University Press, 2011.

Boswell, James. *Life of [Samuel] Johnson* [1791]. ed. R.W. Chapman. 3rd ed.,rev., J.D. Fleeman. London and Oxford: Oxford University Press, 1970.

Charles Wesley: A Reader. ed. John R. Tyson. New York and Oxford: Oxford University Press, 1989.

Complete Jewish Bible. An English Version of the Tanakh (Old Testament) and B'ritt Hadashah (New Testament). trans. and ed. David H. Stern. Clarksville, Maryland, and Jerusalem, Israel: Jewish New Testament Publications, Inc., 1998.

Defoe, Daniel. *Tour through the Whole Island of Great Britain [1724–1726].* ed. Pat Rogers. Harmondsworth, Middlesex: Penguin Books, Ltd., 1971.

Holy Bible, The. Containing the Old and New Testaments Translated Out of the Original Tongues and with the Former Translations Diligently Compared and Revised. The Authorized King James Version. Cleveland and New York: The World Publishing Company, n.d.

Iliad of Homer, The. trans. Alexander Pope.

Volume the First. London: Printed by Charles Rivington, 1760.

Journal of the Rev. Charles Wesley, M.A., Sometime Student of Christ Church, Oxford. To Which Are Appended Selections from His Poetry and Correspondence. 2 vols. ed. Thomas Jackson. London: John Mason, 1849; rpt. Grand Rapids, Michigan: Baker Book House, 1980.

Journal of the Rev. John Wesley, A.M., Sometime Fellow of Lincoln College, Oxford. 8 vols. ed. Nehemiah Curnock. London: Charles H. Kelly, 1909–1916.

Letters of the Rev. John Wesley, Sometime Fellow of Lincoln College, Oxford. 8 vols. ed. John Telford. London: The Epworth Press, 1931.

Manuscript Journal of the Reverend Charles Wesley, M.A. The. 2 vols. ed. S.T. Kimbrough, Jr., and Kenneth G/C. Newport. Nashville: Kingswood Books/ Abingdon Press, 2007–2008.

Moule, Thomas. *The County Maps of Old England [1830].* intro. Roderick Barron. London: Studio Editions, Ltd., 1990.

New and Critical Edition of George Osborn's **The Poetical Works of John and Charles Wesley** *(1868–1872), A.* 13 vols., 21 books. ed. Samuel J. Rogal. Lewiston, New York: The Edwin Mellen Press, 2009–2013

New Oxford Annotated Bible, The. With the Apocryphal/Deuterocanonical Books. ed. Bruce M. Metzger and Roland E. Murphy. New York: Oxford University Press, 1991.

[Newton, John, and William Cowper.] *Olney Hymns, in Three Books*. London: Printed and Sold by W. Oliver, M DCC LXXIX [1779]; rpt. Olney, Buckinghamshire: The Trustees of the Cowper and Newton Museum, 1979.

Parallel Commentary on the New Testament. ed. Mark Water. Chattanooga, Tennessee: AMG Publishers, 2003.

Sermons of Charles Wesley, The: A Critical Edition, with Introduction and Notes. ed. Kenneth George Charles Newport. Oxford: Oxford University Press, 2001.

Wesley, John. *Primitive Physick; or, An Easy and Natural Method of Curing Most Diseases*. London: Thomas Tyre, 1747; rpt. as *Primitive Remedies by John Wesley*. ed. Howard B. Weeks. Santa Barbara, California: Woodbridge Press Publishing Company, 1975.

_____. *Works of John Wesley, The*. 3rd ed., 14 vols. ed. Thomas Jackson: London: Wesleyan Methodist Book Room, 1872; rpt. Peabody, Massachusetts: Hendrickson Publishers, Inc., 1986.

_____. *Works of John Wesley, The. Volumes 1–4. Sermons*. ed. Albert C. Outler. Nashville: Abingdon Press, 1984–1987.

_____. *Works of John Wesley, The. Volume 9. The Methodist Societies: History, Nature, and Design*. ed. Rupert E. Davies. Nashville: Abingdon Press, 1989.

_____. *Works of John Wesley, The. Volume 10. The Methodist Societies: The Minutes of Conference*. ed. Henry D. Rack. Nashville: Abingdon Press, 2011.

_____. *Works of John Wesley, The. Volume 11. The Appeals to Men of Reason and Religion and Certain Related Open Letters*. ed. Gerald R. Cragg. Oxford: At the Clarendon Press, 1975.

_____. *Works of John Wesley, The. Volumes 18–24. Journal and Diaries* (1735–1791). 7 vols. ed. W. Reginald Ward and Richard P. Heitzenrater. Nashville: Abingdon Press, 1988–2003.

_____. *Works of John Wesley, The. Volumes 25–26. Letters (1721–1755)*. 2 vols. ed. Frank Baker. Oxford: Clarendon Press, 1980–1981.

Secondary Sources

Allibone, Samuel Austin. *A Critical Dictionary of English Literature and British and American Authors, Living and Deceased, from the Earliest Accounts to the Latter Half of the Nineteenth Century*. 3 vols. Philadelphia: J.B. Lippincott and Company, 1872–1877.

Blackburn, Bonnie, and Leofranc Holford-Strevens. *The Oxford Companion to the Year*. Oxford: Oxford University Press, 1999.

Blumgarten, A.S. *Textbook of Materia Medica Pharmacology and Therapeutics*. 7th ed., rev. New York: The Macmillan Company, 1937.

Boase, Frederick. *Modern English Biography. Containing Many Thousand Concise Memoirs of Persons Who Have Died between the Years 1851–1900, with an Index of the Most Interesting Matter*. 6 vols. London: Privately Printed, 1897–1921; rpt. London: Frank Cass and Company, Ltd., 1965.

Briggs, Asa. *A Social History of England*. New York: The Viking Press, 1984.

Catalogue of Books (1841), A. Henry G. Bohn. 2 parts (vols.). rpt. and intro. Francesco Cordasco. New York: AMS Press, 1974.

Charles Wesley: Life, Literature, and Legacy. ed. Kenneth C.G. Newport and Ted A. Campbell. London: The Epworth Press, 2007.

Coe, Bufford W. *John Wesley and Marriage*. Bethlehem, Pennsylvania: Lehigh University Press/London: Associated University Presses, 1996.

Courtney, William Prideaux, and David Nichol Smith. *A Bibliography of Samuel Johnson*. Oxford: At the Clarendon Press, 1925.

Crowl, Philip A. *The Intelligent Traveller's Guide to Historic Britain: England, Wales, the Crown Dependencies*. New York: Congdon and Weed, Inc., 1983.

Currie, Robert, Alan Gilbert, and Lee Horsley. *Churches and Churchgoers: Patterns of Church Growth in the British Isles Since 1700*. Oxford: The Clarendon Press, 1977.

Davies, George Colliss Boardman. *The Early Cornish Evangelicals, 1735–1760: A Study of [Samuel] Walker of Truro and Others*. London: S.P.C.K., for the Church Historical Society, 1951.

Davies, Horton. *Worship and Theology in England. III: From Watts and Wesley to Maurice*. Princeton, New Jersey: Princeton University Press, 1961; rpt.

Grand Rapids, Michigan: William B. Eerdmans Publishing Company, 1996.

Fletcher, Charles Robert Leslie. *An Introductory History of England.* 4 vols. London: John Murray, 1920–1921.

Fodor, Eugene. *Britain and Ireland, 1962.* New York: David McKay and Company, 1962.

Green, Richard, and Henry J. Foster. *An Itinerary in Which Are Traced the Rev. John Wesley's Journeys from October 14, 1735, to October 24, 1790.* Burnley, Lancashire: Printed by B. Moore for the Wesley Historical Society, 1907–1908.

Heitzenrater, Richard P. *[John] Wesley and the People Called Methodists.* 2nd ed. Nashville: Abingdon Press, 2013.

Historical Dictionary of Methodism. ed. Charles Yrigoyen, Jr., and Susan E. Warwick. Lanham, Maryland; and London: The Scarecrow Press, Inc., 1996.

Holman Illustrated Bible Dictionary. ed. Chad Owen Brand, *et al.* Nashville, Tennessee: Holman Bible Publishers, 2003.

Jackman, W.T. *The Development of Transportation in Modern England.* 2nd ed., rev., intro. W.H. Chaloner. Cambridge, England: Cambridge University Press, 1962; rpt. New York: Augustus M. Kelley, Publisher/Reprints of Economic Classics, 1965.

Jarboe, Betty M. *John and Charles Wesley: A Bibliography.* The American Theological Library Association/Metuchen, New Jersey and London: The Scarecrow Press, Inc., 1967. Secondary sources.

Langmuir, Erika, and Norbert Lynton. *The Yale Dictionary of Art and Artists.* New Haven and London: Yale University Press, 2000.

Lecky, William Edward Hartpole. *A History of England in the Eighteenth Century.* 3rd ed., revised. 8 vols. London: Longman, Green, and Company, 1883–1890.

Mack, Maynard. *The Garden and the City: Retirement and Politics in the Later Poetry of Pope, 1731–1743.* Toronto: University of Toronto Press, 1969.

Oden, Thomas C. *John Wesley's Teachings.* 4 vols. Grand Rapids, Michigan: Zondervan, 2012–2014.

Merriam-Webster's Geographical Dictionary. 3rd ed. Springfield, Massachusetts: Merriam-Webster, Incorporated, Publishers, 1997.

Oxford Companion to the English Language, The. ed. Tom McArthur. Oxford and New York: Oxford University Press, 1992.

Rack, Henry D. *Reasonable Enthusiast: John Wesley and the Rise of Methodism.* 3rd ed. London: The Epworth Press, 2002.

Redmond, Alvin. *The House of Hanover.* rev. ed. London: Alvin Redman, 1968.

Rogal, Samuel J. *A Biographical Dictionary of Eighteenth-Century Methodism.* 10 vols. Lewiston, New York: The Edwin Mellen Press, 1997–1999.

_____. "Counting the Congregation: Wishful Thinking Versus Hard Reality in the Journals of John Wesley." *Methodist History,* 30:1 (October 1991): 3–9.

Sidney, Edwin. *The Life and Ministry of the Rev. Samuel Walker, B.A., Formerly of Truro, Cornwall.* London: Baldwin and Craddock, 1835; 2nd. ed., London: R.B. Seeley and W. Burnside, 1838.

Southey, Robert. *The Life of [John] Wesley and the Rise and Progress of Methodism[1820].* ed. J. Augustus Atkinson. London and New York: Frederick Warne and Company, 1889.

Taber's Cyclopedic Medical Dictionary, 14th ed. ed. Clayton L. Thomas. Philadelphia: F.A. Davis Company, 1981.

Telford, John. *The Life of the Rev. Charles Wesley, M.A., Sometime Student of Christ Church, Oxford.* Revised and Enlarged. London: Wesleyan Methodist Book Room, 1900.

Trevelyan, George Macaulay. *England under Queen Anne: Blenheim.* London: Longmans, Green and Company, Ltd., 1930; rpt. London: Collins/The Fontana Library, 1965.

Tyerman, Luke. *The Life and Times of the Rev. John Wesley, M.A., Founder of the Methodists.* 3 vols. New York: Harper and Brothers, Publishers, 1872.

Wakeley, Joseph Beaumont. *Anecdotes of the Wesleys: Illustrative of Their Character and Personal History.* New York: Carlton and Lanahan, 1869; London: Hodder and Stoughton, 1900.

Watts, Michael R. *The Dissenters: From the Reformation to the French Revolution.* Oxford: The Clarendon Press, 1978.

Who Was Who, 1929–1940. Volume 3. 2nd ed. London: Adam and Charles Black, 1967.

Index to Citations
from Scriptures

Genesis **5:32** 221; **6:10** 221; **9:27** 221;
  30:8 222; **32:24–25** 222; **41:16** 152
Exodus **14:13** 154; **29:45** 61
Numbers **23:10** 110; **23:23** 141; **24:8**
  221; **25:13** 145;
Deuteronomy **11:29** 74; **20:11** 152;
  27:13 74; **31:17–18** 221; **32:2** 130
Joshua **8:30** 74; **8:33** 74
Judges **3:20** 107; **16:9** 131; **19:6** 218;
  19:9 218; **19:22** 218
Ruth **3:7** 218; **4:5** 97; **4:10** 97–98
1 Samuel **20:3** 128; **25:36** 218; **28:5** 146
2 Samuel **13:28** 218
1 Kings **19:9** 40, 100; **19:12** 40; **19:13** 41;
  21:7 218
1 Chronicles 114; **1:25** 221
2 Chronicles **7:10** 218; **30:9** 144
Nehemiah **1:6** 60
Esther **1:10** 218
Job **4:31–32** 171; **6:18** 123; **17:2** 140;
  22:21 123; **28:28** 110; **29:17** 48; **38:11**
  155; **38:37** 127
Psalms **18:1** 159; **18:3** 159; **18:26** 139;
  22:14 175; **29:2** 76; **33:3** 187; **38:8**
  161; **40:3** 158; **42:2** 152; **42:7** 35; **44:3**
  172; **51:8** 221; **59:9** 115; **68:9** 134;
  68:30 45; **76:5** 146; **77:9** 98, 165; **89:9**
  164; **89:10** 57; **89:15** 133, 172; **89:46**
  221; **90:8** 172; **92:11–12** 128; **96:9** 76;
  100 154; **107:27** 82; **110:5** 174;
  118:15–16 174; **118:23** 86; **133** 222;
  144:15 140
Proverbs **3:8** 77; **15:7** 218; **15:15** 218;
  16:24 77; **17:22** 218; **20:8** 156

Ecclesiastes **7:32** 90–91; **9:7** 218; **9:10**
  42, 118; **12:13** 165
Isaiah **1:16** 116; **6:7** 152, 169; **6:8** 58;
  11:6 92; **12:6** 161; **24:7** 218; **35:8** 188;
  35:9–10 157; **38:13** 221; **40:1** 150, 152;
  40:30 107; **43:2** 117; **45:24** 154; **46:12**
  146; **51:6** 129–130; **53** 185, 197; **53:6**
  169; **54:3:17** 155; **55:1** 40, 170, 188,
  196; **55:7** 184; **55:8** 111; **57:1–2** 130;
  58:1 72; **63:1** 92; **64** 220, 221; **64:1–2**
  220; **64:6** 125
Jeremiah **8:22** 105–106; **9:1** 159; **15:17**
  140; **50:17** 221
Lamentations **1:12** 125; **3:4** 221
Ezekiel **1:16** 118, 219; **5:6** 141; **14:4** 170;
  14:7 170; **18:31** 83, 180, 188; **24:17** 152;
  33:11 111, 180; **37** 100; **37:1–14** 93;
  37:4 31; **39:29** 221; **48** 127
Daniel **6:22** 154; **9:24** 127
Hosea **2:23** 131; **11:8** 116; **14:4** 48, 76,
  118, 164, 181;
Joel **2:14** 198
Amos **4:12** 123
Jonah **4:2** 144
Habakkuk **1:10** 30; **2:6** 174, 221
Haggai **1:13** 107
Zechariah **13:7–9** 75
Malachi **3:2–3** 159
Matthew **1:21** 153–154; **4:13** 61; **4:15–**
  16 114; **5:2–12** 179; **5:12** 156; **5:20** 118,
  154; **5:23–25** 32; **5:44** 79; **5:47** 190;
  7:15 124, 184; **8:13** 145; **9:37** 71; **10:14**
  154; **10:16** 153; **10:25** 77, 159; **10:30**
  172; **11:5** 92, 169; **11:19** 77; **12:43** 42;

13:3–9 217; 13:20 187; 15:22–28 125;
19:26 121; 20:23 74; 22:1 170; 22:6
170; 22:21 145; 23:39 139; 24:12 107;
25:32–33 74; 26:73 82; 28:3 172;
28:18 60; 1:15 152, 178; 2:17 187; 3:35
128; 4:3–9 217; 5:9 162; 10:27 121;
10:46–52 150, 154; 12:34 160, 198;
13:13 61; 13:20 187; 2:35 80–81; 4:18
76; 4:21 77; 6:20–23 156; 6:27 79; 7
45; 7:22 31; 7:34 77; 7:42 158; 8:4–8
217; 8:13 187; 10:23–24 83, 187;
10:29–37 137, 187, 197; 11:9 115;
11:28 114; 12:4 155; 12:15 149; 12:32
73, 187; 13:3–23 197; 13:11–17 157;
14:15–24 75; 15:22 125; 15:32 114;
16:13 183; 16:22 175; 19:42 40; 20:34
135; 20:35–36 116; 21:34 170
Mark 1:15 152, 178; 2:17 187; 3:35 128;
4:3–9 217; 5:9 162; 10:27 121;
10:46–52 150, 154; 12:34 160, 198;
13:13 61; 13:20 187
Luke 2:35 80–81; 4:18 76; 4:21 77;
6:20–23 156; 6:27 79; 7 45; 7:22 31;
7:34 77; 7:42 158; 8:4–8 217; 8:13
187; 10:23–24 83, 187; 10:29–37 137,
187, 197; 11:9 115; 11:28 114; 12:4 155;
12:15 149; 12:32 73, 187; 13:3–23 197;
13:11–17 157; 14:15–24 75; 15:22 125;
15:32 114; 16:13 183; 16:22 175; 19:42
40; 20:34 135; 20:35–36 116; 21:34
170
John 1:29 92, 114; 3:7 38; 3:8 169; 3:16
217; 3:30 111; 4:24 63, 120; 4:35 169–
170; 5:6–7 98; 5:35 111; 6:67 170; 7:6
185; 8:46 114–115; 11:25 188; 13:1 217;
14:1 156; 15:19 217; 22:22 31
Acts 1:4 158; 2:42 114, 157; 3:15 31; 5:31
188; 8:10 143–144; 15:17 180; 16:31
77, 145; 16:34 75; 17:31 194; 18:16

125; 20:21 121; 20:27 194; 20:32 156;
22:3 145; 26:28 165, 166
Romans 1:16 129; 1:18 113; 3:24 94; 4:7
187; 6:11 98; 8:1 94, 171; 8:15 115; 10:2
144; 12:20 168; 14:3 117; 14:17 115,
117; 15:13 75, 172
1 Corinthians 1:23 105; 1:30 76; 2:4 87–
88; 5:8 162; 9:26 125; 13:1–3 41; 13:2
150; 16:9 161; 16:24 144
2 Corinthians 187; 3:18 79; 5:1–4 53;
5:18–19 71; 5:19 87, 142, 147, 174;
5:20 161; 11:3 117
Galatians 3:22 29; 4:14 117; 5:7 48; 6:14
193
Ephesians 2:8 93, 194; 4:20 181; 4:27
144; 4:32 39, 169; 5:14 131, 142, 152,
194; 6:10 107; 6:12 222
Philippians 1:21 80; 1:23 80; 4:6 47
Colossians 1:16 218–219
1 Thessalonians 4:17 86, 156
1 Timothy 1:14 144
2 Timothy 1:13 144; 3:5 90; 3:12 78
Titus 2:10 180, 189; 2:13 180
Hebrews 1:3 71; 2:1 136; 2:3 135; 4:10
114, 197; 4:12 82, 168; 4:14 31, 187;
5:12 154; 6:1 99, 117, 129, 141; 6:5 143;
6:17–18 73; 8:12 82; 10:31 135; 10:35
166; 12:14 127 (2), 165; 13:6 155;
13:22 147
James 5:16 97
1 Peter 1:8 60–61, 80, 109; 2:17 121;
2:21 138; 4:11 154
2 Peter 3:3 30; 3:8 138–139
1 John 1:3 165; 2:15 217; 3:8 165; 4:14 72
2 John 8 127
Jude 25 180
Revelation 1:16 172; 2:10 197; 2:13 125;
3:8 72, 123; 3:12 156; 20:12 174; 21:2
156; 22:20 165

Index of Persons, Places
and General Topics

Abbey Church, Bath 37
"Absolution or Remission of Sins" 173
Act More Effectively 189
Adams, John 178, 187
Adams, Robert 15, 179
Aegean Sea 176
Africa 15, 179
Agape 81
Alabaster 50
Albert Edward 6
Alderney, Channel Islands 128
Allhallows Day 51
Alpraham, Cheshire 70
The Amaranth 66
"Amazing grace, how sweet" 114
"America the Beautiful" 50
American plant species 10
Amoric English 8
Anabaptist teachings 46
Anatolia, Asia Minor 43
Andrew, Richard 91, 168
Anne, Queen 176
Anti-Methodism 2, 19, 33, 34, 56–60,
    95, 117, 132–133, 142, 143, 154–160,
    183, 185, 196, 201
Antinomianism 146, 162, 194
Antiquarian Society 12
Antiquities, Historical and Monumental
    11
"Antiquities in Archaeology" 63
Antiquities in Westminster Abbey 5
Anti-Riot Act (1715) 139, 159, 188
Archaeologia Cornu-Britannica 12
Archaeologica Britannica 7–8

Architectural Illustrations of Cathedrals
    5
Aristotle 122
Arminian Magazine 130, 135
Armorica 214
Arthur, King 15
Arthurian legend 15, 63
Asia 15
assistants 223
Assizes 73, 95
Associate Presbyterian Church, Scotland
    162
Atlantic Ocean 3, 149
Aukland, Durham 69
Autobiography (Franklin) 59, 84

B., Mrs. 56–57, 60
backsliders 173
Bailey 178
Baker, Frank 200
Balliol College, Oxford 38
Bangor, Wales 8
Bant's Cairn, St. Mary's, Isles of Scilly
    179
Baptismal regeneration 14
Baptists 186
Bardsley, Samuel 100
Barrow 169
Baskett, Thomas 189
Bates, Katharine Lee 50
Bath, Somersetshire 12, 37
Beatitudes 156, 179
Beauchamp, Francis 79
Beauchamp, John 78–79

Beckenham, Kent 14
Beckford, William 12
Bedfordshire 12, 13
Benjamin Franklin Papers 85
Bennett, John (1670?–1750) 20–21, 72, 93–94, 120, 150, 151, 187
Bennetts, John 173–174, 189
Berkeley Chapel, London 12
Berkshire 8, 12, 13
Beryl 219
Besore 122
Bethesda, pool of 98
Betony 39
Bible/Holy Scriptures 2, 10, 20, 30, 58, 125, 161, 197
Bibliographer's Manual 7
Bibliotheca Heraldica 5
Bideford 120
Bilbrook, Somersetshire 70
Birmingham, Warwickshire 15, 42
Bishopsgate, London 83
black tourmaline 9–10
Blackwell, Ebenezer 161, 163
Blake, Robert 15, 179
Blatchford, Robert 105
blind letters 4
Board of Ordnance 13
boards 9
Bodmin 26–29, 33, 94, 112, 142, 148, 175, 195
Bodmin Church 27
Bodmin Moor 3, 26, 27
Bohn, Henry G. 6–7
Bolerium 92
Bolton, Lancashire 42
Boniface IV 51
Book of Common Prayer (1662) 45–47, 72, 76, 173
Borlase, George 67
Borlase, John 59, 109
Borlase, Walter 44, 108, 124–125, 171
Borlase, William 8–10, 11, 20, 44, 89, 105, 108, 169
Borough town 66
Boscawen Street, Truro 194
Boscoval House 129, 219
Bose, Dr. 15
Boston, Massachusetts 104
Boswell, James 47
botanical nomenclature 11
Bothe, Thomas del 69
Bottom 26
Boulne-Hurst, Bedfordshire 46
Boyle, J.R. 69
Bradford, Yorkshire 24
Bradford-upon-Avon, Wiltshire 70–71

Brady, Nicholas 164
Brampford Speke, Devonshire 14, 15
Brane tomb, St. Just 169
Brea 29–30
Breage (St. Breage) 30–32, 120
Bretagne (Brittany), France 214
bridge repair 68–69
Bridgewater, Somersetshire 177
Bristol, Gloucestershire 18, 20, 22, 34, 42, 48, 71, 134, 142, 153
Bristol Channel 148, 152, 153, 164, 179
Britain 3, 5, 11, 17, 44, 138; history 12; manufacturers 55; soldiers 127
Britannia Depicta 12, 13
British Channel 153
British Isles 23, 78
The British Librarian 7
British North America 10, 15, 18, 54, 74
Brixton Hill, London 19
Bronze Age 15, 43, 101, 169
Brown Willy 3
Bryher, Isles of Scilly 179
Buckingham, William 133, 134
Buckinghamshire 12, 13
building debt 24
Burkitt, William 21, 153
Burton-on-Trent, Staffordshire 69
Busveal 70, 80, 223
Byrne, W. 12, 13

Cairnes, Cubert 51
calf 214
Callestick (Callestock; Calstock) 32
Calley, John 70
Callington 68
Calvinism 46, 146
Calvinist Methodists 166
Camborne 29, 32–36, 44, 86, 131, 136, 143, 164, 188
Cambridge University 46
Cambridgeshire 12, 13
Came, William 128–129, 147
Camel River 3, 36
Camelford 36–42, 96, 99, 133, 136, 149, 151, 177, 188, 202
Cameron 54
Canary Islands 80
Canorum 57
Canterbury, Kent 15
Cape Cornwall 42
captain 45
Cardinan, Robert de 104
Carew, Richard 7
Carew, Thomas 7
Carn Brae 15, 29, 43–44, 136

Carrick Roads 15, 54
Cary, John 186
Cassock 78
Castle Dore, Fowey 15
Castle Terrible 94
A Catalogue of Books 6, 7
Cayster River, Asia Minor 176–177
Celcius, Olaf 10
Celtic missionaries 63
Celts 11, 44; dialect 6
chaise 41
Channel Islands 128
chantry 120–121
chapelries 104, 166, 184
chapter 8
Charles I 6
Charles II 52, 124, 130, 192
Charles Edward, the Young Pretender
    88, 143, 159, 183, 190
Charleston, Carolinas settlement 104,
    179
Chatham, Kent 34
Cheshire 12, 13
Chester 5
children 164–166, 172
Chinhall, Mr. 170
Chollerford Bridge, Durham 69
Christ Church, Oxford 14, 150
Christian Church 81
Christian Library 122
Christianity 11, 63, 82, 110, 118, 146,
    156, 189, 195
church attendance 169
Church of England 2, 8, 9, 12, 14, 15, 17,
    20, 32, 42, 45, 46, 49, 56, 61, 62, 71,
    93, 100, 121, 124, 150, 154, 157, 169,
    182, 184, 192, 197, 201; clergy 20, 56,
    105, 181, 186, 201; liturgy 47, 201; reli-
    gious societies 18, 210; separation
    from 62, 122; services 59
Church of St. Mary-le-Bow, London 15
church ordinances 121
Church Record 20
church-town 51
Chysauster 15, 152–153
Cicero 32, 167
Cinque Ports 64
City Mall, London 83
Civil War (1642–1649) 6, 54, 130
Clapham, Surrey 14, 19
Claret 47
Clarke 11
Clarke, Adam 147
Classus Plantarum 10
clerical compensation 192
clerical education 122

cliff-top parish 113
Clifford, George 10
Coates, H. 68
Cober River 88
Coinage Hall, Truro 193–194
Coinage Hall Street, Helston 91
coining/coinage town 26, 32, 88, 101,
    104, 124, 191
Coke, Thomas 128
Colan 105
Collector of Customs 162
Collegiate Church of Wolverhampton,
    Staffordshire 108
Collins, John 137–139, 183
Collinson, Peter 9, 10
Commerce 128
Commonwealth period 193
communion 65
Complete History of Cornwall (Hals)
    50–51
Complete Jewish Bible 35
confession 137
conformation 32, 124
Conger-eels 131
Congregationalists 186
Cook, James 129
Cooper 142
Cooper, Samuel 138
copper mines/mining 3–4, 70, 87
Copperhouse Chapel, Hayle 87–88
Cork, Ireland 141
Corker, Robert 185
Cornelly 105
Cornish diamond 4, 9
Cornish grammar 8, 12
Cornish history 7
Cornish language 5, 7, 11, 12
Cornish literature 6–15
Cornish miners 11
Cornish topography 15
Cornwall, Edmund 104
Cornwall, Richard, Earl of 15, 94, 95,
    104
Cornwall Methodist circuits 223
Cornwall Methodist societies 2
Cornweallas 3
corporation seats 193
Corpus Christi College, Oxford 12
Costerdine, Robert 42
Cottenham, Charles Christopher Pepys,
    1st Earl of 14
Coughlan, Lawrence 134–135
County of Durham 69
Court of Arches 14–15
Court of Assizes 94
Coventry, Thomas 61

Coventry, Warwickshire 8
Cowley, Abraham 166
Cragg, Gerald 112
Creed 65, 66
Cripplegate, London 83
Cromlech 102
Cromwell, Oliver 15, 94, 130
Cromwell's Castle, Tresco, Isles of Scilly 179
Crossing the Brook 68
Crowan 24, 34, 35, 44–49, 108, 109
Cubert 49–54, 103
Cubertus 49
Cumberland 12, 13
Cumbria 5
Cunomorus 63
Curnock, Nehemiah 2, 38, 50, 51, 56, 57, 68, 87, 90, 111, 126, 149, 168, 186, 199
Cuthbert parish 49

Dale, James 124
Dalecarlia, Sweden 10
Daniel, Alice 115, 116, 142
Daniel, John 142
Daniell, Thomas 4
Dark Ages 153
Dark Peak 50
Darlaston, Staffordshire 19
Dartmouth, Devonshire 70
Dead Man 111
deal 220
dean 8
Declarations of Indulgence 8
Dedham, Essex 21
Dee River 5
"Defense of Fort M'Henry" 43
Defoe, Daniel 26, 54–55, 64–65, 88, 95, 101, 120, 124, 136, 153, 178, 191
Delabole Quarry 36
Delaware River 59
Dell, William 121–122
Demosthenes 167
Derby 50
Derbyshire 13
Derbyshire, Peak District of 50
Derbyshire, Peak of 50
Destroyer 92
Devonshire 3, 5, 13, 64, 67, 94, 102, 112, 134
Dialogues of the Dead 190
Didsbury College, Manchester 19
dissenters 70, 102, 120, 150, 153, 191, 201
Divine Nature 172
Doddliscombsleigh, Devonshire 61
Dominican monks 192
Donnithorne, Joseph 143–144

Donnithorne, Mrs. 143–144
Doomsdale prison 94
Dore Castle, Fowey 63
Dorsetshire 5
Dover, Kent 64
Downes, John 27, 34
Druids 11, 44, 89
Ducal title 6
Duke Street, Grosvenor Square, London 4
Dunciad 66
Dunstanville, Francis, Lord de 7
Durham 69

E., Kitty 57, 59–60
Earnest Appeal to Reason 180, 195
earthquake 144
East Cornwall 98
East Midlands 50
Ebal, Mount 74
Ecclesiastical reform 202
Edinburgh, Scotland 24
Edward IV 64
Edward VI 104
Edward VII 6
Edward the Confessor 64
Edwards, John 92, 161
Egypt 44
Elizabeth I 15, 54, 104, 176
Ellis, William 146
Elvet Bridge, Durham 69
Emmanuel College, Cambridge 121
England 2, 3, 5, 7, 10, 15, 18, 22–24, 27, 39, 55, 57, 61, 73, 87, 92, 103, 104, 122, 128, 138, 161, 165, 179, 200; book trade 6; collieries 70; counties 8; groat 52; language 166; maps 8; plant species 10; prisoners of war 81, 138; topography 7
England's Topographer 4
English Channel 3, 50, 54, 106, 110, 130, 146
English Counties Delineated 5
English Crown 101
Enthusiasm of Methodists and Papists Compar'd 112
Ephesus 176
Epistles (Cicero) 32
Epworth, Lincolnshire 139
Erasmus (Greek bishop) 135
Erskine, John 174
Erskine, Ralph 162
Essay on Painting 66
Essay on Reason 66
Essay on Satire (Harte) 66
Essays (Knox) 166–167

Essays on Husbandry 66
Essex 14
"Eternal Power! Whose high abode" 187
Europe 43, 44, 52, 61, 87
Eustick, William 172
evangelical clergymen 122
evangelical revival 17
evangelicalism 17
Excursions in Essex 14
Exeter, Bishop of 14
Exeter, Devonshire 13, 27, 61; grammar
   school 61; see of 32, 108, 112, 134
Exeter Cathedral 108
Exeter College, Oxford 9, 37, 61, 89, 109
Exeter Diocesan Visitation Returns 70
Expository Notes on the New Testament
   (Burkitt) 21
Extract of John Wesley's Journal 29
Eynesbury, Huntingdonshire 14

Fairfax, Thomas 54, 121
faith 174
"Faith's Review and Expectation" 114
Fal River 3, 54
Falmouth 54–63, 66, 120, 121, 185, 191,
   202; harbor 123; merchants 55
Falmouth Bay 54
A Fast Sermon 66
Fauna Swecica 11
Fawley, Oxfordshire 14
Fenelon, Francois de Savignac 190
Fenwick, Michael 163
Fetter Lane, London 82
Finchley, London 19
Finsbury Circus/Square, London 83
fishing trade 153
Flamank, George 147
Fletcher, John William 19
Flora Lapponica 10
Flora Swecica 11
Floyd, John 181
flux 47, 118
folio 214
Fonthill Abbey, Somersetshire 12
Fore Street, Bodmin 28
Fore Street, St. Austell 147
Forster, Johann Georg Adam 129
Fortieth Regiment of Foot 74
Fougou 153
Foundery, Hayle 87
Fowey 63–65, 106, 130
Fowey River 63
Fox, George 94
Foy 64
Foyens 64
France 10, 56, 64, 81, 128, 138, 143, 159,

183; language 166; military prisoners
   138
Franciscan friars 192, 202
Franklin, Benjamin 58–59, 84
Frederick the Great 138
*Free and Candid Disquisitions Relating
   to the Church of England* 46–47
free chapel 192
Freeman, Edward Augustus vi
Frome, Somersetshire 32, 37
Front Street, Philadelphia 59
Fundamenta Botanica 10
funds allocated to Cornwall 211–212
Furly, Samuel 39, 142
Furze 35
Fust, H.J. 14

Galloway 6
Gaul 11, 44, 214
Gaunless River 69
Genera Plantarum 10
General Fund 23
General Post Office, London 4
The Gentleman and a Miner 4
Gentleman 's Magazine 12, 173
gentry 72
George II 159
Georgia 37, 104
German Moravians 81
German Pietism 18
Gelman Protestantism 18
Germany 57, 74
Germoe 30, 31
Gilbert, Davies 15
Glanvill, Joseph 37
glossography 214
Gloucester 5
Godolphin, Francis 180
Goldstithney 65
Gonvil and Caius College, Cambridge
   121
Good Samaritan 137, 187, 196–197
Gorham, George Cornelius 14–15
Gorham, George James 14
gospel 118, 122, 184
Gothic architecture 12
Gothic novel 12
Gotland, Sweden 10
Grampound 65–66, 193
Great Awakening 18
Great Britain 124
Great Britain Illustrated 5
Great Supper 75
Greeks 3, 43
Green, Richard 186
Green Court, Trewellard 189

Greenbank Terrace, Falmouth 56
Greenfield, Edward 132, 171
Gregory III 51
Gregory IV 51
Groat 52
Guernsey, Channel Islands 128
Guildford, Surrey 19
"Guinea Catalogue" 6
Gulf Stream 179
Gulval 67, 105, 191
Gulval Cross 67
Gulval Downs 30
Gunnislake 67–69
Gunnislake Bridge 68, 178
Gurney, Samuel 105
Guyon, Marie Bouvier 190
Gwennap 22, 25, 33, 69–86, 91, 112,
  136, 137, 148, 172, 191, 195
Gwennap Green 71, 73
Gwennap Pit 71–72, 82–86, 164, 202
Gwinear 31, 164
Gwithian 86

H., Mr. 123
Haarlem, Netherlands 10
Haime, John 50–51
Hall, Joseph 108
Hals, William 50, 192
Halstead, Essex 108
Hannah 104
Harderwijk, Holland 10
Harper, Andrew 142
Harris, Mr. 34, 35, 86, 143
Harte, Walter 65
Hastings, East Sussex 64
Hathaway, Ralph 180
Hayle 87–88
Hebrews 43
hedge and ditch 99
hedges 165
Heitzenrater, Richard 17–18, 56
Helford River 104
Helston 30, 35, 44, 88–91, 92, 104, 117,
  124, 132, 168, 182, 183, 196
Henderson, Charles 68
Henry II 27
Henry III 15, 94
Henry IV 69
Henry VII 6
Henry VIII 15, 54, 192
Heraldry of Fish 5
Hertfordshire 8
Hervey, James 21
Hethbeth Bridge, Nottingham 69
Hewetson, Henry 5
Hewgoe, Stephen 146

Hierobotanicon 10
High Bridge, Nottingham 69
High Sheriff of Cornwall 7
High Street, Helston 90
High Town, Isles of Scilly 9
Hinde Street, Lewisham 19
"Historical Chronicle" 173
Historical Collections of Matters of State
  61
Historical Survey of the Cathedral of
  Cornwall 12
History of Cornwall (Polwhele) 13–14
History of Eynesbury 14
History of Gustavus Adolphus 66
Hitchens, James 70, 80
Hitchens, James the Younger 70
Hitchens, Samuel 70
Hirchens, Thomas 80
Hitchens, William 70–71
Hittites 43
Hobart, John 160
Hoblyn, William 155, 156, 159, 184, 185,
  196, 198
Holland 57
Holsworthy 120
Holywell 50, 51
Homer 177
Hopper, Christopher 42, 163
Horae Lyricae 187
Hornblower, Joseph 70
Hortus Clifortianus 10
Hortus Upsaliensis 11
Hosken, Joseph 51–54
How, Jasper 153
Hugal, Westmorland 10
Huntingdon, Selina Shirley Hastings,
  Countess of 166
"The Hurlers," Liskeard 15, 101–102
Hurling 19, 171
Hythe, Kent 63

Iliad 177, 221
Illogan 22, 29, 35, 91
Illogan Downs 91
Illogan Highway 91
Illustrations of the Work of Walter Scott
  5
Independents 192
India proofs 14
Innisdgen tomb, Isles of Scilly 15, 179
Ireland 1, 7, 11, 14, 18, 19, 23, 24, 27, 44,
  200, 202; language 167; poets 167
Ireton, Bridget Cromwell 121
Ireton, Henry 121
Irish Methodists 134
iron 43

Iron Age 15, 43, 63, 136, 152
Iseult 15, 63
Israelites 74
Italian, translations from 7
itinerancy: expenses 141; field preaching
     18, 169–170; preaching 21, 22, 30, 167,
     200
Iver, Buckinghamshire 18
Ivy Lane, London 4

Jackson, Thomas 38, 126
Jaco, Peter 117
Jacobites 160, 183; 1715 uprising 139;
     1745 uprising 56
James I 7, 54
James II 8, 88, 177
Jane, Joseph 192
Jersey, Chanel Islands 128
Jerusalem 156
Jerusalem Delivered 7
Jesus Christ 17, 32, 74, 95, 99, 115, 144,
     163, 182
Jesus College, Oxford 8
John V 55
Johnson, Samuel 9, 47
Jones, John (1700–1770) 46–47
Joshua 74
journal extracts 29, 30
Journal of Charles Wesley (Jackson) 38,
     126
Journal of John Nelson 38
Journal of John Wesley (Curnock) 38,
     126, 168
Julius Caesar 58
Justices of Assize 73

Kallan 9
Kalthoeber 12
Keeper of the Records 12
Kendall, Nicholas 106
Kenneggy Downs 92
Kennington Common, Surrey 71
Kent 14, 64
Kenton, Suffolk 14
Kenwyn 14, 108, 194
Keppel, Frederick 134
Key, Francis Scott 43
Kilkenny, Ireland 52
Kimbrough and Newport 105
king 122
King James Version (KJV) 30, 35
King's Bench Prison, London 61
King's Evil 50
Kingswood School 223–224
Kippax, Yorkshire 97
Kirton 121, 219

Kithill 68
Knox, Vicesimus 166
Krill, John 162–163

L., Mr. 114
L., S. 181
Labaree, Leonard W. 59
Ladies' book club 124
Lamb of God 114
Lambeth, London 18
Lancashire 6
Land's End 3, 5, 9, 42, 66, 92–93, 100,
     117, 124, 153, 164, 169, 179, 181, 203
Laneast 20, 36, 93–94, 187
Laneast church 93–94
Lanlivery 61, 144
Lansdowne Hill, Somerset shire 12
Lanyon, Henry 31
Lanyon, Tobias 31
Lapland 10
Large Minutes 23
Last Judgment 137
Latin 20, 125
Launceston 27–29, 36, 37, 39, 42, 65,
     93, 94–100, 134, 176, 186, 190, 202,
     203
Launceston-Camelford road 93, 186
Launceston Castle 15, 94
Launceston town hall 96, 100
Laud, William 121
Lavington, George 112
Law-Death, Gospel Life 162
Lay preachers 201
Lelant 100–101, 198
Lemon, William 30, 70, 151–152
Lent 150
lepers 176
Lestock, Richard 159
Lestwithyel 26
Letters (J. Wesley) 34, 42
letters of orders 131
Lewisham, London 181
Lexicon Cornu-Britannicum 57
Leytonstone, London 19
Lichfield, Staffordshire 8
Life of John Wesley (Tyerman) 126
Life of Samuel Johnson 47
Limerick, Ireland 134, 145, 165
Lincoln College, Oxford 31, 37
Lincoln's Inn, London 7
Lincolnshire 20
Linnaeus, Carolus 9, 10–11
Linne, Carl von 10
Lisbon, Portugal 55
Liskeard 26, 101–103, 147, 186; town
     hall 103

Literary Magazine 9
Little Carharrack 103
Liverpool, Lancashire 19
Lizard Point 3, 103–104, 117
Lloyd, William 7–8
London 1, 6, 7, 16, 21, 22, 33, 48, 52, 83, 87, 92, 94, 109, 112, 119, 122, 124, 129, 140, 141, 143, 146, 147, 149, 157, 161, 167, 194; see of 135
London Moravians 81
London Quarterly Review 20
London Wall 83
Looe 104
Looe River 104
Lord Chamberlain's department 5
Lord Chancellor of England 61
Lord's Supper 130, 144, 151
Lostwithiel 104–105, 106
Love-feast 81–82, 86, 141, 157
Lower Street, St. Austell 146
Lowndes, William Thomas 7
Ludgvan 9, 44, 89, 105–106
Lund, Sweden 10
Luther, Martin 58
Luxulyan (Methrose) 65, 106–107
Lysons, Daniel (?–1800) 12
Lysons, Daniel (1760?–1834) 12, 13
Lysons, Samuel 12, 13
Lyttleton, George 190

M., T. 160
Ma'Carmick, James and Son 105
Maccaronis 83
Maddern, Jennifer Borlase 59, 60
Maddern, John 59, 197
Madeley, Yorkshire 19
Madern Hills 153
Madron 59, 107–108, 185
Magna (-us) Britannia 13, 214
Major, Timothy 160
Mallet, Walter 36
Manaccan 14
Manchester, Lancashire 12, 15, 18–19, 48
"Manderley" 64
Manuscript Journal (C. Wesley) 194
Marazion 30, 34, 66, 67, 108–110, 151, 152
Mark, King 15, 63
Market Harborough, Leicestershire 69
Market House, Helston 91
Market Jew 108
Market Street, Philadelphia 59
Marlborough Grammar School, Wiltshire 75
Mary Magdalene 95
Marylebone, London 4

Master-General of the Ordnance 13
Matthews, Thomas 159, 160
Maurier, Daphne du 64
Maxfield, Thomas 34, 44, 78, 109, 137
May, Edward 82
Meager, Mr. 106, 107
Membership, Cornwall Methodist societies 210–211
Men Scryoha 153
Menabilly estate 63, 64
Menderes River 176
Meriton, John 42, 45, 72, 156
Merther 105
Methodism: circuits 22; classes 67, 105, 170; conferences 21–24, 48; debt 48; itinerancy 17, 200; membership (Cornwall) 22–24, 98–99; mission (Cornwall) 22; preachers in Cornwall 205–210; preaching houses 48, 147; publishing concern 24; societies 24; stewards 96, 133–134, 141, 142, 160–162, 165, 166, 168, 198; trustees 129
Methodist Conference, 70; Form, 129
Methodist Hymn Book (1904) 20
Methodist Magazine 168
Methuen, John 55
Methuen, Paul 55
Methuen Treaty 55
Mevagissey 110–112
Meyrick, Thomas 70
Middle Ages 64
Middlesex 8
Middlezoy 126
milk diet 75, 157
Millard, Henry 33, 160
Milles, Richard 194
Milton, John 19
Mineralogia Cornubiensis 11
Miners' hospital, Truro 191–192
Minutes of Methodist Conferences 21–25, 62, 129, 147
Miracle plays 169
Mitchell 112–113
Mitchell, Thomas 71
Moliere (Jean Baptiste Poquelin) 43
Monmouth, James Scott, Duke of 177
Moorfields, London 83
Moravians 81–82; bands 82
Morecom, Thomas 4
Morgan, Mrs. 112–113
Morocco (leather) 9, 13
Morvah 25, 113–116, 142, 152, 164, 169, 171, 188
Moses 74
Mother church 107–108
Moule, Thomas 4–5, 30, 49

Mount Edgecumbe 116
Mount of Curses 74
Mounts Bay 30, 153
Mousehole 35, 116–117, 127, 175
Mullion 117
Mundic 10

Nance, John 21, 153, 156, 159, 167, 185
National census 27
National Gallery, London 68
Natural History of Cornwall 9, 11
Nature of Saving Faith 174
Neel, William 69
Nelson, John 27, 158, 180
Neolithic 43, 102; chambered tomb 15, 169, 179, 196; settlement 43
New Dialogues of the Dead 190
New Greyfriars Church, Edinburgh, Scotland 174
New Revised Standard Version (NRSV) 35
New Testament 118
New Version of the Psalms of David 164
Newbridge 68
Newcastle-upon-Tyne, Northumberland 18, 22, 156
Newcommen, Thomas 70
Newfoundland 135; fishing industry 120, 178
Newlyn 47, 49, 116, 117, 120, 179
Newlyn East 59
Newport, Gloucestershire 70
Newquay 112
Newton, John 114
Newton Abbot, Devonshire 12
nonconformity 8
Norden, John 8
Norfolk 7, 8, 14
North America 54
North Riding of Yorkshire 92
North Sea 113
North Tamerton 20, 93, 119–120, 186, 187
Northamptonshire 8
Norwich, Norfolk 24, 160, 164; see of 108
Notes on the New Testament (Burkitt) 153
Nottingham 69
Numismatic Society 5

Oblations 192
Observations on the Antiquities of Cornwall 44, 89
Observations on the Islands of Scilly 8–9
Octavo 15
Okehampton, Devonshire 100
Oland, Sweden 10

Old Cornish Bridges and Streams 68
Oldham, Lancashire 175
Olndska och Gothlandska Resa 10–11
Onslow, Lt. Gen. 67
Opie, James 4
"Order for Morning and Evening Prayer" 173
Ordnance 13
Ordnance Maps of Devon and Cornwall 13
Ordnance Surveys of Great Britain and Ireland 13
Oriel College, Oxford 8
Orthodox Church 51
Orthodox Protestantism 18
Otley, Yorkshire 100
outdoor congregations (numbers) 84–85
Oxford English Dictionary (OED) 57
Oxford Methodists 19
Oxford University 7, 20, 21, 46, 137, 167
oyster-fishing industry 178

P., Mr. 76, 91
packets 55
Padstow 27, 63, 148
Painter, Mr. 193
Panegyric 46–47, 167
Pantheon 51
Papists 88, 125, 160
Par station 186
Parable of the Sower 86, 197
Paradise Lost 19
parapet 43
Parliament 6–8, 36, 39, 101, 104, 109, 122, 139, 178; borough 36, 65, 94, 120; elections 160
Parliament of Miners 191
Parliamentary Army 54, 121, 130
parochial 216
Parochial History of Cornwall 15
Parsons, James 167
pastoral scene 195
Paul parish 117
"Peace, doubting heart" 180
Pearce, John 34
Pearce, William 38
Pembroke College, Cambridge 31
Pendeed 108
Pendennis 5
Pendennis Castle, Falmouth 15, 54, 61, 63
Pengreeb 79
Penhale 5, 120
Penryn 56, 59, 62, 88, 90, 120–124, 141, 182, 224
Pentecost 51, 72

Penzance 5, 30, 33, 34, 42, 65, 67, 78, 81, 90, 105, 107–110, 116, 117, 124–130, 138, 147, 152, 158, 169, 173, 179, 185, 234; grammar school 124; Library 105
Penzance Bay 128
Percy, Captain 179
Perfection 140
Perranwell 130
Perranzabuloe 144
Peter II 55
Pharisees 118, 154
Philadelphia, Lydia 72
Philadelphia, Pennsylvania 58, 84
Philistines 131
Phillips, Henry 70, 71
Phillips, William 38
Philosophia Botanica 11
Philp, William 144–145
Pia Desideria 18
Picturesque Excursions in Devonshire 12–13
Pietism 18
Pike's Hill, Falmouth 202
pilchard fisheries 64–65, 104, 110, 120, 130, 131, 153
Pillez 65
Plume and Feathers tavern, Mitchell 112
plundering 24, 53
Plymouth, Devonshire 13, 26, 37, 54, 68, 146, 152, 178, 186
Plymouth Dock, Devonshire 22, 68, 102, 107, 178, 184
Plymouth Passage 130–131
Poems on Several Occasions (Harte) 66
Polkerris 5
Polmassick 5
Polperro 4, 5, 130–131
Polwhele, Richard 13–14, 215
Pompeii, Italy 44
Pool 131–132
Poole, Robert 69, 223
Poole, Dorsetshire 50
Poole Harbour 50
Poole's Hole, Dorsetshire 50
Poor Richard's Almanack 59, 85
Pope 185
Pope, Alexander 9, 66, 177
popery 73
Porkellis 132
Port Gaverne 132
Port Isaac 41, 110, 132–136, 195
Port Isaac Bay 132
Port Quin 132
Port Quin Bay 132
Porth Hellick Down, Isles of Scilly 179

Porthallow 5
Porthcothan 5
Portsmouth, Hampshire 50
Portugal 54, 55
Portuguese merchants 55
postal guide 186
Postbridge, Devonshire 27
practical religion 202
Praed, Mackworth 160
Preacher's Magazine 20
preachers: houses 129; income 141
Predestinarians 74
Predestination 46
Prebendary 8, 37
Presbyterian(s), 153, 166, 186, 192; meeting-house, Bodmin 27
press gang 34
Price (Pryce), William 11–12
Primitive Physick 38, 39
Prince of Peace 136
Princess Street, Truro 191, 222
privateers 58
privilege 26
Probis, Richard 29
Probus 65, 66
Proceedings of the Antiquarian Society 15
Proceedings of the Wesley Historical Society 28, 56
Protestant dissenters 8, 93, 153, 186
Psalms 76
public fast day 159
Pudsey, Hugh de 69
Puritan Commonwealth 52
Puritans 130

Quakers 94, 122
quarterly meeting 90, 106–107, 127, 139, 140, 161, 164
Queen 128
Queen Anne Street, Dunfermline, Scotland 162
Queens' College, Cambridge 14, 93, 142
Quick, Catherine 21
Quintrel, Peter 168

rampart 43
Ram's Head 111
Ramsden Crays, Essex 166
Rankin, Thomas 48, 52, 139, 168
Rashleigh, Philip 63
Rashleigh family 63
Rashult, Smaland, Sweden 10
Rawlings, William 148
Rebecca 64
reconciliation 32

Redhill, Dorking 20
Redruth 11, 15, 29, 32, 34, 42, 43, 52, 69–72, 74, 80, 81, 83, 86, 91, 102, 110, 112, 129, 136–142, 170, 190, 193, 202, 223
Reed, William 38
Reeves, J.R. 70
Reeves, Jonathan 125
Reform Act (1832) 36, 104
Reformation 6
Remains of Japhet 167
Resolution 129
Restormel Castle, Lostwithiel 104
Reynolds, John 66
Rhodes, Benjamin 141
Ribble, Westmorland 6
R[ichard]s (R——ds), Capt. 45
Richmond, Surrey 19
Rigg, James Harrison 20
roads 54
Roberts, James 81–82
Roberts, John 98
Roche 142
Rodd, W. 208, 223
Rodda, Richard 98, 179
Rodmartin, Gloucestershire 12
Rogers, John 33
Rolle, Lord 61
Roman Catholicism 6, 8, 59, 65, 95; doctrine 46; priests 121
"Roman Villas of the Augustan Age" 5
Rome 3; legions 5; monuments 44, 89; period 43
Romney, Kent 64
Rosemergy 142–143
Roseveare, Henry 68
Rosewarne, Camborne 34, 143
Ross, John 32
Rowe, John 36
Rowe, William 30
Royal Anny 13, 70, 71, 109, 183; ordnance department 13
Royal Cornwall Infirmary, Truro 176
Royal Institution of Cornwall 4
Royal justices 73
Royal Navy 34, 44, 54
Royal paper 8, 14
Royal Society 12, 15, 37, 167
Royalists 54, 130; privateers 15, 179
Ruan Lanyhome 12
"Rules of the Band Societies" 97
Runwell, Kent 166
Rushworth, John 61
Russia 57
Russia (leather) 11
Rye, Sussex 64

S——b 126
S——h 126
Sack 80
Sackerly, Thomas 173
sacraments 119, 120, 122, 133, 150, 169
Saducismus Triumphatus 37
St. Agnes 4, 5, 85, 140, 143–145
St. Agnes, Isles of Scilly 179
St. Anthony's parish, Mount Edgecumbe 116, 184
St. Asaph, Wales 8
St. Aubyn, John 109
St. Austell 5, 66, 101, 105, 106, 142, 146–147, 149, 176, 177, 182, 186, 224
St. Blazy 66
St. Buryan 5, 147, 175, 185
St. Catherine's Convent of Mercy 9
St. Cleer 5, 101, 102, 147–148, 186
St. Colomb Major 5, 26, 39, 148
St. Endellion Collegiate Church, Port Isaac 133, 134
St. Ewe 22, 148, 149
St. Finbarrus Church, Fowey 63
St. Gennys 20, 21, 37, 41, 74, 79, 99, 120, 149–151, 195, 223
St. Hilary 24, 151–152
St. Hilary Downs 152
St. Ives 15, 20–22, 25, 28, 29, 32, 33, 52, 66, 81, 82, 87, 89–92, 100, 103, 109, 113, 114, 130, 152, 152–167, 169, 180, 181, 184, 188, 194, 196–198
St. Ives Bay 152
St. James 69
St. James's Park, London 83
St. John's College, Cambridge 32
St. John's, Cornwall 168–169, 186
St. Just 9, 14, 24, 25, 34, 42, 44, 89, 90, 105, 116, 129, 132, 169–175, 181, 189
St. Kubert 49
St. Lawrence 175–176
St. Malin's, Isles of Scilly 179
St. Martin-in-the-Fields, London 8
St. Mary's Chapel, Maidenhead, Berkshire 14
St. Mary's Church, Truro 192
St. Mary's Hall, Oxford 65
St. Mary's, Isles of Scilly 25, 179, 180
St. Mawes Castle, Falmouth 15, 54
St. Meen 27
St. Mewan 176
St, Michael's Mount, Marazion 109
St. Neots, Cornwall 14
St. Neots, Huntingdonshire 14
St. Neots School, Huntingdonshire 14
St. Newlyn 14
St. Peter Port, Isle of Guernsey 128

St. Peter's, Rome 51
St. Petrock 27
St. Samson 105
St. Stephen's Down 176–177
St. Stephen's-in-Bramwell 177
St. Teath 177
St. Tudy 177–178
Saint's Way footpath, Fowey 63
Salford, Lancashire 69
Salisbury Cathedral 8
Salisbury, Wiltshire 34
Saltash 67, 68, 101, 178
Samarian highlands 74
Samuel 104, 179
Sancreed 179, 223
Sancta Maria ad Martyrs, Church of 51
Sandwich, Kent 64
Sark, Channel Islands 128
Savannah, Georgia 81
Savery, Thomas 30, 70
Saxon monuments 44, 89
Saxony 138
Scantlebury, Richard 132–135
Schismatical Methodists 170
Scilly Islands/Isles of 8–9, 153, 179–181
Scoffer 29–30
Scoria 87
Scotland 1, 6, 18, 23, 24, 27, 200; grammar 8
Scottish Kirk 174
Scrofula 50
scurvy 50
Second Letter to the Author of Methodists and Papists Compar 'd 113
Second Street, Philadelphia 59
Secumb 126
Sedgemoor common, Somersetshire 176, 177
Select societies 82, 140, 165–166, 168–169
Selected Works (Dell) 122
Sennen 25, 181
Sermon Before the University of Oxford (C. Wesley), 131
Sermon on the Mount 99
Sermon Register 168
Seven Years' War 138
Severn River 5
Severn Sea 153
Shaftesbury, Dorsetshire 51, 52
Shakespeare, William 58, 64–65
Sheffield, Yorkshire 18
Shell keep 94, 178
Shephall, Hertfordshire 46
Shepherd, William 27, 78, 79, 143, 180
Shincliffe, Durham 69

Shipton, Kent 166
Short Account of the Dearth of Thomas Hitchens 80
Simonds, William 100–101
Simpkin and Marshall 4
Sithney 133, 182
Skirlaw, Walter 69
Sleech, John 14
Slocombe, John 126, 150, 219
Slocumb 126
Smith 126
Smith, John 197–198
smuggling 5, 9, 19, 134, 162
Society for the Propagation of the Gospel 135
Society of Friends 94
Some Account of the Work of God in America 118
Somerset 8
South Wales 87
Southampton, Hampshire 128
Southey, Robert 2, 56
Spain 80, 159, 183
Spanish Armada 15, 179
Sparry marble 9
Species Plantarum 11
Specimen of British Minerals 63
Speculi Britanniae Pars 8
Spelman, Henry 7
Spener, Philipp Jakob 18
spiritual pride 170
spotted fever 79–80
Stable Yard, St. James Palace, London 5
Staffordshire 19
Stanhope House, Atkins Road, Clapham Park 19
stannaries 191
stannary towns 101
Star Castle, St. Mary's Island, Isles of Scilly 15, 179
Star Inn, Penzance 127
Stationers Court, London 4
steam power/engine 30, 70, 152
Stephens, John 153, 155–157, 161
Sticker 182
Sticklepath, Devonshire 95, 150
Stithians 24, 79, 182–183
Stithney 88
Stockholm, Sweden 10
Stone Age 43
Strathclyde 6
Stratton 195
subventions 192
supernumerary 19
surface mining 71
Surrey 14

Survey of Cornwall (Carew) 7
Sussex 14, 64
Sweden 10
Swedish Academy of Sciences 10
Swindells, Robert 163
Symonds, William 159, 184, 185, 196–198
Systema Naturae 10

T., C. 160
T., W. 89
Table of Dates 5
Tamar River 3, 67, 68, 94, 95, 178
Tartuffe 43
Tasso 7
Tate, Nahum 164
Tavistock, Devonshire 22, 68
Taylor, Joseph 110, 167, 194
tea 75, 157
Teddington Road, Twickenham 9
Tees River 69
Telford, Frances Ross 19
Telford, John the elder 19
Telford, John, the younger 2, 19–20, 34, 42, 52, 92, 118, 200
Terrick, Richard 135
Terril, Grace Paddy 138–139
Terril, William 139
Tetcott 119
Theological Dissertations (J. Erskine) 174
Thirty-Nine Articles (1536–1563) 46
Thomas, Rev. 59
Thomson, George 20–21, 41, 74, 150, 151, 157
Three-Cornered Down 91
Tiberius 11
Tiger, HMS 74
tin: coinage 88; ships 88; stamping 191
tin mining 4, 5, 24, 67, 77, 79, 91, 92, 113, 124, 131, 132, 136, 169, 194; riots 36
Tintagel Castle, Bude 15
Tiverton, Devonshire 95, 96, 99
Tolcarn 183
Tolgus tin streaming mill 136
Tolland 61, 62
Tompkins, Henry 34–35
Tonbridge, Kent 166
toothache 96
topography 7
Torpoint 102, 103, 184
Toulon, France 159
Tour Through Great Britain (Defoe) 136
Towednack 184–185, 198
Tower of London 8, 12
Transactions of the Geological Society of Cornwall 14

Treacle 38–39
Treble, John 108
Tredinney 185, 221
Tregavarah Downs 185–186
Tregear, James 173
Tregeseal stone circles 169
Tregony 105; grammar school 105
Tregosse, Thomas 166
Trelights 132
Tremain 5
Trematon Castle, Saltash 178
Trembath, John 70, 79–80, 99–100
Trenode 186
Trenouth 186
Trent River 69
Tresco Abbey, Isles of Scilly 179
Tresco, Isles of Scilly 15, 179
Tresillion 5
Tresmeer 29, 72, 93, 178, 186–187, 190
Treswithian 188
Treswithian Downs 188
Trethevy Stone, Liskeard 102
Trevelyan 5
Trevowhan 188
Trewalder 188–189
Trewegy 190
Trewellard 189–190
Trewint 22, 186, 190
Trezlah 191
Trinity College, Cambridge 7
Trinity Sunday 182
Tristan 15, 63
Tristan Stone, Fowey 63
True Way to the Latin Tongue 7
Truro 4, 14, 28, 32, 39, 54, 55, 61, 62, 65, 66, 71, 105, 112, 130, 136, 143, 148, 182, 186, 191–194, 201
Truro Corporation 192, 193
Tucker, William 80, 133, 217
Tunbridge Wells 20
Turner, John 195, 196
Turner, Joseph 20, 21, 153
Turner, Joseph Mallord William 68
Turnough, John 144
Twelfth Night 64–65
Twickenham, Middlesex 9
Tyerman, Luke 2, 18–19, 56, 83
Tyne River 69
Tywardreath 105, 186

Union of Reason and Revealed Religion 66
United Kingdom 200
United States 43
University of London 20
University of Uppsala 10
Uppsala, Sweden 10

Valletort, Reginald de 178
Valton, John vi
Vathek 12
Velling-Verine 194–195
Verine 194
Veryan 71
Vesuvius, Mount 44
Views of Noble Mansions in Hampshire 5
Villare Anglicanum 7
Virtue, George 4
Viz./videlicet 215
Vowler, James 144–145
Voyage Round the World (Forster) 129

W., Dr. 195
Wadebridge 39, 177, 195
Wainscot 57
Wales 1, 5, 18, 23, 27, 73, 200
Walker, Francis 70
Walker, James 144–145
Walker, Samuel 61–62, 71, 122, 148, 192, 193, 201
Wallis, Mydhope 133
Walpole, Robert 109
Walsall, Staffordshire 59–60
Walter, Bishop of Durham 69
Waltham Holy Cross, Hertfordshire 108
Ward, W. Reginald 38, 44, 50, 57, 61, 68, 102, 133, 140, 148, 149, 160, 174
Ward and Heitzenrater 84, 87, 90, 91, 93, 105, 107, 126, 186, 199
Warleggan 105
Warren, Mrs. 168
watch-night 161, 198
water-spout 35
Watkins, Christopher 175
Watts, Isaac 187
Wear River 69
Wednesbury, Staffordshire 19, 21
Week St. Mary 36, 195, 496
Wellesley College, Massachusetts 50
Welsh language 167
Wendron 132, 183, 196
Wesley, Mary (Molly) Goldhawk Vazeille 31, 118, 119
Wesley, Samuel the elder 19, 20, 93–94
Wesley and the People Called Methodists 126
Wesleyan Methodism 6, 17, 20, 91, 174; Conference 20, 200; Connexion 20; ministry 19; societies 62
Wesleyan Methodist Magazine 20
Wesleyan revival 18
Wesleys in Cornwall (Pearce) 38

West Indies 54
West Saxons 5
West Somerset 5
Westall, William 5
Westell, Thomas 33
Western Societies 22
Western world 51
Westminster Abbey 167
Wheale Vor, Breage 30
Whit-Monday 71
Whitaker, John 12, 215
Whitaker, William 98
Whitby, Yorkshire 24
White Peak 50
Whitechurch, Shropshire 70
Whitefield, George 19, 58–59, 62, 84, 202
Whitford, John 172
Whitsunday 72, 150, 182
Wight, Isle of 104
Wigton, Cumberland 19–20
Williams, Richard 87
Williams, Thomas H. 12–13
Williamson, R. 57
Willoughby, Thomas 69
Winchelsea, Sussex 64
Windermere, Westmorland 10
Windsor 66
wine purchases 105
Winkle, R.B. 5
Woman of Canaan 125
Wood, Richard 134, 135
Worcester 8
Worcester Cathedral 37
Works of John Wesley (Jackson) 126, 149
Works of John Wesley: Journal (1991) 126
Works of John Wesley: Methodist Societies 126
World War II 116
worms, diet of 58
Wright, Richard 98
Wrigley, Francis 141, 146
Wyatt, James 12

Yarm, Yorkshire 69
yearly subscription 23–24
Yeldon, Bedfordshire 122
Yorkshire 18, 27, 143
Youren, Henry 70, 217

Zennor 25, 113, 142, 158, 164, 196–198
Zennor Quoit 196